PLANNING LOS ANGELES

PLANNING
LOS ANGELES

Edited by David C. Sloane

American Planning Association
Planners Press

Making Great Communities Happen

Chicago | Washington, D.C.

TO MY PLANNING STUDENTS
YOUR DREAMS INSPIRE ME; YOUR ACCOMPLISHMENTS AMAZE ME.
—DAVID C. SLOANE

Copyright © 2012 by the American Planning Association

205 N. Michigan Ave., Suite 1200, Chicago, IL 60601-5927
1030 15th St., NW, Suite 750 West, Washington, DC 20005-1503

www.planning.org/plannerspress

ISBN: 978-1-61190-004-0 (pbk.)

Library of Congress Control Number 2012933450

Publication of this book was made possible in part by the generous support of APA's Urban Design and Preservation Division.

Printed in the United States of America

Contents

Chapter 6: Parks and Public Space

Chapter 7: Economic Development

Acknowledgments

David C. Sloane: An edited book is a labor of love, depending on the skills and devotion of many people, most especially this fine group of authors, whom I thank for their generosity, responsiveness, and creativity. I have to single out Todd Gish, who not only provided a great essay but also created three crucial maps. Martin Krieger, Doug McCulloh, and David Yamamoto deserve special thanks for providing photographs that add immeasurably to the book's story. Alan Jutzi, Erin Chase, Kenn Bickness, and Terri Garst from The Huntington Library (San Marino, California), LA Metro's Dorothy Peyton Grey Libraries, and the Los Angeles Public Library helped find and provide illustrations that added materially to the visual success of the book. The book would have been impossible without the truly heroic work completed by the APA staff, especially Timothy Mennel, Julie Von Bergen, and Susan Deegan. My thanks as well to Dmitry Galkin. My dean, Jack Knott, generously provided financial support, and I appreciate all the faculty members and staff of the USC Price School of Public Policy for being my biggest supporters. My fellow board members of the Los Angeles Regional Planning History Group encouraged me to take on this task. Anne Bray helped make the book more conceptually intriguing and visually delightful, and she has filled my life with joy.

Todd Gish: I would like to thank David Sloane, Greg Hise, Kathy Kolnick, and Alan Jutzi for their help with this essay.

Vinayak Bharne: I wish to thank Stefanos Polyzoides for sharing his experiences on the initial Playa Vista master plan, and for his critical comments on this essay.

Dowell Myers et al.: The authors gratefully acknowledge the Los Angeles-based Haynes Foundation for supporting the research that is drawn upon for this chapter.

Lisa Schweitzer: This manuscript benefited from the research support of Dmitry Galkin, Jennifer Lieu, Carina Lieu, and Matthew Kridler. Many thanks to the staff at the Dorothy Peyton Grey Transportation Library for allowing access to the archives.

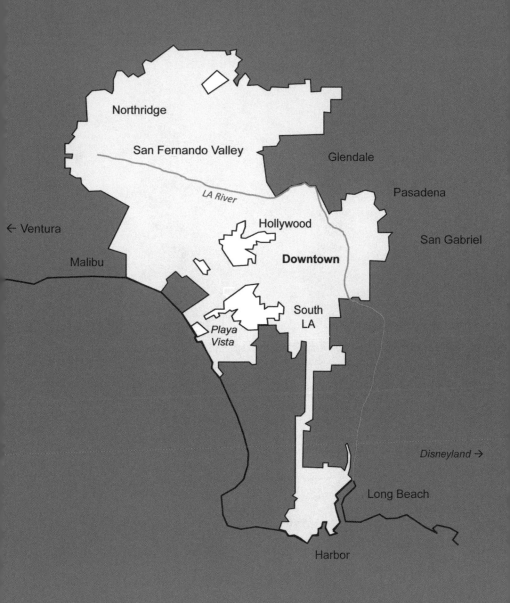

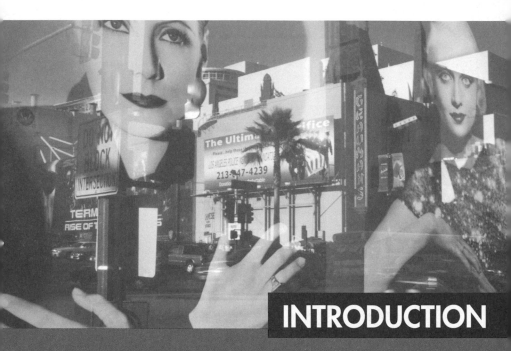

INTRODUCTION

1

Multiplicities/Multiple-cities

David C. Sloane

Outsiders love to hate LA, but which city, among the multiple choices, do they hate? Southern California is an economic giant that produces more than most industrial countries, while inequities abound; poorly paid, ill-housed laborers service luxury homes, elaborate gardens, and garages filled with expensive cars. Propelled by the adoption of new urbanist and smart growth reforms, LA has an increasingly vibrant street life yet is still defined by the car, reflecting the intransigent autocentric infrastructure of the 20th century. The area's homes and streets are spectacularly beautiful, compared rhetorically through the decades to the Garden of Eden; and still, LA is a place where many poor people have to drive a few miles to find a green space where their children can play. LA is a vibrant cultural site that takes its cultural workers largely for granted, offering its enormous pool of artists fewer incentives than almost any American city. And, while regional solutions are difficult to envision here, they are even harder to enact. Given all these contradictions, almost everyone believes Los Angeles is unplanned, and cannot accept that it has a rich planning and development history. They just view Los Angeles as the iconic failure of modern city development.

Those failed relations are central to the story this book tells, and to understanding the evolving narrative of LA. Back in the 1940s, the marvelous Carey McWilliams (1973, 14), author of what is still the best introductory book on LA, wrote, "Walled off from the rest of the country by mountain ranges and desert wastes, Southern California is an island on the land, geographically attached, rather than functionally related, to the rest of America."[1]

The image of LA as island is potentially trite, yet evocatively powerful. Many other authors have mimicked McWilliams's use of it to describe Southern California's separation and isolation; yet for me the power of the image is that it describes the region's transience. The Southern California island continually and unevenly evolves; it does not narrate a static or linear history. For instance, LA is no longer walled off

Figure 1.1. Soccer player in Vista Hermosa Park with the backdrop of downtown's skyscapers, 2011

geographically or at the end of the American cul-de-sac, as University of California President Benjamin Ide Wheeler wrote in 1898 (McWilliams 1973, 134). Yet many Americans still view LA as different, a place apart from the conventional cities of the rest of the nation, partly because of our multicultures and partly because of the persistence of our suburban values.

Figure 1.2. A rooftop pool above Pershing Square in downtown LA is a result of policy and planning creating a coherent strategy of downtown redevelopment.

The turn of America westward toward LA (and toward the Asian east) opened Southern California to the world, making it the prime immigrant gateway of the last half of the 20th century, diversifying its population, and internationalizing its culture—giving outsiders new reasons to be mystified by LA. As Dowell Myers and his colleagues, Steven A. Preston, and others write, the change alters our sense of LA. At one level, it created new (and to the world familiar) islands—such as immigrant enclaves in Monterey Park or Koreatown—but it also set the foundation for bridges across the islands, such as multiracial marriages and transcultural art and architecture that were signals of change (sometimes unwelcome), not only in LA but the rest of the United States. The mountains that separate California from the rest of the United States remain, and the West is still not the East (either in the United States or the world), but the distances have shrunk so that a parade celebrating Chinese New Year and altars commemorating the Day of the Dead feel almost as if they always belonged on the Californian cul-de-sac.

As work by Mike Davis (1990) and others remind us, integration comes unevenly, and usually reluctantly. As Dana Cuff (2002, 14) notes about LA mid-century home construction, "modern housing set itself apart as an island within its surroundings, to its own detriment in the end." Building houses bracketed with front and back lawns, Angelenos moved their family recreation to the backyard and eventually put up fences to gain even greater privacy from the neighbors. After a period of ticky-tacky houses joined by open front yards and sometimes shared driveways, gated communities sprouted, especially in Orange County, further isolating and separating. Master planned communities, such as Irvine or Stevenson Ranch, could be viewed as islands floating in the larger metropolitan sea when seen on aerial photos.

The inequalities that outsiders hate remain, since Orange County still doesn't have an effective public transit system, and gated communities remain common throughout

Figure 1.3. On the 405 going up the Sepulveda Pass, even cars in the southbound carpool lane just sit, waiting for a break in the traffic.

Southern California. Yet one can also see a turn away from that older paradigm in newer developments that are beginning more integrated, denser, and more diversified. Janis Breidenbach reminds us of the Housing Trust in LA, and Vinayak Bharne suggests Playa Vista may illustrate that even wealthier Angelenos are considering homes in denser developments with better parks and more walkable streets. The seas between the islands have not dried, but they have receded.

Finally, of course, outsiders have long viewed LA's adoration of the car as a prime reason to simply shake their heads at the very mention of the place. Indeed, the island vision that seems hardest to shake is that of the driver snug in her car cocoon roaring down the freeway through thousands of other moving islands. This year, "Carmeggedon" became a national phenomenon as commentators comically imagined an LA without cars. The image reinforces the seeming refusal of Angelenos to live public lives, preferring their privacy and intimate, familial relations over ephemeral connections. Movie and television producers love the picture, but LA's critics revel in it even more.

The waters may be receding even here, if very slowly. Lisa Schweitzer suggests that the victory of Measure R, while certainly flawed, could create new transit lines that might result in a new image, that of the bicyclist loading her bike aboard on the Expo Line on her morning commute. That image will not replace the cocooned driver any time soon, but it might compete with it, offering another proof of LA's evolution.

Myths and Mythologies

Changing people's perception of LA, though, is difficult. We, LA's residents, are partly at fault. As Norman Klein (1997) reminds us, LA is a city that has forgotten too much, remembers what is shiny and new, what fits with its image of itself. Of course, every city forgets what it doesn't like and remembers the successes that burnish its image,

Figure 1.4. A Day of the Dead altar at Hollywood Forever Cemetery, 2010

but in LA, the newness of the city makes the forgetfulness seem more unforgiveable and the image consciousness less acceptable. The result is mythmaking at a grand scale, often with very negative results for anyone not rich and powerful.

Cities are filled with myths. Writers, storytellers, old wives, and young children spin them, leaving them behind much like the grand old houses that line the streets of West Adams, Angelino Heights, and other LA districts. Is LA a desert masquerading as a city? Does anyone actually walk anywhere? Were the original settlers "Spanish," or Long Beach the "port of Iowa"? Telling the "truth" from the myths is difficult since they so often are at least partially true. Some, like the racist rhetoric that named the Japanese traitors and African Americans dangerous, were too easily manufactured and took too long to undermine even though they were simply lies. Others, like the GM conspiracy to end the streetcars and the CIA's role in the crack cocaine epidemic that destroyed lives in the 1980s, have elements of truth that make them harder to complicate and retell. Either way, the stories typically belie the paradoxical nature of LA's physical and social environment by overlooking the oppositional interrelationships that shape the city. I think we are better off engaging reality, as messy and disorderly as it is.

For instance, is LA planned, or did it, as so many seem to believe, sprawl out under the direction of greedy, thoughtless real estate developers in stark contrast to New York and the other cities of the Atlantic Coast? Todd Gish responds emphatically, "Call it ugly, call it beautiful, call it dysfunctional—but don't call Los Angeles *unplanned*." The reason is simple, as Greg Hise and William Deverell remind us: "Rather than a city that failed to plan, Los Angeles has been the subject of a surfeit of reports, studies, and proposals." So why do so many people believe the city was unplanned? One reason was that Angelenos wanted to separate themselves from those older cities. When social worker and author Dana Bartlett (1907) hoped that LA could become "the better city," he was imagining a place that wasn't Boston or Philadelphia.

Residents rejected those older cities with their congested streets and disorderly housing. Cuff (2002, 28) reminds us, "From the West, the East was construed as a distinct collection of urban characteristics: besides its severe climate, the East had tenements, high densities, and an associated general overcrowding with all the commensurate health problems." They wanted a different place—a place that (to paraphrase Bartlett) ruralized the city and urbanized the country—long before the freeway made spacious living possible.

Is any other city so powerfully associated with a mode of transportation? Almost everyone accepts that LA is the ultimate sprawling autocentric city; indeed, they believe the car shaped the region, leaving individual drivers cocooned and marooned. Yet, when Bartlett wrote in 1907, the city was already sprawling out, via the nation's most expansive streetcar system. The Pacific Electric and Los Angeles Railway lines covered more than 1,100 miles, reaching from San Bernardino to Santa Monica, Santa Ana to San Fernando, creating the skeleton of the modern metropolis. As Reyner Banham (1971, 220), the Englishman who produced one of the great books about LA, wrote, "the automobile and the architecture alike are the products of the Pacific Electric Railroad as a way of life." Instead of the conventional myth, one might as well argue that the mass transit lines so spread out people, they had to buy a car just to get to all the places Henry Huntington (owner of the Pacific Electric) named after himself.

Figure 1.5. The vine-dripped freeways are modern LA's equivalent of the Roman aqueducts.

The myth that LA was shaped solely by the car is so powerful that many scholars continue to accept it since the car plays such an important role in our image of the city. Architect Charles Moore (1998, 11) summarized its role in complementing the city's art and architecture when he wrote, "If there has come to us a single image of L.A., it is doubtless the tower of City Hall, with the world's first four-level freeway interchange nearby, dripping vines like a Piranesi view of ancient Rome." The twin images reflect each other—City Hall, famous as the imagined home to Jack Webb's character Sgt. Joe Friday on TV's *Dragnet*, and the vines transforming the utilitarian interchange into LA's Roman ruin of the future.

Even more alarmingly, the simple LA story that states the car isolated, fragmented, and separated the city's residents ignores the role of the housing industry, policy makers, planners, and industry. We now know more about the home construction industry's practices (Hise 1999), race-based social and health policy making (Molina 2006), and class-conscious neighborhood building (Cuff 2002). These forces increasingly separated Angelenos through racial covenants and single-use zoning standards, as industry located its jobs on the fringes, attracting growing populations. And they continued to do so even in the recent housing bubble, as Christian Redfearn demonstrates. Did the cars aid the physical growth of suburbs? Sure they did, but that is far from the entire story. Transportation determinism is no better an explanation than the environmental determinism of yesteryear that declared poor people would be fine if we just housed them in middle-class environments.

Marlon Boarnet, Schweitzer, and others remind us that the "multimodal" past that combined walking, biking, cars, and mass transit is also our present and future, defying the myth that LA cannot plan. Aaron Paley and Amanda Berman's chronicle of CicLAvia, the public space extravaganza where over a hundred thousand Angelenos bicycle and

Figure 1.6. The new LA Metro Expo Line on Exposition Boulevard. Long home to the famed "red cars" of the Pacific Electric, the boulevard is once again a transit corridor.

walk streets closed to cars, verify the efforts to close the era of auto supremacy, as do the new transit lines Mayor Antonio Villaraigosa plans to build from Measure R.

These myths feed the ultimate LA planning myth, the one that declares that LA is the anti-city. In her majestic *Death and Life of Great American Cities* (1961), Jane Jacobs viewed LA as the antithesis to her beloved Lower Manhattan, and relied on it as an example of the modern planning she hated. She railed against the city's reliance on the philosophy of "togetherness" that demanded shared values and did not appreciate the simpler, ephemeral relationships of public life. Even before Jacobs, LA had become the iconic representation of sprawl, a message driven home by William Whyte's (1958) evocative metaphor of bulldozers from LA meeting those from San Bernardino somewhere many miles east of downtown. After Jacobs's initial attack, other commentators followed suit, especially during the early years of the antisprawl campaign and the birth of new urbanism. LA became the capital of sprawl, infamous for its freeways and suburban lifestyle. Was LA a city? Yes. Was it a place that embraced urbanity and valued public life? No.

Scholars have exploded the popular image of LA as a collection of (bedroom) suburbs in search of a city. Most prominently, Greg Hise showed in *Magnetic Los Angeles* (1999) that many suburbs, such as Westchester and Pacoima, were constructed not for their bedrooms but for their jobs, as industrial suburbs with housing and services. Becky Nicolaides (2002) and others chronicled the rise and complexity of vibrant places and commercial activities ranging from the blue-collar neighborhoods in Long Beach and San Pedro to the suburban homesteads of the San Fernando and San Gabriel valleys.

When Breidenbach reminds us that a majority of LA households have *never* owned their homes, a central myth of LA's popular story crumbles. How can the majority be rent-

Figure 1.7. At Playa Vista, higher-density housing rises out of the plain near the Pacific Ocean in an area famous for its expensive single-family houses.

ers in a city where home building and single-family residential zoning are central pillars of the sprawling autocentric society? Margaret Crawford further undermines the myth by documenting the city's everyday urbanism, where vendors walk the streets, home own-ers sell goods in their yards, and the homeless live in public places. The nostalgia for a long-lost suburban Arcadia veils the rich public culture of Broadway's Latino marketplace and the domino partners playing in Monterey Park neighborhoods. Perhaps we need to revise our understanding of planning Los Angeles and reconsider the multiplicities of experiences. Perhaps, then, we will remember what should not be forgotten and talk less about what is ephemeral, glitzy, and image rather than substance.

A Horizontally Dense Metropolis
If we are willing to reconsider the "anti-city" myth, we might be able to start seeing LA anew. My USC colleague Gen Giuliano was the first person I heard describe LA as a "horizontally dense" city. Unlike conventional cities, epitomized by New York City, where the center is very dense, and the city becomes less dense as it spreads outward, Los Angeles is not quite as dense at its middle but stays dense for long miles as it stretches to the horizon. Much of this density is infill development and is relatively recent—over the last half-century—but the foundation for the horizontally dense metropolis is older.

Planning and urban design scholar Ann Forsyth (2005, 72) has argued, "In areas like Southern California . . . a new kind of metropolitan area had very obviously come into existence during the early part of the twentieth century." She rejects the idea that these places were simply the "regional cities" Clarence Stein, Lewis Mumford, and other

1920s planning commentators imagined built out of dozens of "neighborhood units" that Clarence Perry envisioned. (Talen 2008 provides a nice summary of these ideas.) People live in multiple cities, Forsyth argues, more akin to Kevin Lynch's (1960) nodes than "a multicentered city set in a landscape of agriculture and open space." Residents "engulfed" in that now-mature urbanized region move from one center to another to do a business deal, take their children to school, eat at a new restaurant, and visit a museum. As one planner Forsyth interviewed said, "there is no central something." The description sounds suspiciously like the sprawling, disconnected narrative of the anti-city, but the reality is much denser and more fluid than that myth purports.

Such decentralized, regional living comes at a price—that island culture with which we began. As Jane Jacobs, Charles Moore, Robert Fogelson, and Mike Davis have noted, in LA places are either intimate or foreign, safe or dangerous, protected or public—and Angelenos are not as adventurous as others in crossing those boundaries. Jacobs (1961, 72) was most disparaging: "Los Angeles is an extreme example of a metropolis with little public life, depending mainly on the contacts of a more private social nature."

Davis (1990) was most pessimistic, drawing the portrait of a city controlled by powerful interests who care little for the people who live there and construct a built environment that fits their corporate or elite needs. He brilliantly demonstrates the unforgiveable planning around Bunker Hill that exemplified contemporary "fortress architecture," but frustratingly he could not see the everyday urbanism that subverted the intentions of downtown interests, creating places like Broadway, which morphed from the center of Anglo nightlife in the 1940s to a Latino marketplace by the 1980s. Certainly, LA was, and is, a place of social inequity, as Davis so effectively described, but it is also a place of amazing adaptability and social support—although the physical environment, particularly in the city's poorer neighborhoods, could provide more assistance.

Figure 1.8. Pershing Square squats in downtown, unloved by almost all.

Figure 1.9. Families gather in Elysian Park, one of LA's too few parks. Angelenos love the ones they have.

Jacobs was also distraught about LA's public spaces, arguing that Pershing Square, the city's central downtown park, was indicative of the city's disdain for public life. The 1992–1994 redesign by Mexican architect Ricardo Legorreta did little to improve the place Moore (1998, 21) had earlier called a "hot five-acre rooftop." Here, Loukaitou-Sideris documents the city's disappointing park infrastructure, showing the limited availability, inequity accessibility, and resulting lower use. While she finds room for optimism in the development of parks near downtown, in South LA, and in Santa Monica, she calls for innovation—in designing parks that better fit the needs of immigrant communities (not just soccer-playing adolescents) and in utilizing spaces that would integrate play into the routine of everyday life in the city. Recently, LA officials have advocated for borrowing the "parklet" idea from other cities such as San Francisco. Parklets could be developed on major thoroughfares—suggesting again the end of the era of auto supremacy—in places that have few available large lots often needed for fully developed parks.

Given such innovations, the realities of everyday urbanism, and the clear signs that street retailing has made a comeback from the nadir period of the enclosed shopping mall, Jacobs's disparaging vision may itself be receding. However, the physical environment of gated communities, 150-foot-wide suburbanesque streets (in the city), and policies that limit vending and valorize project development (over parks, agriculture, and gardens) will remain barriers to fully developing the city's civic culture.

The Endless Game of Politics and Planning

Progress seems in the air; then another big project comes up and we seem to slip backward toward an earlier style of planning. We all accept that planning is political, yet in Los Angeles, many feel that politics is planning. Recently the Los Angeles City Council met to consider supporting a new football field adjacent to

Figure 1.10. Almost all of LA's cultural icons, including the Getty's Terrace, are scattered across the city, accessible only by car or poor transit service.

the convention center and LA Live. As with so many planning decisions in the city, the conversation did not start with the city's plan for the area, because the city did not have a specific plan for southwest downtown, even though the area has been a visible growth center for the last generation or more. A narrowly drawn specific plan does exist for the Los Angeles Sports and Entertainment District, but it barely includes the area affected by the proposed football stadium. Instead, developments seem driven by private interests which too often can influence public will, such as with the new law that exempts projects (like the stadium) over $100 million from parts of the California Environmental Quality Act process. Local politicians control the pace and scale of development by approving individual developments—whether they fit into a plan for the area or not, without a clear vision of the plan for the city or region.

Figure 1.11. *LA's billboards bombard us with visual messages of fast food, violence, and sexism—save for a short time in 2010 when art replaced commerce.*

Too often the result is that the city and the region suffer. On the city level, good buildings, like Disney Hall and the Los Angeles Cathedral, end up standing isolated from one another in the urban fabric. The political and planning focuses are on spotlight developments, such as LA Live, rather than on creating a rich self-sustaining urban scene. The areas that do not get as much attention, say the fashion and toy districts on the southeastern side of downtown, hold amazing economic power, as Elizabeth Currid-Halkett demonstrates. The fashion district and its sister arts districts around the region play a crucial role in the postindustrial economy, yet only now are downtown interests focusing more on them. Poorer areas, such as Angelino Heights and Highland Park, long ignored by city officials, receive attention when they appear ripe for development because of the recentralization of population and transit-oriented development.

Occasionally the city is more systematic, such as with the most successful development policy of the last generation, the Adaptive Reuse Ordinance (1999) that Ken Bernstein discusses. This ordinance not only brought new housing to a downtown largely bereft of middle-class and luxury units, it also helped stabilize (temporarily at least) thriving manufacturing and retail districts, such as the flower market and meat distribution center, which emerged away from the glare of development politics. These more successful planning examples too often still increase inequity, as has the development downtown of almost exclusively luxury condominiums.

The politics of planning pervades the region, although the smaller cities seem to have better success in developing coherent envisioning strategies and managing the inherent conflicts created by competing projects. As Alan Loomis and Sam Gennawey relate, Glendale, northwest of LA's downtown over the Santa Monica Mountains, has attempted to compete with the other cities and districts in the San Fernando Valley and with those across the LA basin by redesigning its downtown and approving the Americana at Brand. The two decisions seem almost diametrically opposed—trying to make downtown more walkable and active even as the largest new shopping mall in the region opens. Yet such contradictions are common in LA, where the designs are rarely pure, the aspirations never uncomplicated, and the population often strives for polar opposites.

Lark Galloway-Gilliam and Josh Sides describe changes in South LA, which has few of the resources that are easily accessible to a resident of Playa Vista, just north of LAX near the beach. Yet residents in South LA face the same compromises as in Glendale. South LA residents are struggling to control the increase in obesity in their community. One innovative approach passed by the LA City Council was to place a moratorium on new stand-alone fast-food restaurants for two years to give residents time to develop a comprehensive plan. Critics complained the moratorium wouldn't work and would take jobs away from youth who might work in the fast-food franchises. So residents were faced with the choice: Do you want the jobs associated with fast food to disappear in an area where young people have few employment options and development has been stalled for decades? Or, do you choose to allow fast food to dominate the food system, leaving residents with few healthier alternatives and resulting in persistent obesity rates, sky-high diabetes diagnoses, and premature deaths? The planning and development decisions in many communities are not simple equations.

William Fulton shows how Ventura County, on the fringes of the metropolitan region but squarely in the bulls-eye of new growth and development, has decided to use urban boundaries as a means of resolving such dilemmas by managing change at a county level. Jennifer Wolch and her colleagues discuss how a "green vision" would help

Figure 1.12. The port's tall cranes stand as sentries lining the harbor's entrance, reminding us of the region's emergence as a Pacific Rim giant.

municipalities and the region reconsider conventional development and move toward sustainability. And, in her discussion of the LA and Long Beach port plans for improving the horrible environmental cost of the largest port complex in the United States, Meredith Drake Reitan reminds us of how one change can affect the entire system (for good or bad), and the limitations of local authority to alter existing conditions.

On the regional level, as Robert Leiter and Elisa Barbour and Kenneth Topping show, the inability of the political players to work together limits the capacity for solutions that stretch over political boundaries. Whether it's worries about the lack of regional seismic planning or the future of our infrastructure, the answers seem just beyond reach since no one will cede power. Just as the refusal of the chamber of commerce in 1930 to accept a regional parks authority robbed LA of parks and parkways, critical improvements to land use and sustainability are held up today.

Residents' frustration with the politicians' mode of development, and the planners' lack of clear vision and power, came to a boil in the 1990s, when several parts of LA (Hollywood, the Harbor, and the San Fernando Valley) threatened secession. Juliet Musso evaluates one of the outcomes of that voters' revolt, the new Neighborhood Council system. While she concludes that the system has been an uneven success, the councils represent a further puncturing of an older style of development and planning. As she shows, in highly functioning neighborhoods, developers now understand that they need to negotiate with the neighborhood council, not just the local council office.

Goetz Wolff suggests that such negotiations are only part of a broader shift in the economic development environment. He argues that the rise of an effective community-based network of organizations has altered how business can be done in the city. Yes, power still speaks (as the march of the football stadium against all good reason exemplifies), but in a growing number of cases across a broad range of neighborhoods, community action is making a difference.

Galloway-Gilliam and Gilda Haas provide examples of the movement. Local activism can have an impact, as communities fight back against the presumption of growth-oriented planning controlled by developers and politicians. The pioneering Community Benefits Agreement negotiated with the developer of LA Live and the fast-food moratorium leading to changes in the LA General Plan framework suggest that things can improve, even as they remind us how hard it is to change things.

Bland or Beautiful?

Few cities in the world are in a more beautiful natural setting than LA. Even today, the 19th-century booster claim that one could ski in the mountains in the morning, eat lunch in the city, and swim in the ocean in the afternoon—all under glorious sunlight that warmed the visitor and resident year-round—is not fanciful, even if traffic makes it seem arduous. The surrounding mountains, rivers, beaches, and canyons are stunning in their diversity, accessibility, and natural beauty.

Amid this natural splendor, we have built a city that many commentators view as an eyesore. Mike Davis most brutally critiqued the region's development processes, but even Charles Moore (1998, xxi), who generally wrote joyfully about LA, revealed, "Here in Los Angeles the shape of the city is soft at the edges, piled layer on layer, cloud on cloud, composing a hazy pattern of amenity that leaves only a few special places unengulfed, survivors in a paradise awash." The search for paradise left few natural

Figure 1.13: Grand Avenue is a set of buildings dreaming of an urban place.

places untouched and created miles upon miles of undifferentiated housing. Reyner Banham declared the LA "plains" (that area south of the Santa Monica Mountains, stretching from Hollywood to San Pedro, Santa Monica to Boyle Heights) a service area supporting the magnificence of the hills and beaches. As *Los Angeles Times* architectural critic Christopher Hawthorne (2011) recently pointed out, the "plains, for a huge and growing percentage of the population, *are* Los Angeles." Just as Banham overstated the ease of mobility, planners underestimated, as Vinit Mukhija shows, the difficulty of altering the conventions of development when they tried to create concentrated nodes as part of the 1970 plan.

Meredith Drake Reitan's essay on the supergraphics ordinance shows the continuing debate between beauty and commerce. Billboards and supergraphics have become so valuable to developers that negotiations about their inclusion in major developments is now a given. Unlike other jurisdictions that ban them (Beverly Hills) or heavily tax them (New York City), LA is the Wild West, where thousands of billboards, many of them illegal (untaxed and unpermitted) desecrate—or is it illuminate?—the landscape. Since owners can get anywhere from $5,000 to $150,000 per month rent for spaces on their buildings, the temptation to violate an ordinance that brings minimal fines is like asking a surfer to pass up the perfect wave.

Altering conventional processes and producing a greener vision, such as the one Wolch and her colleagues discuss, demands hard choices and a commitment to policies that support environmental solutions, including envisioning a new LA. The Friends of the Los Angeles River have suggested that a river that looks like a river is only a small start in connecting life to work and play and establishing Los Angeles as the Garden of Eden to which Topping alludes. Yet the river could also serve as a new spine for a clean technology industry as well as a new symbol of a revitalized city that looks beyond commercial projects for its self-image.

An Urban Place That Remains Firmly Suburban

Balancing the public's continued desire for a suburban metropolis that is not too dense, is not too fragmented, and offers amenities without endangering precious lifestyles, is an enormous challenge. Even as South LA residents pray for more development that will bring healthier restaurants and full-service grocery stores, other places in Southern California are trying to better manage, slow, or even stop growth.

Simon Pastucha's description of LA's Urban Design Studio raises a last point about the beauty and blandness of LA. I find Grand Avenue the most frustrating place in the city. The street is home to some of our most spectacular recent architectural triumphs, with another coming in 2013 when the Broad Museum opens. Disney Hall, MOCA, the Los Angeles Cathedral, and the Colburn School represent together an array of finely designed, very usable spaces. They sit atop Bunker Hill, which remains one of the foremost examples of urban renewal's limitations.

For 20 years, I have been leading walking and bus tours down the street, infuriated by the lost opportunities to build an urban place at our civic and cultural center. LA is a global city with millions of residents where the civic leaders seem firmly committed to a planning vision that rejects the disorder and energy of a great city. When one walks by Disney Hall, the experience is breathtaking and slightly discomforting. Unless you have a lot of money to spend at Patina restaurant, Disney Hall stands in physical isolation from its surroundings. Similarly, the breathtaking Los Angeles Cathedral and the adjacent MOCA are situated in isolated spaces with no surrounding restaurants, shops, or other activities. MOCA's restaurant is at its lower level, completely disconnected from the street (just as the Los Angeles County Museum of Art has its restaurant inside its courtyard, and the Getty Museum's lovely café demands a ride on a monorail). So the tours I lead walk through the Disney Hall lobby and stream away to the next "star architecture" project, without a stop for ice cream, lunch, or any other activity.

Charles Moore recognized the issue when he wrote about the architectural star from the previous generation, the Music Center, also on Grand Avenue, next door to Disney Hall. Moore (1998, 15), skewering the building's pretentiousness and its aspirations to serve as the centerpiece of LA's acropolis, and then noting, "the designers might have remembered you have to *get* to an acropolis." Instead, "the main access to the Music Center is up from the basement parking. Otherwise you crawl up some emergency stairs that allow you to feel you've arrived at the service entrance. You feel really silly if you've gotten all dressed up." Why are so many of our great buildings so physically isolated from the street, set amid so much blank space, and conceptually cordoned off from other activities? Deluded by the dream of the "better city" without the disorder and congestion of earlier models, LA too often falls back on the suburban mentality that separates and isolates rather than integrates and congregates.

Organization of This Book

Trying to view LA is a challenge for the editor as well as the tourist. Just as the tourist must decide between Disneyland or Universal Studios, mountains or beaches, the editor must make choices about what gets discussed. I decided that more voices are better than fewer, risking that readers might find the book too fragmented, just as Robert Fogelson (1993) found the city. LA fascinates us—this book's professors, professionals, and photographers—because of its confounding contradictions and demanding physical and social realities, so a book about planning LA requires a multiplicity of voices to portray the cacophonous quality of LA. A diversity of voices and visions is better than a coherent narrative dictated by a single or a small number of authors and artists, even though some readers may wonder about other voices that could be included or how they can fit all the voices together to "understand" LA. A book can only provide insights—snapshots in our increasingly visual world—that can help visitors and residents alike as they experience the city. So the only way to present Los Angeles is as a mulitiplicity, with multiple cities and multiple perspectives competing for attention.

The book is divided into six sections representing conventional planning concerns: history, demography and populations, land use, transportation, parks and open space, and economic development. Within each of the sections, an author has provided an overview essay that is supplemented with a series of essays on specific topics relevant to that field. These essays include the examination of a specific development, such as Playa Vista; a plan, such as the Glendale Downtown Specific Plan; a policy, such as the Adaptive Reuse Ordinance; and an exploration of events, such as the 1992 Civic Unrest. Punctuating the sections are short explorations of innovative, sometimes alternative projects or places, such as the downtown Civic Park and Leimert Park's KAOS Art Center.

Most Americans seem to view LA with dread, reflecting Robert Redford's derisive opinion, "If you stay in Beverly Hills too long you become a Mercedes." Outsiders' perception of LA is more likely to be its superficiality—surfer dudes and buxom blondes, Valley girls and movie moguls, or a suburban family sitting around its backyard barbeque in a drab neighborhood of ticky-tacky houses. Angelenos sometimes reinforce this perception by being self-deprecating to the point of needing to boost LA, as if it needed to be the biggest, the best, the most amazing, the next, new, postmodern city. Out here on the "island on the land," residents still feel a sense of separation even in an age of airplanes and the Internet.

The description of LA as an illegible landscape with a superficial society is, though, actually unintelligible for many of us who live here. We know LA is teeming with innovative planning projects, experimental media and visual arts, intriguing housing and community development concepts, technological and environmental advances, pioneering street and conventional theater, all set in an ethnic and racial mash-up representative of a 21st-century urban reality. People around the globe wear clothes, play games, buy home features, adopt bits of language, and listen to music pioneered on the streets and in the communities of Southern California. Readers will find surprises and unexpected complexities in these essays; they will also find humor, innovation, and controversy. The city and its surrounding region frustrate, vibrate, and demand that we contemplate, even as they too seldom relate, enough to make any visitor take pause, look around, and find something that excites or repels, making LA always engaging.

HISTORY OF PLANNING

2

Challenging the Myth of an Unplanned Los Angeles

Todd Gish

LOS ANGELES GREW UP SUDDENLY—PLANLESSLY—UNDER THE
STIMULI OF THE ADVENTUROUS SPIRIT OF MILLIONS OF PEOPLE
AND THE PROFIT MOTIVE. —LOUIS ADAMIC[1]

PLANNING IN LOS ANGELES? IN THE WORLD'S EYES THIS IS A
SELF-CANCELLING CONCEPT. —REYNER BANHAM[2]

Call it ugly, call it beautiful, call it dysfunctional—but don't call Los Angeles *unplanned*. The British scholar and honorary Angeleno who wrote the second epigraph above concluded: "this has always been a planned city." A long record of public and private planning for this city and region is found in archives and policies, streets and neighborhoods, contradicting an enduring urban legend of LA as the quintessentially unplanned metropolis—the great cautionary tale for anyone interested in good city building.[3]

Why the persistent myth of an unplanned LA? First, the cliché of a somehow improvised metropolis is just one component of a larger urban mythology of the City of Angels as unique: exceptional as a place not only on the ground but also in the imagination.[4] On the one hand, the city has been obsessively promoted for well over a century (starting with booster advertising in the 1870s) via repetitive, compelling, and frequently inflated promises of beautiful scenery, ideal climate, economic opportunity, and idyllic lifestyle.[5] On the other hand, works of *noir* literature and critical theory describe a bleak, dystopic LA of perverted souls, corrupt institutions, and exclusionary society (McWilliams 1973, Davis 1990). The myth of an unplanned LA fits *both* versions of this unusual story: generations of newly arrived real estate entrepreneurs, platting one leafy suburb after another for home owners of every stripe and unencumbered by downtown bureaucracy; or greedy developers clearing out cheap farmland on an ever-moving urban fringe, effectively mandating automobile ownership and congested commutes, all without input or resistance from impotent (or complicit) local officials. In either scenario, planning ranges from nonexistent to inadequate to incompetent.[6]

Second, the distinction between the *making* and *implementing* of plans means that a long line of them for LA—a regional open space network, a "City Beautiful" civic center, a downtown people mover, a system of helicopter transit stations—somehow do not count because they were not executed (LA City Planning Commission 1928, 1944, 1954, 1955). But many plans were, and their legacy on the ground is there for good, ill, or indifference. "Bad" (or poor or failed) planning is still planning. Indeed, some of the very features of the Angeleno urban landscape now considered shortcomings are evidence of one era or another's state-of-the-art planning.

Third, sheer size hides the reality of planning. "Los Angeles" is now a city of 468 square miles, a county of 4,084 square miles containing some 88 municipalities, hundreds of unofficial communities, and vast unincorporated territory. And in the minds of some, LA is a massive region extending even farther (Figure 2.1). This vast scale is not new: in 1933, participants at an international meeting of architects and urbanists analyzed same-scale plans of major cities. Maps depicting Paris, London, Berlin, Rome, Barcelona, Detroit, Baltimore, and others covered from one to a few panels. The great array of panels describing LA "produced a monstrosity of oversize" that dominated the exhibition space.[7] Then and since, the absence of a totalizing order for a place of nearly incomprehensible size can render invisible all the various plans and planning for smaller sections.

Figure 2.1. Los Angeles City Planning Commission map, ca. 1922. The name "Los Angeles" has long held multiple geographic meanings: city, county, and region.

Fourth, the standard U.S. planning history chronology favors established eastern and midwestern municipalities, depicting a rich past of innovative plans by distinguished practitioners: Frederick Law Olmsted and Robert Moses in New York City; William Penn and Edmund Bacon in Philadelphia; Olmsted and Daniel Burnham in Chicago; Pierre L'Enfant, then Olmsted (Jr.) and Burnham in Washington, D.C.; Alfred Bettman in Cincinnati; George Keller in Kansas City; and Harland Bartholomew in

St. Louis.[8] As LA supposedly broke the mold of the "traditional" city with its climate, culture, and geography, so it somehow *just grew* without planning, according to the stereotype. This partiality by scholars has delayed research into West Coast urbanization and planning—and ignored an impressive list of national experts working in LA and a growing literature discussing it.[9]

None of the myth-challenging counternarrative to follow is to equate the City of Angels with the City by the Bay, the Windy City, the Motor City, or others. Local specifics of timing, geography, climate, culture, and demographics distinguish each place. One signature aspect of LA is its vast, diffuse physical form; this condition emerged relatively early, as a collection of streetcar settlements linked to a dense urban core via transit lines. The arrival of the automobile as a *force majeur* came later but easier to LA as a result of the dispersed, low-density pattern already in place. Despite particulars, LA has at least one thing in common with San Francisco, Chicago, Detroit, and the rest. Over time, the city, county, and region have been the object of intense work by many planners: public servants, private professionals, civic leaders, and others attempting to apply the best city-building practices of their day to local conditions.

Planning before Planners

Los Angeles was planned from its founding. El Pueblo de Nuestra Señora la Reina de los Angeles was established in 1781 as an outpost for the Spanish colonial government quartered in faraway Mexico City. This and other newly planted North American settlements—such as St. Augustine and Santa Fe—came under the jurisdiction of Spain's Laws of the Indies, a detailed program for development, administration, and society (Crouch, Garr, and Mundigo 1982, chap. 3). The rules were many, though only some were followed; but the planning was there in a pattern that shaped subsequent city building. Los Angeles became a Mexican city in 1821, then a city in U.S. territory in 1848. Municipal officials throughout the 1850s sought to sell off some of the city's lands, hiring government surveyors to create accurate maps of the town core and surrounding territory (Robinson 1948, chap. 15). Part cadastral survey and part subdivision plat, these de facto plans were crucial to the next phase of land sale and development, and generative of the city's urbanization pattern over the next century. Their most striking feature was the orientation of new property lines to the compass points, breaking sharply with the diagonal orientation of the original *pueblo* pattern—a contrast still evident along the western edge of downtown where the two converge.[10]

Intensive real estate activity and business expansion have famously played a large part in the urbanization of LA.[11] But no city has grown simply via unchecked private enterprise—not even LA.[12] In every city, before coalescence of a defined planning profession or municipal planning agencies, a range of urban actors performed a variety of tasks we now call "planning" (Teaford 1984, Hammack 1988, Schultz 1989, Revell 2003). Lawyers, engineers, architects, landscape architects, social reformers, doctors, nurses, realtors, and journalists served as advisors to local government, as consultants to civic or business organizations (who lobbied local government), or simply as advocates and activists. Local officials themselves were the most influential of these proto-planners. In the name of public administration and public works, the ordinary business of surveying, regulating, and servicing the expanding metropolis fell to elected city council members and county commissioners. Once approved, tasks and assignments were then carried out by the municipal engineer, district attorney, county sheriff, building official, or outside consultant.

Los Angeles City Council members achieved the seeming impossible as well as the routine as they dealt with matters ranging from major infrastructure projects to the provision of basic services, streets and infrastructure, nuisance complaints, safety, and protection of public and private property. Two major public works projects accomplished in the first decade or so of the 20th century fundamentally transformed the region's future. The Los Angeles Aqueduct cost about $24 million (1907 dollars) and extended 223 miles north to the Owens Valley, tapping a plentiful and reliable source of water for the increasingly hydro-challenged city. Miles away to the south, work at the harbor on the Port of Los Angeles quickly turned the growing metropolis into a global *entrepôt*, at a crucial nexus where continental railroad lines met international shipping lanes. Both aqueduct and port required extended political wrangling involving multiple jurisdictions; land acquisition and public financing; coordinated engineering, design, and construction; and, once complete, operations and administration. These massive pieces of infrastructure were clearly cases of urban (even regional) planning, accomplished by proto-planners pulling the various levers of a diversifying municipal apparatus, concerned with future growth and order in the built environment (Erie 1992).

More routinely, Angeleno proto-planners working to ensure the safety and prosperity of their municipality considered much more modest public improvements. Typical council business in the 1890s, for example, included hearing property owner petitions for infrastructure: some sought street openings and grading to connect remote parcels to the urban grid, while others petitioned for access to water from the river or to connect to the growing municipal sewer system. Many "public" improvements in this period were paid for privately, often by property assessment on affected parcels.[13]

Regulating private property was another common task. The city council passed ordinances aimed at multiple aspects of construction (height, material, location, layout) to limit the impact of fires in certain districts. Building codes led to wider controls, and Angeleno officials pioneered early land-use regulation—years before New York City's zoning ordinance of 1916.[14] As LA grew in population, commerce, and industry, conflicts between neighboring property owners multiplied. Plaintiffs' nuisance claims, ranging from the aesthetic to the life-threatening, were answered in one localized ordinance after another, for years. Then, between 1904 (when the council prohibited new industrial uses in one part of the city) and 1910 (when the council finished carving the municipality into nominal residential and industrial districts), these proto-planners extended and transformed long standing nuisance law into a broader application of land-use controls over large urban territories that gained national attention—and provided a test case for zoning advocates across the United States.[15]

Progressive Urban Reform

The conventional narrative of American planning history begins with progressive urban reform in the first two decades of the 20th century, when several loosely related advocacy movements worked to improve conditions of health, sanitation, housing, civic beauty, and recreation in cities (Scott 1971; Boyer 1978, chaps. 15–19;

Krueckeberg 1983; Teaford 1986). Progressive Angelenos fully participated in this early planning work; they were linked to other reformers via trade publications and national conferences, and they contributed to a nationwide discourse touting the latest strategies. Visitor Jane Addams, founder of Chicago's famed Hull House, spurred concerned Angelenos in the early 1890s to establish a local college settlement association to aid poor working and immigrant families (Koslow 2001). In 1905, muckraking journalist Jacob Riis, author of the landmark *How the Other Half Lives*, an exposé of vile Manhattan tenement conditions, spoke to a packed Los Angeles auditorium on the evils of congested slum housing.[16]

These and other visitors found a rapidly changing city. Between 1900 and 1920, population grew more than fivefold: the city from 102,000 to 576,000, and the county from 170,000 to 936,000.[17] Robust economic activity and industrial development brought growth and aggravated crowding, congestion, and poverty as thousands of poor and working-class families jammed into ramshackle housing. Pundits warned of inaction: "As foreign immigrants pour into our rapidly growing city . . . Los Angeles will find itself a second New York," the worst condemnation possible, given Gotham's dreadful reputation for social alienation and physical squalor (LA County Housing Commission 1908–1909, 4). In 1907, the brand-new LA Housing Commission responded by targeting house courts—the region's pervasive, horizontally configured form of slum housing—in its comprehensive housing ordinance, one partially modeled on tenement regulations in New York City.[18]

Some reformers viewed the ugliness of slums and ordinary blight as a stain on the city's appearance—an absolute emergency for Angeleno boosters loudly and continuously publicizing their city to the nation as a virtual paradise. The Los Angeles Municipal Arts Commission was appointed in 1903 to ensure civic beautification. Its mission, aligned with those in other cities, fit boosters' promotional goals and included urging enforcement of signage laws and making recommendations for tree planting and streetlight installation (LA Municipal Art Commission 1904).

City Beautiful plans became the hallmark of progressive urban design, as municipal governments and civic associations nationwide pursued the state of the art in capital improvements (Wilson 1989). Street patterns, park groupings, and public buildings all formally composed in a grandiose axial layout characterized the ideal (Burnham and Bennett 1970; Hines 1974, chaps. 7, 9, and 14).

Ambitious arts commissioners convinced the city council to hire nationally recognized design consultant Charles Mulford Robinson in 1906. His sweeping proposal included a new civic center, train station, grand boulevard, and public gardens.[19] Fanfare greeted the plan's release in 1909, but authorities facing tight public budgets and resistant property owners declined to carry it out. A decade later and beyond, other City Beautiful designs were proposed—one for a vast civic center district downtown that would contain city, county, state, and federal facilities and expansive public spaces.[20] Meanwhile, in nearby Pasadena, Burnham protégé and Plan of Chicago coauthor Edward Bennett proposed his own Beaux Arts plan for the upper-middle-class enclave in 1923 (Scheid 2009). The Pasadena plan was implemented and still guides development there; the LA plan remained on the shelf.

The booming City of Angels needed more than just stately public buildings and attractive parks; advocates knew it needed comprehensive planning. Initially, private volunteers had driven planning reforms; now, local governments began appointing citizen commissions to advise policy makers on specific problems and solutions. In 1910, a quasi-public city planning committee was appointed; in 1915, a privately organized city planning association was formed of local notables, who lobbied the city council for an official commission. Their work paid off in 1920 when a group of well-connected civic leaders—instructed to "dream dreams and see visions . . . of the better city to be"—was appointed, forming the new Los Angeles City Planning Commission.[21] Pragmatics quickly trumped visions, however, and planning work focused on street improvements, public facilities, and more articulated and effective zoning and subdivision rules.[22] Continued growth had weakened land-use regulations in a piecemeal fashion: officials faced "chaos among the property owners . . . due to the fact . . . no one knows what to build or where."[23] Yet the process continued. A new city charter in 1925 increased funding and authority and created a city planning department to support this and other commission work (Figure 2.2)

Figure 2.2. Los Angeles City Planning Department report frontispiece, ca. 1925. The Planning Department's self-representation literally frames a map of the booming metropolis showing the city as a hub for every form of modern transportation.

Regional Plans and Planning

Farsighted planners recognized the need to work at an even larger scale: the multijurisdictional metropolitan region. The legendary Plan of Chicago had shown the way, with its ambitious proposal for regionally integrated transportation and open space extending beyond city limits and even state lines (Burnham and Bennett 1970). In the late 1920s, the nonprofit Regional Plan Association (RPA) published the massive Regional Plan of New York and Its Environs, with a scope reaching into New Jersey and Connecticut and aiming to accommodate an additional 10 million in population by the 1960s.[24] Some Angelenos admired this level of ambition.

By 1920, Greater Los Angeles already extended for many hundreds of square miles and included smaller cities such as Torrance, Santa Monica, Inglewood, Long Beach, Pasadena, Glendale, Whittier, Pomona, and many more unincorporated towns. Most were linked to the "parent" City of Angels by a growing network of streets and highways, as well as a radial web of interurban rail transit with more than 1,100 miles of track reaching into four counties. Everything was expanding: more people, more traffic, more development.

In 1922—just as New York's RPA was getting to work—the board of supervisors established the Los Angeles County Regional Planning Commission (LACRPC), making it among the first public metropolitan planning agencies in the United States. Its mission was to (1) better control new development in unincorporated county territory and (2) work with constituent municipalities to coordinate items such as land use, circulation, and flood control, despite conflicting "home-rule" politics between jurisdictions (LA County 1931).

Multiple plans were produced—some by the LACRPC, some by private organizations—to address the most urgent challenges facing the region, with mixed success (Robbins and Tilton 1941). Automobile and truck traffic congestion and connectivity across the metropolis were huge and growing concerns, as the use of private vehicles only continued to escalate. As a result, much regional planning focused on highways and circulation (Bottles 1987, Roth 2007, Axelrod 2009). The Traffic Commission of the City and County of Los Angeles hired national experts Frederick Law Olmsted Jr., Harland Bartholomew, and Charles Cheney to produce the 1924 Major Traffic Street Plan. Its provisions for a vast grid of new and widened streets was largely implemented, though a steady rise in auto use quickly nullified any imagined traffic reduction. Highways remained a main focus of LACRPC into the 1930s and '40s, and its planners produced a master plan of highways and laid the groundwork for subsequent state and federal highway planning in the area (e.g., LA County 1929 and 1931, LACRPC 1941).

Implementation of other regional plans was only partial—or nonexistent. In the late 1920s, for example, the Olmsted and Bartholomew firms were again hired, this time by the powerful Los Angeles Chamber of Commerce, whose booster elites worried about the lack of attractive parks in a place promoted for its environmental qualities (see Hise and Deverell in Chapter 6). The result was a visionary document proposing a vast countywide system of new parkways, open space preserves, and beachfront improvements, as well as a new state-level agency with taxation authority to ensure long-term funding (Olmsted Brothers and Harland Bartholomew and Associates 1930). This plan was relegated to the shelf due to its steep fiscal and political aspirations, though some individual recommendations eventually made their way into later park and highway planning.

In the years that followed, Angeleno planners and developers drew upon leaders of the emerging profession as well as concepts popular nationally and internationally. Figures such as Olmsted Jr., Bartholomew, Clarence Perry, and Clarence Stein either influenced developments or actually worked in LA. Far from being unplanned, the city and its suburbs often displayed lessons learned from the exemplars of what was considered good planning (Hise and Deverell 2000).

Subdivisions and Neighborhoods

The regulation of land subdivision became increasingly critical into the 1920s and 1930s, as widespread automobility and worsening urban congestion prompted continuing extension of the urban grid outward and the multiplication of satellite suburbs beyond the fringe of many U.S. cities. Sophisticated developers providing for community functions were uncommon, and public planning authority to require such was still limited; any landowner could still easily purchase a tract, subdivide it into many lots with few restrictions, start selling, and move on to the next.[25] The resulting hodgepodge, replicated time after time and mile after mile, suffered multiple problems: (1) unbalanced land uses emphasizing single-family housing to the exclusion of apartments, shops, schools, and parks; (2) traffic problems caused by unaligned local streets; (3) pedestrian dangers due to a shortage of sidewalks and multiple crossings; and (4) a perceived lack of interaction among people moving to areas underserved by such basics and amenities. Los Angeles became famous for a disorderly process that was common all over the United States (e.g., Zunz 1982, Harris 1996, Sandweiss 2001). (See Figure 2.3.)

For the 1929 Regional Plan for New York and Its Environs, sociologist Clarence Perry devised his "neighborhood unit" concept as a replicable template for the laying out of discrete, multifunctional neighborhoods. The unit was sized for a population

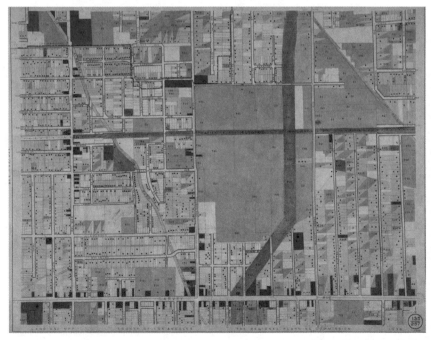

Figure 2.3. Los Angeles County Regional Planning Commission land-use survey, 1936, showing a southeastern part of the county. By the 1920s and '30s, the combination of population growth, expanding automobile use, prolific land subdivision, and limited land-use regulation transformed many agricultural areas, worrying city and county planners concerned about disorderly growth.

of 5,000 to 6,000, with proposed shops and apartments located along major arterials and home sites on minor internal streets, all to be centered on a park, an elementary school, and neighborhood institutions. Perry's plan recognized the automobile as both an accessibility solution and a safety problem, and he worked to locate the heaviest vehicular traffic at the unit's periphery. Overall, the wide range of functions, carefully laid out in modules of appropriate size, was intended to encourage positive social formation of the kind found in established urban neighborhoods (Committee on the Regional Plan of New York and Its Environs 1929, 7: 34–35; Perry 1939, chap. 3).

Between 1924 and 1928, more than 72,000 new lots flooded Los Angeles County's real estate market, and Angeleno planners embraced the neighborhood unit as quickly as their counterparts did elsewhere (LACRPC 1929). In a 1931 publication of the LACRPC, an idealized, hypothetical layout for a self-contained town titled Community Plan of 1000 Acres was presented as the latest thinking to guide small-town officials and large-scale developers. Aside from minor deviations, the plan is plainly a cluster of six of Perry's neighborhood units woven together.[26] (See Figure 2.4.)

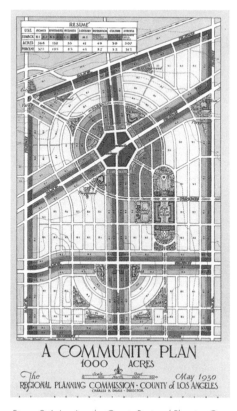

Figure 2.4. Los Angeles County Regional Planning Commission, proposed community plan, 1930. When one of the area's last surviving Mexican-era ranchos went on sale, the county published a community plan promoting the latest in best planning practices: neighborhood units, transitional zoning, and a hierarchical street pattern.

Similarly, a neighborhood unit plan was described in a 1932 report of the LA City Planning Commission as a "typical example of . . . zoning as applied to a quarter-section of the San Fernando Valley section of the city" (LA City Planning Commission, 1931–1932, 12). Angeleno planners rendered this version as easy to implement as possible by (1) removing sites reserved for open space and institutions and (2) eliminating Perry's asymmetrical layout of varying block shapes and curvilinear streets. Both modifications were significant: a shortage of park land was high on residents' list of urban complaints, and this move only worsened the problem. The geometric aspect was similarly pragmatic. The unit was an exact square, a half-mile on each side, matching Perry diagram's 160-acre size while clearly adopting the quarter-section land increment so common in real estate transactions.

Decades later, dozens of square miles in the Valley had been developed as (modified) neighborhood units. Mile after mile of boulevards alternate with secondary streets lined with low-rise apartment buildings, punctuated every half-mile by a small corner store or minimall and every mile by a larger strip center—all forming an expanded tartan grid of activity buffering internal quadrants of single-family houses on tertiary residential streets.

Garden City, USA

English reformer Ebenezer Howard's bold Garden City concept proposed a regional system of new, small cities, surrounded by landscaped greenbelts and connected by modern transportation—providing planners everywhere with another, more daring strategy to address growth (Howard 1965). Each constituent city would be self-contained with the full range of urban functions, not simply another bedroom suburb. An entire system of complete but dispersed settlements was appealing to both theorists and practitioners. Adherents of Howard's vision built a couple of model garden cities in England, and American enthusiasts followed suit with their own versions, which attracted interest from urban reformers, private developers, and others. Two of the best-known built examples in the United States are Forest Hills Gardens in Queens, New York (1910), planned and designed by Frederick Law Olmsted Jr. and Grosvenor Atterbury, and Radburn in Fair Lawn, New Jersey (1929), by Clarence Stein and Henry Wright. Howard's boldest communitarian ideas about urbanism were dropped, resulting in attractive, well-designed housing amid lavish open space, occasionally with some community facilities but rarely with any industry or other jobs-related component (Perry 1939, 209–13; Stein 1957, chap. 2).

Though Los Angeles cannot be described as a garden city (or system), Howard's concept for dispersed, well-designed settlements has appealed to generations of regionally minded Angelenos. In the 1910s, the city's housing commission lauded the concept as a wise use for vast stretches of open land: "Along these miles bordering the rapid transit systems will be built the garden cities of the future."[27] By the 1920s, city and regional planners looking for strategies to decongest the increasingly sprawling but still centralized structure of Greater Los Angeles considered a diffuse pattern of self-sufficient satellite communities designed with the automobile in mind as one solution (Axelrod 2009).

Two decades later, a master plan for the vast San Fernando Valley recommended a "'regional city' [with] a number of well-planned and moderately sized communities of reasonable density, separated by agricultural areas, the whole bounded by a well-developed system of parkways and highways." In text Howard himself could have penned, the plan proposed "compact communities planned to have all the amenities of a country town . . . to be wholly self-sustaining . . . and encircled by agricultural greenbelts."[28] And as late as 1970, the proposed Concept Plan for the entire LA municipality (see Vinit Mukhija's essay in this chapter) was "characterized by centers of high density development, interspersed by low density areas of areas of parks and single-family neighborhoods, and connected by an integrated transportation network" (LA City Planning Dept. 1969–1970 and 1974). Neither comprehensive plan was implemented, but the long-standing allure of the idealized garden city settlement strategy for bringing order to a vast terrain was evident in both.

A few of the many suburban towns around core cities such as LA were promoted as garden cities. Few, if any, met the ideal described by Howard, but a number of them bore resemblance to the model versions built by his adherents.[29] In 1911, for example, businessman Jared Torrance set about developing an eponymous, self-sufficient "modern industrial city" of jobs, housing, commerce, and open space well-situated in southwest Los Angeles County near a rail line connecting downtown to the harbor.[30] The developer hired Olmsted Jr., who laid out an axial plan centered on a new rail station, business district, and park. This core anchored a larger plan that carefully separated industrial, commercial, and residential land uses; noted architect Irving Gill designed many of the public buildings. Angeleno reformer Dana Bartlett approved of the plan: "In the garden city of Torrance . . . will be a city liveable for those who move from the smoky, dirt-begrimed industrial regions of the older city. It will seem like entering a new world."[31] Initial progress was slow, but Torrance eventually became a fully functioning city.

The more focused garden suburb found a home in LA, too. Baldwin Hills Village is a remarkable example, implemented with help from Clarence Stein (1957, chap. 9; Wong 2001). This project, in Stein's words, "was to demonstrate the practical possibilities of spacious homes and surroundings in an orderly community . . . using the basic features of the Radburn idea: superblock, homes facing central greens [and] pedestrian and auto completely separated" (1957, 190). The 64-acre village contains 627 attached apartment units, along with garages, service structures, and community buildings all deployed in a finely calibrated hierarchy of lush outdoor spaces (private gardens, semipublic courts, recreation areas, and public greenways). Stein saw this Angeleno adaptation as the pinnacle of his work on this kind of housing: "At Baldwin Hills Village . . . the Radburn Idea was given its most complete and most characteristic expression" (1957, 189). No less an authority than Lewis Mumford praised the project as "an outstanding example of good planning" (1961, 432ff.). Many large-scale garden apartment projects proliferated in the years before and after World War II, including Wyvernwood near East Los Angeles and Lincoln Place in Venice. Each was related in concept to Baldwin Hills Village (and Radburn), but none fully employed its complete inventory of sophisticated components (Sansbury 1993).

Urban Renewal and Redevelopment
The push for central city renewal in the 1940s defies another myth—that of a center-less LA, "a collection of suburbs in search of a city" (McWilliams 1973, 235). A large and vibrant downtown did exist and, as in many American cities, parts of it had become degraded over time by slum housing, abandoned buildings, crumbling infrastructure, failing businesses, and a declining tax base. Bunker Hill—a knoll at the edge of the growing city—was developed as an exclusive residential district starting in the 1880s (Longstreth 1998; Davis 2000, chap. 3; Bottles 1987, chap. 7; Foster 1971). Flourishing for decades as an elite enclave, the neighborhood declined as commercial activity gradually expanded around it (Pugsley 1977, Loukaitou-Sideris and Sansbury 1995–1996). By the 1930s, its aging mansions had been carved into rental flats or replaced by residential hotels and apartment buildings; its population by this time was densely packed and relatively poor, with crime and disease rates comparatively high. Suburban competition only made matters worse for the aging

downtown: as development resumed after World War II, real estate investors showed little interest in this area when vast new sites waited on the Westside and in the San Fernando Valley.[32]

Federal remedies for urban ills were devised in the U.S. Housing Acts of 1949 and 1954 to help state and local governments. Newly created redevelopment agencies used new tools to acquire, assemble, reconfigure, regulate, and resell property—making them public developers. Relying on visual cues of physical obsolescence and ignoring less visible community ties, planners declared entire districts blighted, cleared them by wholesale demolition, and (often) replaced them using modernist design on a large scale in places such as Boston's West End, Chicago's Hyde Park, and LA's Bunker Hill (Parson 2005, chap. 5).

The Los Angeles Community Redevelopment Agency (CRA) was established in 1948, with CRA planners turning their attention to Bunker Hill in the 1950s. Officials and elites hoped to attract major corporations to a new acropolis of business downtown but worried that "the headquarter offices of major companies will not locate in Los Angeles as long as only hit and miss opportunities are provided in terms of planning for their needs."[33] Apparently the ideal locations for new corporate command posts were not only large, construction-ready sites but also ones amid compatible land uses and serviced by new infrastructure. The project area covered a vast 136 acres—the largest at the time in the nation—and reconfigured some 326 lots into 25 large parcels on widened avenues. Multiple plan drafts were produced and revised during the decade with the intent of creating a cohesive new district. The 1958 plan approved by the city council proposed a catalog of essentials common to renewal projects across the nation: "ultramodern office buildings of 20 stories or more; apartments and hotels, multi-decked parking structures, landscaped plazas, separated vehicle and pedestrian movement and other modern features."[34]

On Bunker Hill itself, original occupants were evicted by the thousands, buildings bulldozed by the hundreds, parcels reconfigured, and streets improved. But further progress was slow and implementation stalled at several points, as reluctant landowners, litigation, federal regulations, and an uncooperative real estate market conspired to keep many sites vacant for decades.[35] Only four parcels had been developed by the late 1960s, and a majority of parcels would not be built upon and occupied until the 1980s. Even today, Bunker Hill still holds a few vacant lots among its huge collection of modern (and postmodern) building complexes and plazas. The city council reacted to the problems and delays by denying approval for another, even larger redevelopment plan nearby. Only the recent surge in housing construction and residential conversions of old office buildings has managed to breathe sustained activity back into downtown LA.

Conclusions

By the 1950s, Los Angeles City Planning Department offices were a destination for visiting planners.[36] In the 1960s, worsening structural inequality and social exclusion experienced by minority communities, highlighted in the infamous Watts riots, gave participatory planning a much-needed urgency and boost. After 15 years of broad participation and preparation, the city's massive new general plan was adopted in 1974, proposing dense subcenters surrounded by low-density residential neighborhoods, all woven together by a new transit system. Though that system never material-ized, a renewed interest and impetus for major public transportation improvements for the region was reborn; the county Metropolitan Transportation Authority now oversees this expanding work, helping to reshape many parts of the metropolis. The CRA (www.crala.org) now oversees well over a hundred projects that provide renovation, rehabilitation, and services rather than clean-slate demolition and wholesale rebuild-ing. And regional land-use and transportation strategies are conceived and proposed by the Southern California Association of Governments (SCAG; www.scag.ca.gov), the nation's largest council of governments—one that includes six counties, 190 mu-nicipalities, and more than 19 million residents.

Greater Los Angeles has been planned since its beginning. Plans ranging from ambitious to timid, with scales from large to small, have been implemented or al-lowed to languish. Practitioners have responded to similar problems, been guided by the same concepts, applied the same tools, and pursued the same goals as their counterparts in other cities, and not just recently. At about the time Thomas Jefferson was devising the National Land Ordinance for survey and settlement of U.S. territo-ries, the first Angelenos were in the process of applying Spain's Laws of the Indies to their new *pueblo*. Just after Chicago's proto-planners had accomplished nothing less than reversing the flow of the Chicago River, their counterparts in Los Angeles began construction of a massive aqueduct that would hydrate their city from more than 200 miles away. While Daniel Burnham was designing a City Beautiful civic center for Chicago, Charles Mulford Robinson was doing the same for LA. Frederick Law Olmsted Jr.'s plan for Forest Hills Gardens in New York was done just before his work on the suburban towns of Torrance and Palos Verdes Estates. When New York City's comprehensive zoning ordinance was enacted, Angeleno officials were more than a decade into administrating their city's use districts. Both New York's RPA and the LACRPC were established the same year. Clarence Perry's neighborhood unit concept was published in the Regional Plan for New York and Its Environs just before a close variant appeared in two major LA planning documents. Clarence Stein's application of garden city ideas at Radburn, New Jersey, and the subsequent federal greenbelt cities program was soon followed by his work at Baldwin Hills Village. Later, as bull-dozers leveled old neighborhoods for replacement with modernist towers in Boston's West End, LA's Bunker Hill met a similar fate. Planning theorist Kevin Lynch consulted with the Los Angeles City Planning Department in the 1960s on its comprehensive plan preparation (LA City Planning Dept. 1966).

More recently, new urbanist Andres Duany planned the neotraditional towns of Seaside and Celebration in Florida, not long before his work on the thousand-acre Playa Vista project in West Los Angeles and the Downtown Strategic Plan. Transit-oriented development champion Peter Calthorpe's plans for San Diego, San Jose, and Sacramento just predated his development study for Downtown LA's South Park district and visioning work for SCAG. Finally, as smart-growth advocates around the nation have encouraged higher urban density and infill development to help curb sprawl, Angeleno officials have adopted a small-lot subdivision ordinance with the same objectives.

Besides the long-standing East Coast favoritism among American urban scholars, another slant has hindered an understanding of planning in Los Angeles. What historians call presentist bias—20/20 hindsight, some might call it—insists on looking at historical events through a contemporary lens, projecting current values onto people and institutions in the past and disregarding the context in which they operated. Typically, historical actors fail the modern test. In this case, planning orthodoxy's 21st-century disapproval of automobile-oriented design, low-density suburbs, land-use segregation, and modernist high-rise downtowns indicts or negates the work of practitioners performing what were the profession's best practices in the first two-thirds of the 1900s.

This ahistoric view props up the myth of an unplanned or ill-planned LA by forgetting important facts (Hise and Deverell 2005): (1) widespread public opinion about the region's extensive transit system was quite hostile by the 1910s: "General perception of the automobile as a democratic piece of urban technology influenced [the] support [of] automobile transit as an alternative to the inefficiency and seeming corruption of the railways" (Bottles 1987, 15); (2) continued mixing of residential and commercial land uses was commonly considered injurious to public health, family life, and property values in the early 1900s—devising a legal means to separate these primary urban functions was the *raison d'être* of planning theory and praxis in this period; (3) similarly, urban concentration and high population density was considered harmful—expansion into suburban towns and satellite subdivisions was already common and accepted around U.S. cities, serving most economic classes. In this historic context, then, planners in and around LA were doing their jobs—and doing them well.

To think of LA as unique is to sequester it from discourse. Dismissing it as un-planned or badly planned is a cliché useful to pundits but useless to professionals and observers seeking nuanced debate on public policy and urban development. LA's particular form has not resulted from absent or bad planning but from generations of "good" planning—the best practices of their day, promoted by the profession and variously applied to specific areas and subject to local circumstances of geography, climate, politics, economics, and culture, just as in every city. In plans and regula-tions, planners required a host of new features for the growing metropolis, block by block, subdivision by subdivision: single-use zoning; larger lots; wider streets; and greater provisions for parking. They laid out mile after mile of new infrastructure for automobiles, buses, and trucks (streets, bridges, grade separations, freeways) while essentially leaving rail transit on its own. And they mapped out and authorized the clearance of old neighborhoods to make room for new freeways and downtown renewal projects. All of this constituted *good planning* in the decades between 1920 and 1970, when the city planning department reported: "Los Angelenos enjoy their single-family homes and transportation mobility. . . . 'Concept Los Angeles' [the gen-eral plan] says that the City must commit itself to protecting its unique features and life style" (LA City Planning Dept. 1969–1970). In this way, the City of Angels may offer more useful lessons in how to anticipate negative outcomes than it does general complaints about where we went wrong. For example, might today's creation of new high-density, mixed use transit villages bring future problems that we cannot foresee today but should try to?

The corrective storyline of a planned LA makes no claim of an efficient, balanced or beautiful metropolis. And it certainly makes no case for a socially integrated city (e.g., Leavitt 1997, Deverell 2004, Fong 1994). The voices of ordinary Angelenos, now critical to the planning process, were mostly missing throughout the period covered in this chapter, though elites' concerns were normally addressed in some form. Indeed, planners and public officials in the City of Angels have long faced the same complicated urban problems facing their counterparts all over the nation—and that is the point. Population growth, environmental concerns, economic imperatives, limited resources, social relations, public budgets, private interests, fickle voters, political agendas, and technological changes have shaped every city and its planning in particular ways. The same is true here.

Regulating Visual Blight

Meredith Drake Reitan

In the 1960s, Tom Wolfe called it "electro-graphic architecture." Reveling in the neon that flashed, popped, and danced wildly along LA's boulevards, Wolfe saw a new language emerging—one that made built surfaces subservient to the graphics, logos, and brand names they displayed (Wolfe 1968, 47–50). Today in LA, billboards are an especially hot topic, generating vocal opposition from neighborhood activists, preservationists, and home owners associations and passionate appeals for free speech and economic freedom from supporters.

"This is good," says Bill Roschen, president of the LA City Planning Commission. Only the second architect in 90 years to lead the commission, Roschen has worked tirelessly to raise awareness of the links between architecture and planning in the city. For Roschen, the controversy surrounding billboards, digital displays, and supergraphics—the large plastic signs that drape entire buildings—are positive indicators that the public cares about planning and that it especially cares about urban design.

For a number of years, the city has regulated billboards with a series of ordinances that placed limits on signage. Key provisions were designed to "reduce visual clutter" by shrinking the amount of advertising allowed, prohibiting billboards in some neighborhoods, and strengthening the enforcement of existing signage laws. Recent ordinances have allowed for the discretionary review of particular sign projects and, more controversially, created special sign districts that allow more flexible regulations in some neighborhoods because of their "exceptional commercial intensity" (LA Dept. of City Planning 2009). An important condition of the sign district is that in order to erect a new billboard or display, a sign must be removed from another part of the city. In this way, planners hope to concentrate signage in areas considered most appropriate.

Roschen argues that this clustering of signage has the potential to reinforce place-based identities. Some neighborhoods, such as Hollywood, have a long history of elaborate billboards and signs. Yet billboards can also overwhelm public space. For some, what has emerged in the designated sign districts is too slick and too static to be compared to the "wild and baroque" signs that so enchanted Wolfe. Yet for Roschen, the regulation of signage is just one of a number of elements along a continuum of urban design. He feels that regulation, though controversial, is the perfect vehicle for more expanded, citywide conversations about urban design goals.

Income from signage is an important consideration for developers. Since the average billboard can generate advertising revenue in the range of $14,000 per month for regular and $128,000 per month for digital in a highly viewed location, billboards not surprisingly have strong support among developers, who see them as a way to lessen investment risk. Roschen hopes that, through good urban design and careful consideration, a balance can be struck between signage and the existing urban fabric.

The 1970 Centers Concept Plan for Los Angeles

Vinit Mukhija

Los Angeles is usually viewed as the archetypal unplanned city. Many scholars, however, have challenged this narrow perception by emphasizing the impressive concerted efforts of market actors in organizing its development (Hise 1999, Weiss 1987). Although Los Angeles is recognized for being at the vanguard of implementing zoning in the country (Fogelson 1993), its public planning efforts to comprehensively guide the growth of the city are rarely acknowledged. I draw attention here to the Centers Concept, initiated in the mid-1960s to provide a more restrictive spatial framework for development in the city. Triggered by the growing traffic congestion, smog, and redevelopment pressures, the concept was developed with extensive public input and offered a bold, comprehensive vision to restructure LA's growth as a polycentric region. The Centers Concept subsequently became the guiding vision of the city's General Plan. By targeting development and density in the right places, the General Plan aimed to protect the city's single-family neighborhoods from redevelopment, while actively channeling growth to a pattern more optimal for public transit and less driving.

The Centers Concept deserves more recognition in the planning literature. A departure from planning's conventional focus on urban dispersion, it signaled a polycentric metropolitan pattern with nodes of activity and marked the institutionalization of public participation in the city's planning decision making. The concept's key insights, underlying objectives, and planning approach are still relevant. Implementing the concept, however, has not been easy. Steering growth and restructuring land uses is always a challenge; it has become even more so in a city where the market demand for development has distinctly slowed down. Unyielding, neighborhood-based opposition to additional density or change compounds the difficulty. Here, I discuss how the landmark Centers Concept was developed in a city not known for planning, share its key attributes, and assess how it continues to play a significant role in influencing planning efforts and debates in LA.

Planning the 20th-Century Metropolis

High density and the congestion of cities played a pivotal role in the rise of the profession of planning (Sloane 2006). Housing reformers and early 20th-century planners were galvanized to action by the poverty, density, and unsanitary conditions of inner-city tenements and the growing congestion and pollution of the industrial city. Led by Lewis Mumford, Catherine Bauer, Henry Wright, Clarence Stein, and other "regionalists," the objective of urban dispersal and deconcentration became the driving force of planning, architecture, and urban policy in the United States.

The 1920 census formally announced arrival of a new kind of city, with LA making its first appearance in the list of top 10 cities in the country (Table 2.1). In contrast to the established cities of the East Coast and the Midwest, LA was writing a very different urban history that eschewed the urban norm of density and the hub-and-spoke pattern of industrial cities. Most of the large cities had eight to nine times LA's density. Frank Lloyd Wright, the modernist master, with several LA-based commissions, was influenced by the city's suburban style of development in proposing his Broadacre City. As in Wright's proposal, LA had a relatively flat density gradient, too. By "1930 the ratio of population density between the central city and the outlying suburbs was less than 3 to 1 in Los Angeles, compared to 30 to 1 in San Francisco, 26 to 1 in New York, 23 to 1 in St. Louis and 15 to 1 in Philadelphia, which was then considered a sprawling city of single-family homes" (Fulton 2001, 129).

With its high car ownership rates, LA was a leader in the automobile revolution. By 1930, there were two cars for every five people in the city (Hall 1988, 283). In 1930 the Olmsted brothers and Harland Bartholomew, sponsored by the LA Chamber of Commerce, developed a metropolitan plan covering 1,500 square miles and proposed a land acquisition and development strategy of public parks, playgrounds, and beaches in a regional network (Hise and Deverell 2000). The proposal recognized and privileged the dominant position of LA's single-family homes and automobiles, and it made a virtue of its dispersed and sprawling growth pattern, but it was never implemented (see Hise and Deverell).

The idyllic LA was not immune to the travails of congestion. In the 1920s, congestion was centered around downtown, but by the late 1930s, as employment decentralized, it was dispersing (Fulton 2001). Planners at both the county level (LA Regional Planning Commission) and the city level (LA City Planning Commission) had started thinking of LA's growth as a polycentric, regional dispersion with downtown as the center surrounded by satellite subcenters (Hise 1999, 186–215). Planners were guided by a definite "trend toward concentration in small communities." The city's 1944 Master Plan for the San Fernando Valley built on this insight and proposed a series of self-contained communities as potential urban nuclei (Hise 1999, 192–93).[1]

Los Angeles's growth politics, however, were in favor of development. The city continued its spectacular trajectory of growth. Within 40 years, it became the third-largest city in the country (Table 2.1). Its density also increased more than threefold, but the increases were evenly distributed. With its robust population growth came a tremendous rise in the number of automobiles in the city—and unfortunately also in the city's notorious smog and traffic congestion. By the mid-1960s, home owners associations were actively fighting development projects, particularly in the hillsides, and demanding growth control measures and public participation in decision making.

Table 2.1: The top 10 cities and their densities in 1920 and 1960			
1920			
Rank	City	Population	Density (People/square mile)
1.	New York	5,620,048	18,796
2.	Chicago	2,701,705	14,013
3.	Philadelphia	1,823,779	14,248
4.	Detroit	993,078	12,748
5.	Cleveland	796,841	14,128
6.	St. Louis	772,897	12,670
7.	Boston	748,060	17,197
8.	Baltimore	733,826	9,289
9.	Pittsburgh	588,343	14,745
10.	Los Angeles	576,673	1,577
1960			
Rank	City	Population	Density (People/square mile)
1.	New York	7,781,984	24,697
2.	Chicago	3,550,404	15,836
3.	Los Angeles	2,479,015	5,451
4.	Philadelphia	2,002,512	15,743
5.	Detroit	1,670,144	11,964
6.	Baltimore	939,024	11,886
7.	Houston	938,219	2,860
8.	Cleveland	876,050	10,789
9.	Washington, D.C.	763,956	12,442
10.	St. Louis	750,026	12,296
Source: U.S. Census			

A key signal of change in the city's politics was the election of Marvin Braude as a LA city council member. Braude, who is still well regarded in the city for his leadership and support for preservation in the Santa Monica Mountains, was the president of a Westside home owners association and an antigrowth champion (Fulton 2001).

As the public demanded more growth controls, city planners revisited the idea of strengthening existing nodes of activity to promote a polycentric urban form and spatially restructure the city. They were also influenced by successful precedents of new, intense nodes within LA's existing urbanized areas. In the mid- to late-1940s, Metropolitan Life Insurance developed Park La Brea, a 160-acre housing development with more than 4,000 residences in town houses and towers. In the late 1950s, planning started for another large project, Century City (Garvin 1996). Century City was developed as a "city within a city" on the 263-acre back lot of 20th Century–Fox studios. It combined a residential community with a center for regional employment, shopping, and entertainment.

Los Angeles was not unique in this approach. In New York, the proposed plan for Lower Manhattan in the late 1960s also recommended the development of a new, mixed use center within the city. The federal government too embraced the idea of developing new towns or centers within existing cities as a growth strategy. Through Title IV of HUD Act of 1968 and Title VII of HUD Act of 1970 it offered to provide a "federal guarantee for up to $50 million in obligations issued by developers of approved new communities as well as up to $20 million in interest-free loans" (Garvin 1996, 298). These endeavors suggested that the planning tide was turning from its conventional emphasis on dispersal, and the strategy of actively promoting polycentric development was beginning to receive institutional support.

The Centers Concept

The Department of City Planning released its Centers Concept for restructuring the city's urban form in January 1970. It recommended to the city council that the proposal be approved and adopted as the basic framework for the city's new General Plan.[2] Although the proposal was known as the Centers Concept, it drew on four alternatives—Centers, Dispersed, Corridors, and Low Density—developed and publicly released by the planning department in September 1967 as Concepts for Los Angeles (LA Dept. of City Planning 1967). As the proposal noted, "none of the four original alternatives was found to offer a unique and completely satisfactory basis for the General Plan. The Concept most closely resembles 'Centers' but has been drawn from all four, as well as other sources" (LA Dept. of City Planning 1970, 7). The 1967 concepts paper, which included urban design scholar Kevin Lynch as a key consultant, focused on housing density options, spatial structure, transportation framework, and open space network as the defining policy variables. It examined how the variables came together to generate distinct alternatives.

The Centers option emphasized both single-family and high-density housing, and it aimed to develop a city of highly urban character, which at the same time preserved the single-family lifestyle option. The Dispersed alternative focused on single-family and low- and medium-density housing. The Corridors option proposed medium-density corridors developing radially from the core, with single-family housing still dominating the market. The Low Density alternative explored the feasibility of capping the city's population at four million and limiting most of its housing to single-family lots.

By the time the planning department synthesized these ideas into its Centers Concept proposal, more than 60,000 people had participated in the planning exercise (Hamilton 1986, 501). To build popular support for the proposal, the planners emphasized the continuing importance of single-family housing in the fabric of LA and promised to hold most of the city's single-family neighborhoods inviolate from zoning changes. At the same time, the Centers Concept proposed a network of 29 centers with high- and medium-density housing. Perhaps most ambitiously, the proposal took a metropolitan approach and suggested a total of 48 centers spanning the extant 77 cities and the unincorporated County of Los Angeles. (The county now consists of 88 cities.) This proposal was the last time the city explicitly suggested a detailed growth and development framework for the entire county.

The proposed centers included a core similar to the current transit-oriented developments (TODs), intense development within a quarter-mile radius of transit stations. Unlike modernist, monofunctional zoning centers, the centers were envisioned to have mixed uses, including housing, through "multiple function structures." The renderings of the structures, and the suggestion to use air rights to permit development over the streets, indicated the influence of the megastructures of the 1960s. The rooftops, much like today's green roofs, were to serve as landscape plazas. And, in an idea of its time, pedestrian circulation was proposed to be grade-separated in a "nearly complete separation of vehicles, transit, and pedestrians" (LA Dept. of City Planning 1970, 14). In addition to the central core, the centers were to comprise nodes of medium-density housing and other land uses. Unlike those in the core, the land uses in the nodes would develop a specialized orientation. Most nodes were physically contiguous with the core, but when they were spatially separated they were to be known as satellites (see Figure 2.5).

The Centers approach allowed the preservation of the city's single-family stock, which many residents and policy makers considered the true spirit of the place, while addressing the notorious smog and necessity for car travel through a public transit system focused on the centers. The concept called for the rehabilitation of old single-family neighborhoods but suggested that a small minority of them could be redeveloped at a higher density, including with town homes. It also proposed additional medium-density housing on the freeway frontage and in the nodes and satellites of centers. The cores of the centers were to be limited to high-density housing. The concept proposed that larger households occupy the lower-density housing; families with children were not expected to live in the urban centers (LA Dept. of City Planning 1970, 23).

The centers would form the skeleton for the region's proposed rail rapid transit system, with a secondary rail system connecting the cores to their nodes. Bus services of local feeder lines were proposed between centers and their adjoining hinterland of suburbs. The car remained king in LA, but the city's retail strip malls were out of favor. In some cases, the strips were to be phased out; in others, their retail concentration was to increase. The city's industrial districts would continue along its railroads and freeways and were expected to provide almost 900,000 jobs (LA Dept. of City Planning 1970, 28). The concept also emphasized a network of mostly small-scale open spaces—limiting the need for expensive land acquisition—as a landscape framework for knitting together the city and the region. Much like the current Los Angeles River Revitalization Plan, the concept noted the potential for developing recreational parks, lakes, and streams along the river, which it referred to as the "flood control channel" (LA Dept. of City Planning 1970, 30).

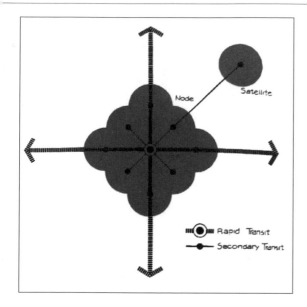

Figure 2.5. Conceptual diagram of a Center, from the 1970 Centers Concept Plan

The Enduring Legacy of the Centers Concept in Los Angeles

The Centers Concept's adoption as a part of the General Plan in 1974 was a landmark event in a city with a contentious historical relationship with institutionalized planning. Although the plan has been less successful in restructuring the urban form of the city, it helped establish the agency of planning in shaping contemporary U.S. cities and is still influential in LA. It also correctly identified many of the city's key planning issues. First, its dispersed pattern of development has made organizing a viable public transit system difficult, while heavy private automobile use has made traffic congestion a citywide feature. A polycentric spatial structure of intensively developed centers would help address this. It continues to be one of the region's key planning goals, particularly with California's new state-mandated emphasis on addressing greenhouse gas emissions and climate change through integrated land-use and transportation planning. Second, the role of public participation in decision making was established. Since residents of LA's single-family homes dominate the political process, it also acknowledged the visceral hold of the single-family lifestyle on planning ideals in the city. Third, authors of the concept were ambitious and recognized that a regional approach was warranted. They knew, however, that implementing a metropolitan plan would be difficult and presented their ideas for the other cities in the county as suggestions.

The Centers Concept, nonetheless, had some shortcomings. It did not anticipate the relative slowdown of growth in LA and the rise of community opposition to density and urban centers. First, planners overestimated the city's population growth. Although LA, unlike many older cities, continued to grow—becoming the country's second most populous city in the early 1980s—its rate of growth in the 40 years following the concept slowed down considerably from the frantic pace set in the four decades leading up to the proposal. As Table 2.1 indicates, from 1920 to 1960 the city's population grew more than fourfold. Between 1970 and 2010, how ever, its population increased by a little over a third (Table 2.2). Although its density increased similarly, LA is now one of the denser large cities. In 1970, its density was a little more than half of the median density of the top 10 cities. Now, conversely, its population density is close to twice the median density of the top cities. The trend suggests that the city cannot count on significant increases in its population and overall density.

Second, planners did not adequately anticipate the magnitude of opposition to density. Home owners associations challenged inconsistencies between the city's General Plan and its zoning ordinance. Consequently, the Los Angeles Superior Court asked the city to reduce its zoning according to the General Plan. In 1986, Proposition U received 69 percent of the vote in the city, cutting in half the allowed intensity of commercial zoning in most of the city.[3] The downzoning made it impossible for many of the centers proposed in the General Plan to develop intensely. The city grew, but most of its growth followed a dispersed pattern, and congestion worsened.[4]

Finally, neighborhood-based resistance to density and the downzoning contributed to limiting the supply of housing, which raised the cost of housing and has played a role in the city's lower growth rate. Moreover, the strategy of the Centers Concept made the flawed assumption that larger households with children would be able to afford and live in single-family housing, and thus it did not adequately address the housing needs of LA's low-income families. Builders of high-end housing consistently outbid affordable housing developers, particularly in the centers. With the dearth of modestly priced housing, the poorer residents of the city have employed informal strategies, including overcrowding and illegal garage conversions, to make housing

Figure 2.6 Low- to medium-density town house development

Table 2.2: The top 10 cities and their densities in 1970 and 2010

1970			
Rank	City	Population	Density (People/square mile)
1.	New York	7,894,862	26,343
2.	Chicago	3,366,957	15,126
3.	Los Angeles	2,816,061	6,073
4.	Philadelphia	1,948,609	15,164
5.	Detroit	1,511,482	10,953
6.	Houston	1,232,802	2,841
7.	Baltimore	905,759	11,568
8.	Dallas	844,401	3,179
9.	Washington, D.C.	756,510	12,321
10.	Cleveland	750,903	9,893

2010			
Rank	City	Population	Density (People/square mile)
1.	New York	8,175,133	26,821
2.	Los Angeles	3,792,621	8,092
3.	Chicago	2,695,598	11,842
4.	Houston	2,099,451	3,502
5.	Philadelphia	1,526,006	11,380
6.	Phoenix	1,445,632	2,798
7.	San Antonio	1,327,407	2,880
8.	San Diego	1,307,402	4,020
9.	Dallas	1,197,816	3,517
10.	San Jose	945,942	5,359

Source: U.S. Census

affordable. Such informal infill strategies have further contributed to LA's dispersed pattern of development, which has not helped the conceptual goal of developing intense centers in the city.

To address some of the housing supply and affordability concerns, in the mid-1990s the city revised its General Plan framework and supplemented the idea of intense development in centers with dense transit corridors (LA Dept. of City Planning

1995). However, there is not sufficient development demand in the city to allow for both intensely developed centers and corridors. The original Centers Concept might still better serve as the primary blueprint for LA's growth and development in the 21st century. The ideal number of centers and their appropriate intensity of development mostly likely need to be revised. Successfully steering growth will mean limiting building opportunities in some parts of the city and requiring a minimum intensity of development in targeted areas. The biggest challenge for planners in LA is to find creative and more successful approaches to address Angelenos' distrust of change and density. They must convince residents of a grand bargain that preserves the fabric and density of most parts of the city but also welcomes new intense development in the right places.

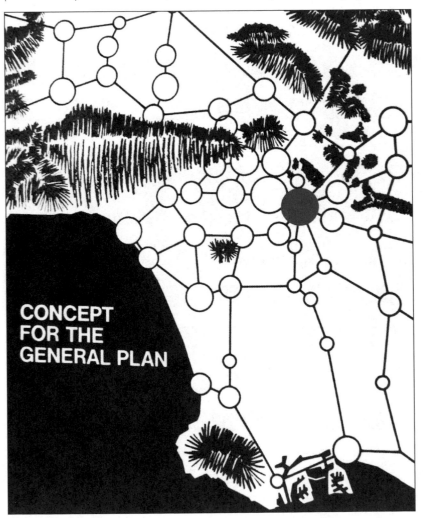

CONCEPT
FOR THE
GENERAL PLAN

Figure 2.7. The Centers Concept

LA's Love-Hate Relationship with Nature

Kenneth C. Topping, FAICP

Throughout a century and a half of urban growth, LA and the surrounding region have exhibited a love-hate relationship with nature. Millions have sought Southern California as a place to secure new opportunities, raise families, and live out their lives. Mild winter days and dry summers, coupled with easy access to beaches and mountains, established Southern California as a virtual Garden of Eden.

Yet a dark side has accompanied this love affair with LA, most notably:

- Water taken from remote sources and brought great distances to spur growth
- A semiarid landscape transformed into unsustainable green lawns and golf courses
- Riverbeds constricted and paved with concrete linings and bottoms
- Fires ravaging nearby hills and mountains where people built to maximize views
- Air filled with pollutants from automobiles and trucks
- Lurking seismicity, the region's ultimate environmental challenge

Throughout, proponents of growth have ignored the basic lesson that nature pushes back. Experts tell us the region is "11 months pregnant" with the next great earthquake, nature's ultimate payback. What Southern California needs now is a transformative reconciliation with the natural world.

Race to Eden

Southern California has grown into a sprawling metropolitan region of 21 million people stretching from Santa Barbara to San Diego, framed by mountain ranges and the Pacific Ocean. Successive cycles of growth were stimulated by westward U.S. migration, immigration from other countries, and a booming industrial economy. This massive transformation was propelled by the region's mild climate, an abundance of arable and developable land, and the importation of water as well as its strong infra-structure and an urban growth machine that effectively marketed the region as an ideal tourist and residential destination.

LA's moderate winter and summer temperatures encourage year-round outdoor activity. A region that started as an agricultural giant, with thousands of square miles planted in citrus and avocado orchards, among other bounty, became a center of suburban residential growth. Ebenezer Howard's vision of "Garden Cities" evolved into its own peculiar expression in the form of tract after tract of 50-by-100-foot lots, with single-story bungalow or ranch-style homes, neatly manicured lawns, and back-yard pools and patios. Small town centers that started and flourished as agricultural hubs, connected by Henry Huntington's privately developed regional streetcar system, became the nodes for the region's massive post–World War II growth when the or-chards were replaced with houses and shopping centers.

The region's benign climate spurred a flourishing tourism, health spa, and resort industry along the coastlines, within the valleys, and along the foothills. The snow-capped San Gabriel and San Bernardino mountains tower above the basin and valleys, offering quick escapes for skiing and sledding. Hundreds of miles of beaches and coastline are equally accessible for year-round outdoor recreation.

Yet Southern California has been transformed into a vastly sprawling, somewhat faceless region where hundreds of incorporated cities have no visible identity other than city limit signs, presenting an urban design challenge in reestablishing a sense of place for individual communities. Behind this transformation is an ongoing battle with nature, waged by those still wishing to overcome, rather than accommodate, the environment.

Water from Great Distances

Following westward extension of the railroads in the late 19th century, LA flourished, growing from about 5,000 people in 1890 to more than 100,000 by 1900. Exter-nal water procurement began in the early 1900s and continued through the 1960s, including three major projects:

- The Los Angeles Aqueduct (bond funded, 1905 and 1907) brought water from the Owens Valley, 215 miles from the city, then extended to Mono Lake, 280 miles distant (bond funded 1930)
- The 242-mile Colorado River Aqueduct (bond funded 1931, completed 1941) following legislation in 1927 forming the Metropolitan Water Dis-trict of Southern California (MWD)
- The State Water Project (SWP) (bond funded, 1960) brought Northern Cal-ifornia water through the California Delta (completed 1973), augmented by the Coastal Aqueduct (completed 1997)
- The imported water stimulated further growth. Within a decade following construction of the Los Angeles Aqueduct, the city had more than a half-million residents and surpassed the population of San Francisco for the first time.

With the new Colorado River Aqueduct and the SWP, LA's population ex-ploded; it rose to just under two million by 1950, halfway to its present level of four

Figure 2.8. Opening of the California Aqueduct, November 5, 1913

million people. By 1970, the counties of Los Angeles, Orange, San Diego, and Ventura had tripled their combined population to a total of 10 million. By 1999, MWD was providing 60 percent of the water used by nearly 18 million people living in coastal counties from Ventura to San Diego.

Southern California is not unusual in its dependence upon water from other regions (see Hise and Deverell). For example, more than 60 percent of urban and agricultural water use in the San Francisco Bay and the South Coast hydrologic regions, and 30 to 60 percent of water used in the southern Central Valley, is met by imports from elsewhere. Recent environmental lawsuits have impeded the extent to which these regions may continue to draw water from distant sources through the California Delta.

The warming of the oceans and atmosphere is now diminishing these external water supplies by altering the water cycle, with earlier snowmelt reducing the snowpack—a primary source of California's annual water supply—and less water storage in distant mountain ranges. During the past two decades, Southern California has experienced severe droughts. This prospect has underscored the realization that Southern California must adapt to climate change, among other things, by reducing its reliance on imported water and increasing conservation of sources within the region.

Paving the Rivers

In the early part of the 20th century severe flooding took a heavy toll on lives and property. As a result, the Los Angeles Flood Control District was formed in 1915. Empowered by the Los Angeles County Board of Supervisors to provide flood protection, water conservation, recreation, and aesthetic enhancement within its 3,000-square-mile territory, it operates a system of dams, levees, and 500 miles of open channels, 2,800 miles of underground storm drains, and an estimated 120,000 catch basins. The two primary watercourses—the LA River and the San Gabriel River—have been seriously confined by dams and channels mostly built by the U.S. Army Corps of Engineers after disastrous floods in 1938.

In the early 1800s the LA River flowed west from the plaza to Ballona Creek near Venice. A flash flood in 1825 altered its course southward. Currently, the LA River flows 50 miles from the western San Fernando Valley eastward past Griffith Park, turning near downtown, and flowing south to the Pacific Ocean at Long Beach. Originally a free-flowing river meandering over undeveloped alluvial plains, the LA River was the city's primary water source prior to construction of the Los Angeles Aqueduct. Most of the river channel is narrow and treeless. Concrete lines the channel walls and bottoms except for the Sepulveda Basin retention facility, a three-mile reach east of Griffith Park known as Glendale Narrows, and the last few miles near Long Beach. During predominantly dry seasons, actual flows are only a few inches in depth. During the winter rainy season, flows are heavy and deep, rising high up the concrete embankments.

The San Gabriel River also once flowed freely across undeveloped lands. Now its controlled and mostly paved channel goes for 60 miles through five dams from deep within the San Gabriel Mountains southwest through Whittier Narrows, where it joins the Rio Hondo River in a dual flood control basin and then proceeds separately southward to Long Beach Harbor.

In recent decades, interest has grown among environmental and recreation stakeholder groups for natural restoration of portions of the rivers (see Wolch et al.). They hope to remove concrete channel bottoms and allow more continuous stream flows to encourage natural vegetation and wildlife to flourish and to install pedestrian and bike trails to promote active recreation in flood control rights-of-way.

Physical obstacles to softening and greening the LA and San Gabriel rivers are substantial. The rivers and their tributary creek channels have been significantly narrowed to enable development on adjoining alluvial land. Both rivers are significantly constrained laterally by the presence of freeways along substantial stretches. While they include unlined basins designed for limited percolation into groundwater basins, their primary function by design is to maximize runoff for flood protection purposes. Any changes require not only involve significant reengineering but also securing the assent of authorities, particularly the County Department of Public Works and the U.S. Army Corps of Engineers.

However, in July 2011, U.S. Environmental Protection Agency administrator Lisa Jackson declared that the entire LA River can be considered as "traditional navigable waters" under the Clean Water Act. This action overturns a previous ruling by the U.S. Army Corps of Engineers that only four miles of the LA River were navigable, and opens the door to a variety of future restoration actions. Environmental advocates are seeking similar measures to "green" the San Gabriel River. The fundamental question is whether federal and county flood control bureaucracies will support or resist such initiatives.

Living with Wildfire
Over the decades, development has pushed higher and higher up the slopes of the hills and mountains in search of vistas. The brush-covered Hollywood Hills and

- Malibu areas provide extraordinary views of the Pacific Ocean and San Fernando Valley. Further east in the San Gorgonio Mountains, alpine communities such as Lake Arrowhead and Big Bear Lake are destinations for quick recreational getaways and convenient commuting to San Bernardino and Riverside.

Not surprisingly, during the past half-century wildland fires have occurred with increasing frequency in hilly and mountainous areas near populated areas of Southern California. From 1950 through 2009, Los Angeles County experienced 42 state and federally declared fire disasters, while San Bernardino County had 23, Riverside County 20, Ventura and San Diego counties 17 each, and Orange County 12.

Over the past decade, a series of devastating wildfires burned in locations identified by fire management specialists as Wildland-Urban-Interface (WUI) areas. Wildland fires in 2003 destroyed 5,671 structures, resulting in $917 million of structural damage, mostly in Southern California WUI areas. In October 2007, wildfires displaced nearly one million residents, destroying thousands of homes and taking 10 lives. The Station Fire of August 2009, which occurred in national forest above La Canada, resulted not only in loss of substantial watershed ecosystems but also in devastating mudflows through suburban streets and homes following subsequent rains.

Fire is obviously an integral component of Southern California's ecosystem. Its cascading consequences should lead to a reexamination of development practices in WUI lands. Yet as growth continues to push further into environmentally sensitive habitats, a serious question remains whether Southern California communities can learn from these repetitive fire disasters to more effectively design streets, neighborhoods, and homes to minimize wildfire losses in WUI areas.

Cleaning the Air

LA's well-chronicled infatuation with freeways led to a need to reduce smog from all sources for health protection purposes, as overseen by the Southern California Air Quality Management District at the regional level and the California Air Resources Board (CARB) at the state level. Over the past several decades, substantial progress has been made in regulating air emissions from a variety of automotive and industrial sources. Until recently, however, state and regional air quality regulations did not address carbon emissions, now recognized as a prime contributor to global warming and climate change. In 2006, the California legislature enacted Assembly Bill 32, the California Global Warming Solutions Act (2006), which called for CARB to execute a program to reduce greenhouse gas (GHG) emissions by 25 percent by 2020. Passed in 2008, Senate Bill 375 mandated each metropolitan planning organization (MPO) to develop a "Sustainable Communities Strategy" identifying how California's GHG reduction targets would be met for the respective region. Although land-use planning is not the subject of the legislation, regional target-setting processes are likely to impinge on development decisions and strengthen regional planning. Ultimately they will have the force of law through the California Environmental Quality Act and state regulations.

The Southern California Association of Governments (SCAG), is responsible for advising state and federal transportation agencies on freeway and highway improvements. Under SB 375, SCAG is now tasked with setting GHG emissions-reduction targets for the region, requiring new attention to smart growth principles. SCAG will need to actively promote measures such as mixed use, increased densities, infill hous-

Figure 2.9 Erosion above the Pacific Coast Highway in Santa Monica

ing, extension of the Metro rail system, and greater reliance on transit-oriented development to meet the targets, providing an opportunity to pursue the transformation of Southern California communities into a regional pattern distinguished by unique visual identities, less reliance on the automobile, and more harmony with nature.

The Next Great Quake

Seismicity remains a major environmental concern. Minor earthquakes occur frequently in California with little consequence. However, major events periodically create substantial losses of life and property. The magnitude 7.9 Fort Tejon earthquake occurred along the San Andreas Fault in 1857, before urbanization. Experts tell us such great quakes return about every 150 years, meaning Southern California is now overdue for a recurrence. The 1994 magnitude 6.8 Northridge earthquake, with $48 billion in direct and indirect losses, was a wake-up call for the anticipated "Big One." The March 2011 Japan triple disaster (earthquake, tsunami, nuclear) has provided a further stark reminder of Southern California's vulnerability.

The possibility of a catastrophic event in Southern California poses key public policy challenges:

- Retrofitting seismically vulnerable structures
- Upgrading outmoded lifeline infrastructure
- Pre-event planning for postdisaster recovery and reconstruction
- Tsunami preparedness planning in low-lying coastal areas

Newer inventory would fare reasonably well given increasingly stringent state building codes. However, older buildings could collapse and kill occupants before

Figure 2.10 The site of an ocean-view house that burned in the Malibu fires of November 1993

they have time to flee. Southern California retains a large inventory of buildings constructed before stricter structural codes standards were adopted, including soft-story apartments, nonductile concrete buildings, and a sizeable proportion of pre–World War II homes with weak foundations. Unless action is taken soon to retrofit seismically vulnerable buildings, substantial loss of life could occur.

Potential impacts on water systems could be severe due to outdated design and deteriorating conditions of existing systems. The 2008 Great ShakeOut preparedness exercise, which was based on a magnitude 7.8 Southern San Andreas earthquake, anticipated long-term water outages. Earthquake-induced water, oil, and gas pipeline ruptures could lead to widespread urban and wildland fires, depending upon weather conditions. Substantial public investments are needed to strengthen such lifeline infrastructure and to educate the public on possible obstacles to response and recovery efforts in areas with damaged, destroyed, or disrupted water systems.

In short, a catastrophic earthquake would pose significant challenges for restoring people's lives, restarting economic engines, repairing infrastructure, and creating sustainable redevelopment. California has made significant statewide advances in disaster mitigation, preparedness, and response planning. However, relatively little progress has been made toward encouraging local and regional planning for disaster recovery.

The American Planning Association (Schwab et al. 1998) advocates for pre-event recovery planning, arguing that waiting for a major disaster to happen before addressing recovery often invites serious postdisaster recovery delays. Advanced recovery planning can help communities take more effective preventive actions, expedite recovery, recapture market share, and rebuild more sustainably.

Los Angeles had this experience with an earthquake Recovery and Reconstruction Plan prepared in the late 1980s and implemented after the 1994 Northridge earthquake. The plan helped the city act more effectively and more expeditiously during the postearthquake recovery (Olshansky et al. 2005). Pre-event planning is now needed to address issues related to tsunami and nuclear power plant evacuation and hazard mitigation.

Toward a Transformative Future

Los Angeles and the Southern California metropolitan region need to make friends with nature, and the sooner the better. Reconciliation requires more effective regional planning placing resilience and environmental adaptation as uppermost considerations.

However, in Southern California, regional entities such as MWD and SCAG have shown limited interest in remediation beyond the confines of their traditional water supply and highway planning programs. Both entities have common interests, but above all is the urgent need to form a collaborative regional planning mechanism that deals effectively with resource management and environmental adaptation concerns in Southern California. A regional resource management agency mechanism could help facilitate LA's reconciliation with nature. Such an entity would help localities recognize the impacts of climate change, reduce reliance on imported water, enhance water conservation, promote more sustainable urban landscaping, encourage greening and softening of the rivers, give adequate attention to fire-safe development in WUI areas, minimize reliance on carbon-emitting automobiles, and permanently reduce earthquake risks before the next great quake through structural and lifeline retrofits, as well as undertake pre-event recovery planning.

Like LA's love-hate relationship with nature, this idea contains an inherent contradiction between the desire for local control and the envisioned regional benefits. Whatever mechanism is chosen, the challenges are real and will remain until effectively addressed.

Neighborhood Councils

Juliet Musso

Although in the popular imagination LA is a city without neighborhoods and with a "social capital deficit" (Brown and Ferris 2002, 7), the city has a major neighborhood council (NC) initiative. This system has three notable features. First, the reform was enshrined in the city charter, giving it a stronger legal stature. Second, a cadre of neighborhood activists mobilized and promoted the development and implementation of the NCs in the face of a reluctant city government, giving the NCs a strong grassroots character and a history of contention and tension vis-à-vis city departments. Third, the controversy over the political legitimacy and accomplishments of the NCs continues a decade later. The LA experiences speak to the tensions around local control, social equity, and inclusion in planning and community service delivery and suggest a need for continued attention to structuring arenas for community engagement around land use.

The Context of Reform: Countering the Politics of Secession

The NC system was created by a 1999 charter reform and now consists of 98 independently elected NCs certified by an appointed Board of Neighborhood Commissioners. These councils provide advisory input on policy making, budgeting, service delivery, and land use, receiving from the city $45,000 each for annual operations. The NCs operate within areas that average approximately 40,000 in residential population (see Figure 2.11). The creation of the neighborhood councils was accompanied by other reforms, including the creation of Area Planning Commissions intended to decentralize planning review.

The political context of the reform strongly influenced the development of a relatively autonomous but poorly supported system of councils that frequently function reactively to city policy and land use. The NCs emerged out of a charter reform process resulting from the threatened secession of the San Fernando Valley, Hollywood, and the Harbor communities of San Pedro and Wilmington. The council system must

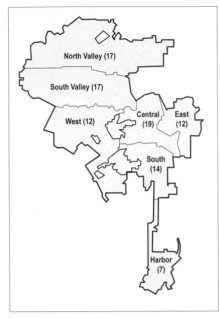

North Valley (17)

South Valley (17)

West (12)   Central (19)   East (12)

South (14)

Harbor (7)

Figure 2.11 Los Angeles community districts

be considered, on the one hand, an outgrowth of the uneasy dynamics between downtown political agents characterized by an institutionally weak mayor seeking greater strength and a small but powerful city council and, on the other hand, the fragmentation of the city's many regionally distinct communities with variant economies and local political cultures (Box and Musso 2004, Sonenshein 2006). The reform in effect served as a containment strategy that had only mixed city hall support, which fostered some resentment among NC organizers, while, paradoxically, mobilizing their engagement in the nascent system.

The charter reform process unfolded as a political struggle between the city council and the mayor, who advocated rival charter commissions. Neighborhood governance received particular attention during the charter development process. Recognizing that rival proposals would be unlikely to receive voter approval, the two commissions ultimately compromised on a reform proposal that increased the powers of the mayor, created the Area Planning Commissions, and mandated a citywide system of NCs with purely advisory powers.

Tensions surrounding land-use and development issues were particularly prominent in the secession and NC movements, along with perceptions about inequities in service delivery (Box and Musso 2004, Hogen-Esch 2001, Sonenshein 2006). Community activists sought formal control over land use, complaining repeatedly that they did not know developments were occurring until "the bulldozer was coming down the street." NCs did not get formal power over land use but gained an "early warning system" to provide advance information on issues under consideration by city councils and commissions, a participatory budgeting process, and regular meetings with departmental general managers.

The system required more than three years to plan and implement, and it developed in a highly decentralized and largely self-organized way, with local community activists writing bylaws and drawing jurisdictional boundaries. Implementation focused on requisites for the certification of councils, with limited attention to procedures for involving the NCs in city planning or policy making (Musso et al. 2011).

The resulting NCs were hybrid organizations endorsed and regulated by the city but with a strong grassroots character and unpaid volunteers. The councils enjoy relative autonomy from the city, which has a role largely confined to certification, audits of expenditures, and support for NC elections. The NCs have varying structures, political styles, and practices. Some have boards that are elected at large; others elect board members within designated geographic districts or stakeholder categories. NCs commonly address policy and planning issues through standing committees that review issues and bring recommendations to the elected board for an advisory vote.

The evolution of the system also produced NC coalitions and alliances. One long-standing alliance, the Los Angeles Citywide Alliance of Neighborhood Councils, serves as a clearinghouse for information on issues affecting NCs. In January 2011, for example, LA's deputy director of planning and an advocacy group representative made a presentation on the city's restructuring of the zoning code, and a Community Redevelopment Area staff member discussed proposed state changes to its policy. The Los Angeles Neighborhood Council Coalition initially was an attempt toward a formally structured congress of NCs, but it continues as a coalition to provide support and information on neighborhood issues. Other alliances are geographic in character (e.g., Valley Alliance of Neighborhood Councils, Harbor Alliance of Neighborhood Councils). In addition, an alliance called PlanCheckNCLA serves as the oversight committee for a pilot program around NC engagement in and information around land-use issues. This fluid landscape serves to support political networks that disseminate information across the city and mobilize NCs to address citywide issues.

Neighborhood Councils and Politics in Los Angeles

The implementation of the system has stressed notification and information dissemination to the NCs. The development of an electronic notification system makes all city council and commission meeting agendas accessible electronically 72 hours prior to meetings. Moreover, the planning department has an independent early notification system that provides electronic notification of all planning applications and other materials for any one of its seven planning areas, responding to NC concerns that city notification is not sufficiently fine-grained.

Any effort to generalize about the impact NCs have on city planning and policy is difficult given the limited development of procedures for their engagement, the scale of the Los Angeles system, and the relative autonomy and variation among them. Nevertheless, two key observations are possible (Musso et al. 2011). First, the system descriptively overrepresents higher-income home owners relative to the residential population of LA. Second, a survey of the social network relationships developed during the system's implementation suggests that NCs have continued to develop horizontal networks that support political mobilization, although their relationship to community stakeholders has been less strong.

Board Member Characteristics and Issue Orientation

A critical question is the representative legitimacy of the NC boards; specifically, whether they are descriptively or substantively representative of their communities. Do they "look like" or "speak for" their constituent communities (Pitkin 1972, Guo and Musso 2007)? A frequent concern cited during the NC reform campaign was that NCs would serve the NIMBYist concerns of middle-class residents, in effect formally recognizing home owner associations.

Surveys undertaken during different stages of the development of the system confirm that the characteristics of NC boards differed on average from those of the city as a whole. For example, a 2006 survey found NC board members were wealthier; underrepresented Latinos relative to their proportion in the city population; had very high rates of citizenship; and had longer tenure in their communities (Musso et al. 2007). As Figure 2.12 suggests, the descriptive underrepresentation of Latinos and overrepresentation of whites on NCs is pronounced even compared to other forms of citizen engagement, including the regional appointees to the Area Planning Commissions.

Moreover, in the 2006 survey, 63 percent of NC board members said they represented home owners. When required to identify with a single primary stakeholder affiliation, half of all respondents identified themselves as representing home owners, even though, according to the 2010 Census, only 38.2 percent of the city's housing units are owner-occupied.

Many studies have demonstrated similar socioeconomic biases among individuals involved in volunteer activities (Verba et al. 1995). Nonetheless, the relatively high socioeconomic status and high rates of home ownership and long tenure of NC board members foster a strong interest in land use and planning relative to other issues that may be of concern to LA residents broadly, such as public safety and education. As Figure 2.13 illustrates, NC board members strongly emphasized land use and transportation relative to a random survey of likely voters, who placed more emphasis on education. This suggests a possibly stronger orientation toward social issues.

Thus, despite provisions in the city charter that specifically mandate NCs to represent "many diverse interests in communities," to "reflect the diversity" of their communities, and to ensure that no "single stakeholder group may comprise a majority" of the board, the NC system has developed a dominant orientation toward the interests of home owners. This places NCs at odds with both business and property developers and low-income housing advocates.

An important question is whether the NCs can nonetheless represent communities on substantive issues. Councils might be constituted to engage their constituents in a participative fashion that could encourage deliberation and discussion of diverse standpoints. An evaluative content analysis of bylaws of 40 NCs conducted midway through the implementation process suggests considerable variation in whether NC structures support broad participation (Musso et al. 2007). Some bylaws appear

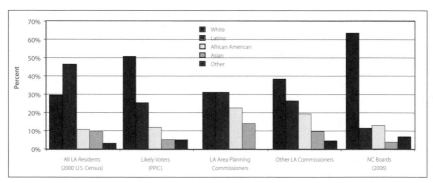

Figure 2.12: Race/ethnicity of neighborhood council boards compared to other forms of participation.
Source: Musso et al. 2007

to encourage general participation, allowing broad engagement of stakeholders in committees and open board meetings. Others have replicated city council structures in which board members control committees and board meetings, providing only limited opportunities for public input.

Neighborhood Councils as Political Networks

A second way of inferring the likely political character of the NC system is to consider the character of the relational ties that develop as a result of engagement in the system. Several network relationships arguably support the effective functioning of the NC system, as illustrated in Figure 2.14. Cumulatively these network relationships can be understood to develop the social capital critical to the effective function of governance systems (Putnam 2000, Galaskiewicz 1979, Granovetter 1973, Son and Lin 2008).

First, ongoing interactions with stakeholders are important to convey information about community needs to NC board members and support substantive representation. Second, NC board members should build strong internal relationships in order to support governance capacity in the form of trust and commitment critical to collaborative activities. Third, connections to city agencies and actors will facilitate the trans-

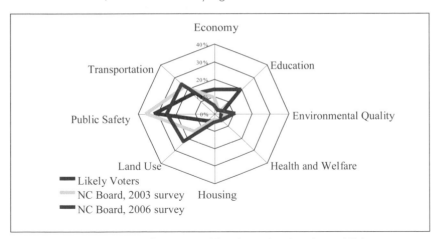

Figure 2.13 Neighborhood issues of concern, as defined by NC board members and likely voters. Source: Adapted from Musso et al. 2007

mission of information and help to develop mutual understanding and shared goals. Finally, relationships across the city, linking NCs to one another, provide opportunities for the dissemination of knowledge and model practices, as well as forming capacity for political mobilization and collective action.

Network surveys suggest the NC system has had mixed success in developing the strong relationships that foster social capital and political efficacy. Between 2003 and 2006, NCs apparently did not substantially increase their level of contact with community stakeholders. Board members asked to report how many community stakeholders they had contacted within two weeks of their most recent board meeting averaged 2.3 contacts in 2003 and 2.0 stakeholder contacts three years later. While the "optimal" level of stakeholder engagement is not clear, the results suggest stagnation in community outreach. NC committee and meeting attendance apparently declined during the same period, while board members cited outreach as the most challenging aspect of the system.

This relatively thin level of engagement in the community is likely attributable to several factors. A catch-22 may be operating, as a narrow focus on land use may not appeal to a broad stakeholder audience. Furthermore, given the large size of NC communities and their volunteer character, the task of outreach may simply overwhelm their organizational capacity. The structural approach of many NCs may discourage participation, as many NCs require stakeholders to fill out speaker cards and wait until the end of a lengthy evening meeting to provide input.

A thin pattern of relationships seems to exist between NC boards and city agencies and political actors. In the same surveys, board members reported contacts to city offices in the two weeks preceding a board meeting of 2.3 and 2.4, respectively. This result would appear to be a missed opportunity to forge relationships between board members and city officials that could support their role as mediating organizations. These weak relationships are likely attributable to the city's support of the system largely consisting of information dissemination, leaving NCs using the same processes as the general public to engage public officials. While some council members send field staff to attend NC meetings, others maintain distance, and many departmental general managers have little or nothing to do with NCs.

In contrast to these weak "vertical" networks, the reform has resulted in a significant increase in citywide networking across neighborhoods. As noted, NCs have developed a number of alliances within regions and across the city. The surveys show a substantial increase in contacts across boards, from less than half a contact on average in 2003 to two in 2006. Evidence also exists of citywide mobilization in response to city policy issues, including a proposed Department of Water and Power (DWP) rate increase, opposition to an extension of city council term limits, and, most recently, against a proposed charter amendment that would require installation

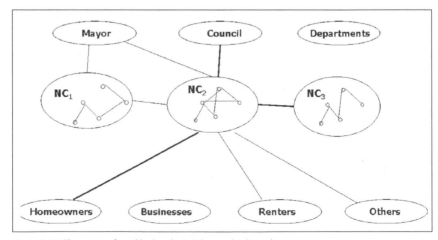

Figure 2.14 The variety of neighborhood council network relationships

of solar power in city buildings. Thus one clear effect of the reform is a horizontal network of NC actors that serves as a reserve of political power that can be tapped to mobilize on a citywide level.

Implications for Community Engagement in Land Use

The overall impact on planning and land use of LA's NCs, operating in a multitude of economically and culturally diverse communities, is unclear. Certainly the city's electronic notification system and PlanCheck pilot program disseminate information more broadly about specific development proposals and proposed land-use policies. Further, most NCs have land-use committees that monitor land-use and development controversies. Are community stakeholders utilizing this increased capacity in a primarily oppositional fashion, as opposed to engaging in proactive planning to shape land-use decision making? While some developers and affordable housing advocates apparently view the NC system as an obstacle to development, NC members acknowledge the limitations of their role. As a volunteer from the Westchester Neighborhood Council expressed it, "We can only encourage [developers] to come see us. There's no power in 'Just say no.' Instead, 'Just say what?'"

A 2006 survey found that NC activities are diverse and vary across the city. Figure 2.15 summarizes the proportion of self-reported activities around land use, community assistance (e.g., grants to local organizations); beautification (e.g., tree planting or graffiti removal); citywide issue advocacy (e.g., DWP rate increases); events (e.g, community festivals); outreach; and other activities. The distinction between land-use and proactive planning is between engagement of a specific proposed development or broader community planning standards.

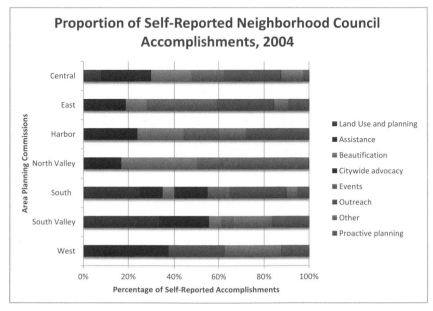

Figure 2.15

A complex picture of engagement in planning and land use emerges. South Valley NCs, for example, reported the highest number of land-use-related accomplishments and the second-highest number of proactive planning accomplishments (half of all reported accomplishments). The South Los Angeles and South San Fernando Valley areas cited land use more among their achievements. The Harbor area reported the most accomplishments related to proactive planning, reflecting ongoing engagement with community advisory committees, such as meetings on a proposed Bridge to Breakwater project, an improvement plan for the San Pedro waterfront.

Proposed LAX airport expansion and large-scale residential developments such as Playa Vista have awakened West area stakeholders regarding increasing density. About 1,200 people attended a community meeting on the controversial Playa Vista project cosponsored by the Mar Vista Community Council, Grass Roots Venice, and Westchester/Playa Del Rey. The Westchester/Playa Del Rey NC conducted a charrette to envision Lincoln Boulevard as a mixed use corridor, and it has undertaken efforts to beautify the Sepulveda corridor.

A survey of the Department of Neighborhood Empowerment project coordinators also revealed regional differences. For example, the East Area NCs provided input into the Silver Lake–Echo Park community plan as well as "built a sense of community" by securing an additional bus route and planting trees. The South Valley coordinators cited opposition to locally undesirable land uses, including a proposed meat-processing facility, a dump site, alcohol resale permits, a fast-food restaurant, and a motel. North Valley NCs focused on community beautification and improvement, such as installing public art, replacing playground equipment, paving streets, and trimming trees, as well as opposing the proposed Sunshine Canyon landfill contract extension.

South LA NCs were active in opposing unwanted land uses including a homeless shelter, motel, slaughterhouse, and a dump site. Without regard to context, one could assume this to be a classic example of NIMBY behavior, yet this area of the city has historically been disenfranchised, and the prevailing attitude appears to involve feelings of frustration that the community is a social services provider of last resort. At an August 2004 Area Planning Commission meeting convened by the city to present a proposed inclusionary zoning ordinance, Dorothy Fuller, secretary of the 8th District Empowerment Congress, articulated community sentiment by stating: "The 8th district has endured a downward spiral. The NIMBY syndrome, things that people don't want in the city of LA, find their way into the 8th district. . . . Exclude the 8th district—we've been the brunt—and we don't want it anymore." This reaction also explains the reason South LA residents blocked additional liquor permitting, an issue that finds particular resonance there.

In sum, while NCs have become active participants in land use, they do not represent a monolithic NIMBY opposition to development. Neighborhood councils engage in many activities that are complementary to development, including community events, beautification, and outreach. The character and orientation of land-use involvement appears to vary regionally due to differences in capacity, historical relationships to the city, and community attitudes toward development.

Going Forward

These survey results raise important issues about the value of LA's local community empowerment. Because of improved information dissemination, the city arguably encourages land-use controversies to surface earlier and promotes discourse among affected parties. However, NC boards may not hear or represent the full array of community viewpoints and interests in addressing development because of the lack of diverse representation.

Two sets of reforms are needed to build greater representative legitimacy and deliberative efficacy into the NC system. First, the city should provide support and incentives intended to increase diversity within the NC system. For example, LA might learn from Minneapolis, which has targeted grant programs that require local community councils to engage a broad cross section of the community in collaborative planning (Fagotto and Fung 2006). Another model is the participatory budgeting program in Puerto Alegre, which provides programmatic grants in part based on demonstrated community involvement in participatory deliberations (Baiocchi 2001).

Second, the city should consider incorporating more carefully structured deliberative processes for engaging NCs with city officials (see Musso et al. 2011, Bryer and Cooper 2007). The lack of strong mediating ties between local stakeholders, NC boards, and city agencies relates at least in part to the lack of structured processes and forums for engaging city policy and planning issues. Berry et al. (1993) stress the importance of putting in place "political innovations" to support engagement of citizen and city. Similarly, Fung (2004) argues that effective democratic reforms demand the delegation of powers to local groups with associated expectations and accountability mechanisms. LA has not done this. LA has invested in an information provision system—as required by charter—but largely ignored the means of deliberation or engagement of the NCs with city decision-making processes.

Everyday Los Angeles

Margaret Crawford

Around 1990, my colleagues and I recognized that something new and important was happening on the streets of LA.[1] What we saw around us contradicted the widely accepted (even among Angelenos) image of the city as "autopia," a place notorious for its complete absence of street life, an urban feature ridiculed in numerous jokes and even commemorated in the rock song "Walking in LA"—with its repeated lyric of "nobody walks in LA." Sometime during the course of the 1980s, this had changed. The city was still car-oriented, but its sidewalks and parking lots had exploded with new and surprising activities. Recent immigrants sold oranges from median strips; vendors lined up along sidewalks, offering everything from tamales to tube socks. Other vendors hijacked the chain-link fences that surrounded vacant lots to display rugs and flags for sale. In spite of restrictive regulations, mobile food carts and trucks moved across the city, selling everything from fresh fruit to bacon-wrapped hot dogs. Outside of Home Depot and paint stores, day laborers gathered, available for employment. A new building type appeared all over the city on corner sites vacated by gas stations: the minimall. Cheaply built and designed for quick, convenient, automotive commerce, minimalls quickly attracted immigrant entrepreneurs. Their plastic signs, juxtaposing English with Hangul, Thai, and Armenian characters, served as an index of the city's rapid demographic shifts as it became a major destination for global immigration.

Even familiar places demonstrated an unexpected capacity for shape shifting, such as the auto body shop on La Brea Avenue that closed down in the late afternoon to be reborn as an outdoor *taqueria*, grilling up *carne asada* to attract passersby. In quiet neighborhoods, residents transformed their driveways or lawns into weekend retail venues. As garage sales proliferated, some active streets turned into the second-hand equivalent of a mall.

In the course of conducting their daily lives and earning a living, all of these people had, inadvertently, created a new urban landscape. In many different ways,

Figure 2.16. A down-on-his-luck street vendor

they activated and humanized neglected and desolate parts of the city, filling them with people and life. Women wearing aprons and selling homemade food domesticated sidewalks and parking lots, making them seem more like home. Cheap rugs covered the harshness of chain-link fences, their soft textures and bright patterns evoking a multiplicity of urban living rooms. During the O.J. Simpson trial, the slogans on T-shirts sold on the street provided a running commentary on shifts in public opinion. Mobile food vendors created temporary restaurants in different parts of the city, bringing unexpected groups of people together for a meal. Garage sales made private lawns into public places. Unlike the previous generation of auto-oriented commerce, based on impersonal mechanisms like drive-through windows, this new commerce required human contact and interchange as part of the transaction.

The liveliness of the urban life around us heightened our dissatisfaction with the prevailing modes of urban design. Even in LA, most urban designers, pursuing their own design agendas, seemed unaware of the city around them and displayed little interest in the people who lived in it. In the early 1990s, both the discourse and the practice of urban design in LA consisted entirely of concepts and places conceived in nearly complete opposition to the city as it actually existed. New urbanism, looking to the past to create neotraditional towns complete with compact centers and walkable neighborhoods, was surprisingly popular. Although sprawling LA would seem like an unlikely home for this movement, its advocates promoted Playa Vista, a new development on the west side of the city, as an alternative model for urban development. They claimed that density and self-containment would reduce car use and encourage community.

More avant-garde designers engaged in speculative practices, which encouraged "deconstructing" urban space through mapping and layering to produce new urban forms. In different ways, both seemed equally formulaic and abstract, generic

Figure 2.17. Playing for tips on the street

approaches that ignored the rich human meanings around us. The urban design projects that actually got built adhered to traditional concepts of public space. After multiple design competitions for the location, Mexican architect Ricardo Legorreta's 1990s redesign of Pershing Square, a historic plaza that was once the focus of downtown LA, still remained largely empty. CityWalk, a pedestrian mall designed by Jon Jerde as a collage of historic Los Angeles streetscapes, was far more popular but was not a real street, just part of the Universal City theme park.

In response, we decided to propose a new set of urban design values. We wanted urban design to have an empirical, not a normative, starting point, accepting the city as it actually was instead of reimagining it as planners and designers thought it should be. We also wanted to place urban residents and their daily experiences at the center of the enterprise.

We decided to call this "everyday urbanism." Unlike other terms, such as "informal," "everyday" could contain many different layers of meanings. Some of these we selectively borrowed from French philosophers such as Henri Lefebvre and Michel de Certeau, who had theorized everyday life in interesting ways. Both saw the ordinariness of the everyday as uniquely leveling, since every person, whatever his or her income or status, has his or her own everyday experience. This observation was important since, although many Angelenos connected these phenomena exclusively with recent immigrants, we found everyday urbanism over the city. Beverly Hills, for example, became a hot spot for permanent garage sales. Home owners who were "upside down" in their mortgages often took to domestic retail, sometimes selling new items to help pay their mortgages. This forced the city—worried about its image—to start restricting garage sales and requiring permits.

Although clearly not everything about everyday urbanism was positive (the ubiquitous orange sellers, unfortunately, were not free agents but more like indentured workers, selling fruit to pay off the "coyote" who brought them across the border) we optimistically felt that the urban transformation we saw around was hopeful, particularly in a city in the midst of a recession and beset by rapidly changes in its racial and ethnic makeup. More than just survival mechanisms, they demonstrated new and inventive ways of appropriating and using urban space. At the very least, they deserved attention and analysis.

To make this point to a wide audience, we published a book that featured hand drawings, photographs, and hyperrealistic models, all experiments in how to represent everyday life. Monacelli Press published *Everyday Urbanism* in 1999.[3] We quickly found ourselves at odds with a broad range of prevailing professional and academic opinion. Planners in Southern California cities, including LA, saw the activities we described not as positive examples but as regulatory problems to be controlled. Indeed, many of these activities, from street vending to permanent garage sales, violated city codes. Since we focused on vernacular practices, architects were generally indifferent. When it came to buildings, however, the American Institute of Architects took a stand, beginning a campaign to ban minimalls, which most of its members considered to be "urban blight." Progressive thinkers like Mike Davis objected to our optimistic appraisal of the city's public and political life. Davis's *City of Quartz: Excavating the Future in Los Angeles* (1990), and David Rieff's 1991 *Los Angeles: Capital of the Third World*, depicted the city in apocalyptic terms, seeing minimalls and street vendors as symptoms of a collapsing public realm and a multiethnic city hovering on the verge of implosion.

Yet over time, it turned out that Everyday Urbanism encapsulated a widespread but not yet articulated attitude toward cities. Urbanists in LA and around the world were already paying attention to many of the same things. By accepting and analyzing these urban practices, Everyday Urbanism gave a name to a way of engaging with the city. This produced, in addition to a design approach—uppercase Everyday Urbanism—a lowercase everyday urbanism, now a widely accepted term to positively describe ordinary places and activities. By 2004 the concept had acquired such wide resonance that Doug Kelbaugh, dean of the University of Michigan School of Architecture, declared that Everyday Urbanism was one of the three dominant urban design paradigms.

Over the years, LA's everyday urbanism has continued to expand and intensify. Now recognized as a permanent dynamic in the city's development, it has justified our optimism that it was a positive contribution to the physical and social life of the city. A significant "trickle-up" effect can be observed. As informal practices moved up the food chain, they influenced the middle class, which then not only accepted but even applauded them.

The battle to legalize street vending, which seemed to be on the verge of success 20 years ago, is once again on the city's agenda, this time with a much better prognosis. This campaign is the result of an informal alliance of hipsters, foodies, and immigrant vendors that began when vendors started appearing outside of late-night clubs. Adopted by gourmet chefs, food trucks and carts of all kinds, once known as "roach wagons," have become a popular part of the city's food scene. Their popularity has legitimized immigrant vendors. In spite of competition from trucks operated by top chefs, the winner of the 2010 Vendy awards for best street food was Nina Garcia, who has sold her Mexico City–style quesadillas from a card table in the parking lot of Big Buy in Boyle Heights for two decades. Her victory, celebrated by restaurant

Figure 2.18. An ice-cream seller, working in the shade

critics and foodie blogs, demonstrates how the entry of middle-class, often college-educated cooks into the world of street vending has upgraded its image among the middle-class public. The extent of their support became clear in 2008, when public outcry from all over the city forced Los Angeles County officials to abandon efforts to restrict food trucks.

Similarly, the efforts of University of California–Los Angeles researchers and advocates to study and support day laborers have produced an even more dramatic transformation in their image. Once perceived by the public as criminals and loiterers, day laborers sometimes now benefit from municipal and corporate hiring sites, which recognize their value as an official part of the labor market.

Planners have started to recognize the ways in which temporality can transform urban space, adopting different forms of temporary urbanism such as pop-ups and mobile events to enliven desolate areas and serve as "eyes on the street."

As different immigrant communities prospered, they took on a larger role in shaping the city's built environment. In Koreatown and the San Gabriel Valley, developers draw on models from Seoul, Hong Kong, and Taipei to densify suburban landscapes with high rises and innovative minimall prototypes. While upgraded multistory and monumental minimalls now host banquet halls and Hilton Hotels, their lowlier cousins continue to be popular destinations for Angelenos seeking the city's best ethnic food. As its realm continues to grow—despite commercial megaprojects such as The Grove and LA Live or efforts to produce traditional urban forms such as Grand Street—everyday urbanism, ordinary yet omnipresent, will continue to be a major force shaping LA.

Dedicated to John Chase (1953–2010), the first Everyday Urbanist

The City as Textbook

Meredith Drake Reitan

Most young people don't know anything about urban planning. If you talk to planners, most of them stumbled upon the profession, often long after high school or even college. Remarkably, the Los Angeles Unified School System has embarked on developing the third high school in the nation to feature an urban planning program of study, joining the New York City Academy of Urban Planning and Milwaukee's School for Urban Planning and Architecture.

The East Los Angeles Renaissance Academy of Urban Planning and Design (ELARA) is one of five academies located at the newly constructed Esteban E. Torres High School, the first high school to be built in East LA in 85 years. ELARA supports 16 teachers and close to 400 students in grades 10 to 12. In addition to state-required courses such as math, history, and English, the school offers elective courses in GIS, architectural drafting, and geography. Students are specifically encouraged to connect to the city beyond the classroom. For example, during a recent field trip along the Gold Line from Pasadena to downtown LA, students were paired with urban planning professionals. The tour gave students not only the opportunity to observe LA but also to experience the city in a physical way as they wound their way from the East LA Civic Center Metro Station, through Boyle Heights, Little Tokyo, and along Olvera Street. Along the way, students discussed urban culture, the built environment, and economic development with planning professionals.

While none of the school's teachers is a trained urban planner, they rely on a broad base of community and professional support. Graduate students from UCLA's planning program have helped run workshops, and the nonprofit LA Education Partnership helped to craft the curriculum and get the pilot idea approved. Martin Buchman, an English teacher at ELARA, led the effort behind the school and the curriculum.

Planning professionals often complain that community members and policy makers misunderstand their work. Organizers hope training programs such as ELARA's will produce a few practicing planners while helping a new generation of LA residents become more knowledgeable civic leaders.

For additional background, see Berg 2011.

EVOLVING DEMOGRAPHICS

3

Metropolis of Dispersed Diversity

Dowell Myers, Anna Jacobsen, Sarah Mawhorter,
and Joshua Wheeler

Los Angeles is undergoing dramatic demographic changes with major consequences for planning. Not only are residents the intended beneficiaries of planning, but they also play pivotal roles in reshaping the city, serving as housing occupants, service consumers, workers, voters, and community members. The overarching goal of planning is to promote public well-being, so it is important for planners to understand their local and regional constituents and engage them in the planning process. Perceptions of LA have quickly become outdated as demographic changes have unfolded over the past two decades. To help planners see the extent of these changes, we focus here on four demographic trends revealed by the 2010 census—in race, immigration, age, and housing. Similar trends are transforming cities across the United States.

It is difficult to define the boundaries of LA. Regional planners assume that LA comprises the whole of Southern California, extending from the Pacific Ocean to the borders with Arizona and Mexico. We use the more practical boundaries of Los Angeles County, which, with a population of nearly 10 million, is the largest of any county in the nation and exceeds most states. This boundary contains the City of Los Angeles, with a 2010 population of 3.79 million, as well as 6.03 million suburban residents. For our analysis we utilize the 2010 census where possible and the 2009 American Community Survey for all other social and economic characteristics. Any trends are constructed with information from 1980, 1990, and 2000 censuses.

Los Angeles stands out for its racial and ethnic diversity. The county no longer has a dominant racial or ethnic majority; its residents are all minorities. Further, LA's spatially dispersed diversity contradicts the model of a central city dominated by minority groups surrounded by suburbs dominated by a white majority. The county has a relatively even balance between city and suburbs on other key demographic dimensions, such as immigration, income, poverty, and housing costs.

Los Angeles has been one of the principal gateways for immigrants since 1970. More than one third (35.7 percent) of the regional population is foreign born, three times the national average of 12.5 percent in 2009. Still, the flow of immigrants to LA peaked in 1990, a decade before the United States, and has fallen since. Today, the average LA immigrant is long settled, with corresponding progress toward integration.

While many urban commentators focus on race and ethnicity or immigration, LA is undergoing dramatic aging of its population, as are most U.S. cities. In many ways age changes are the most significant demographic dimension for planners since so many behaviors and service needs differ among age groups, not simply between retirees and workers but also among children, teenagers, and young adults.

All of these major demographic changes—race, immigration, and age—affect the residential patterns of the population. We briefly explore differences in household formation that are generated by population growth. The changing composition of new households shapes the demand for new apartments or single-family homes and variations in home ownership and renting.

Race and Hispanic Origin

Los Angeles's rich ethnic diversity has been fueled by migration from other parts of the United States and immigration from Latin America and Asia. Since 1980, the non-Hispanic white and African American or black shares of Los Angeles County residents have declined, while the Latino/Hispanic and Asian shares have grown.[1] Between 1980 and 2010, Latinos increased in number from 27.6 percent of the population to 47.7 percent, and the numbers of Asians grew from 5.6 percent to 13.7 percent. Whites' share fell from 52.9 percent in 1980 to 27.8 percent in 2010, and blacks' share fell from 12.4 percent to 8.3 percent.

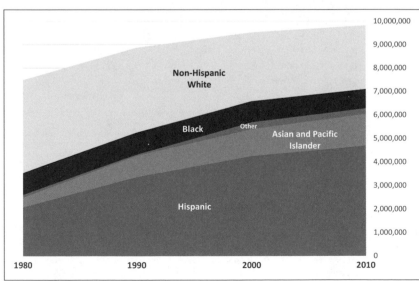

Figure 3.1. Racial and ethnic populations of Los Angeles County, 1990–2010. Source: U.S. Census, 1980, 1990, 2000, 2010

The greatest changes occurred in the 1980s and 1990s, with relatively minor changes in the last decade.

Though whites' share fell dramatically, most of the change was due to rapid growth in the Latino and Asian populations rather than large declines in the white population (see Figure 3.1). Between 1980 and 2010, the Latino population more than doubled, growing by 126.9 percent, and the smaller Asian population more than tripled, growing by 223.9 percent. At the same time as immigration from Latin America and Asia accelerated, white birth rates fell and white and black migration from other parts of the United States slowed. Still, the white population was reduced in absolute number by 31 percent in the 30 years between 1980 and 2010, and the black population declined by only 12 percent. Offsetting white and black declines, Latino and Asian population growth accounted for 151.8 percent of the total population growth.

LA's racial and ethnic populations are increasingly evenly distributed between the central city and suburbs. Overall, 39 percent of all Los Angeles County residents lived in the central city from 1980 through 2010 (see Figure 3.2). An even balance of each ethnic group between city and suburbs would reflect this same proportion. In 1980,

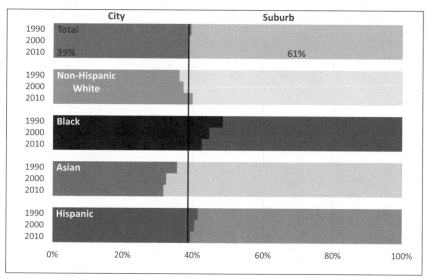

Figure 3.2: Percentage of the population of each race or ethnicity living in LA city or suburbs, 1980–2010. Source: U.S. Census, 1990, 2000, 2010

the white population was slightly skewed toward the suburbs, but by 2010 the white distribution matched the county average. Meanwhile, the share of the black population living in the central city steadily declined. In 1980, 54 percent of blacks lived in the central city. By 2010 only 43 percent of blacks lived in the central city, closer to the county average. The growth of the Asian population since 1980 was strongly concentrated in the suburbs, whereas Latinos have been evenly distributed between the county and the city. Not every city and neighborhood in the region has an even ethnic

Diversity Dispersed Between City and Suburbs

In terms of measures of diversity, the City of Los Angeles and its surrounding suburbs have certainly moved toward greater uniformity over the last two decades. This uniformity is reflected in a city-suburb convergence in the percent of people of color (i.e., groups formerly known as minorities who consist of all those other than non-Hispanic whites) and is reflected also in high share of foreign-born residents in both the city and suburbs.

The percentage of people of color increased in both the city and the suburbs between 1990 and 2000 (see Figure 3.3). In the following decade, the suburbs outpaced the city, and by 2010 the suburban share of people of color matched that of the city, suggesting a dispersal of diversity around the county.

The percent of foreign-born residents illustrates another important change occurring over the last 20 years. Between 1990 and 2000, the percent of foreign-born in the city and suburbs increased at nearly identical rates. By 2000, however, the foreign-born shares hit a peak; while the suburbs maintained its percentage of foreign-born residents at 33 percent through 2010, the city experienced a slight decline in its foreign-born percentage, falling from 40.9 percent in 2000 to 39.7 percent in 2009.

To further understand the remarkable dispersal of diversity throughout the region, we compare the top 20 most populous cities across the United States and compare

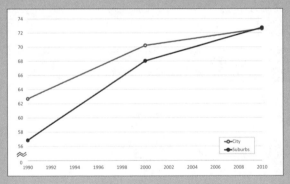

Figure 3.3: Percent people of color, 1990–2010. Source: U.S. Census, 1990, 2000, 2010

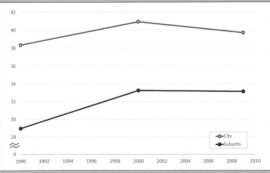

Figure 3.4: Share foreign-born, 1990–2010. Source: U.S. Census, 1990, 2000; American Community Survey 2009

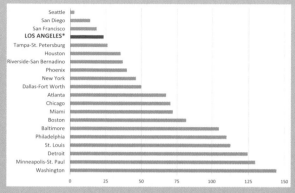

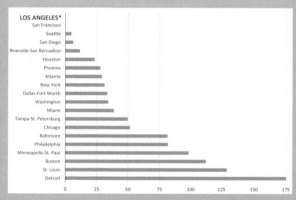

Figure 3.5: Difference between city and surrounding region— top 20 metropolitan areas, 2009, relative poverty of city to MSA (top) and proportion people of color (bottom). Source: American Community Survey 2009

them with their surrounding regions, as defined by their Metropolitan Statistical Area (MSA). (In defining the Los Angeles MSA, we exclude Orange County, which was recently added to the definition by the Census Bureau, and instead we retain the traditional definition of solely Los Angeles County, which has a total of 88 municipalities.)

The top 20 cities are compared to their broader regions in terms of several dimensions often thought to distinguish the residents living in cities and suburbs. These include poverty rates, proportion minorities or people of color, percent foreign-born residents, and median housing values. The rate for each central city is expressed as a percentage above or below the rate for the whole MSA. Figure 3.5 shows how similar a city is to its larger region on two of these indicators, poverty rates and people of color as a share of population. Cities that diverge from their regions have a longer bar. Cities that are most similar to the rest of the region are closest to zero at the center axis. For example, the poverty rate is 10.6 percent in the City of Seattle and 10.3 percent in the larger MSA, so the city's rate is nearly the same as the broader region, reflected by a bar slightly above zero. By contrast the 2009 poverty rate, in Washington, D.C., was 18.4 percent in the city and 7.5 percent in the MSA, giving the city a rate 144 percent above the suburbs, reflected by a much wider bar than Seattle. This shows that

Washington is the most dissimilar from its wider geography (not that it has the highest poverty level).

Consistently, characteristics of residents in the City of Los Angeles closely reflect those of residents in the larger region. On the poverty indicator, LA has the third smallest difference between city and surrounding region. On the percent people of color, LA has the smallest difference from surrounding region of all the large metropolitan areas. For indicators not shown, Los Angeles has the fifth-smallest difference on percent foreign-born and the fourth-smallest difference on median house value. Our interpretation of these data is that LA has evenly dispersed diversity. LA is certainly not marked by stereotypical wide variations between the central core of a city and its neighboring suburbs. While other cities might come closer to their regions on selected measures, LA is virtually unique in that it comes close to the surrounding region on all indicators examined. Other regions in California share this feature of dispersed diversity, unlike the urban structure familiar in the eastern half of the United States.

mix. Los Angeles is a polycentric city, with many areas dominated by only one or two ethnicities. As evident from Figure 3.2, however, every major ethnic group has very substantial representation in the suburbs outside the actual city.

Immigration

In the streets of LA, signs in Spanish, Korean, Chinese, and a dozen other languages make it plain that this is a city of immigrants. Over one third of Los Angeles County residents are immigrants, three times the national average of 12.5 percent. But immigration has not been a constant force in LA. The flow of immigrants has slowed, and immigrants from previous decades are becoming well-established Angelenos. The implications of these changes have not been fully explored.

Immigration to the United States surged in the 1970s and 1980s, and LA was a prime destination because of its strong demand for labor and its location near Mexico and facing Asia. Since 1990, the annual flow of immigrant arrivals in LA has fallen back below 1980 levels (see Figure 3.6). The recession in the early 1990s hit LA hard, and immigration was further discouraged by stronger border controls, high housing costs, and stricter enforcement of labor laws.[2] Immigration to the United States as a whole increased to a peak in the early 2000s. New destinations with better jobs and cheaper housing attracted more immigrants. This slowdown in the rate of immigration to LA, echoed a decade later in the United States as a whole, has caused a shift in the immigrant population.

Fewer newcomers are arriving, and previous immigrants are becoming longer-settled residents of LA (see Figure 3.7, page 76). In 1980, 60 percent of immigrants had arrived in the last 10 years, but by 2008 only 30 percent were newcomers. In 1980, only 20 percent of immigrants had lived in the United States for 20 years or more, but by 2008 more than 40 percent had. Immigrants often arrive with few advantages: they are poor, jobless, and homeless, with limited English abilities. But most do not stay that way for long. Research shows that immigrants make rapid progress toward finding work, saving money, purchasing a home, and other achievements

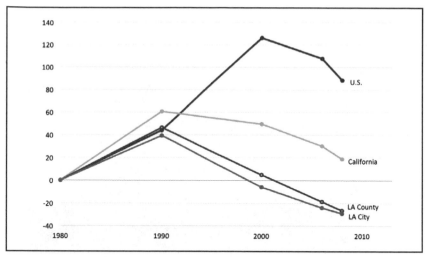

Figure 3.6: Percentage change since 1980 in annual immigrant arrivals. Source: U.S. Census, 1980, 1990, 2000; American Community Survey 2006, 2008

(Myers and Pitkin 2010, Gabriel and Painter 2008, Bean and Stevens 2003, Alba and Nee 2003). A longer-settled immigrant population contributes to LA's maturity, productivity and prosperity (Myers et al. 2010).

The upward mobility of LA's increasingly settled immigrants has practical effects on home ownership. The longer immigrants have lived in the United States, the more likely it is that they will own a home (see Figure 3.8, page 77). For example, immigrants who arrived in the 1980s had a 19 percent home ownership rate in 1990, which rose to 35.9 percent in 2000 and 45.4 percent in 2009. This upward trajectory is remarkably consistent for immigrants who arrived in different decades, regardless of their starting point. In the first 10 years after arrival, immigrant home ownership rates rise by an average of 16 percent, and in the second 10 years home ownership rates rise by an average of 11 percent. Different immigrant groups buy homes at different rates. Latino immigrant home ownership rates rise slightly more slowly than average, and Asian immigrant home ownership rates rise more quickly. Buying a home is a solid investment in a community, requires financial stability, and goes hand in hand with other benefits like participation in social networks, steady employment, and tax contributions.

Few immigrants entered the United States in the 1940s, '50s, and '60s, so most immigrants living in the United States in the 1970s and '80s were recent arrivals. Immigrants who arrived in LA in 1980 came to a truly foreign land, with few resources to help them find their way. Today, previous immigrants greet new immigrants, helping them navigate the complexities of urban life and find a job and home. The ratio of long-settled immigrants to new immigrants shows how the immigrant landscape has been transformed (see Figure 3.9, page 77). In the 1980s and 1990s, for every recent immigrant in the previous five years there was less than one immigrant who had been in the United States for more than 20 years. Today, four long-settled immigrants

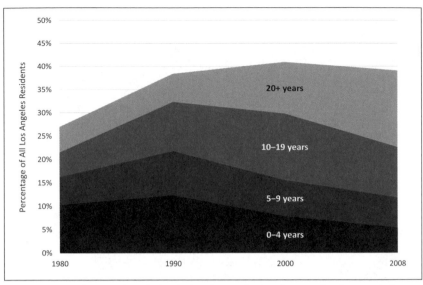

Figure 3.7: Foreign-born population by length of residence in the City of Los Angeles. Source: U.S. Census, 1980, 1990, 2000; American Community Survey 2006, 2008

reside here for every recent arrival. This "helping hands ratio" is calculated by country of origin, since the networks that benefit newcomers form through common language, culture, and imported ties of family and friendship (Portes and Zhou 1993). For every nationality, the helping hands ratio has shot up since 1990. The increasing proportion of settled immigrants is good news for all current and future LA residents.

Emerging Patterns in Age

Age is the great modifier, acting as the backbone to shifts in race and immigration. Age is also the great unifier; 10 years from now, each of us still alive will be 10 years older than we are now. As such, changes in age structure are widely used by planners to foresee population shifts. With this understanding planners apply demographic perspectives to develop policies that meet the future needs of changing populations.

Age is a dynamic force: a population growth of 100,000 in a given decade has different impacts depending on whether it happens in children, young adults, middle-aged adults, or seniors. Growth in LA has been focused in different age groups in different decades. Planners and policy makers, not to mention the general public, have not always recognized how different changes in past, current, and future decades can be. The divergent trends are best shown in Figure 3.10 (page 78), three successive charts comparing population growth or decline by age group as observed between 1990–2000 and 2000–2010 and as projected by the California Department of Finance for 2010–2020.

While Los Angeles County has experienced a modest population growth of 3.1 percent (299,267) in the last decade (2000–2010), that growth has not been

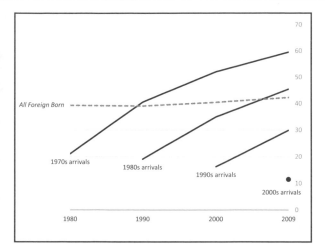

Figure 3.8: Immigrant
home ownership rates by
arrival cohort, Los Angeles
County, 1980–2009.
Source: U.S. Census,
1980, 1990, 2000;
American Community
Survey 2009

equally shared among age groups. Clearly, from 2000 to 2010 Los Angeles County experienced a significant upswing in the number of its residents ages 50 and older. This growth is the result of the maturing baby boom generation. The largest gains were observed in the following age groups: 50s (+33.9 percent), 60s (+37.3 percent)—the baby boom generation—and 80+ (+29.1 percent), their parents.

The more dramatic and somewhat unexpected change during this time period was the decline in the total number of children under age 10, which fell by more than 260,000 (−16.9 percent). Also significant was a loss of more than 160,000 adults aged 30–34 (−10.1 percent)—the "missing" parents of the "lost" children.

Such significant loss in this age group is still surprising considering trends observed during the 1990s. Between 1990 and 2000, Los Angeles County saw a growth of more than 150,000 children under the age of 10 (+11.2 percent). Furthermore, while the maturing of baby boomers was looming, its effects were not yet felt, and the net

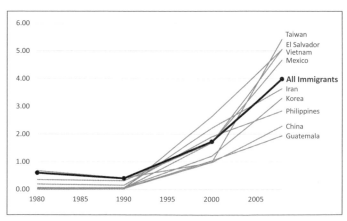

Figure 3.9: Los
Angeles County
helping hands:
ratio of long-settled
to new immigrants
by country of
origin. Source:
Myers et al. 2010

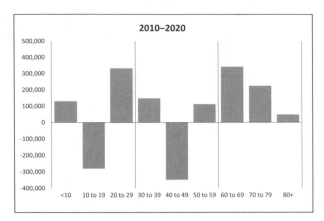

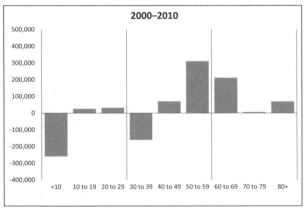

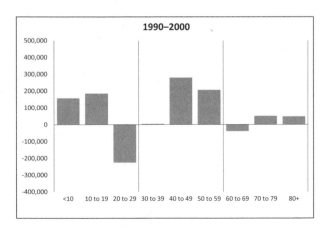

*Figure 3.10:
Los Angeles County
population growth
or decline by
age group. Source:
California Dept. of
Finance 2010*

growth in the number of residents over 60 increased by a mere 4.8 percent (55,000) during the 1990s compared to a 23.1 percent growth seen during the 2000s.

By 2020, the number of residents over age 60 is expected to continue to grow, increasing by more than 612,000 (+36.7 percent). With an expected growth of just over 86,000 (+1 percent), however, the population under 60 will not be able to keep pace.

LA may grapple with a severe shortage in its replacement workforce as the boomer group reaches retirement. This scenario is perhaps best represented by the "senior ratio"—the ratio of older residents (65+) to working-age residents (25–64). In LA the senior ratio is projected to more than double between 2000 and 2030 (Figure 3.11, page 80). While these changes represent a pattern that is emerging across the United States, the problem is even worse in LA. Whereas the senior ratio is poised to increase in the nation from 23.8 to 42 between 2000 and 2040 (an increase of 76.5 percent), in LA it could soar from 18.8 to 43.6 (an increase of 132 percent).

The impacts of an aging population on social services and Medicare are widely recognized, but less appreciated are the economic impacts of having fewer workers and more opportunities for minority youth. A less welcome impact may be the potential imbalance between too many seniors and not enough young buyers, which has been termed the "generational housing bubble" (Myers and Ryu 2008). Planners need to recognize the implications of these issues and begin to consider what strategies will be required to serve the needs of an increasingly older population.

Residential Patterns

Changing demographics are directly expressed in changing residential patterns. Planners use three principal indicators to understand housing: household formation, multifamily versus single-family stock, and tenure (owning or renting).

Household Formation

Population growth translates directly into a need for housing units via household formation. A household is defined simply as an occupied housing unit, and each unit has a householder who is the principal owner or renter of the unit. The probability that a person is a householder is given by the headship rate—the number of householders of a given age divided by all the people of that age.

Figure 3.12 (page 81), showing 2010 headship rates in Los Angeles County, illustrates that 15-to-24-year-olds are remarkably similar in their low headship rates across all ethnic groups, between 5 percent and 13 percent. The largest jump in headship then occurs as these young people transition into adulthood at ages 25 to 34. At this point some interesting trends begin to develop among the races, the most notable being that blacks and non-Hispanic whites have higher rates, 42.6 percent and 45.5 percent, than Asians and Latinos, at 33.8 percent and 29.9 percent. Another interesting divergence between these ethnic groups is witnessed among 45-to-54-year-olds. For Asians and Latinos this is where headship reaches its apex and stays flat for successive age groups, but headship rates continue to escalate for whites and blacks.

In general, the higher the headship rate, the more housing units are needed for people at that age. However, one key consideration is how changes in population offset headship rates. An important example of this is seen where the chart displays

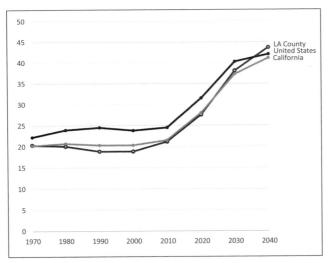

Figure 3.11: Senior ratio: 65+ per 100 working age (25–64). Source: California Dept. of Finance, U.S. Census Bureau, and authors' calculations, 2010

a bump in rates for 75-to-85-year-olds. This rate is a function of a contraction in the population at that age without a simultaneous loss in householders. In other words, widows and widowers continue to maintain their households. This appears to happen more significantly for whites and blacks than it does for Asians and Latinos, which may be evidence of a greater likelihood among the latter groups to move back in with their children following the death of a spouse.

Although significant tendencies are revealed by the 2010 headship graph, planners need to grapple with how changes over time will impact future housing needs. To better comprehend how headship is transforming, Figure 3.13 presents the changes in per capita headship rates by age from 2000 to 2010 for the entire Los Angeles County population.

Obviously, the last decade in LA has been marked by a consistent decline in headship. This decline was most pronounced among 25-to-34-year-old householders, a decline of 5.2 percent since 2000. Potential explanations for the emergence of this trend include an increasing probability for young adults to remain within a parent's household or a tendency to double up within new households. Because the decrease in headship is happening for young adults, who usually form the most new households, this change may have crucial implications for planners as they try to assess the growth in housing needs for the coming years.

Multifamily Housing

Fundamental to planners' success at overcoming the challenges of an aging population will be their ability to address shifts in living arrangements. Planners accept that the prior notions of households composed primarily of nuclear families will begin to shift drastically in the coming years. In calling for increased development of mixed use, walkable neighborhoods, many planners anticipate increased demand from the growing number of single-person households and dual-income, no-children households who often prefer amenity-proximate, urban dwellings.

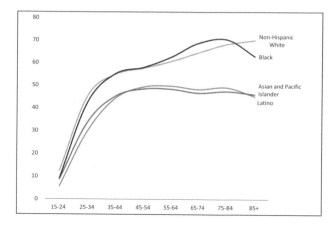

Figure 3.12: Los
Angeles County
headship percent per
capita, 2010. Source:
U.S. Census Bureau,
2010

Construction permits are often an indicator of the future projections of developers, even if those might reflect outdated expectations. Permits show what is anticipated to be in demand. Figure 3.14 (page 82) shows the number of permits for new construction of single-family homes (one housing unit) and multifamily housing (buildings with two or more housing units). Beginning in 2003, the number of permits for multifamily housing began to grow in Los Angeles County, and by 2006, 60 percent of all permits were for multifamily units. While the construction industry was clearly affected by the Great Recession, provisional data for 2010 indicate an uptick in new construction, particularly multifamily.

These market trends are often attributed to either consumer preferences or government policies favoring low-density development. Widely overlooked are the major demographic swings that change who is demanding what kind of housing. The upswing in apartment construction is consistent with the change in age structure shown in Figure 3.10. During the 1990s, the LA region lost more than 200,000 residents in their 20s, which was followed by a small gain in the 2000s and by an anticipated 300,000 gain in the 2010s. Past research has shown than trends in the size of the 20-to-34-year age group are crucial for supporting new apartment construction (Myers and Pitkin

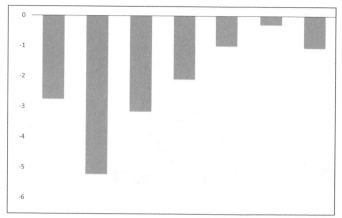

Figure 3.13: Los
Angeles County
headship per
capita, changes by
age, 2000–2010.
Source: U.S.
Census Bureau,
2000, 2010

2009). After a decade or more of lessened demand, when multifamily construction fell to abnormally low shares in California and nationwide, the apartment revival is under way, both in LA and nationwide. This potential demand will not necessarily be met by developers, because availability of credit has been severely constrained by the economic recession. In addition, residents often object to multifamily construction because they dislike density and congestion, and because they are shocked by the increase in apartment construction compared to the low years of the 1990s.

Housing Tenure

Ominous changes are under way in the nature of demand for home ownership. On the surface all is calm, because the home ownership rate in Los Angeles County has held steady since 1980 in the range of 48 to 49 percent, excepting the temporary upswing during the housing bubble. In addition, home ownership rates are highest for older residents, as shown in Figure 3.15, so that the aging of the population has tended to prop up home ownership. Of the 1.5 million home owners, nearly half (48.7 percent) are now over the age of 55. Massive home sales are to be expected in the coming decade because of downsizing and sell-off by older home owners, based on cohort trends from 2000 to 2010 (Pitkin and Myers 2011). In Los Angeles County, the net loss of home owners in this decade is anticipated to be 17 percent of those currently ages 55 to 64, 29 percent of those currently ages 65 to 74, and 66 percent of those ages 75 and older. That volume of sales will require an increased number of home buyers, and these will be heavily drawn from the ranks of Latinos who dominate the younger ages. As seen in Figure 3.15, the home ownership rates of Latinos are lower than whites (or others), and their rates have been dropping in the last decade. Nonetheless, Latino home buyers will determine the fate of the housing market in LA. Whereas white home owners declined in number by 70,517 in the 2000s, Latino home owners were the major growth sector to take up the slack, increasing by 79,700.[3] This trend was supplemented by 35,822 additional new owners from all other sources combined, yielding a total growth for the decade of 45,005 home owners in LA.

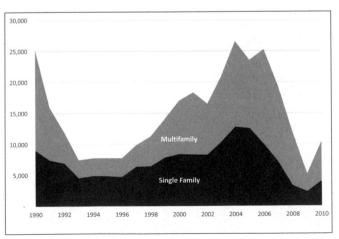

Figure 3.14: New construction permits by housing type, Los Angeles, 1990–2010. Source: U.S. Census Bureau, 1990–2010

Aging white home owners and young Latinos have common interests. While some have pointed to a growing divide between ethnic groups and generations, the new evidence suggests a growing partnership through home ownership, a willing exchange between sellers and buyers (Pitkin and Myers 2011). The clear challenge for the future will be how to pick up the growing slack from the increased sell-off by older home owners. "Who is going to buy your house?" has become an important question for all of us.

Policy solutions to strengthen home ownership are twofold. On the supply side, the sell-off by older home owners can be slowed by making communities more elder friendly in their services and urban design (promoting greater walkability and sociability). These environmental changes will help people stay in their homes longer (Myers and Ryu 2008). On the demand side, the home-buying capacity of the younger generation needs to be strengthened by programs to improve job skills and promote higher education. Cultivating a stronger base of future home buyers will help the older generation as much as the young.

Integrated Demography

Studying the evolving demographics of the city is not a separate, stand-alone topic. Rather, an understanding of local demography should be integrated into broader economic, social, and political processes that determine planning and policy directions. Planners could usefully adopt the perspective of "integrated demography," applying demographic trends, as well as demographic perspectives and tools, to the solution of broader problems.

As we have demonstrated in the case of housing, application of demographic analysis leads to better understanding about the rate of household formation, the future course of home buying and selling, and the need for a denser urban form

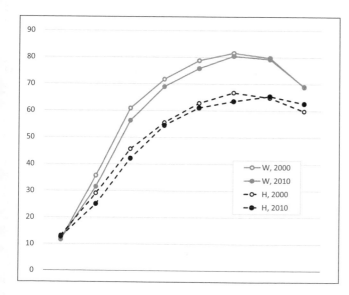

Figure 3.15: Home ownership rates by age, whites and Latinos in California. Source: U.S. Census Bureau, 2000, 2010

composed of a mixture of single-family and multifamily housing units that reflects the evolving population and its needs. This practical outcome for business and government flows from demographic changes.

Extending this further, the integrated approach includes not only consumption projections but also public perceptions and political responses, featuring demography as both cause and effect, and also as interpretive lens on public debates. People are the subject of demography and at the same time active decision makers with opinions about demographic changes. Planners can usefully contribute to the public dialogue by helping citizens and leaders better understand themselves and the changes around them. Planners can also contribute crucial technical advice through the projections that help people see ahead and encourage them not to allow trends from the last decade to guide future decisions. In a dialogue with the public, planners become counselors about the meaning of demographic trends.

The product of demographic analysis in planning should be more than a stack of facts. The primary product is a narrative that describes demographic changes—past and future—explains their impacts on society, interprets popular misconceptions about those changes, and ultimately aims for improved public understanding of alternative policy directions.

Conclusion

The demographics of LA have evolved dramatically over the last two decades. Racial and ethnic changes have culminated in a majority-minority demography, and this pattern of ethnic diversity is dispersed nearly equally between the city and suburban region. Perhaps LA has entered a postdiversity or postminority era, as if these population distinctions may lose much of their prior resonance.

Sharper changes have focused on immigration and changes in the foreign-born population. A newer event for many other regions in the nation, immigration has been the most prominent factor of social change in LA for more than a generation. Today we find that the arrival of new immigrants in LA has declined and that immigrants are longer settled, a tremendous shift from 20 years ago. These long-settled immigrants have the potential to provide "helping hands" for newcomers.

Los Angeles may lead the nation in diversity and immigration, yet in the area of aging it mirrors many other metropolitan areas. Baby boomers live throughout the country, and at every stage in their lives they have wielded overwhelming social, economic, and political power. Our contrast of three decades of change in age groups provides a perspective that can be usefully applied in other cities. Policy makers and city builders often have trouble seeing beyond the present or recognizing the demographic underpinnings of past trends. This myopia can lead to misguided and opportunistic diagnoses of urban change, and planners have a special duty to educate the public about these dynamics (Nelson 2006). The three-decade diagram (Figure 3.10) could prove useful in many other cities.

Population is so closely linked to housing that the census collects the two sets of information together. Age differences create profound changes in the types of housing people desire (Myers and Pitkin 2009). As one example highlighted here, sharp changes in the number of 20-somethings have led to major swings in apartment construction. Similarly, the aging of the baby boomers leads first to rising home ownership in late middle age and then to massive sell-offs in retirement years. Finally, a bright spot not commonly recognized about immigrants is the major degree to which they move up into home ownership. This upward mobility will help LA to absorb the impact of the aging baby boomers.

Our urban areas are shaped by the "population factor" of Alonso (1980). Our analysis of LA can be replicated with similar data for any region in the United States. The planning profession has opportunity to play a major leadership role in interpreting demographic changes for the benefit of local residents and leaders.

The Ambiguous Legacies of the 1992 Riots

Josh Sides

There is no precise yardstick for tragedy. Horrible things happen, and we try our best to measure their impact—in lives lost, property destroyed, dreams denied. But 20 years after the LA riots of 1992, despite our best efforts, we are no closer to having a unified synthesis of their meaning than we were in the days and weeks following the tragedy.[1] We can, however, observe significant changes in the institutional and cultural landscape of South LA in the two decades since then.

In the wake of the riots, planners, politicians, investors, and community leaders offered up good-hearted and ambitious proposals to alleviate the chronic problems of unemployment, poverty, high morbidity and mortality rates, social isolation, and physical abuse at the hands of law enforcement agents in the region. However, very few of these proposals ushered in fundamental changes to the circumstances of life in the South LA region, particularly for its African American residents. And ultimately, the most enduring change in South Central LA over the past two decades—its transformation from an infamous black ghetto to a predominantly Latino immigrant community—was never planned. In many respects the story of South LA since 1992 is a cautionary tale, one that reminds us of the profound limits of planning and policy making in regions of extraordinary demographic dynamism.

The Riots

In retrospect, the LA riots appear to have been inevitable. By the early 1990s, few of the great promises of the civil rights era of the 1960s or the Tom Bradley era of the 1970s and 1980s had been fulfilled. Unemployment remained alarmingly high—as much as 25 percent among young black men—rates of drug addiction and alcoholism soared, and gang violence exacted a staggering toll on the residents of South LA (DiPasquale and Glaeser 1998, 70; Johnson and Farrell

1993). In 1991 and 1992—the macabre banner years for homicide in LA—more than 3,200 people were murdered in LA, most of them young black men.

Then, in March 1991, television screens across the world broadcast the videotaped footage of Los Angeles Police Department officers raining down 56 baton blows on African American motorist Rodney King. Two weeks later, television viewers watched another act of sickening violence when a Korean grocer shot and killed an unarmed 15-year-old black girl named Latasha Harlins after an altercation over a bottle of juice. In October, the grocer was convicted of manslaughter and served no jail time. Finally, on April 29, 1992, a jury in Simi Valley, one of the most remote and whitest suburban areas of LA, acquitted three of the four officers involved in beating Rodney King. The response in South LA was loud and immediate: That night, thousands of South LA residents, both black and Latino, took to the streets, starting a four-day riot that destroyed more than 1,000 buildings, injured 2,500 people, killed 58, and ultimately resulted in $1 billion in damage and 16,000 arrests (Shaffer 2002; Gottlieb et al. 2005, 179).

Rebuild LA

Before the riots had even concluded, Mayor Tom Bradley and Governor Pete Wilson announced what would become the most high-profile and ambitious response to the Los Angeles riots: Rebuild LA. An "extra-governmental task force" that later became a nonprofit corporation, Rebuild LA sought to harness the power of the private sector where, presumably, the public sector had failed. Bradley assembled a team of 80 top business and political figures under the leadership of Peter Ueberroth, the former baseball commissioner who had brilliantly managed the first privately financed Olympic Games in LA in 1984. But Ueberroth's exuberance may have been his downfall, as Rebuild LA repeatedly overpromised and underachieved.

Among those promises was the creation of 57,000 new jobs within five years, primarily through the construction of badly need grocery stores. A commitment by the Vons supermarket chain to build 12 new stores in the riot-torn region was the centerpiece of that promise. But the supermarket industry—roiled by mergers, labor disputes, and new demands for larger facilities—proved to be precisely the wrong industry to jumpstart South LA's flagging economy. Vons soon reneged on its commitment.

Ten years after the riots, a careful survey by scholars at Occidental College concluded that there was no net gain in supermarkets in South LA. As one group of scholars has fairly concluded, "Rebuild LA was less an agenda than a series of pronouncements."[2] Thirteen months after his appointment, Ueberroth left Rebuild LA. The organization limped along for several more years, achieving a few modest victories before closing its doors permanently in 1997 (Park 2004).

Liquor Store Abatement

Campaigns to mitigate the proliferation of liquor stores in South LA have met with greater, if much quieter, success than the Rebuild LA campaigns. As was the case throughout urban America since the 1950s, liquor stores were greatly overrepresented among retail establishments in South LA. Historically, their presence has created two grievances among African Americans, the first being that residents must pay higher prices for foodstuffs in liquor stores than they would in larger stores, and second, that the surfeit of alcohol aggravates community health by encouraging alcoholism.

Almost a decade before the riots, a group of African American residents of South LA organized the Community Coalition for Substance Abuse Prevention and Treatment to tackle the "the liquor store menace." Led by Karen Bass, a community activist and future member of the U.S. House of Representatives, the Community Coalition scored an important victory by compelling the city to intensify its issuance of conditional use permits, which allowed residents greater control over the hours, location, and even the lighting of proposed liquor store establishments (Sloane forthcoming).

Because liquor stores served as the flashpoints for so much of the violence in the riots—about 200 of South LA's 728 liquor stores were destroyed during the melee—they became prime targets for policy reform in the months and years after 1992. Most significantly, the Community Coalition secured the support of prominent council members in rejecting traditional "fast-track" approval for liquor store reconstruction. They defeated an assembly bill designed to limit community involvement in the rebuilding efforts and prevented almost all of the 200 liquor stores destroyed in the riots from reopening (Park, Watson, and Galloway-Gilliam 2008). Today, South LA is still burdened with far more liquor stores proportionally than affluent regions of LA (U.S. GAO 2006, 134). But the LA riots triggered significant policy changes in the realm of "social hazard" zoning that have arguably enhanced, however modestly, the quality of life in South LA.

Tax Incentive Initiatives

As with liquor abatement, the concept of empowerment zones, in which employers received government incentives to operate in impoverished areas, predated the 1992 riots. But the concept also gained much more currency as a result of the riots, and in 1993 it became a hallmark of the Clinton administration's urban policy in the Empowerment Zones and Enterprise Communities Act of 1993. Using this program, California's own Enterprise Zone program, and the Los Angeles Revitalization Zone (also created in 1993 in response to the riots), employers could receive federal tax credits, wage credits, capital gains deductions, city business tax waivers, and Department of Water and Power subsidies.

With this laundry list of generous incentives, one might expect there to have been an employment revival in South LA. However, most research on the impact of the enterprise zones, both nationally and in LA, suggests that they were not effective at luring employers to impoverished areas. A frank assessment of the federal empowerment zone in LA, conducted by the Government Accountability Office, found no appreciable economic growth or reduction in unemployment in the target area (Spencer and Ong 2004, Dowall 1996). And in the Los Angeles Revitalization Zone, investment appears to have come only in the form of permit applications to make repairs in buildings lightly damaged by rioting and had no positive effect on larger scale investments (Independent Commission on the LA Police Dept. 1991, iii, iv, xix).

Explanations for the failure of the empowerment zone concept abound: too many homeless people were included in target areas; large businesses could not find sufficiently large parcels for their operations; businesses that took advantage of low-interest loans often defaulted. But there is also that great unreported variable: perception. Probably no combination of tax incentives and favorable loan terms would have spurred investment in an area perceived to be rife with crime and prone to riots.

Police Reform

The televised beating of Rodney King and the subsequent hearings of the Independent Commission on the Los Angeles Police Department (Christopher Commission) ushered in some of the most sweeping changes in LAPD history. Those changes fundamentally transformed the historically violent relationship between the LAPD and the residents of South LA. When Tom Bradley assembled the Christopher Commission less than one month after the beating of King, he sent the clear message that the "culture" of the LAPD would have to change, and the commission's report detailed just how insidious that culture was. Among other discoveries, the commission found that "a significant number of officers in the LAPD repetitively used excessive force against the public and persistently ignored the written guidelines of the Department regarding force"; "the problem of excessive force is aggravated by racism and bias"; "the failure to control these officers is a management issue"; and "the complaint system is skewed against complainants." This last point was illustrated by this stunning statistic: of the 2,152 citizen complaints of excessive force between 1986 and 1990, "only 42 were sustained" (Cannon 1997, 592).

As a result of the commission's report, the LAPD—although sometimes haltingly—instituted dramatic reforms, most specifically in the area of use of force. These changes were accomplished through extensive training for new recruits, the introduction of nonlethal weapons like pepper spray and beanbag rounds, and the virtual abandonment of the side-handled metal baton (Leovy 2002). Just as important, Chief Bernard Parks instituted reforms to the citizen complaint process, requiring all complaints to be formally investigated by Internal Affairs or the LAPD chain of command—where they had formerly been swept under the rug. By 2002, 15 percent of all complaints against officers were sustained, compared to the 2 percent documented by the Christopher Commission.[2] And in 2005, the police commission began posting abridged summaries of all use-of-force incidents on its website. This level of transparency and accountability would simply have been unimaginable prior to the King beating and subsequent riots.

A New South Los Angeles

As the campaign to "fix" South LA in the wake of the riots proceeded on many fronts, Angelenos generally understood them to be campaigns to help African Americans in South LA. After all, "South Central" LA—its official name before the city council changed it to South Los Angeles in 2003—had become virtually synonymous with black crime, poverty, and gang violence.[3] The music, film, and fashion industries had freely capitalized on the "South Central" name since the rap group NWA popularized the term in their wildly popular 1988 album, *Straight Outta Compton*. But one oft-quoted statistic from the riots stuck out like a sore thumb: 51 percent of those arrested were Latino, while only 38 percent were African American.[4] Closer observers had already noticed that, as of the 1990 census, Latinos already constituted 45.5 percent of the population of South LA (Cannon 1997, 585). And subsequent censuses only confirmed what was easily visible on the ground. By 2000, Latinos represented 58.5

percent of the population of South LA; by 2010, they represented 66.3 percent. In 2010, the "black district" of South LA was only 31.8 percent black.

As much as African Americans lamented the loss of a traditionally black community—and many lamented this loudly—the Latin Americanization of South LA was an economically advantageous development. "What salvaged Los Angeles in the mid-1990s," the journalist Lou Cannon has written, "was a burst of economic activity led by Latino immigrants."[5] The infusion of Mexican and Latin American families, who appear to have a high rate of labor force participation, represents an increase in what economists call "purchasing power" in those communities. Harvard economist Michael Porter, founder of the Initiative for a Competitive Inner City, has been beating the drum about inner-city purchasing power for the last decade, concluding, in 2006, that inner-city residents in the United States spent $122 billion on retail annually. In the first decade of the 21st century, developers and retailers have responded to this rising Latino purchasing power by building stores, malls, and housing developments in areas once regarded as off-limits for prudent investors. In South LA today, there are approximately a dozen Starbucks stores, those bellwethers of discretionary income.

Simultaneously, the demographics of black LA have transformed in ways that improve the purchasing power of South LA even as they disrupt the coherence of a "black community" in the region. Thousands of poorer African Americans "priced out" by the bullish real estate market of the late 1990s and early 2000s left the city for more affordable markets in Riverside County, the Antelope Valley, and Nevada. And a healthy proportion of middle-class blacks have been migrating, since the 1990s, to southern cities like Atlanta and Charlotte, where black entrepreneurialism is ascendant, southern culture has been redefined for the better, and housing prices are significantly lower than they are in LA.

At the same time, however, the African Americans who have remained behind are generally more solidly middle class than their departing counterparts. One quick indicator of this reality is the modest increase in black family median income, relative to the countywide median, over the last decade.[6] Perhaps more significantly, they have exhibited an extraordinary commitment to affirm their political and cultural influence on the region through dozens of campaigns and events, including the recent "Fix Expo Campaign" to bring a light-rail stop to the thriving black arts community of Leimert Park.

If the demographic trends of the last 20 years are any indicator, we can reasonably expect South LA to be about 20 to 25 percent African American by the time of the 2020 census, and at that point there may be no longer any visible legacies of the riots of 1992 in South LA. Instead, one might find an extraordinarily diverse and highly integrated community of Californians for whom the anger, despair, and violence of 1992 seem as antiquated as the days of Jim Crow.

Tinker-Toy Urbanism

Meredith Drake Reitan

James Rojas believes that everyone is an urban planner because everybody has a sense of how to improve the physical environment. After serving for 12 years as a planner at the Los Angeles Metropolitan Transit Authority, Rojas has recently reinvented himself as an artist, traveling the world with suitcases full of found objects to engage individuals from all walks of life with the planning process. For Rojas, the city is a visual and sensual experience that frames urban issues. More important, he argues, this experience should be the point of entry for all planning discussions.

By mid-2011, Rojas had facilitated more than 120 workshops and created 30 interactive city models. He employs a pedagogical method of project-based learning, where participants retain more information by engaging the full range of their senses. Rojas taps into participants' emotional responses to the city with the goal of making the planning process more visual, tactile, and playful. Workshop exercises let participants investigate, discover, and explore their relationship with the built environment. Familiar, nondescript objects allow participants to be comfortable even as they are creative. Green yarn becomes grass, blue poker chips become the ocean, and hair rollers become apartments or office buildings. The final results have no scale, no maps or terms to learn, and no wrong or right answers.

After the models are created, workshop participants are asked to explain their ideas to the group. Since they frequently interject their own experiences, memories, and thoughts of place (both real and imagined) into these discussions, the explanations are often the most interesting part of the workshop. Their reflections connect participants to one another, allowing them to creatively engage in the planning process.

Participants gain satisfaction from the workshops because they are able to translate their visions and ideas into physical form. As Rojas explains, all we need is to provide people with tools and a voice since they are, already, all urban planners.

Minority-Majority Suburbs Change the San Gabriel Valley

Steven A. Preston, FAICP

It wasn't supposed to be this way, they thought. The citizens gathered at a public hearing in one of the 31 cities in the San Gabriel Valley were of a certain age and a certain generation and most particularly a certain demographic profile. They had come to the meeting to protest an unwanted transformation of their community.

They were confused by the profusion of signs in languages they did not understand. They were upset by the sudden arrival of Chinese *dim sum* houses, noodle parlors, and *boba* tearooms—and the loss of familiar steakhouses, coffee shops, and traditional credit retailers. In other communities it might be the *panaderias* that replaced bakeries or the emergence of Armenian banquet halls. In each case, "their" suburb was being transformed from one with an Anglo population and culture into one with an emerging dominant minority culture.

A few miles away from the meeting with the protesters, a different scene played out as families, young couples, teens, and seniors shopped along Valley Boulevard, a street at the epicenter of demographic change in the southwestern San Gabriel Valley. Families gathered for a sweet treat at a tea room, for lunch at a popular restaurant, or settled for a late-night foot massage session. A few doors away, a gaggle of foodies from LA's Westside descended on the next "hot spot" for a bowl of rice noodles, meat, and vegetables. In the San Gabriel Valley, Asian and Pacific Islanders (API) were reshaping the cultural landscape.

Its temperate climate, visual setting, and access to downtown LA make the San Gabriel Valley a fine place to live, with communities worth fighting to protect. The battles are for control over public and private spaces and the extent to which culture influences concepts of urbanization, spatial distribution, and physical design. Still, those battles are just part of an evolving story. Long before the minority-majority suburbs sprung up across the landscape, the San Gabriel Valley had seen successive waves of change.

Wei Li first described the concept of the "enthoburb" in a 1998 paper, followed by additional research focusing on Chinese communities in and outside of traditional "Chinatowns" (Li 1998). But in the San Gabriel Valley, these enclaves moved beyond minority status to create minority-majority communities. In March 2010, *New York Times* writer Timothy Egan reported from the San Gabriel Valley on eight Asian-dominated ethnoburbs along a 25-mile swath. These communities, he noted, citing Li, are "suburban in look, but urban in political, culinary, and educational values, attracting immigrants with advanced degrees and ready business skills" (Egan 2010).

The Backstory

The San Gabriel Valley spreads out at the base of the San Gabriel Mountains, a rich, fertile alluvial plain that 100 years ago inspired *plein air* impressionists to capture the unique color and light of its landscapes. It is, as every television viewer who watches the Tournament of Roses parade knows, a picture-postcard backdrop. Not everyone knows, however, that the first European settlements in Los Angeles County occurred here in 1771, 10 years before the *pueblo* of Los Angeles itself was founded near the site of a Tongva indigenous settlement.

Franciscan missionaries built a small collection of adobe structures adjoining, and protected by, the Mission San Gabriel Arcángel, in part because there was a good source of water, the gold of the arid West. The haphazard urban form of our contemporary streets around the mission is no accident: They represent the almost wagon-wheel-like spokes of roads radiating out to points across the valley floor. LA's initial urban form was defined by King Phillip of Spain in the Laws the Indies (1573). However, only after acquisition by the United States in 1848 did the first small "American" settlements in the valley appear (Lexington, now El Monte; and later, the Indiana Colony, now Pasadena).

The Indiana Colony's 1874 founding gave rise to Pasadena, the valley's dominant city, in 1886. Like much of Southern California, the valley benefited by promoting California as a healthful environment, drawing tourists and invalids in equal measure. The San Gabriel Valley quickly became home to an affluent network of small communities, fueled by a form of "gentleman farming" that evolved into the principal economic engine of its time: citrus ranching.

Groves spread out across the "frost-free" citrus belt between Pasadena and Riverside, typically focused around a transportation break point—where a north-south main street crossed an east-west train line and where produce from the packing houses could be loaded. Dominated by the "citrus aristocracy," these areas produced a profusion of modest, attractive, leafy middle-class settlements of substantial brick buildings, charming bungalows, and picturesque churches that defined the valley's urban form—obscuring, however, the Mexican immigrant laborers who were necessary to pick, sort, wrap, and ship the fruit. The dominant culture was Anglo, white, and largely of Midwestern origin (McWilliams 1973, 205–26).

So long before the current generation of demographic change, successive waves of immigrant peoples—Tongva, Spanish, Mexican, and American—had already repeatedly reshaped the San Gabriel Valley's landscape.

A new wave of change arrived after World War II, as immigrants came to LA successively from the South, the East, Mexico and Central America, and Asia. Anglo suburbs like Compton became African American (and now, increasingly Latino) communities, and working-class neighborhoods in Bell, Bell Gardens, Maywood, and Huntington Park became Latino-majority cities. The first minority-majority suburbs within the San Gabriel Valley were Latino beginning in the 1960s. As an increasingly well-educated generation of young Mexican American and other Spanish-speaking families sought to capitalize on their stake in the American dream, they moved to communities like El Monte, South El Monte, and Baldwin Park, where a cadre of Latino leadership moved into positions of political influence, and to communities like Monterey Park and Montebello, which were seen as steps up the economic ladder. These suburbs were not the historic towns of the citrus aristocracy; they developed later, were located more often along the southern edge of the San Gabriel Valley, and had stronger ties to industry.

API cultural influences in the San Gabriel Valley unrolled along an entirely different track. As war and economic and cultural upheaval in Southeast Asia upended the social, economic, or political order in a host of countries, increasing numbers of immigrant families moved to Southern California. They found their own particular brand of paradise in the San Gabriel Valley, with distinct implications for planning and land-use decision making in those communities.

The Start of the Minority-Majority Suburbs in the San Gabriel Valley

There had always been a significant Asian American presence in the San Gabriel Valley—Chinese railroad workers and Japanese strawberry growers and nurserymen had found homes here despite exclusionary laws at the turn of the 20th century and the internment of Japanese families during World War II. But a new generation of residents, coming from places like Hong Kong, Taiwan, and China—principally ethnic Chinese but also some Vietnamese, Korean, and other Southeast Asian—began moving into the San Gabriel Valley in significant numbers following the fall of Saigon in 1973 and the opening of Southeast Asia to commerce, a relationship clearly visible through the extensive trade that passes through the ports of Los Angeles and Long Beach.

Starting with the suburban community of Monterey Park, incorporated in 1923 in the low-lying, rolling hills just north and east of East Los Angeles, these communities spread: north to Alhambra; northeast to San Gabriel, Rosemead, Temple City, and Arcadia; and across the southern flank of the San Gabriel Valley to take in large swaths of Rowland Heights, Hacienda Heights, Walnut, and Diamond Bar.

With their arrival came a cultural transformation that has changed the look and feel of these communities, dramatically enhanced the educational focus, created new economies around international tourism and trade, and created conflict between the established belief structures of these communities and their newest residents.

Demographic Change in the San Gabriel Valley

Today's San Gabriel Valley is neither the natural paradise encountered by the Tongva nor the agricultural wonderland of the past century. A fully urbanized region, it accounts for more than two million people and 400 square miles—one-fifth of Los Angeles County's population, with nearly 40 percent of its incorporated jurisdictions.[1] Some 550,000 households reside there.

The San Gabriel Valley Council of Governments reports that the valley is among the most ethnically diverse areas in Southern California, noting that:

- the valley's two million residents are 44 percent Latino, 27 percent Caucasian, 25 percent API, and 4 percent African American.
- pre-census analysis projected that in 2010, the demographic composition of the valley would be 48 percent Latino, 25 percent API, 23 percent Caucasian, and 4 percent African American.
- the region is also distinguished by significant linguistic diversity. Spanish is the most commonly spoken language in 10 of the San Gabriel Valley's 31 incorporated cities (Azusa, Baldwin Park, El Monte, Industry, Irwindale, La Puente, Montebello, Pomona, Rosemead, and South El Monte), and Chinese is the most commonly spoken language in three cities (Alhambra, Monterey Park, and San Gabriel).
- other languages spoken include Korean, Tagalog, Vietnamese, Arabic, Armenian, and Japanese.

In the decade between 1990 and 2000 alone, Caucasian populations have decreased relative to growing Hispanic and Asian populations:

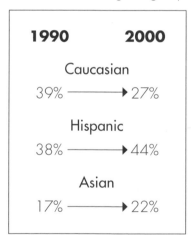

1990   2000

Caucasian

39% ⟶ 27%

Hispanic

38% ⟶ 44%

Asian

17% ⟶ 22%

3.16. Growth of minority populations in the San Gabriel Valley between 1990 and 2000. Source: San Gabriel Council of Governments n.d.

Planning in Minority-Majority Communities
Regulatory Environment
The earliest battles were fought over signs in communities like Monterey Park in the 1980s, where discord over the use of Chinese characters on signs ignited a battle that gets played out to this day in communities all over Southern California. The issue has occurred with such frequency that the National Asian Pacific American Legal Consortium has issued a guide to battle "English-only" laws and restrictive sign regulations (National Asian American Pacific Legal Consortium 2003). Other battles have occurred over private "VIP" rooms in restaurants, nonconforming divisions of commercial space, and property maintenance.

Among the most interesting changes is the influence of *feng shui*, the ancient Chinese tradition of arranging spaces and activities in ways that promote the fortuitous flow of good energy, or *chi*. Routine actions such as checking a residential plan or a commercial enterprise get interesting when city planning, building, or design standards run counter to cultural practices. Traditional beliefs around Chinese numerology result in requests to local building departments to adjust address numbers to produce a more fortuitous address. In Arcadia, a leafy suburb east of Pasadena, the city's practice of making these accommodations for a modest fee became a matter of public debate when the *Los Angeles Times* wrote an article explaining the practice (Ni 2011). (These requests are often granted as long as the adjusted number does not interfere with the correct numerical sequencing of that street.)

Economy

In many cases, the advent of a large class of new businesses has provided a boost to the economy. In cities like Alhambra, San Gabriel, Monterey Park, and Rosemead, the advent of Chinese, Thai, and other Southeast Asian dining experiences have made this subregion the darling of food critics. In 1999, *The Atlantic* first recognized the emerging cuisine culture of these communities as a serious generator of visitors and capital (Schwarz and Schwarz 1999).

In other cases, it's the shopping, fueled by the valley's importance as a Pacific Rim trading center. For most of the last decade, a single shopping complex, the San Gabriel Square, generated more in sales tax revenue than the entire length of the city's principal commercial street, Las Tunas Drive. Just down the street, the San Gabriel Superstore fills a former Target store with a host of smaller retailers.

Still other uses have grown in combinations that create land-use controversies of their own. In Temple City, a profusion of wedding gown shops, tux rental shops, and bridal emporiums serving a largely API clientele caused an uproar when their clustering threatened retail variety on that city's principal shopping street. Throughout the valley, the proliferation of foot massage establishments has created controversy, especially when police or code enforcement officials found that those establishments were offering full-body massage and, occasionally, something more. Recent changes in California law have led San Gabriel Valley cities to reexamine out-of-date laws governing foot- and full-body massage establishments, both popular pursuits in the API community; San Gabriel, a community of four square miles and 41,000 residents, has 45 such establishments.

A more disturbing aspect in some communities is the practice of "maternity tourism," in which affluent Chinese mothers pay up to $35,000 to travel to the United States for prenatal care and to give birth. While the practice is mostly reported in national media in terms of its connection to issues like immigration reform, the impacts at the local level are more fine-grained: the establishments are often opened surreptitiously in a private house, apartment building, or airspace condominium, often without any business licenses or building permits. They are often discovered only when an aggrieved caller reports an unusual number of pregnant women going in and out of a private house. The establishments challenge traditional zoning code definitions of boarding houses, hospitals, assisted living facilities, and other uses; the traditions associated with the practice are rooted in traditional Chinese values about childbirth and child rearing.

Spatial Distribution

Because larger cities in China often have denser residential and commercial environments, the dominant form of new development has found an uneasy balance between physical and spatial norms in the homeland and those of the adopted home. Enclosed courtyards stand in for traditional front yards; smaller units in denser configurations are popular in both residential and commercial architecture.

Urban Design

Architectural design is often the unfortunate victim of an economy that rewards production. Many architects serving the immigrant community operate on fees as low as 3 percent of building value, compared with rates of 10, 12, or 15 percent elsewhere. The products are designed to minimize costs and often run afoul of communities' expectations for enhanced design.

There is great affection in the immigrant API community for the romanticized history associated with the Spanish and Mexican eras, but architecturally this desire often gets translated into poor replications of popular Southern California styles: small, boxy stucco buildings with tile roofs stand in for the elegant fantasy of mission revival and Spanish colonial revival architecture, often with disproportionate entries and colonnades intended to signal the owner's wealth and status. In commercial architecture, the appearance of large, two- and three-story shopping arcades with little street presence and deep parking wells were the result of traditional zoning codes that had not anticipated this form of development and were not prepared for it when it arrived. Since then, San Gabriel Valley communities such as Rosemead, Alhambra, and San Gabriel have moved aggressively to redefine development standards around more pedestrian-scale, transit-oriented values.

Education

San Marino's unified school district was recently characterized in a *Los Angeles Times* report as the highest-scoring in the state, but even less affluent communities with large Asian American populations place a significant emphasis on education. The emergent API communities of the San Gabriel Valley have placed their emphasis on educational attainment, with local school districts showing significant improvements in scores and a high demand for extracurricular and enrichment programs designed to better position their families to secure good college and university choices.

Community Engagement

Many San Gabriel Valley cities were unprepared for the manner in which unprecedented demographic change would affect notions of planning in their communities. The impact on planning is significant. Historic cultural aspects of Chinese culture have caused API residents to tread cautiously where government is concerned. Despite rapid growth in API populations throughout the valley, the number of local elected leaders is trailing their percentage of the population. Planning and community development departments are identifying the need for translation services in Mandarin, Cantonese, Vietnamese, and Korean dialects. Group facilitation processes are being altered to address the needs and interests of a dominant Chinese and API community.

As in many cultures, the greatest conflicts arise when immigrant populations, fearful of engaging their local elected officials because of bad experiences they have had in their home countries, choose to withdraw from participation in public processes. Attempting to draw these residents out to participate in public processes is often time consuming and unsuccessful. In other cases, distrust of government bureaucrats, differing cultural norms for giving "gifts" to public servants, and the cultural imperative to "save face" can create tensions and complexities for planners who are negotiating with new audiences in styles that are unfamiliar to them. Planners are forced to define planning within a framework of diverse, competing cultural values.

Housing
Asian immigrants have invested their money in neighborhoods that Caucasians might see as declining but which immigrant families, coming as they do from less stable environments, see as a stable investment. As a result, a visual tour of neighborhoods suggests a high degree of "bootstrapping"—large houses popping up between modest bungalows of another era, designed with two-story-high porticos meant to show the relative affluence of their owners in neighborhoods that would normally be defined as depressed.

Land Values
API investment has helped drive land values. Four years ago, San Gabriel—where the largest part of new investment has been at the hands of the Chinese community—saw the county's third-highest rate of growth in assessed valuation, exceeded only by Santa Monica and Beverly Hills and tied with Pasadena. In last year's assessor's report, seven of the 10 cities with the fastest growth in valuation were in the San Gabriel Valley (LA County, Office of the Assessor 2010). Affluent San Marino, with its attraction to API buyers, was the only wealthy community in Los Angeles County that has not seen home prices fall during the recession (Beale 2011).

A Peek into the Future
Early results from the 2010 census suggest that growth in API populations will continue. First-generation immigrant communities are likely to mature into second-generation communities with substantially increased influence, as Asian American political leaders move into positions of power. Community organizations such as the Asian Youth Center, started as two decades ago as a United Way project for immigrant youth but now boasting a staff of more than 40 working in locations throughout Los Angeles County, demonstrate the prominence and donor power of API community networks.

San Gabriel, Monterey Park, and Walnut all have elected API mayors or council members as well as members of the state assembly. With the advent of stronger political representation and a growing class of young, talented multilingual planners coming out of the county's three accredited planning programs, expect to see planning programs and processes that are increasingly developed by those communities rather than ones aimed at them.

LA Housing Stories

Janis Breidenbach

Each city has its own housing stories. These stories highlight the contours and conflicts around where and how housing is planned and built. These stories put into relief the parameters of what is possible and permissible within the constraints of politics and culture. They are an important, if often overlooked, part of our larger narratives around city building. They tell us not only about where we live, but about who we are. They tell where we site our housing, what types of housing we do or do not permit, how big, and how little. These are some of LA's housing stories.

These stories collide with the broader image of housing in LA. When most people think of an iconic LA home, two images arise: the first is a home in the hills with majestic views; the second includes miles of subdivision tracts with similarly beige-hued houses strung out in the flat lands. These images reflect our view of LA as a "city of homes," where ownership is everything. They also belie reality since the City of Angels is a city of renters, not home owners. The real story of LA housing should be illustrated with a photograph of a multifamily unit filled with renters.

The home ownership rate in LA has rarely surpassed 40 percent. From about 33 percent in the 1930s, it reached a peak of 46 percent in the 1950s, aided by a trans-formed mortgage finance system that allowed middle- and working-class families to purchase homes. By the 1970s, it started shrinking again. The 2009 American Community Survey found that only 39 percent of us were home owners (U.S. Census Bureau 2010). Sadly, the Federal Reserve Bank of New York has introduced the notion of a "home ownership gap"—the difference between official rates and effective rates when accounting for the negative equity resulting from the implosion of the housing bubble; as I write this in mid-2011, LA's effective rate may be as much as 5 percent less than the official one (Haughwout et al. 2010), pushing the rate back to 1930s levels.

Given our renter/home owner ratio, one would conclude that renters should have a material voice in our city-building conversations. Yet the reverse has been the norm. The voice of our non–home owner majority has been heard only when broader economic, political, and demographic phenomena are in conflict. The results have rarely have favored the majority, yet they are some of LA's most interesting stories.

The Ballad of Chavez Ravine

In 1949, Chavez Ravine held three contiguous neighborhoods and roughly 2,000 residents in the steep hills to the northwest of downtown LA. Some of the housing in the ravine was made up of small, middle-class homes; much was "substandard" in an area with few city services or amenities. Sequestered from the rest of the city by its terrain, the residents were predominantly second-generation Mexican Americans mixed with Southern European immigrants and African American migrants from the South—many of whom settled there because they were denied housing elsewhere (Parson 2005).

Chavez Ravine sits high above the LA basin, with some spectacular views of the city. After passage of the 1949 Housing Act, the Los Angeles City Housing Authority (CHA) was anxious to rid the city of "slums" and produce housing for its burgeoning population of World War II veterans and Midwestern transplants. With $100 million from the federal government and eminent domain powers from the state's redevelopment law, the CHA proposed that Chavez Ravine be transformed into Elysian Park Heights—a huge project incorporating single-family homes, larger apartment buildings, a cooperative, and public housing. Renowned architects Richard Neutra and Robert Alexander were called upon to design the project (Hines 1982). When completed, upward of 10,000 people would have called Elysian Park Heights home. The project would be a "modern city" achievement of design and development, meeting the CHA's goals of "making a better world" (Parson 2005).

What family stories would have unfolded within this ambitious project? What would these stories have told us? We will never know. It was never built. Even as the project was in its planning stages, powerful real estate interests, the *Los Angeles Times,* and Cold War McCarthyism combined to kill it. Home builder Fritz Burns and conservative attorney Frederick Dockweiler led the new Committee Against Socialist Housing, which funded a referendum on the project. The CHA project manager and others were called out as communists; when the manager refused to answer questions regarding his political affiliation, he was fired (Parson 2005). For 10 years afterward, the future of Chavez Ravine was contested, through two mayoral elections, two lawsuits, and two local referenda. In 1959, the land was turned over to Walter O'Malley and the newly transplanted and renamed Los Angeles Dodgers baseball team (Anderson 2007).

Chavez Ravine is a housing tale of who we were—and were not. The complexities of a multiyear conflict involving public housing, anticommunism, and powerful real estate interests have been simplified into a David versus Goliath saga of the last resident refusing to leave her home to make way for Major League Baseball. The longer, broader conflict raised questions of where we allow people to live and to what lengths we are willing to go to enforce land-use decisions. The ballad of Chavez Ravine was not only about public housing or a baseball stadium but about a conflict over city building—who has a seat at the table and how decisions get made and for whom.

The story of Chavez Ravine is one of loss for the immigrant and migrant renters—a story that reflects that generation's conflicts over where and for whom housing would be built. Racial covenants and other forms of discrimination shaped how and where housing was built and who lived where even as LA residents filed some of the first legal challenges to these practices (Rasmussen 2006). Such barriers to adequate housing due to discrimination were an ongoing frustration and, if not the only trigger, definitely contributed to the urban riots of the 1960s, including Watts in 1965.

Shifts in the City

In the decades that followed, after such discrimination was found unconstitutional, other structural factors continued to limit the affordability of housing in LA. The LA region's economy was damaged when heavy industry and the associated middle-class jobs started to leave, which happened just as property values went through the roof and immigration soared. The city had a housing crisis; tenant organizers and advocates went into action.

By the late 1970s, rent inflation sparked serious community organizing and a demand for rent control, especially after the passage of Proposition 13 drastically reduced property taxes but not rents. Indeed, Jerry Brown, in his first stint as governor, established a statewide "hotline" for tenants that received 12,000 calls per day (Gottlieb et al. 2005). In LA, the Coalition for Economic Survival and the Gray Panthers kept up the pressure until the city council passed the Rent Stabilization Ordinance in May 1979 (Dreier 1997). One of the significant highlights of LA's rent control story is how organized constituencies with different agendas came together to fight for affordable housing. Housing tenure and cost became a strong bond crossing ethnic, cultural, and geographic boundaries.

Figure 3.17. Just as the destruction of Chavez Ravine removed affordable housing, the massive redevelopment of Bunker Hill eliminated a grand old neighborhood in favor of modernist planning for a new downtown.

In the 1980s LA's deindustrialization became globalization, and the city transformed into what Saskia Sassen terms a global city—a "strategic site" in the global economy, a place where the "command functions" are located (Sassen 1994). The middle class shrunk as heavy industry's jobs left, replaced by what Sassen (2000) describes as the new "urban proletariat"—lower-skilled immigrants and women—who found jobs in a burgeoning service economy that grew with and around global city institutions. By the end of the decade, LA's wage gap had two poles: high end and low end. Not surprisingly, a housing affordability gap followed suit.

However, the lessons on coalition building from the rent-control struggle had been well learned. Indeed, as grass grows through the cracks in a sidewalk, during the next decade new and transformed actors emerged out of the interstices of a changed city to come together in a new coalition—a "civil society from below." The result, Housing LA, was another unique LA story.

Housing LA

Not an organization in its own right, Housing LA was (and is) an ongoing coalition, consisting of relationships between and among a number of important city constituencies concerned about housing cost and quality, type, and tenure and—from a planning perspective—about where and for whom housing is built. Its first campaign—the reason for its formation in 1997—was to establish a $100 million citywide Housing Trust Fund (HTF). Although tenant organizations and the tenants themselves were the face of the campaign, two other major partners played key roles; they either had not existed 20 years earlier or had been almost completely transformed.

The first partner was a new collective organization of nonprofit affordable housing developers, often referred to as Community Development Corporations (CDCs). A hard-to-define constituency, CDCs can be analyzed as either an industry or social movement—and sometimes as both. Distinct from for-profit developers, CDCs operate with a "double bottom line," utilizing their real estate finance acumen to build and manage housing that is affordable *and* sequestered from the larger market. Their organizational lineage stems from the policies and programs of the War on Poverty, through which they took on the task of rebuilding neighborhoods and eradicating poverty.

The vast majority of LA's CDCs were birthed between 1985 and 1995. They vary in their specific missions: some work only in certain geographies, others build citywide; a few are based in ethnic communities; a few are faith-based. Some CDCs not only develop but do their own design, property/asset management, social service provision, and community organizing. The backgrounds of CDC leaders differ, but more than a few call upon the heritages of Jane Jacobs and Rosa Parks. They are competent civic negotiators who know the importance of advocacy and—when necessary—are not averse to conflict.

If organized CDCs were the "new kid," Housing LA's "old-timer" partner was the labor movement. Los Angeles has never been a union town. What union density existed in the 1970s and 1980s had been significantly reduced due to deindustrialization, antiunion animus, and a lack of aggressive organizing. By the mid-1990s, aggressive organizing efforts by immigrant-led campaigns in the service sectors had started a turnaround. They won campaigns that would have been unthinkable in prior years. Janitors, hotel workers, security guards, and in-home supportive services workers joined their respective unions—and won contracts (Gottlieb et al. 2005). In a single election, 75,000 in-home supportive service workers joined the labor movement, the largest union election since Ford's River Rouge factory workers joined the United Auto Workers in 1941 (Meyerson 1999).

Housing LA's diverse constituencies brought a new dimension to housing activism in LA. The campaign understood the role of affordable housing as a core dimension in what the city had become and what kind of city it could be. Housing LA was not demanding charity; it was claiming its place as an integral part of the development process in LA. Campaign leaders were clear—they were working to gain resources for affordable housing but also to have a voice in what is built, how it is built, by whom, and for whom.

The campaign was conceived and formed in late 1997 with a three-year timeline to achieve the Housing Trust Fund. The first two and a half years were spent building support for the HTF among the July 2001 mayoral candidates. Six months after Mayor James Hahn was elected, he announced the HTF on January 17, 2002. Although not planned, the date of the announcement was the anniversary of the devastating 1994 Northridge Earthquake that had destroyed 25,000 units of housing (much of it multifamily renting at the low end of market).

These three stories unfolded in different times within evolving political, economic, and social realities. In contrast to the struggle over Chavez Ravine, the rent control and Housing LA campaigns were citywide. As opposed to the rent control battle, Housing LA raised contentious questions about how and where growth and development were going to occur, as well as how we keep existing housing affordable. Housing LA thus is not just a story of what happened but also a precursor of how city-building stories may unfold in the future.

The Next LA Story? Climate Change, Land Use, and Affordable Housing

In 2008, the California legislature passed SB 375, the Sustainable Communities and Climate Protection Act, with a policy goal of increased land-use density as a way of reducing vehicle-miles traveled, one of the main contributors to greenhouse gas emissions in California. SB 375 will ultimately contribute to LA's city-building conversation through its pertinent—if convoluted—planning requirements. Going forward, metropolitan planning bodies must develop Sustainable Community Strategies (SCS) that link regional land-use and transportation policies, while local governments must pay increased attention to where affordable housing will be sited as they prepare state-mandated housing elements—one of the seven elements of their general plans (Adams, Eaken, and Notthoff 2009). Although affordable housing policies are not required to comport with SCS, without conformity, certain incentives—including transportation resources—may not be forthcoming. This circuitous process will form one of the parameters in upcoming city-building conversations.

This loop—from SB 375 through SCS and regional transportation plans, combined with local housing elements that tie back to the allocation of transportation funds—provides an opening for affordable housing organizers to question the limits of the market and the role of land-use policy when it comes to shelter for those who have been historically excluded not only from the results of land-use planning but also from the planning process itself.

Of course, the specifics of future opportunities and conflicts of the next LA housing story remain unknown. Land-use tools that increase affordable housing have arguably been a greater source of conflict than resources. Mixed income, or inclusionary, housing has been a contentious policy in California, even as about 40 percent of the state's localities have ordinances governing it. After the HTF campaign, Housing LA attempted against great resistance to pass an inclusionary ordinance. After a multiyear effort the vote was scheduled then stopped by a successful lawsuit that argued inclusionary requirements violated the state's stringent limits on rent control—itself passed in the aftermath of earlier successful rent control campaigns (Scott 2009).

In early 2011, a proposal to allow reduced parking around transit stops was on its way to passage when legal aid lawyers realized that it could easily lead to demolition of rent-controlled housing and—absent inclusionary requirements—the exclusion of low-income people from transit-adjacent housing. More of these policy "surprises" surely await us in the future.

Development patterns will shift as we move toward a less suburban and more urban future; our demography and economy will change as well. Los Angeles's housing will still be built within the constraints of terrain and climate, politics and culture, but although our terrain will stay more or less the same, the other parameters may be drastically different. However, we will still have to decide where and for whom we build homes, whether we accommodate home owners or renters, where we increase density, and where we limit it. How we resolve these contentious issues will create LA stories that will, again, tell us who we are.

Finding Public Space
on Private Beaches

Meredith Drake Reitan

The beach is the region's most extensive public space, stretching along the coastline from Santa Barbara to the Mexican border. The beach is also a place of conflict, with wealthy property owners trying to enhance their privacy by limiting public access and environmentalists concerned about further development and the extensive use by a growing population. From 2007 until 2010, the Los Angeles Urban Rangers highlighted the possibilities and the problems associated with the beach by going on safari in Malibu, home to some of the coast's most desirable beaches. Combining local knowledge and cheeky irony, the group highlighted the shifting boundary between public and private space in one of LA's wealthiest areas.

The Malibu Public Beach Safaris were designed to show visitors how to legally and safely park, walk, picnic, and sunbathe on Malibu's 27 miles of public beach, 20 miles of which are adjacent to private beachfront development. One can legally walk only below the mean high-tide line, although the on-the-ground policy is that the public can walk on any dry sand (i.e., below the last high-tide line). As their brochure suggests, the Urban Rangers safari includes a "public-private boundary hike, sign watching, a no-kill hunt for access ways, and a public easement potluck."

The founding members, Jenny Price, Sara Daleiden, Therese Kelly, and Emily Scott, came together in 2004 for the Art Center College of Design's gardenLAb, an exhibition of environmentally themed arts groups. The group adopted the persona of park rangers since Scott had worked as one. They created a mock campfire circle around which they could talk about urban topics, including downtown redevelopment, freeway landscaping, and display behavior on Hollywood Boulevard. When performing, these architects, artists, academics, and freelance journalists fully inhabit the ranger personality, complete with faux-ranger costumes and that particularly upbeat way of talking. Their performances straddle the boundary of art and civic engagement, raising issues of environmental equity, access to public spaces, and people's relationship to nature.

LAND-USE AND ENVIRONMENTAL POLICIES

4

One Hundred Years of Land-Use Regulation

Andrew H. Whittemore

The history of land-use and environmental regulation in LA is a story of winners and losers. Early leaders of the 20th century in planning and real estate, however, viewed land-use regulation as "an exact science": a practice that through the select elimination of private abuses could deliver maximized prosperity.[1] Already in 1931, William Munro, then president of the National Municipal League, lamented that "whenever a question of rezoning comes up, the issue is not usually approached from the standpoint of what the city needs, but of what the private owners desire and what their immediate neighbors feel disinclined to let them have" (Munro 1931).

Munro's observation is not particularly surprising since a plentiful body of literature has told the story of the parochial management of zoning and planning.[2] In LA, four historical sets of winners and losers characterize the politics of land-use and environmental regulation "regimes," each having different impacts on the built form of the city.[3]

Speculative real estate interests governed the first regime, which lasted from the advent of zoning in 1921 until the mid-1930s. With the collapse of property values in the late 1920s and the founding of the Federal Housing Administration (FHA) in 1934, a new phase in the history of land-use regulation ensued as the FHA expanded the accessibility of the single-family home and planners reformed zoning to accommodate large-scale community developers and their buyers. However, as land prices rose, developers turned increasingly to infill development, and home owners groups dug in their heels, initiating four decades of home owner preeminence. In this third regime the great majority—if not all—alterations to the zoning code decreased development possibilities in the city; the introduction of statewide environmental regulation also greatly bolstered the preservationist prerogative. In the last decade, housing advocates and traditional development interests have combined to challenge home owner preeminence, expanding development possibilities in order to both address housing concerns and increase profits.

Districting: Prelude to Zoning

In 1909 the entirety of the city outside of 25 industrial districts was established as a residence district prohibiting "any trade, calling, occupation or business."[4] This legislation represented the culmination of a half-decade of "districting," a form of land-use regulation involving the exclusion of commercial operations from designated residential areas. Districting began in 1904 with the proscribing of laundries—operations often owned by recent Asian immigrants—from three residential districts.[5] In the subsequent years the city introduced residential districts excluding stables, brickyards, and various other nuisances, creating an elaborate regulatory landscape.

Districting had several shortcomings: most significantly it did not stop the overbuilding of the city by speculators in either residential or industrial districts. Big developers feared the market instability that unlimited production could generate; the real estate industry, in LA and elsewhere, preferred the scarcity produced by stricter regulation. "Now," stated J. C. Nichols, developer of Kansas City's exclusive Country Club District, "if in developing our subdivisions, we can limit the quantity of certain classes of property, if we can create the feeling that we have a monopoly of that class of property . . . we are assisting in the sale of that property" (Weiss 1987, 65–66). Developers hoped that smaller, sloppier competitors would be cut out by comprehensive planning and zoning that promised to make the startup period of projects more cumbersome (ibid., 19). The city council founded a city planning commission in 1920.

The Speculator's Regime

In October 1921 the LA City Council created five zones designated by letters "A" through "E," with "A" proscribing any use but single-family homes, "B" proscribing nonresidential uses, "C" proscribing industrial uses, "D" proscribing only the most noxious industrial uses, and "E" being unlimited.[6] However, planners, their allies in big real estate, and home owners would struggle to implement the more restrictive zoning categories as small-scale speculators sought to undermine them.

In devising a citywide zoning scheme, planners in LA drew upon design schemes such as that of Clarence Perry, whose ideal "Neighborhood Unit" called for single-family homes to be protected on quiet interior streets, with commercial activities and apartments clustered at the edges along major arterials (Perry 1929 and 1939). Los Angeles planners were determined to separate uses by zoning arterials predominantly for multifamily use, with commercial uses located in clusters at major intersections and interior streets reserved for single-family residences and public facilities.[7]

Zoning represented a far more stringent regulatory regime than that of districting. Planning commission members repeatedly took to the local press to explain the need for zoning to disgruntled speculators.[8] The small-scale speculators whose profits depended on getting more out of limited resources opposed more restrictive zoning categories intended to contain commercial and multifamily residential uses. A battle ensued over how much of LA would be restricted to residential and how much would be open to commerce.

Complicating the zoning debate was the construction of 48 radial routes and 36 interdistrict, 74-foot-wide thoroughfares, designed by LA's transportation planners (Olmsted, Bartholomew, and Cheney 1924, 34–46). City planning engineer

Thomas Coombs condemned them as unaccommodating for any use, calling them the most injurious mistake the city had ever made (LA Dept. of City Planning 1929–1930, 49). Property owners on these streets insisted their properties be zoned for commercial use since the levels of noise and dirt made them inappropriate for residential construction. The real attraction, of course, was profit: property values jumped as much as 300 percent on upzonings to commercial use (Buck 1924).

Even when the planning commission refused a property owner's request and advised more restrictive zoning, the owner still had options. In a city council elected on a nonpartisan basis, favors were not hard to buy. The council ended up deciding that most major roads should have commercial frontage. The planning commission's *Annual Report of 1928* reported that 5.8 percent of the city's land was used for commercial purposes while 13.4 percent was zoned for it (LA Dept. of City Planning 1927–1928, 6). In 1928 the ratio of commercially to residentially zoned land in boomtown Los Angeles was 25 percent—the average in other cities was 9 percent. This "overzoning" would frustrate planners and their allies in big real estate into the Depression.[9]

Even where planners achieved concentrated shopping districts, elected officials interfered by "spot zoning" (or rezoning) lengthy strips of frontage for commercial use. Spot zoning involved granting "exceptions," as variances were then called, for

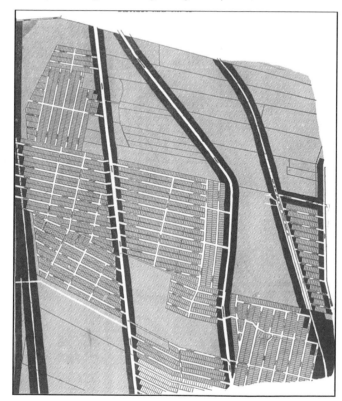

Figure 4.1. The weakness of planners against speculative interests meant that boulevards in even semirural areas, such as this one near Culver City in 1925, were zoned for intense commercial development. Source: City of LA, City Council 1925, District Map no. 13

a single property. Because zoning restrictions at the time almost entirely consisted of use restrictions, exceptions were functionally similar to zone changes. Resident groups criticized spot zoning as "a notorious condition which seeks to exploit the majority property owners for gain, promoted by a few paid lobbyists and workers, who are subverting the cause of justice for the benefit of their secret employers."[10] The planning department and Municipal League publicly condemned lobbyists who paid council members to override the planning commission's recommendations against exceptions.[11] In the 1930s, LA district attorney Buron Fitts called the council's oversight of the city's zoning a "racket" that "eclipses any other form of asserted corruption yet brought to our attention" and launched an investigation.[12]

The result of the haphazard application of the zoning code was that even as the growing city increased in total valuation, it ended up with miles of vacant frontage. By 1929, LA's valuation had surpassed that of Chicago's Cook County, yet the value ultimately failed to materialize in development, and it evaporated with arrival of the Depression. The overzoning meant that too much area was zoned for commercial activity, and builders were wary of building residences adjacent to potentially egregious commercial uses—the result, the Realty Board noted, was the "economic waste" of the vacancies.[13]

The overzoning adversely affected not only commercial buildings but the development of strong residential neighborhoods. The *Los Angeles Times* theorized that the prospect of commercial traffic was driving home owners to other jurisdictions.[14] One realtor wrote that single-family districts were being pushed "to a circle far outside that which would reasonably be expected" (Bush n.d., 24). The situation meant that public investments often went unused; William Munro pointed to empty schools in former residential districts invaded by industry. He observed: "No one thinks to ask whether the [zoning] change, if made, will increase or simplify the difficulties of municipal administration" (Munro 1931, 203–4). The solution was to strengthen zoning restrictions, but many property owners were not eager to downzone.[15] According to the Guaranty Building and Loan Association of Hollywood, the fact that owners paid

Figure 4.2. Vacant commercial lots on Wilshire Boulevard, 1928. Source: City of LA, Dept. of City Planning 1927–1928, 8

higher taxes on commercially designated land only increased their hopes for eventual development.[16]

Other interests actively protested overzoning. The Los Feliz Improvement Association and Hollywood Chamber of Commerce persuaded the mayor to veto the rezoning of Los Feliz Boulevard to a commercial thoroughfare, arguing that "city planning would be a farce if every subdivider or owner of vacant lots that might bring a higher price for business purposes, is allowed to disregard the interests of the home owners in residence districts."[17]

The Depression did not end the problem, as spot zoning and overzoning continued.[18] By 1933 only 4.8 percent of the city's zoned land was zoned for single-family use, down from 9.5 percent five years earlier, although 58.9 percent of zoned land was developed for this use. The amount of commercial zoning was also up from 13.4 percent to 19.1 percent, although only 9.2 percent of zoned land was used for commercial purposes.[19]

The Community Builder's Regime

The planners' ideal city came closer to realization when the Federal Housing Administration (FHA), founded in 1934, began to require lending standards for the reception of federally insured amortized mortgages. The FHA, in grading neighborhoods from "best" to "hazardous," assumed mixed use blocks to be volatile and the socially and physically homogeneous single-family district to be stable. A good score from the FHA depended on the containment of intensive uses and protection of low densities advocated by planners.[20] The FHA overwhelmingly denied mortgages in areas of older construction, areas that were not zoned, or where the proximity of less restrictive zoning threatened investments in low-density residential construction. The FHA's policies provided LA planners with a persuasive case that zoning more land for single-family use and insulating it from more intense uses was the best way to assist households to achieve home ownership and stimulate growth (LA Dept. of City Planning 1934–1935, 17–20).

In 1935, the city conducted a property survey of its central 100 square miles and concluded that much single-family property was not up to par with FHA standards (ibid., 20). Change was slow at first: from 1936 to 1938 the council moved 14.3 miles of street frontage from multifamily designations into single-family "R-1," 6.4 miles from business designations to residential ones, and 1.82 miles of frontage from industrial designations to various less intensive ones. In total in this period, 25 miles of frontage was shifted to more restrictive designations versus 0.6 miles to less restrictive ones (LA Dept. of City Planning 1937–1938, 15). This shift in policy aided big developers and home owners while it tended to injure their common opponent, the fly-by-night speculator who might buy a zone change and pursue a noisy, traffic-generating use next to its subdivision (Weiss 1987).

While planners and big real estate developers agreed on protecting single-family districts, in other areas they differed. With the prospect of so much FHA-spurred growth, the planning department for the first time made an effort to coordinate development with planning. The city undertook areawide rezonings principally focused on downzoning: rezoning multifamily "R-4" as "R-2" or "R-1" and accommodating commercial districts with the local commercial "C-1" designation rather than general commercial "C-2."[21] Planners intended that the long-range planning for the San Fernando Valley would preserve profitable agricultural uses while containing urban areas in concentrated nuclei.[22] Real estate development interests disagreed.

Developers convinced city leaders to adopt the 1955 Master Plan for the San Fernando Valley, which more than halved the amount of land in agricultural zones (LA Dept. of City Planning 1954–1955, 20). The FHA-backed community builder reigned supreme. Trends in zoning were now toward providing for lower density rather than concentration, culminating in the 1955 introduction of a "RE" Residential Estate zone, a zone mandating large minimum lot sizes.[23]

By the mid-1960s most of the agricultural land preserved in the Valley by the 1955 plan had disappeared, and the Valley's urban areas melded into a single mass. As the city advanced ever closer to the natural growth boundaries of the mountains and the ocean, land costs rose, and multiunit construction passed single-family construction in unit volume in 1957 for the first time since the 1920s (LA Dept. of City Planning 1957–1958, 10). However, the new building trends presented a problem in a city where civic leaders and home owners were accustomed to homogenous stretches of single-family development. They eventually turned on the developer-driven regime since it no longer served their interests.

The Home Owners' Regime

Until 1960, Angeleno home owners fell in step with big developers. Zoning, promoted by the city's big real estate interests, afforded home owners protections beyond what districting or covenants could give them. The FHA's policies satisfied both big developers and home owners by presenting an incentive against overzoning and spot zoning. After 1960, however, home owners groups found something to dislike not only in the speculators seeking to construct a service station on every corner but with many of the big developers, who had built communities just like theirs. As undeveloped land dwindled in LA and its vicinity, developers began to pursue denser infill development in already built-up areas, breaking the trust they had with home owners.

The first gains of home owners groups were in expanding height district regulation. In 1962, in light of one riling proposal for an apartment building, the Los Feliz Improvement Association successfully petitioned to create a new height district more limiting than any current alternatives.[24] Associations from various other wealthy areas of the city in the Valley and on the Westside joined them, hoping tighter regulation would protect vistas, one of many increasingly assumed inalienable assets of property ownership.[25] Since then, two even more restrictive height districts have been introduced at the behest of home owners.[26]

The successful imposition of height restrictions fed home owners' appetite for more restrictions. When the city expanded the regimen of exclusive residential zones in the 1960s, adding four large-lot "RE" zones, some neighborhoods would settle for nothing less than the new zoning designations.[27] One group of home owners condemned upzoning to "R-1" as promoting slum development even though the costs of new homes would be in line with others in the area.[28] Home owners were evidently demanding that their neighbors live at least as well as they did. A 1962 case closing a rock quarry despite no clear alternative use for the property led to a rush to protect industrial uses (R. Jackson 1981, 35). This culminated in the creation of the "MR1" and "MR2" Re-

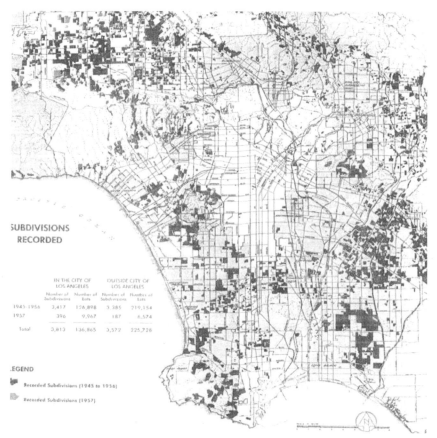

Figure 4.3. Subdivisions recorded in Los Angeles County, 1945–1956. The city's background is white; the county's is gray. The concentration of subdivisions in the upper left corner is in the San Fernando Valley. Source: City of LA, Dept. of City Planning 1956–1957, 10

stricted Manufacturing districts in 1970—industrial areas exclusive of residential uses— designed to "to protect industrial land for industrial use."[29]

The rise of the home owners immediately influenced citywide politics. In 1961 Valley council member Patrick McGee based his mayoral campaign on what the *Los Angeles Examiner* called his "unusual councilmanic record of being an almost constant dissenter . . . featured by his opposition to almost every development proposed."[30] On the home owners' side was a sense of moral authority due to their supposed attention to nonmaterial values of community. "Nobody is making a buck out of this homeowner association," the *Los Angeles Times* quoted one activist in the midst of a development battle (Burleigh 1967). Indeed, activists in the Valley's Sherman Way neighborhood separated their values from those of developers and city officials by condemning high-density zoning as "monetarily prized" (Secor 1964).

The power of the home owner even affected land-use policies in the inner city. While the city council halved parking requirements in downtown in 1962, such policies became increasingly restrictive elsewhere in the city. In 1965, the city effectively doubled parking requirements in all residential zones.[31] Again in 1970, the city council overrode a mayoral veto to pass an ordinance increasing required parking spaces by increasing room counts, an ordinance the department of city planning described as "so restrictive as to be detrimental" and the Building Industry Association warned would come at a cost of 7,000 units per year.[32]

Even as the city council relaxed restrictions after the Watts riots to allow foster homes and Head Start facilities, their overall policy limited the construction of affordable housing by focusing on protecting single-family districts.[33] The result was that the combination of high land costs, density restrictions, and parking requirements were forcing developers to charge higher prices for housing units. Already in 1963, builder Ray Wyatt complained that restrictions forced him to price units out of the range of the majority of consumers: "We are forced to build 75% of our houses at prices 15% of our customers can afford" (Seaver 1963, 195).

Figure 4.4. A sample Residential Planned Development (RPD), 1966. Source: City of LA, Dept. of City Planning 1965–1966, 12

Nothing aggravated home owners groups as much as Planned Unit Developments (PUDs), locally termed Residential Planned Developments (RPDs). RPDs allowed developers to cluster allowable density over a large area into smaller, compact forms, leading planners to hope they would produce more affordable units.[34] The issue came to a head in 1966 when a county grand jury indicted developer Bryan Gibson on charges of grand theft and conspiracy to pay $51,000 in bribes for a conditional use permit to build 900 units in a town house–style RPD in the San Fernando Valley's Chatsworth district (Einstoss 1966).

Public faith in City Hall dropped abruptly, and the case became a general trial of planning in the city. The resulting Citizens' Committee report presented recommendations calling for, among other things, regular area-by-area revision of the General Plan, the conformance of zoning with the General Plan, and standardized processing for conditional uses and RPDs.[35] Charter amendments of 1969 largely delivered on the recommendations, although not, significantly, on zoning's conformance with the General Plan.[36]

The planning department undertook area-by-area reviews, termed Community Plans, with the aid of a local advisory group (LA Dept. of City Planning 1971–1972, 3). Home owners groups influenced the process by calling for significant zoning rollbacks. Also at this time, the planning department released the first citywide conceptual plan, Concept Los Angeles. The Concept Plan called for preserving areas of single-family construction and containing growth in high-density mixed use concentrations. Planning Director Calvin Hamilton sought to bring the Concept Plan in line with home owners' demands, endorsing the department's own zoning rollback study. The resulting 1972 study advocated a zoning capacity reduction of 35 percent for a 1990 population capacity of 4.1 million (LA Dept. of City Planning 1972, 55).

Critics thought 4.1 million was far too permissive for a city of 2.8 million people. Instead, area planning workshops started discussing *no* growth as a realistic alternative.[37] The logic of the antigrowth movement was that growth accommodation was really growth stimulation, that permissive zoning was a self-fulfilling prophecy maintained by regulators at the behest of wealthy developers. The Department of City Planning argued that this "inhumane" position "ignored the nature of population increase," and that more stringent zoning would merely force growth elsewhere.[38] Unfortunately for antigrowth advocates, the 1972 rollback study, although incorporated into land-use plans, was toothless as long as the city could get away with not enforcing the General Plan.[39] Antigrowth advocates attempted to bridge this gap by getting the 1978 state legislature to pass Assembly Bill 283, requiring that LA's zoning conform to its General Plan by July 1, 1981.[40] The General Plan was finally implemented when a case filed by a coalition of 42 Westside and Valley home owner organizations gave LA until March 1988 to make its zoning consistent with its General Plan (LA Dept. of City Planning 1985a, 16).

The California Environmental Quality Act (CEQA), passed in 1970, represented another significant challenge to developer preeminence. In 1972 the California Supreme Court ruled in *Friends of Mammoth v. Board of Supervisors* that CEQA applied to all projects permitted by any government agency in the state, a ruling that resulted in performance-based evaluations for nearly all new development.[41] These evaluations were intended to identify existing natural and man-made resources at development sites and to require the mitigation of significant impacts on these resources.

In 1987 a court decision was handed down in favor of the Friends of Westwood, who had sued the city to force the compiling of environmental impact reports (EIR) for large-scale projects. Although state law was clear on the subject, city policy had remained somewhat ambiguous.[42] The city immediately made it policy to conduct EIRs for all projects over 45,000 square feet generating 500 or more car trips per day or having 25 or more residential units.[43] Three years later a city ordinance mandated a site-plan review process for all projects meeting these thresholds, and in addition required the planning department to review a proposal's compatibility with abutting properties and consistency with zoning, the General Plan, and any applicable redevelopment plan.[44]

Empowered home owners took to the review of development proposals with gusto, using site-plan review as a mechanism to water down development proposals or make them infeasible. This suppression of new development arguably came at the cost of further displacing development and any of its negative impacts to fringe locations, and discouraging local benefits from development (Council on Development Choices in the 80s 1983, 17). Developers and their allies derided these new urban engineers as NIMBYists: cynical home owners who refused to measure potential negatives of development against potential benefits to themselves and others.

Already in 1980, researchers found that statewide, developers were "overdesigning" to avoid triggering EIRs, thus contributing to the inflation of housing costs (Small and Knust 1980, 46). A recent article put it simply: "Go to almost any planning conference in California, and you are likely to find sessions about how CEQA prevents good planning. Viewed exclusively through an EIR, a high-density infill project often looks worse than a low-density greenfield subdivision" (Shigley 2010, 15). In other words, the costs of mitigation could deter less determined, less financially equipped developers altogether, sending them to less populated and less regulated jurisdictions—ironically, contributing to the impacts of sprawl.

Home owner power culminated in 1986's Proposition U, a measure that halved allowable floor area ratio from 3:1 to 1.5:1 in commercial and manufacturing zones in the city's prevalent "Height District 1." This district covered about 85 percent of commercially zoned areas (Connell 1986a, Kaplan 1986). The proposition's supporters were able to gain a nontraditional ally in low-income minority areas by linking their cause with that of the Concerned Citizens of South Central Los Angeles, who were fighting a trash-burning operation in their area (Connell 1986a). However, many in the city's low-income communities may have supported the initiative for a different reason: *Community Democrat* publisher Willard Murray believed the proposition would not stop development but direct it out of high-income areas and cause it to be more evenly spread (Connell 1986b).

When the proposition passed, the low-slung commercial boulevards of LA, for better or for worse, were frozen in time. For planners, a voter initiative with so much power seemed a compromise of the city's planning traditions. The American Planning Association's 1986 Los Angeles conference was welcomed by the *Los Angeles Times* with the words: "Welcome to Los Angeles Planners: R.I.P." (Kaplan 1986).

Given the growing limitations on construction it was not surprising that housing costs rose. Further exacerbating the housing situation was Proposition 13, a 1978 statewide measure restricting cities' and counties' ability to raise taxes on residential property. As a result, residential construction lost much of its appeal as a source of revenue generation.[45] The expansion of regulation in the 1970s and 1980s was complemented by limited measures to provide more affordable housing options. The city's 1971 "15% ordinance" required all developments of five or more units made feasible pursuant to a zone change or conditional use permit to reserve 15 percent of total units for low-income buyers.[46] Regulators had prohibited homes with zero-lot lines since the Yard Ordinance of 1935; now (in 1984) they agreed to a town home zone.[47] They also permitted more permissive zoning for mobile homes and accessory dwelling units limited to two persons over 60 in single-family zones pursuant to the state's 1981 "Granny Bill" (SB 1160) (Birkinshaw 1982).[48] In a boon for artists, a

Figure 4.5. Ventura Boulevard, 1987. With Proposition U, Angelenos prevented the further infringement of high-rise development in residential areas.

downtown live-work ordinance allowed residential and limited commercial uses to occur in the same building.[49]

In 1982 the state mandated a density bonus of 25 percent if developers reserved 10 percent of units for lower income households or 25 percent of units for low- or moderate-income households. Developers in large cities had little interest in the density bonus because it could not overcome the barrier of high land costs (Taylor 1981). By 1987, 72 density bonus projects had produced only 3,520 rental units, 22.4 percent of which were priced for moderate-, low-, or very low-income earners.[50] The city argued that density bonuses produced the negative impacts of density without creating enough affordable units, and suggested targeting them solely to low- and very low-income households. This became state law in 1989.[51]

The Housing Element of 1986 reported that the combined effects of Proposition 13 and zoning restrictions meant that housing turnover was slow, and when new units were added to the city's supply or older units came onto the market, they tended to go to the highest bidder; that bidder was inevitably not a low-income earner (LA Dept. of City Planning 1986, 46). The potential home buyers of Southern California may have deserved to take advantage of the region as much as previous generations, but unfortunately for them many were left outside a land-use decision-making process dominated by home owners and fiscally minded planners.

The Balanced Regime

Antigrowth activists arguably still dominate the city's planning scene. The single-family house, opined Robert Greene in 2003, had become a revolutionary force in the past quarter-century (Greene 2003, 28). From the proliferation of large-lot zoning and parking requirements, to Proposition U and the "institutionalized NIMBYism" of site plan review, the story of land-use regulation in LA was for the better part of the late 20th century written by suburban preservationists (ibid.). As of 1990, lower-income

Figure 4.6. Development resulting from "Residential Accessory Services" zoning, Hollywood, 2010

South LA had had an impact on liquor store regulation, but not much else. Meanwhile, a housing crisis has blossomed across the metropolis, forcing middle-income households into inland counties and the poor into overcrowded housing. As dismal as the LA situation is, reforming land-use regulation in some adjoining municipalities was nearly impossible. A 2008 housing study of the Westside, coauthored by the Los Angeles Department of City Planning and the planning departments of four other Westside cities, found that whereas 72 percent of the population resides within the city limits of LA, 79 percent of local housing production since 2000 was within the city (Westside Cities Working Group 2008, 75).

The Citywide General Plan Framework of 1996, although it officially replaced the quarter-century-old Concept Los Angeles, basically reiterated the goals of the old plan.[52] The vision called for by the Framework did not prove popular among Valley and Westside home owners (LA Dept. of City Planning 1985b, 185–91). Dissatisfaction culminated in the Valley's attempted secession in the early 2000s, an effort one editorial in the Valley's *Daily News* called a "smokescreen" for the desire of Valley home owners to exercise greater control over land-use decisions.[53] The Valley was partially placated with the creation of Neighborhood Councils (NC) by the 1999 charter. These are voluntary, nonmandatory organizations intended to enhance community presence in decision making.

The NCs were a shadow of a grander vision that would have had them control land-use matters (City of LA 1999, Article IX). Reform Commission member William

Weinberger feared that a decentralization of zoning power would introduce suburban exclusivity to the city: "If each community decided they didn't want any commercial development in their plan, that would have an effect on the entire city" (Rohrlich 1998). As a result of these anxieties, the NCs became official advisory community liaisons to city hall: less powerful than initially planned, but still influential.

The city is fortunate the Reform Commission felt as it did: a 2007 University of Southern California study painted a bleak picture of decentralized democracy in LA. The NCs, the study found, had failed to become representative of their communities. (See Juliet Musso's essay in Chapter 2.)

The efforts of home owners to restrain building helped produce an acute housing crisis. The federal government's Center on Budget and Policy Priorities found in the late 1990s that the LA area suffered a shortfall of 300,000 units at the end of the decade, making the city's units the second most overcrowded housing in the nation, second only to neighboring Orange County. The City of Los Angeles played no minor role in the crisis, with half of the shortfall blamed on the city (Haefele 1998, 15). Fifteen percent of the county's households were considered overcrowded in 2001, triple the national average (Southern California Studies Center and the Brookings Center on Urban and Metropolitan Policy 2001, 25). The Southern California Association of Governments reported at the time that only 8,000 housing units were being produced in the city per year at a time that 60,000 were necessary to alleviate the cost of housing (Meyerson 2001, 20).

The antigrowth achievements of the previous decade left limited prospects for change. The General Plan Housing Element of 1994 reported a capacity for 958,237 more housing units assuming a 100 percent build-out (LA Dept. of City Planning 1993, 60). However there were economics to consider—whether or not allowable densities would permit developers to recover land costs. There was also the issue of how much Angelenos were willing to allow. Despite the supposed room to grow, only 84,255 multifamily units were added in the 15 years following 1994, not even 14 percent of the estimated multifamily build-out. In contrast, 21,888 single-family units were added in the same period, 65 percent of the single-family build-out (Construction Industry Research Board 2010). An evident bias remains in what gets permitted in LA.

The meager rate of housing construction in the city has propelled an increasingly conspicuous and illegal overcrowding problem. Already by 1990 an estimated 40,000 to 50,000 illegal dwelling units existed in LA, housing 200,000 people.[54] In 1997 a joint task force recommended the rehabilitation of illegal units with city funds and granting the improved units temporary occupancy permits. Home owners groups balked at the measure, one saying it was "gutting the Los Angeles zoning code through the back door"(Bernstein 1997).

As one response to the crisis, the city convened a Housing Crisis Task Force (1999), which introduced some notable new zoning designations.[55] Describing the city's capacity for new residential development at "nearly zero," the Task Force's Land Use and Planning Sub-Committee delivered recommendations on the zoning code, processing, and incentives for affordable housing (LA Housing Crisis Task Force 2000). Delivering on these recommendations has required to some extent getting around Proposition U, a move not unnoticed by neighborhood groups. In 2002 the city created two new "Residential Accessory Services" zoning designations that permitted ground floor accessory limited commercial uses through vertical subdivision.[56] These regulations could replace the commercial zoning affected by Proposition U while preserving the possibility of commercial uses, and restore the residential potential of sites where Proposition U had removed it. By 2010, implementation had resulted in the provision of 10,900 units (Blumenfeld 2010).

A 1999 ordinance established procedures for the adaptive reuse of economically unviable commercial or industrial buildings built before the 1974 institution of modern building codes downtown and in the adjacent Westlake district.[57] The 2002 Adaptive Reuse Incentive Areas Specific Plan expanded the scope of the Adaptive Reuse program to other historic commercial areas of the city, including Hollywood.[58] In early 2010 the department of city planning estimated that the adaptive reuse ordinance had produced 9,156 units (Blumenfeld 2010).

The adaptive reuse program, along with the long-in-progress approval of standards for home occupations in 1996, signaled a shift toward land-use control through performance standards.[59] Arguably LA's zoning policy has developed flexibility over the past 20 years. A quarter-century after Proposition U, one narrative out of city hall does not seem to dominate discussion in regard to planning. The complaints of suburban home owners over limited clout in city hall seem out of touch considering that an actual group of have-nots do not live in single-family homes on the Westside but in various valleys and deserts of Southern California distant from preferable locations or in overpriced and often overcrowded rental units in the denser parts of the region.

Council member Ed Reyes has summarized the situation somewhat pessimistically: "LA today is a tale of two cities, with the haves protected by City Hall, and the have-nots left to fend for themselves" (Greene 2003).

Conclusion

Four distinct regimes characterize the history of land-use and environmental regulation in LA. The first phase, lasting from the initiation of citywide districting legislation until the first half of the Depression, was distinguished by the supremacy of speculative real estate interests. The intervention of the FHA starting in 1934 initiated a new phase, as it made low-density development of residential property more profitable by greatly expanding the accessibility of the single-family home. However, the outward pace of development created a predicament for future urbanization, considering the natural growth boundaries of the region. As the suburban population matured in the 1960s, home owners groups, attached to unchanging conditions as the basis of their homes' values, began to challenge developers intending to capitalize on demand in developed areas. Through the election of antigrowth candidates to the city council, the home owners of the Valley and the Westside were able to impose their preferred model of growth on the entire city.

Arguably, LA may in the last decade have begun to experience a third shift. The shrinking share of home owners and a growing population for whom the housing market presents no affordable options has generated enough anxiety to present a challenge to the home owners' regime. It has been a short time since the introduction of many strategies for the promotion of urban infill and accommodation of population, and it could be argued that we have not seen significant results. In addition, critics are correct when they point out that too much of this development does not serve the people who need housing the most. On the bright side, the first decade of the 21st century may finally have been the decade in which planners and legislators seem to be trying to expand the definition of the public served by land-use regulation.

Almost New Urbanism

Vinayak Bharne

Los Angeles, long derided for its notorious suburban sprawl, in fact boasts a rich history of neighborhood making. From its early 20th-century streetcar suburbs like Boyle Heights and Angelino Heights, located along Pacific Electric trolley stops, and the rectilinear subdivisions of Pasadena's rustic Bungalow Heaven, to the iconic verdant curving streets of Beverly Hills and the Olmsteadean sea-facing communities of Rolling Hills and Palos Verdes, LA has a great stock of traditional neighborhoods that compare with the best in the country.

The world's image of LA, however, is dominated not by these exemplars but by an endless plain of "ticky tacky houses. . . . slashed by endless freeways" or by its 50-year-old landscape of unprecedented sprawl (Banham 1971, 143). Circa 1942, fueled by massive postwar migration, LA saw sweeping infrastructural changes through freeways, airports, and flood control that induced rapid land development. By 1960, its rail system was dismantled and the new federal mortgage program induced the proliferation of single-family housing at an unprecedented pace, covering the entire basin with homogeneous growth. Industrialized production churned out new communities like Westchester near the LA airport, Panorama City in the San Fernando Valley, and Lakewood in Long Beach, relentlessly repeating garage-dominated, single-family houses and residential pods centered on wide dead-end streets. Architectural dingbats tried even more than the occasional tower "to cope with the unprecedented appearance of residential densities too high to be subsumed within the illusions of homestead living" (ibid., 159).

It is against this backdrop that one must understand Playa Vista, an enlightened development vision to revive Southern California's lost community traditions, question the planning regulations that had devastated the LA landscape for more than half a century, and search for an alternative to this failure of postwar development. In 1978, the Summa Corporation (managed by Howard Hughes's heirs) announced it would develop the former site of Hughes's airport and factory, located between Venice and Marina del Rey. It prompted one of the most protracted development battles in LA history, with opponents claiming that the project would destroy the fragile Ballona Wetlands west of Lincoln Boulevard along with serious traffic and air pollution consequences. In 1989, after gaining control of Summa, Maguire Thomas Partners, which had led the ambitious Bunker Hill redevelopment downtown in the early 1980s, assembled a carefully selected team to design a new 1,085-acre, mixed use village inspired by the great prewar neighborhoods of the region. The team consisted of Moule & Polyzoides, Moore Ruble Yudell, Duany Plater-Zyberk/Architects and Urbanists, Olin Partnership/Landscape Architects, and Ricardo Legorreta as architect.

Vision

The process that generated the Playa Vista master plan was a radical departure from the mainstream planning practices of its time. In response to regional growth and local concerns, the developer initiated an outreach process inviting community input from the same people who had opposed previous efforts on the site. Three charrettes in 1989 negotiated a broad set of mutually agreed criteria for the development: the restoration of the degraded wetland, the establishment of height standards compatible with surrounding communities, and the reduction of traffic impacts from the development. It was also decided that Playa Vista would be a pedestrian-friendly community with pocket parks and basic amenities located within walking distance of each dwelling, and that its average density would be 24 dwelling units per acre in contrast to the four to 10 dwelling units per acre of the typical sprawl tract (Chase 2005, 122).

Figure 4.7. Mixed use buildings in Playa Vista

Unlike the earlier Summa scheme that had covered the entire site with development, this plan proposed no development south of Jefferson and west of Lincoln, preserving a large portion of the wetland as a "natural window" into the project.[1] Water from the neighborhoods would be harvested, passively cleaned through a riparian habitat along the project's southern edge and eventually discharged into the wetland to replenish its dying ecosystem. Two districts and five neighborhoods were organized as a network of interconnected streets and blocks consistently punctuated by a variety of parks and greens. The streets were narrow to slow down traffic speeds. The blocks were designed to never exceed 400 feet in length and structured with an alley network that clarified their fronts and backs and provided garage entry from the lot rear, thereby creating a curbless sidewalk for rich pedestrian life. The blocks were sized to be platted with lots of diverse sizes that would contain various building types and generate a rich and heterogeneous townscape in contrast to homogeneous sprawl tracts. This was a genuinely exciting idea for one of the largest urban infill projects in the region.

The details of the plan's physical components were not conceived hypothetically but derived from a deep study of local prewar precedents. Recognizing the paucity of available information, the team measured and photographed streets within the region, documenting their building setbacks, sidewalk widths, carriageways, and views both from the middle, as seen from a car—and sidewalk, as seen by a pedestrian (Polyzoides 1997). These studies were organized empirically into groups sharing formal characteristics, creating a catalog of street standards that guided the design of the Playa Vista grid.

The plan was organized on two regional highways, Jefferson and Lincoln boulevards; three regional connectors, Bay, Teal, and Centinela avenues; and the principal internal collector, Runway Avenue. The residential streets within neighborhoods were initially conceived as narrow, 30-foot carriageways with parking on both sides and 14 feet of travel space. They were eventually expanded to 36 feet to respond to buildings of higher densities. All these proposed streets were deviations from the existing city standards. Faced with the dilemma of challenging the city on all deviations or saving the residential streets, Maguire Thomas chose the latter and received approval for the smaller street dimension—much to the chagrin of the fire department, which continued to resist the standards (Polyzoides 1997).

The design team also documented a range of traditional Southern California housing types that had remained ignored in postwar development: duplexes, triplexes, quadruplexes, town houses, and courtyard housing. They were classified according to their objective physical criteria—access, open space, internal circulation, spatial organization, and parking—and organized as a gradient of residential densities between the extremes of the single-family house and tower. Their minimum lot dimensions were carefully calibrated and coordinated with the block depths and widths to allow for optimum platting flexibility. This housing spectrum would provide many alternative living options, becoming the essential DNA of a type-diverse neighborhood fabric. This means of achieving density through a typological menu, rather than an exclusive floor area ratio and coverage mechanism, was one of the plan's most ingenious ideas.

These studies in part became the foundations of what we now know as the new urbanist movement. In fact it was during the design of Playa Vista that the idea of forming the Congress for the New Urbanism emerged. Playa Vista therefore continues to be seen by many as the original poster child of new urbanism in LA. But one must remember that during its design—even though the Florida panhandle village of Seaside had been designed a decade earlier by Duany Plater-Zyberk under the rubric of neotraditionalism—the now established and tested model of traditional neighborhood development (TND) was significantly infant. Even so, Playa Vista's master plan did contain most components of what would today be classic TND—representing a fantastic opportunity to apply traditional town planning principles at the scale of a metropolitan region.

There was, however, one important missing implementation dimension. There was no officially adopted vision-specific code to uphold the master plan's standards. Such a code would have provided a regulatory framework to ensure, among other things, a conscious and varied density distribution through the specific building types, and their setback, size, length, height, and frontage, for a rich and varied townscape. But with environmental activists arguing whether the project should have happened at all, the master plan took five years to obtain approval and was further tied up by lawsuits. Discussions on a code had begun, and as a planned unit development, Playa Vista was entitled to one, but Maguire Thomas—after years of litigation—decided to relinquish the project in 1997. Playa Vista eventually won the suit, but at the heavy price of losing its visionary developer..

The master plan consequently found itself within the mainstream planning channels, and the lack of this alternative regulatory mechanism became responsible, as much as anything else, for the Playa Vista we see today. The new owners, Playa Capital, a group led by Goldman Sachs and Morgan Stanley, hired a management team from Orange County, and land was sold to and developed by 15 separate

Figure 4.8. Apartments in nontraditional architectural idioms in Playa Vista

Figure 4.9. Mediterranean-style apartments and town homes with varied massing, rooflines, and porches

builders (Pristin 2007). In the absence of a vision-specific code or a town architect, the original intentions and standards were compromised, with subsequent workshops concluding that much of the project had to have four stories in order to be profitable (Newman 2004). Playa Vista sunk into the cleft between its initial sophisticated planning intentions and the lethargies of conventional development.

Realization

In 1996, Playa Vista's initial master plan had called for 13,085 residential units, five million square feet of office and studio space, 600,000 square feet of retail space, 750 hotel rooms, and more than 500,000 square feet of educational, civic, cultural, and public uses.[2] Today, its completed first phase has more than 3,000 rental and ownership units housing more than 4,000 residents and employees. Its recently approved second phase will feature 2,600 units, 200 assisted living units, 50,000 square feet of office space, 195,875 square feet of retail space, and 40,000 square feet of community amenities including a fitness club and pool.[3] The original plan's outlines are clearly discernible, and, despite the shift in development attitudes, many of the original planning principles have endured: buildings form a street edge, there is an emphasis on public landscape, and there are stores and transit within walking distance of the homes.

But for its original authors, Playa Vista today is nothing less than a new urbanist tragedy. They are not entirely wrong. The wide streets are a far cry from the intimate original hierarchy. The residential fabric is dominated by conventional apartment buildings, some "pretending to be row housing," others literally extruded stacking diagrams with building walls insulated from the narrow sidewalks by thick planting or berms (Newman 2004). The architecture embodies Orange County housing at Barcelona densities, employing the usual tricks to veneer what is essentially mainstream development. There is less typological and more stylistic variety, but even so the eventual effect is more of an aggregate of site-by-site developer projects rather than a coherent townscape. The very frontages that make traditional Southern California neighborhoods so charming—porches, stoops, forecourts, and porticoes—remain blatantly missing, making Playa Vista a flat neighborhood diagram with a half-baked and largely street-skeptical architectural dimension.

What is also missing is a strong transit corridor within or around the community, and LA's long-standing weakness in alternative transit forms makes Playa Vista even more vulnerable to the limitations of an exclusive four-wheel-dominated street grid. While the relationship of urban design and transit in this very location may raise complex questions due to its distance from downtown versus its proximity to the airport, the development's incompleteness remains insufficient to justify a public investment in rapid bus or rail.

But that said, Playa Vista is not sprawl. People really do walk on its sidewalks. The landscape in the streets and parks is mature, rich, and ample and dominates the visual experience of the place. There is a high ratio of open space to development, and the built forms do help define the greens. The urban formalism of linear parks and visual terminations is evident and readable. There is a housing mix for all incomes, with 25 percent of units held aside for moderate- and low-income renters and buyers; this housing does add critically needed units in LA. The promised public amenities are also all there: a library, fire station, police drop-in station, and community center.

Playa Vista's developers also claim that all the historic Ballona Wetlands have been protected and that when the state completes its acquisition of all land west of Lincoln Boulevard and north of the Ballona Channel, more than 750 acres will be preserved as parks and open space. They also claim to have designed an innovative stormwater collection system and a natural stormwater filter in the adjacent 26-acre freshwater marsh located at the southeast corner of Lincoln and Jefferson. More than 3,000 native trees and 10,000 native shrubs and grasses have apparently been planted in this marsh, transforming it into a popular stopover for more than 200 bird species.[4]

Additionally, Playa Vista claims to be facilitating more than $125 million in transportation infrastructure improvements in the surrounding community. By purchasing five natural-gas-powered buses, it is extending the Santa Monica and Culver City bus lines to major employment and entertainment centers such as the Fox Hills Mall, Marina del Rey, UCLA, and Century City.[5] It has started a clean-fuel summer Beach Shuttle service to enhance traffic flow to and from the ocean, with a future year-round low-emission shuttle system also in the works. Playa Vista will not feature as a ranking example in the annals of new urbanism, but even so it still outshines most, if not all, mainstream LA development.

Legacy

From the standpoint of what it should have been, maybe Playa Vista is a lost opportunity. It does affirm the virtues of a street grid but also proves that great neighborhoods are hardly two-dimensional planning diagrams but carefully conceived physical places—street by street, lot by lot. But then Playa Vista's failed new urbanist vision is not alone. Numerous new urbanist greenfields in other parts of the country have been similarly compromised due to the lack of coding, ineffective public-private partnerships, or the indifference of municipalities and makers toward new directions and standards. If Playa Vista was too progressive for 1990s LA, then it represents as much the myopia of Southern California's development culture as the infancy of new urbanism as a revisionist planning methodology not yet prepared to navigate a calcified administrative and planning system.

Playa Vista also suggests the place of new urbanism as a nationally influential planning movement that is still struggling to find its "official" stronghold in LA. One must recall here a tandem and equally ambitions planning effort—the Strategic Plan for Downtown Los Angeles.[6] Both efforts that could have charted new planning directions were compromised in their own ways. But even though the Strategic Plan has not been officially implemented, downtown's renaissance, as seen over the past few years—with numerous modest projects bringing people back into the city's historic heart—is an unofficial implementation of its ideas. New urbanism or not, the point is that by retaining several original values, both projects have affirmed the virtues of a nonutopian urbanism for Southern California. Playa Vista in this sense can be seen as the scout that paved the way for things to follow and the numerous nonutopian planning and urban design projects currently changing the region's face can therefore be read as its legacy.

Would Playa Vista have been different had it been initiated today? Recent greenfield projects provide an ambiguous answer. Monrovia Nursery, originally designed as a TND in Azusa, was reduced to a conventional suburban design by the approval process; Riverpark in Oxnard has a relatively decent single-family and town house stock, with narrow streets and alleys; and Parklands in Ventura has an approved TND code, even though it took six years to get there.[7] Los Angeles has come a long way over the past two decades. The same bureaucracies that fueled LA's placeless landscape are now supporting a renewed interest in street design, walkability, and mixed use infill development through new street ordinances, sustainability guidelines, and a growing web of transit. In a time when LA is standing up for humane urbanisms, perhaps Playa Vista, if initiated today, might have had a different destiny.

Playa Vista reminds us that compromises are indeed the bread and butter of the art and practice of city making. It affirms that great urban design is eventually only as good as the planning and regulatory mechanisms that support it. The question therefore is: where does one draw the line between compromises that are acceptable versus those that are not, and who eventually decides what that least common denominator should be? All said and done, Playa Vista does represent the beginnings of a crusade against 50 years of urban nihilism—and that in itself is enough to make it worthy of attention and praise. Thus, the task at hand is to commend and celebrate its successes while simultaneously excavating its original intentions to understand why they failed—and to strive toward creating the engines that will realize those intentions for a better future in LA and beyond.

Glendale's Downtown Specific Plan

Alan Loomis

Like many similar midsized American downtowns, the 200-acre center of Glendale (population 195,000) is a tapestry of successive development trends from the past century. The city's architectural icons—the art deco Alex Theatre, a neoclassical post office, and the Works Progress Administration–era city hall—were built in the boom era following municipal incorporation in 1906, when Glendale boasted it was the "fastest growing city in America." After the Depression and World War II, a series of new modern office buildings housed the expansion of municipal government and local financial institutions.

But in the mid-1960s, urban renewal was inaugurated with the removal of the LA–Glendale streetcar tracks. During the 1970s, construction of the 134 Freeway bifurcated downtown, and six blocks were leveled for the suburban-style Galleria shopping mall. A "bricks, banners, and bollards" attempt to revive downtown's main street, Brand Boulevard, immediately followed. In the 1980s and early '90s, the logic of suburban office parks produced a skyline of high-rise office towers and single-purpose parking structures. When a strategic vision for a mixed use downtown was adopted in the mid-'90s without a corresponding change in zoning standards, its implementation was dependent upon specific development deals. By the end of the decade, downtown saw its first mixed use experiments, with projects named the Exchange and Marketplace that combined cinemas, restaurants, and retail. Finally, the construction of The Americana at Brand brought a mature "lifestyle center" to the downtown, with its collage of boutique retail, restaurants, cinema, housing, and a Vegas-style fountain. The cumulative result of this layered history is a downtown that is the functional and vibrant center of the region's third-largest city but still less than the sum of its parts.

Designed to incorporate, mend, and unify the disparate development trends and policies that generated the existing skyline, Glendale's Downtown Specific Plan is a proactive urban design strategy for a mixed use, transit- and pedestrian-oriented downtown. Intended to eliminate ambiguity or confusion about the form of desired development, the plan outlines a comprehensive and integrated framework of policies, requirements, guidelines, and incentives. This is in contrast to the old commercial-only central business district zoning standards, which were never amended to eliminate conflict with the goals of the previous Downtown Strategic Plan and Design Guidelines. Enabled under the unique provisions of California legislation that permit the creation of specialized area plans, the Downtown Specific Plan expresses both the city's vision for downtown and its implementation standards.

Informed by and respectful of the placemaking concepts articulated by proponents of form-based codes and new urbanism, the plan is free of these ideological constraints or positions. Instead, city staff produced the plan with an eye toward implementation. As a result, the plan itself is an easy-to-read "manual" expressed through an integration of graphics and straightforward, rhetoric-free language. Organized front to back along the typical development and design process—beginning with programmatic concerns, proceeding to issues of building mass, and eventually working toward details and implementation procedures, the plan sets the physical standards and guidelines as well as land-use regulations, and establishes policies for economic development, streetscape improvements, transportation development, parking, pedestrian amenities, open space, preservation of historic resources, and public art.

In contrast to the plans of many neighboring cities, Glendale's Downtown Specific Plan does not specify development targets or limits as measured by number of units, commercial square footage, or maximum densities but instead outlines the desired physical vision of the downtown. As such, the plan articulates a number of urban design parameters, including:

- A new pattern of height limitations to sculpt the skyline with respect toward views to the surrounding mountains and historic landmarks
- A focus on open space and the ground level of buildings that enhance the pedestrian experience into a coherent network of public space
- Height and density incentives in exchange for features and uses that expand downtown's role as an economic center, diverse residential neighborhood, and architecturally exciting environment, including green building, affordable housing, public open space, historic preservation, and adaptive reuse

Shortly after its adoption in late 2006, nearly a dozen projects totaling nearly 1,500 residences, of various architectural styles and scales by national and local architects, were entitled under the plan's standards and guidelines. Most of these projects, which included a number of high-rise luxury condominium and hotel proposals, fell victim to the recession that immediately followed. However, the plan has proved equally adept in guiding the more modest mid-rise studio apartment developments of the postbubble economy. Since 2010, a midmarket hotel and nearly 600 apartments have been entitled under the plan's streamlined two-step review process. Unlike the condominium projects proposed during the housing boom, the apartment buildings are now under construction, evidence of the plan's policy coherency, user friendliness, and flexibility.

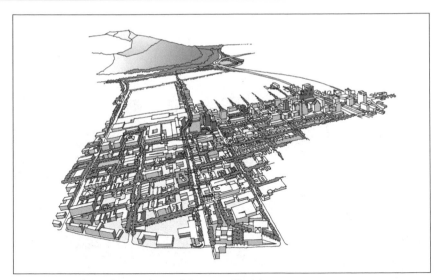

Figure 4.10. Rendering of an aerial view of downtown Glendale

Creating such opportunities for infill housing development within the downtown is one of the key policy features of the Downtown Specific Plan. Faced with mounting political pressure to prevent or limit growth in established neighborhoods and surrounding hillsides, Glendale made a conscious choice to focus future residential development toward the downtown and other transit-oriented infill locations that had previously been zoned for commercial uses only. This strategy is consistent with the Southern California Association of Governments' Regional Compass Growth Plan (also known as the Compass 2% Strategy Plan), a blueprint for housing the additional five million people expected to live in the greater LA area over the next 20 years. The plan calls for more than 400,000 new housing units to be built along existing transportation corridors and commercial centers, thus increasing transit use by 50 percent and reducing vehicle miles traveled by 35 percent but affecting only 2 percent of the region's land-use patterns. In Glendale, the downtown plan is expected to accommodate approximately 3,000 new apartments and condos otherwise destined to be built in surrounding neighborhoods, where residents would have had to drive to the downtown's jobs, stores, and cultural sites.

Underpinning this infill development strategy is Glendale's Downtown Mobility Study, produced by Nelson/Nygaard Consulting Associates of San Francisco. It gathers under a single umbrella the full range of best practices in transportation planning. Each of these—a free bus shuttle, parking benefit districts, in-lieu fees, and transit-priority streets, among others—is adapted from an extensive catalog of case studies and local research, and tailored to the physical vision articulated by the Downtown Specific Plan.

The mobility study's recommendations outline a series of incremental steps designed to wean Glendale from its addiction to cars. Following the suggestions of Donald Shoup's seminal book, *The High Cost of Free Parking* (2005), Glendale began by

Figure 4.11. Glendale has implemented market-based parking policies.

adjusting its parking management policies. To encourage drivers to "park once" in the city's public garages, the city installed new digital pay stations and restructured meter, lot, and garage fees to integrate all public parking resources into a single market-based price structure. The first 90 minutes in the garages are free and significantly cheaper thereafter than the more desirable, but less plentiful, on-street parking spaces.

Almost immediately, downtown Glendale became a textbook model of Shoup's theory, and occupancy rates for the premium on-street parking on Brand Boulevard dropped from always full to 85 percent, quickly ending the perception that downtown Glendale did not have enough parking. In support of this new policy, the city also launched a comprehensive wayfinding program, designed around the internationally recognized blue circle–p parking logo.

Additionally, the city reformed its downtown parking requirements from suburban-based ratios to standards more appropriate to a mixed use urban environment and codified incentives for developers to reduce their parking demand even further with in-lieu fees, additional bike parking, transportation demand management programs, and other techniques. The city is now taking steps to improve its other mobility options by installing real-time next-bus information at transit stops, upgrading streetscapes with trees and pedestrian lights, and building a citywide bicycle network incorporating wayfinding signs, sharrows (street marking indicating a shared lane for cars and bicycles), and road diets (either reducing the size or number of lanes to promote alternative transportation).

For this comprehensive integration of urban design and mobility policies demonstrating a local application of the 2% Strategy, SCAG gave Glendale its highest honor during its inaugural award program for exemplifying "how communities can implement Compass Principles to encourage mutually supportive land use decisions and transportation investments."

Despite this visionary stance, many of the policies adopted with the Downtown Specific Plan were not clearly developed, and the city was forced to create new procedures as developers made proposals utilizing these policies. For example, the plan introduced a "one percent for art" requirement, but the guidelines and the review process for evaluating public artwork were not considered until the design team for a new hotel included an artist. The plan also provides height and density bonuses in exchange for LEED (Leadership in Energy and Environmental Design) green building certification, but it did not resolve the chicken-or-egg problem of how to grant planning entitlements based on construction techniques that cannot be verified until after the building is completed. While these procedural problems were worked out by staff and developers as needed for specific projects, this ad hoc approach introduced an element of uncertainty into the development process that the plan was designed to avoid.

The Downtown Specific Plan also lacked a robust and meaningful economic strategy, perhaps because it was drafted during the heady days of a boom economy. Nonetheless, the plan's focus on the physical form has proved to be a usable foundation and flexible framework for subsequent planning and economic development initiatives in recent years. With the recent closure of the 15-year-old Mann Cinema and demise of many big-box retailers such as Borders, Tower Records, and Mervyn's, the two-block area surrounding the "100 percent" corner at Brand Boulevard and Broadway—downtown's two signature commercial streets—was effectively emptied. Recognizing that the retail market was dramatically contracting, the Glendale Redevelopment Agency decided to recast this area as an "art and entertainment district" through an art-in-vacant-storefronts program and a coordinated retenanting and redevelopment scheme. While such cultural districts are common in many cities, Glendale lacks this concentrated mix of theaters, nightclubs, art galleries, music clubs, and spin-off restaurants and bars that create a focus for nightlife and visitor trade.

Dubbed "Maryland Off Broadway," the district is an economic development, planning, and urban design strategy for reimagining Maryland Avenue, one block from Brand and Broadway and home to the city's first, but now largely vacant, mixed use complexes. Endowed with a luxurious and well-designed streetscape, Maryland is both relatively narrow and short at two blocks long. This compact scale is ideal for creating the sense of congestion that gives entertainment districts their energy or "buzz." Additionally, the street is anchored at either end by existing civic and cultural venues—the Alex Theatre to the north and the Central Library at the south. Conveniently, both buildings are located at sites that, as a result of shifts in the downtown street grid, terminate views up and down the street, further enclosing the district's activity and creating unique opportunities for prominent entrances or landmark architectural features. Although neither the theater nor the library has obvious pedestrian connections to Maryland today, improvements planned for the district are designed to give both buildings a more prominent presence.

To the north, the Downtown Specific Plan and the Maryland Off Broadway strategy envisioned that new development in the parking lots surrounding the Alex Theatre would connect its historic Brand Boulevard forecourt to Maryland Avenue with uses complementing the theater's programming. Through a public-private partnership, the

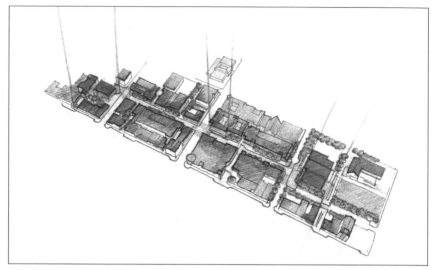

Figure 4.12. Aerial view of the arts and entertainment district

city enticed Laemmle Theatres, a popular LA-based art-house cinema chain, to anchor a mixed use building on this site. Translating a $2.6 million public subsidy into $11 million of private investment, the Cinema Lofts project will incorporate new back-of-house facilities for the Alex Theatre, 42 apartments, a restaurant, five movie screens, and a prominent theater marquee designed to create a visual icon for the district.

Figure 4.13. Street-level collage of the district

Figure 4.14. Rendering of the public plaza leading to the Central Library

Views south on Maryland Avenue currently end in the side facade of the Central Library, a brutalist-style building designed in 1972. A $10 million renovation plan will remake this view into a prominent public plaza, with grand stairs leading into the library's main reading room through a new north entrance. A site for public art, street performances, or temporary exhibits, this plaza will improve pedestrian crossings from Maryland to the library and serve as a gateway between the art and entertainment district and Central Park further south.

The city is also investing more than $5 million to completely rebuild Central Park, removing and consolidating surface parking lots, driveways, and alleys and replacing them with new pedestrian promenades between Maryland Avenue and other destinations in the area. The cornerstone of this project is the Museum of Neon Art, an independent institution with one of the largest collections of vintage neon advertising and artwork in the nation. After decades of operating out of temporary locations in downtown LA, the museum will find a permanent home at the midpoint of a new *paseo* between The Americana at Brand and Central Park. The paseo is designed to showcase the museum's collection, and its signature neon "diver" sculpture will be poised to leap off the building into a reflecting pool, fed by dripping neon water from a vintage plumber sign in the shape of a faucet.

Hoping to expand the presence of the Museum of Neon Art with inventive applications of neon, LEDs, and other contemporary lighting effects, the city also adopted a "creative sign" ordinance to encourage unique and playful signs. Additionally, the city enacted a series of legislative incentives and code amendments to facilitate and promote the district, replacing discretionary conditional use permits with over-the-counter standards for specific uses supported by licensing procedures for entertainment operators and promoters. Attempting to cut through the red tape, the Maryland Off Broadway strategy aligns the city's planning permits and procedures with its expressed urban design and economic development policy.

Although the city committed more than $18 million for public improvements and subsidies to launch the Maryland Off Broadway district, the response from the private sector is more than double this investment. The first private development in the district, Broadway Lofts, is under construction for completion in 2013. A $30 million, six-story

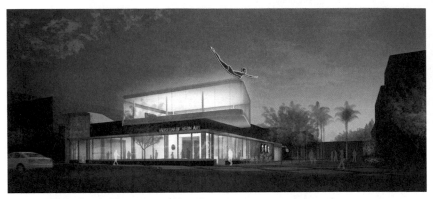

Figure 4.15. Rendering of the Museum of Neon Art

building located at a site formerly occupied by Circuit City, it includes a full-service, entertainment-oriented restaurant along with 208 residential lofts and studios marketed toward a young urban professional population. Other projects, from the Cinema Lofts to new restaurants, total another $15 million of private money.

Because of the foundational policies provided by the Downtown Specific Plan, the Maryland Off Broadway district strategy jumped from concept to groundbreaking within the four-year time frame of a single council election cycle. This fleet-footed response to changing economic conditions is possible because the Specific Plan was drafted not only around broad-based goals and open-ended use regulations but precise urban design and architectural standards. The plan's easy-to-read graphic format makes the document a practical tool for aligning varying development proposals with the vision and requirements of the city. Instead of attempting to manipulate project density and uses through a lengthy and expensive discretionary entitlement process, design review in downtown Glendale is based on how effective projects are in furthering the city's policy goals for an economically vibrant, mixed use, pedestrian-oriented downtown. Additionally, as the region's and country's assumptions about mobility shift, the Downtown Mobility Study offers an outline for incrementally building the integrated multimodal transportation system necessary to support this vision.

More important for Glendale, the implementation of the Downtown Specific Plan has pioneered urban design-based planning policies. Its ongoing success establishes the precedent for an ambitious Community Plan program, which is extending similar placemaking strategies to all of Glendale. As in other cities in greater LA and nationwide that are largely built out, in Glendale almost all planning issues are also urban design problems, and the city is creating new planning polices to recognize its diverse mix of suburbs, hillside subdivisions, village centers, industrial districts, urban housing, and commercial corridors.

Regreening the LA River

Meredith Drake Reitan

If most Angelenos visualize the Los Angeles River, they see graffiti, concrete, and urban refuse. But if the Friends of the Los Angeles River (FoLAR) succeed, this often overlooked space will soon be the site of kayak trips, fishing families, and riverfront picnics.

The Los Angeles River, which encompasses more than 830 square miles of urban watershed, originates at the confluence of the Arroyo Calabasas and Bell Creek in the San Fernando Valley and travels all the way to San Pedro Bay, a distance of about 51 miles. Once home to steelhead and grizzlies, the Los Angeles River meandered through wetlands, marshes, willow, alder, and sycamore, providing desperately needed water for the region.

When the U.S. Army Corps of Engineers completed the LA flood control project in the late 1930s it essentially replaced the river with the world's largest storm drain. Over the ensuing decades, the river that had once been the sole water supply for LA disappeared from public consciousness. Instead, it was a "flood control channel"—a no-man's-land, surrounded by fences and "no trespassing" signs.

In 1986 a small group began speaking on behalf of the river. With the belief that effective advocacy, education, collaboration, and imagination could accomplish great things, FoLAR (http://folar.org) set out to change reality. Their first official act was to cut a hole in the fence and declare the river open. Since those early days, the group's mission—to protect and restore the natural and historic heritage of the Los Angeles River through inclusive planning, education, and wise stewardship—has meant that FoLAR has been at the forefront of many river-related victories.

Most recently, after extensive lobbying from FoLAR and other supporters, the U.S. Environmental Protection Agency declared the whole length of the LA River to be "traditional navigable waters," an official designation that enables the agency to apply elements of the Clean Water Act to the concrete-lined waterway. In making its decision, the EPA looked beyond whether the river's flow and depth could support navigation to consider the river's potential for recreational uses and public access. The EPA also considered the river's susceptibility to restoration and the presence of ongoing restoration and educational projects. As Lewis MacAdams, the poet, writer, and cofounder of FoLAR suggests, "the EPA has essentially redefined the LA River and its values."

The river's new designation was one of a series of victories, including the development of the Los Angeles and San Gabriel Rivers Watershed Council, the city's principal forum for discussion of the rivers' future. Another was the creation of new community parks at the Cornfield Yards, a 30-acre parcel of land between Chinatown and the river, and at Taylor Yard, a 220-acre former railroad yard with more than two miles of living riverfront near the Latino neighborhoods just north of downtown, an area sorely lacking in parkland.

FoLAR hopes that these successes will lead to other parks, including the Piggyback Yards, 130 acres on the city's last active rail yard. FoLAR has collaborated with local architects, planners, and landscape architects, including Michael Maltzan Architecture, Perkins+Will, Chee Salette Architecture Office, and Mia Lehrer to transform the river by reshaping its channel, replacing the concrete bed with a soft bottom, and slowing the flow to allow vegetation to grow. Piggyback Yards would help protect communities downstream by serving as an overflow during Southern California's sporadic flood season. During the remainder of the year, the area would serve as a park with lawns, sports fields, paths and trails, gardens, playgrounds, fountains, and performing arts spaces. While the Union Pacific Railroad currently has no plans to give up Piggyback Yards, as MacAdams said in a 2010 *New York Times* article, the transformation of the rail yard into a park "may not happen in my lifetime," but "someone had to start the process."

Planning as a Tool for Battling the Fast-Food Invasion

Lark Galloway-Gilliam

Despite spending approximately 16 percent of the nation's gross national product on health care—more per person than any other nation—the U.S. life expectancy of 78.37 years ranks 50th in the world (CIA 2011). The situation is worse for the 800,000 residents of South Los Angeles, whose life expectancy is on average eight years less (75.2 to 77.0 years) than that in healthier sections of the city (83.6 years), for a ranking to approximately 86th in the world (LA County Office of Health Assessment and Epidemiology 2010). Disparities in life expectancy have historically been linked to differences in public health, medical care, diet, and prolonged exposure to hazardous conditions. South LA represents the convergence of the failure of these systems. Yet residents of South LA have not lost hope. Instead, they are trying to use planning and other methods to change the physical and resource environments so people can live healthier, longer lives.

Planning has historically been closely aligned with public health and has played a major role in eradicating the transmission of disease, thus reducing morbidity and mortality in the United States through improvements in sanitation and the separation of functions (Duhl and Kristin-Sanchez 1999, Sloane 2006). With advances in medicine, public health focus shifted to individual behavior change and the promotion of immunizations. The federal and state governments assumed authority over automobile and highway safety, air quality, and the health risks associated with product safety such as food, alcohol, and tobacco. Today, however, the leading causes of death in the United States are associated no longer with the transmission of disease but rather with chronic conditions such as heart disease, strokes, and cancer, for which medical interventions are only part of the remedy (Kochanek et al. 2011). Policy makers and health professionals are calling for new prevention strategies in an effort to control costs and improve the population's health.

Compelling evidence exists that the built environment plays a significant role in what ails America, particularly in lower-income, racial, and ethnic communities such as

South LA. Decades of urban neglect and decay have given rise to a movement toward urban sustainability, smart growth, and new urbanism. Local jurisdictions once again play a distinct role in improving health through planning and land-use policy. What is often missing from this new model—where pedestrian-centered neighborhoods meet economic sustainability and social activities—is a response to inequalities in the built environment and its impact on the health status of racial and ethnic populations.

The passage of a city ordinance in December 2010 to regulate the density of fast-food restaurants in South LA is an example of the role and power of local government and city planning in helping to eliminate health disparities.

Health Disparities

Home to the largest population of African Americans and a major point of entry for new immigrant populations, South LA is Los Angeles County's most diverse racial and ethnic geographic region. This diversity extends to income level and educational achievement along very blurry neighborhood boundaries. The comparative statistics between South LA and LA County are staggeringly tragic. South LA has:

- The highest rate of adults diagnosed with diabetes (12 percent), hypertension (29 percent), and death due to coronary heart disease (217 per 100,000 population)
- Twice the rate of preventable hospitalizations due to congestive heart failure, hypertension, and both long- and short-term diabetes complications
- The highest rate of adult (35 percent vs. 22 percent) and childhood obesity (29 percent vs. 23 percent) (LA County Dept. of Public Health 2009)

The relationship of obesity to a wide range of preventable and chronic diseases has generated national concern about nutrition (Boone-Heinonen et al. 2011). South LA residents have among the highest rates of fast-food consumption in Los Angeles County, with 42 percent of adults reporting eating fast food at least once a week and only 13 percent consuming the recommended five servings of fruits and vegetables per day. The rates are more startling for children: 53 percent eat fast food at least once a week and 55 percent drink at least one soda or sugar-sweetened drink per day. To understand the disproportionately high rates of risk behavior and disease, we must look beyond individual behavior and examine the food resource environment.

South Los Angeles Food Resource Environment

Not surprisingly, research links the proximity and density of fast-food restaurants with higher rates of fast-food consumption. Eating fast food is associated with a higher intake of calories, fat, sodium, sugar, and sugar-sweetened beverages and the associated weight gain and insulin resistance (Bowman and Vinyard 2004). The overabundance of fast-food restaurants makes it more difficult for individuals to meet dietary recommendations (Baker et al. 2006). Community Health Councils (CHC), a community-based nonprofit health advocacy and policy organization, conducted a comprehensive assessment of South LA's food retailers and restaurants (Lewis et al. 2005). The findings were consistent with national research showing that urban, lower-income, and racial or ethnic minority communities have more fast-food restaurants and fewer healthy food outlets like supermarkets than more affluent and predominantly white communities (Morland et al. 2002, Block, Scribner, and DeSalvo 2004). While the California Health and Safety Code regulating the preparation and sale of food limits the authority of local public health agencies to safeguarding sanitation standards and the grading of retail food facilities, state law gives local jurisdictions police power to enact zoning ordinances in the interest of public health.[1] The research provided the catalyst and rationale for a 2008 initial moratorium on the permitting of new stand-alone fast-food restaurants in South LA.

Planning and Racial Inequalities

South LA, like many inner-city communities, has fallen victim over the last 40 years to housing segregation and a devolution of the physical and economic infrastructure. While the passage of the Fair Housing Act in 1968 allowed for the western migration of African American and Latino families, "white flight" continued de facto housing segregation along racial and ethnic lines. Housing covenants were replaced by "redlining" by banks and insurance companies, causing the systematic devaluation of property values. The white middle-class and business migration resulted in a redirecting of planning resources and attention away from the inner city to suburban and outer urban neighborhoods. Major manufacturing corridors were abandoned with the exodus of businesses to suburbs and the demise of large-scale manufacturers. Minimalls, undercapitalized small businesses, absentee property owners, and large swaths of abandoned lots replaced business districts once lined with car dealerships and major retail outlets. Older communities and their shallow commercial districts became anyone's playground as boundaries became blurred and new industrial uses bled into residential areas with few constraints. The blatant and systematic wholesale divestment by the private sector and absence of public policy was punctuated by the 1965 riots and 1992 civil unrest.

The state of South LA's environment was aggravated by the city's failure to use planning to protect and promote the area. LA's 35 community plans make up the city's Land Use Element. The community plans are intended to coordinate development, yet the three community plans for South LA have not been updated in more than a decade. The West Adams–Baldwin Hills–Leimert Community Plan Revision was last done in 1998; the South Central Los Angeles Community Plan Revision, were and Southeast Los Angeles Community Plan Revision were updated in 2000.

The existing plans are limited in scope, focusing on issues of aesthetics, economic development, and the compatibility, cohesion, and transition within and between residential, industrial, and commercial uses. Redevelopment took precedence over planning along commercial corridors, thus contributing to chaotic development when it occurred.

Additionally, the city's ordinances and specific plans illustrate the lack of investment and prioritization of this region by policy makers and planners. Few ordinances and only three out of 44 specific plans affect South LA:

- Crenshaw Specific Plan (Ordinance No. 176,230, 2004) provides standards for the Crenshaw corridor to promote controlled development/redevelopment, encourage economic revitalization, assure a balance of commercial land uses, preserve and enhance community aesthetics, and promote a high level of pedestrian activity.

- Conditional Use Approval for the Sale of Alcoholic Beverages (Ordinance No. 171,681, 1997) regulates and reduces the high density of retail outlets selling liquor by requiring the review and issuance of a conditional use permit for the use of a lot in the area for an establishment dispensing (for sale or other consideration) alcoholic beverages.
- North University Park (Ordinance No. 158,194, 1983) protects and enhances the buildings, structures, sites, and areas of historical architectural significance in the North University Park neighborhood.

The liquor policy was a pioneering effort to use planning regulation to respond to issues of safety and the presence of nuisances in the community, issues only indirectly related to the actual sale of alcohol, such as the physical disorder that occurs frequently around liquor stores. The others are focused on aesthetics, not the fundamental issues confronting the area.

A change in planning leadership and philosophy led to a more active engagement with local communities, including the initiation of community plan updates and eventually the moratorium. Former planning director Gail Goldberg and a small team of innovative planners, including Faisal Robles and Reuben Caldwell, took the bold step to go beyond the regulatory requirements to embark on a multiple-stage process of soliciting input from a broad cross section of community stakeholders. In addition to hosting community workshops, the South LA planning team began attending local neighborhood council meetings and the CHC Food Policy Roundtable Coalition to gain a better understanding of the impact of the built environment on the health of the community. The community, aided by training from a wide range of community-based organizations and department staff, had become more sophisticated in its understanding and use of planning and design concepts. As a result, it identified a wide range of issues far beyond the standard list delineated in the previous community plans, including the lack of healthy food retail.

As a result of the shift, the city accepted the responsibility for addressing both the health of a community and inequalities in the health resource environment. The result was the adoption of an interim control ordinance (ICO) placing a moratorium in 2008 on the issuance of permits for new stand-alone fast-food restaurants in the West Adams–Baldwin Hills–Leimert, South LA, and Southeast LA community plan areas. City council members Jan Perry and Bernard Parks introduced the ordinance in direct response to disproportionately higher rates of health disparities in South LA and gaps in the nutritional resource environment exposed by the CHC assessment. The report by the planning department indicated that the overconcentration of fast-food restaurants in the three planning areas is "detrimental to the health and welfare of the people of the community."[2] The passage of the moratorium is arguably the first use of zoning to regulate fast-food based on health concerns. In addition to regulating the density of fast food restaurants, the moratorium and final ordinance sought to preserve limited land for development that contributes to the health of the community, including addressing the shortage of full-service grocery stores.

Fast-Food Ordinance

The ICO was designed to provide sufficient time for the city to study and incorporate appropriate permanent regulatory controls on new fast-food restaurants in the three South LA community plans. The ICO was extended twice to the maximum two-year limit. However, the city's fiscal crisis delayed the completion of the community plan updates, thus jeopardizing the adoption of a permanent ordinance. In the absence of a new community plan, CHC initiated a campaign to build community support for another solution. Despite agreement among policy makers and the community that it should be permanent, the moratorium expired on September 14, 2010.

The planning department worked quickly with the local city council and city attorney office to find an alternative vehicle. The planning department presented the option of adopting an amendment to the city's General Plan as an alternative to the community plan update. With the support of the council offices and community advocates, the city council adopted the amendment on December 8, 2010.

The amendment went beyond the initial moratorium and increased the distance requirement for exemptions from 750 feet to at least a half-mile from existing fast-food restaurants. The General Plan Amendment requires new stand-alone fast-food restaurants to meet six criteria to address their overconcentration and requires design and landscape guidelines to mitigate their visual impacts on the community. The restaurants must:

- Be located in at least a half-mile radius, or 2,640 linear feet, away from any existing fast-food restaurant;
- Provide a continuous building wall along the street frontage and sidewalk;
- Have a height, bulk, and mass that is compatible with the surrounding area;
- Locate parking at the rear or sides of the building and have it partially screened from view by a 36-inch decorative wall or landscaping;
- Landscape at least 7 percent of the surface parking lot area; and
- Have an adequate trash disposal plan to control litter.

The ordinance is limited. Properties in some parts of South LA are exempt, as are fast-food restaurants in mixed use buildings, shopping centers, and malls. So is the replacement of an existing fast-food restaurant. (The new restaurant must meet the other five criteria.) During the two-year moratorium (which occurred during a severe recession), the city received approximately 10 inquiries regarding new stand-alone fast-food restaurants, but none materialized into an application. However, approximately a dozen new fast-food restaurants were allowed to open in mixed use developments or shopping centers.

Next Step

The adoption of the General Plan Amendment is but a first step in a much larger policy agenda for improving the health of communities such as South LA. The health crisis in South LA necessitates a more comprehensive approach to planning health equity. Completion of the community plan updates must be a priority for the city. The updates should include additional protections such as limiting the density and proximity of fast-food restaurants near schools and other sensitive receptors, further consideration of the exclusion of fast-food restaurants in strip malls and minimalls, and incentives for the development of healthier food retailers.

Community advocates, planning staff, and the planning commission are now working toward the incorporation of a broader set of health policies in the city's General Plan. This effort will take into consideration issues of access to and the equitable distribution of health care facilities, healthy food, open space, hazardous sites, and more. These changes will require significant community input, public and private participation, political will, and dedicated resources from the city.

Such successes and aspirations are threatened by continuing city budget cuts that have further compromised and reduced the staffing needed to bring the community plans to completion. Currently, only three staff members are assigned to South LA. Greater balance and equity must be reached in the allocation of planning resources to streamline the permit and entitlement processes against the tremendous need for strategic planning and design of underresourced communities.

Adopting and implementing the latest model for urban design is not enough. Plans must be customized to the unique needs of each community with the goal of improving health and ensuring health equity. Perhaps the real measure of the effectiveness of city planning should be the health of its most unhealthy community.

More Than a PSA

Meredith Drake Reitan

Many communities have an abundance of fast-food outlets, while healthy options are scarce. One of the goals of Public Matters (www.publicmattersgroup.com) is to flip this reality. However, as Mike Blockstein and Reanne Estrada, the group's principal and creative director, will tell you, they are not involved in corner store conversions; rather they do Market Makeovers. Beyond simply adding fresh food to store shelves, Public Matters aims to create a viable consumer base for healthy options by using innovative art and media practices to integrate the public into neighborhood-based projects. Their approach weaves together planning, place, and participation with the goal of long-term change, and it recognizes that improvements are not simply a function of the physical environment but entail changing the idea of the "market" in an economic and symbolic sense.

A strategic but playful use of rhetoric, both in terms of language and visual style, sets their projects apart. Rather than produce typical public service announcements, Public Matters uses new methods, many adopted from its visual art background, to send its message. The ultimate goal is to inform the process as well as the end product, and the team works closely with students, municipal groups, community leaders, and others to accomplish this aim.

The Market Makeovers (www.marketmakeovers.org) program began as a collaboration of the South L.A. Healthy Eating Active Community Initiative, high school students at the Accelerated School, and Public Matters. Using two corner stores as case studies, the team cleaned, painted, and reorganized the store to highlight healthy food options. Simultaneously, the program developed an online toolkit for community members. The website hosts videos made by high school students and other user-generated content. It provides information on healthy eating and advice on how to replicate the projects. The resulting website reaches a national audience of public health practitioners, advocates, community activists, educators, and policy makers.

Blockstein says Public Matters brings a sense of place into planning, so that community members are not just invested but also feel affection for the places they live.

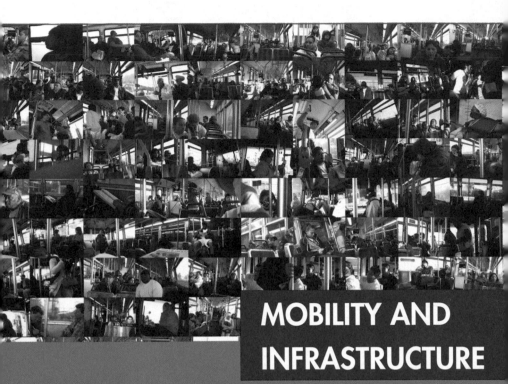

MOBILITY AND INFRASTRUCTURE

5

Back to the Future in Transportation Planning

Marlon G. Boarnet

Few things are as synonymous as cars and LA. Yet 30 years have passed since the pop group Missing Persons sang about an LA where driving was ubiquitous. In the ensuing decades, the image of LA as a car capital has not faded, but the reality is now far different. The metropolitan region that was an early adopter of the automobile and modern freeways is still pioneering the future of transportation planning. That future, though, will resemble not the recent past but the era that predates the interstate highways. Cars will not lose their dominance—far from it—but to understand the current and future LA transportation landscape requires a much broader perspective.

The construction of the U.S. Interstate Highway System following passage of the 1956 National Defense and Interstate Highway Act marked a brief period of time when transportation planning was top-down, centralized, focused on large infrastructure projects, and largely severed from place-based political pressures. The financing systems and institutional framework for transportation planning in the United States date to the 1956 Act, and cities and metropolitan areas have taken decades to catch up with the reality that interstate construction largely stopped by the early 1970s. After a long hiatus, the place-based political pressures that defined transportation planning and bound it with land use have reemerged, and nowhere is that reemergence more evident than in LA. The region has embarked on an infrastructure investment agenda that includes six new rail transit (BRT) lines programmed over the next 10 years, a maze of bus rapid transit and express bus corridors, pedestrian plans for even the most exurban municipalities, and billions of dollars in sales tax revenue allocated to transit. Yet this is not a modal story but rather one about the rebirth of local context and planning in transportation.

The Context

Post–World War II transportation and urban development in the United States have been of one type: auto-oriented. Looking forward, the car and auto-oriented land uses will continue to dominate, as no other mode provides the same advantages in terms of travel time, cost, and convenience. However, the car's dominance will not be monolithic. Ideas that would have been laughable 20 years ago, such as neighborhood vehicles, "road diets" that remove street lanes, bicycle-oriented development, and bicycle-sharing plans, are being implemented in niche markets throughout the LA metropolitan area. Integrating pricing into transportation demand management—politically toxic and strongly resisted 20 years ago—is also making inroads. The transport world is transforming from a "one-size-fits-all" model of auto-oriented infrastructure and associated land development to a model with meaningful variations on that theme.

This paradigm shift is occurring in two ways. For the past two centuries, transportation planning has been bound up with changing transportation technologies. Virtually every generation from the early 19th century to the mid-20th century saw the development of new technologies that lowered the cost of passenger transportation and hence decentralized urban settlement. Cities evolved as transportation shifted from walking to horsecar to electric streetcar to early automobile to the interstate system (Muller 2004, Vance 1991).[1] These changes led to a common expectation that transportation costs would fall over time. Yet intrametropolitan passenger transportation technology has largely been unchanged for the last half-century, and as congestion delays have increased, transport costs (factoring in time costs) have risen (Glaeser and Kohlhase 2004, 208–210). The first paradigm shift is the movement of transportation away from new infrastructure to the more mundane task of marginally improving the movement of persons within cities.

The second paradigm shift flows from the first because, for the first time transportation is not primarily about building infrastructure to support a new technology but instead about applying innovations and improvements where possible, using existing technologies.[2] The growing popularity of "older" modes—rail transit, walking, bicycles—is a natural result. This shift brings to the fore the traditional place-based politics that were obscured by higher-level, centralized government planning and funding during the interstate highway era. Transportation access confers costs and benefits across the landscape, and those localized economic advantages and disadvantages create a place-based forum for political decision making. As transportation becomes more local, the politics of place will become more visible.

Transportation in Metropolitan Los Angeles

At the turn of the 20th century, metropolitan LA boasted one of the premier interurban passenger rail systems in the world, the Pacific Electric. That system, like virtually all U.S. transit systems of the time, was privately owned. The tie between land use and transportation was tight. The rail transit system made it possible for real estate developers and land speculators to develop outlying areas by providing access, and the increased land prices made possible by transportation access were captured by the landowner and developer. Wachs (1984) notes that LA's characteristically dispersed urban form first emerged in the early 1900s with the Pacific Electric connecting downtown LA to Santa Monica, Long Beach, Newport Beach, Santa Ana, Ontario, San Bernardino, and the San Fernando Valley. This sprawling region spanned almost 100 miles end to end, with the emerging settlements of the time little more than towns separated by vast expanses of open land. As Wachs notes, the major centers and spatial extent of the present metropolitan LA were recognizable by the 1920s, and the development in the last three-quarters of the past century "consisted of filling in the spaces between outlying centers associated with important stations on the Pacific Electric."

Los Angeles was an early adopter of the automobile. By 1919, it had one car for every nine residents—more cars per capita than any other large city in the United States. By 1929, that ratio had tripled, as the city had about one car for every three residents. That boom occurred during a decade when LA's population more than doubled—from 577,000 to 1.24 million (Wachs 1984). Los Angeles was truly the nation's first automobile city.

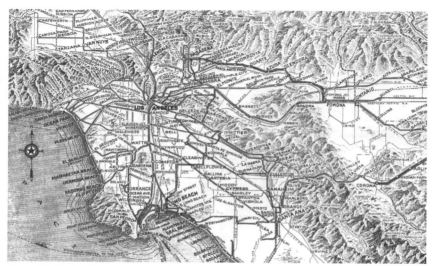

Figure 5.1. The Pacific Electric Railway, the nation's largest in the early 20th century, created the region's development skeleton.

The implications for the rail transit system were predictable. Pacific Electric traffic peaked in 1924, and 1931 was the last year that the system's revenues covered operating costs (Adler 1991). The years between the wars and the period immediately after World War II were difficult times for passenger rail across the United States. The automobile drew customers away from transit, fare box revenues declined, and many systems responded by deferring maintenance and reducing service quality, which further prompted people to shift to car travel. The net result was financial distress in the usually privately run rail transit systems of the time. From the mid-1930s to the mid-1950s, LA and California officials debated how to respond to this financial crisis.

In other American cities, transit shifted from private to public ownership, often in a reduced form, and typically that shift required identifying public revenues that could fill the gap between the fare box take and operating costs. Danielson and Doig (1982, chap. 7) discuss that transition in New York City. The same possibility was debated in LA. While many factors conspired to preclude the choice of public rail operations in postwar LA, place-based economic competition was a key factor. By the end of World War II, LA's bedroom suburbs, first incubated by the region's interurban rail system, had grown into cities and communities with their own economic interests. The executive director of the Chamber of Commerce of South Gate (a city approximately 10 miles south of downtown LA) stated the matter clearly in 1950, saying that his city's residents:

> are not interested in getting to downtown Los Angeles, but we have 30,000 employees in the City of South Gate who live in various sections of metropolitan Los Angeles. We are just as much interested in getting those men and women back and forth to their employment as we are in getting them to downtown Los Angeles for any other reason. May I be brutally frank and say that we are a lot more interested in getting our employees back and forth to work than we are getting our citizenry to leave our own merchants in the City of South Gate and go downtown to Los Angeles to spend their money (quoted in Adler 1991, 74).

The ideal transport system for South Gate and other outlying economic centers would be grid-oriented and would facilitate the movement of customers and employees to decentralized jobs rather than focus inwardly on the downtown. These pressures reduced political support for publicly financed rail transit. In 1948, the Los Angeles City Council voted 8–6 against the creation of a rail rapid transit district, and more generally during the 1940s and 1950s the political coalition needed to provide public support for the failing private rail operations was stymied by a loose coalition of outlying economic centers whose interests favored freeways over transit. In 1961, the Los Angeles Metropolitan Transit Authority (Metro) eliminated service on the last of what had been the Pacific Electric lines, making LA the largest U.S. city without a rail transit system (Adler 1991).

With the passage of the Interstate Highway Act, the LA region embarked on an ambitious freeway-building plan. Early proposals envisioned a grid that would place freeways approximately four miles apart throughout the metropolitan area (Taylor 2000). While that system was never fully built, the massive federal funding (nine federal dollars for every state dollar) led to an explosion of highway building. California opened more freeway miles from 1957 through 1959 than it had built in all previous years, and centerline highway miles in the state doubled again from 1960 through 1964 (Taylor 2000, 210). From 1956 to the early 1970s, transportation was a massive, centralized program of highway construction. The generous federal match and the increased revenues provided by the new highway trust fund encouraged states to build the interstate system quickly. In the initial rush, questions of place and issues of local politics were largely subsumed to the imperatives of the infrastructure construction project (see, e.g., Taylor 2000).

That era, which many current planners view as "normal" for transportation, was, in broader historical context, highly unusual. Before the interstate era, urban transportation had been about places and context, balancing a mix of modes and characterized by financing systems and plans that interwove the needs of settlements, persons, and mobility in dense locales. The centralized planning of the interstate highways, with routes sited with single-minded attention to mobility (often intermetropolitan mobility) and with little consideration of land use, was a dramatic departure from earlier

Figure 5.2. The freeway system improved mobility—and created havoc for local neighborhoods.

practices (Taylor 2000, Brown, Morris, and Taylor 2009). Los Angeles, and the entire country, has spent the past few decades slowly backing out from the heady days of highway building and reassessing planning in light of the more common realities of place-based competition and interactions between land use and transportation.

The Seeds of a More Localized Transportation Planning

The interstate highway years seeded three factors that eventually propelled the return to a more local approach to transportation. The first seed was fiscal pressure. The gasoline tax finance system that infused funds into the Interstate Highway System was, particularly for urban highways, unsustainable in the long run. Unlike property taxes (the highway finance instrument that the gas tax displaced during the two decades from the 1930s to the 1950s), gas tax revenues do not increase as the cost of urban land and hence right-of-way costs (Taylor 2000). Nor have fuel tax revenues kept pace with improvements in vehicle fuel economy or inflation (Taylor 2006, 281). The resulting fiscal pressures provided strong motivation for county, special district, and other local governments to eventually look elsewhere for transportation revenues, a trend that played out particularly strongly in California. By 2005 all of the larger metropolitan counties in the state had enacted local sales tax increments to fund transportation (Crabbe et al. 2005).

The second seed was environmental regulation. The state's efforts to regulate pollution from cars began early, as LA's legendary smog, and the basin's geography, which traps ozone in atmospheric inversion layers, contributed to air-quality issues that galvanized public opinion (Boarnet and Crane 2001, 22). The Los Angeles Air Pollution Control District, the first such body in the nation, was created by a vote of the Los Angeles County Supervisors in 1947, following the passage of enabling state legislation (South Coast Air Quality Management District [SCAQMD] 1997). The district was the predecessor to the SCAQMD, which regulates stationary sources of air pollution (industrial plants and the like) in the greater LA region and which is responsible for the largest population of any such body in the United States. California regulated automobile tailpipe emissions as early as 1961, almost a decade before the 1970 Clean Air Act (CAA) Amendments gave similar authority to the U.S. Environmental Protection Agency (EPA) (Boarnet and Crane 2001, 22–23). Since the 1970 amendments, California has been granted a waiver to exceed EPA emission regulations. Most recently, the state has enacted possibly the nation's most ambitious greenhouse gas–emissions regulatory framework through Assembly Bill 32 and Senate Bill 375, which requires coordinated metropolitan land-use and transportation planning to achieve greenhouse gas–emission reduction targets. The net effect has been long-standing attention to environmental issues amid a regulatory structure that generally enjoys public support and is administered by professional agencies with decades of experience and continuity.

The third seed has been the growth of the LA region, accompanied by increasing population densities (Fulton et al. 2001) and the resulting traffic congestion. The Texas Transportation Institute consistently ranks LA among the most congested urban areas in the nation (Schrank, Lomax, and Turner 2010). While people can take many actions to avoid congestion, including locating to the less congested urban fringe and driving at off-peak hours, the available congestion measures (e.g. Schrank, Lomax, and Turner 2010, Boarnet, Parkany, and Kim 1998) and

Figure 5.3. Environmental pressure began increasing with the horrible smog attacks of the 1940s; in this photograph from 1964, only the tops of downtown's skyscrapers are visible above the smog.

Figure 5.4. Congestion pricing signs, such as this one on I-15 in San Diego County, represent new ways planners are trying to improve regional mobility.

anecdotal evidence suggest that the Glaeser and Kohlhase (2004) proposition about rising passenger transportation costs inside urban areas describes the LA region well.

These three seeds combine to produce a context where vehicle travel is expensive in time cost and in the attention to air quality externalities, and the funds available for street and highway infrastructure cannot keep pace with the cost of building new infrastructure to meet travel demand. In the face of those pressures, construction of new highways in California slowed to almost a standstill by the 1970s (Taylor 1995 and 2000; Brown, Morris, and Taylor 2009). Since then, policy makers have worked at the margins, making improvements where possible, thinking multimodally and creatively in ways that more readily tie transportation to the needs of places and relationships with land use. That experimentation and innovation has proceeded in two phases. The first phase still reflected the earlier era's focus on infrastructure, with efforts to find local revenue sources to fill the gaps in state and federal funding. The second phase has been a more creative attempt toward a contextual, locally informed view of transportation that includes important variations on the automobile and highway infrastructure themes.

The First Phase of Local Innovation: Local Option Sales Taxes and County-Level Infrastructure

The shortfall of gasoline-tax highway funds led to a proliferation of county sales tax measures to support transportation projects. Since 1980, 20 California counties have passed referendums that add a sales tax increment, almost always an additional half-cent, to the state sales tax rate to fund county transportation projects (Crabbe et al. 2005). This facilitated a wave of local transportation innovation as counties proposed transportation packages that were tailored to local (county) needs and could obtain voter support.

In LA, mass transit is financed through three half-cent sales tax increments, passed in 1980 (Proposition A), 1990 (Proposition C), and 2008 (Measure R). All of Proposition A sales tax revenues are for transit operations or rail system development, with 40 percent of the revenues devoted to bus operations per Metro board policy. Proposition C revenues, similarly, are devoted exclusively to transit or transit-related projects, with the exception of the 20 percent returned to local communities within Los Angeles County. Measure R devotes 20 percent of the most recent half-cent sales tax increment to highway capital projects, 15 percent to local return, and the balance to transit capital or operations (LA Metro 2009, 59.)

In contrast, the sales tax increments in the outlying counties have been primarily for highways. Orange County passed Measure M, its half-cent transportation sales tax, in 1990, and in 2004, renewed it for 30 years.[3] Measure M devotes 25 percent of sales tax revenues to transit (Orange County Transportation Authority n.d.). Riverside County passed its half-cent sales tax, Measure A, in 1988 and extended it in 2002, with 15 percent of the funds devoted to transit (Riverside County Transportation Commission 2002 and n.d.). The pattern, not unexpected given the realities of urban development, is that the outlying counties have focused more heavily on streets and highways, with Los Angeles County focusing local resources almost exclusively on new transit infrastructure and operations. As highway and right-of-way costs increase and as developable land becomes scarce in the more outlying counties, one can expect shifts toward infrastructure that supports alternatives to the automobile outside of Los Angeles County.

In Los Angeles County, the most recent sales tax increment, Measure R, will create $40 billion in projected revenue over 30 years (LA Metro 2009). Metro's long-range plan commits funds to six new rail transit lines scheduled to open by 2019, and within a few years the city should see construction of three new rail transit lines simultaneously. In total, the six lines planned for the next decade will increase the Metro rail network from 79 to approximately 120 miles, making it larger than the current Washington, D.C., Metro system.[4]

The LA rail system represents a shift from largely federal and state revenue sources to mostly local finance. In the early days of postinterstate highway rail transit construction, the federal government was often the dominant revenue source. Pickrell (1992, 167) provides evidence that of the eight new rail systems that opened in the United States in the 1970s and 1980s, seven had federal funding shares that exceeded half of forecasted construction costs. That federal involvement was likely a legacy of thinking from the interstate era, when transportation of all kinds was viewed as naturally a national project. Pickrell (1992, n. 18) notes that in some cases, the federal funds were interstate highway funds that were "traded in" for transit capital funding. Yet urban rail systems serve cities and metropolitan areas, and while not denying the importance of cities to the nation, one would expect a pattern of increasingly localized finance and planning of rail transit such as had been typical before the interstate highway era. Los Angeles has illustrated that devolution of rail transit finance to the local level. The first wave of Metro rail projects, those completed as of 2009, were paid 38 percent with local revenue, while the six lines scheduled to open in the next decade are projected to be funded 60 percent from local sources (Table 5.1).

Figure 5.5. The East LA Gold Line and other rail projects reflect new priorities around transportation.

In the 1980s, Orange County confronted the same fiscal pressures that led Los Angeles County to sales tax increment financing. While a well-developed highway system covered the northern half of Orange County, only one limited access highway served the rapidly growing southern part of the county. The Orange County Master Plan of Arterial Highways, dating to the 1970s, had envisioned a network of new highways to accommodate population growth in the southern half of the county, but prospects for federal or state funding were nonexistent by the 1980s (Boarnet, DiMento, and Macey 2002, Boarnet and DiMento 2004). In response, the county formed two special purpose agencies with the authority to build the new highways with bonds repaid from tolls and development impact fees. From 1993 through 1999, the Transportation Corridor Agencies (TCA) opened 51 new centerline miles of toll road in Orange County, a massive infrastructure program during the generally quiescent highway building period of the postinterstate era (TCA 1999, 3). The interstate highway system was funded not by borrowing but out of current gasoline tax revenues—ironic in that long-lived infrastructure was paid for in cash, rather than financed. The TCA toll roads were a return to preinterstate bond financing methods and presaged current discussions about infrastructure banks and other methods to use borrowing authority to build transportation infrastructure.

At the same time that the TCA were being organized, similar pressures led to even more startling innovation in the northern part of Orange County. In 1989, as part of a compromise, the California legislature passed Assembly Bill 680, which raised the gasoline tax (desired by Democrats) and authorized up to four privately financed highway projects (desired by Republicans).[5] This compromise was the last time the per-gallon gasoline tax was increased in California. Carpool lanes were being planned at the time for the median of State Route 91, which connects job-rich Orange County to the inland residential suburbs of Riverside County, but no funds were available to build the lanes. As part of an open call for private highway franchises under the provisions of AB 680, the privately held California Private Transportation Company (CPTC) proposed to build and operate the approximately 10 centerline miles as toll lanes. The lanes, which opened in 1995, were remarkable both for being wholly privately owned roads and for being the first application of congestion pricing in the United States.[6] Because the SR-91 toll lanes were adjacent to their unpriced completion, congestion pricing was part of the business plan from the earliest days of the CPTC proposal (Boarnet, DiMento, and Macey 2002). CPTC felt congestion pricing was essential to maintain its promise of an uncongested driving experience. While congestion pricing is anything but common, the demonstration effect of the SR-91 lanes moved it into the realm of realistic discussion, and congestion-priced lanes now exist in San Diego and Houston (see U.S. DOT n.d.; Harris County Toll Road Authority n.d.a and b). Los Angeles County is proceeding with construction to accommodate a one-year pilot project to allow congestion-priced solo-driver vehicles onto the high occupancy vehicle lanes on the I-10 El Monte Busway and the I-110 Harbor Transitway.

The Second Phase of Innovation: Smaller and More Context Based
With time, the combination of fiscal pressures and a growing focus on community quality of life led to more localized efforts that are very different from the large infrastructure construction programs of the first phase of innovation. The earliest

Table 5.1: Los Angeles Metro Rail Lines, funding sources, and opening dates

Existing LA Metro Rail Lines

Line	Opening Date	Total Projected Capital Cost [1]	Projected Local Expenditures[1,2]	Local Share
Red Line	1993	$1,400	$ 515	36.79%
Red Line segment 2	1996	$1,800	$ 217	12.06%
Red Line segment 3	1999–2000	$1,300	$ 217	16.69%
Green Line	1995	$ 718	$ 612	85.24%
Blue Line	1990	$ 877	$ 877	100.00%
Gold Line	2003	$ 859	$ 431	50.12%
Gold Line eastside extension	2009	$ 898	$ 161	17.88%
Total		$7,852	$3,029	38.58%

Future LA Metro Rail Lines, scheduled to open before 2020

Line	Projected Opening Date (LA Metro fiscal year)	Total Projected Capital Cost [1]	Projected Local Expenditures[1,2]	Local Share
Expo Line phase I	2011	$ 862	$ 64	7.42%
Expo Line phase II	2015	$1,300	$ 947	72.85%
Gold Line extension	2017	$ 851	$ 836	98.24%
Crenshaw/LAX Line	2018	$1,700	$1,500	88.24%
Regional Connector	2019	$1,073	$ 388	36.16%
Westside subway extension	2019	$1,950	$ 973	49.90%
Total		$7,736	$4,708	60.86%

Source: LA Metro 2009

Notes: ([1]) in $ millions; ([2]) local expenditures are those that are not from state or federal sources.

Figure 5.6. A separated bicycle lane in Long Beach

examples of this second phase were village-oriented commercial centers. Some were pre–World War II downtowns that reflected earlier neighborhood designs, such as Old Town Orange or the downtown in Torrance. In other places, declining downtowns were redeveloped with a focus on pedestrian friendliness—Santa Monica's Third Street Promenade and Old Town Pasadena are examples.

For years, such neighborhoods were quaint residential villages or popular entertainment and shopping destinations, evoking an earlier era. As interest in neighborhood level transportation–land-use planning increased from the 1980s forward; a wave of transit-oriented land uses was developed around the region's new rail transit investments. Hollywood, after years of decline, was the site of major joint development projects on and near property owned by Metro. At the Hollywood and Vine Red Line station, the transit-oriented joint development included 375 apartments (of which 20 percent are leased at below-market rates), close to 60,000 square feet of retail, and a 300-room luxury hotel with 114 condominium units. At the Hollywood and Highland station, a Metro joint development project included 390,000 square feet of retail, a 640-room hotel, and the 3,500-seat Kodak Theatre, home to the Academy Awards since 2001. Other joint development programs have been built throughout the region.[7]

These projects have served as exemplars of locally conceived and implemented transportation innovation over the past few years. Consistent with the emerging trend toward context and experimentation, these projects go beyond the 1990s concept of transit-oriented development (TOD). For instance, Long Beach has announced its intentions by mounting a sculpture of an antique bicycle on its city hall, with an inscription proclaiming that the town is "the most bicycle friendly city in America" (Barboza 2010). In 2000, Long Beach developed a bicycle master plan, which was undergoing updates in 2011 (City of Long Beach n.d.). In addition to typical bicycle infrastructure, such as 35 miles of new bicycle lanes and over 2,000 bike racks citywide, the city has pursued more innovative projects:

- One traffic lane was removed from downtown portions of Broadway and Third Street to accommodate separated bicycle lanes shielded from car traffic by planters and parallel parking (Bike Long Beach 2011).
- "Sharrow" or shared bicycle and vehicle lanes in the beach neighborhood of Belmont Shore allow bicycles and cars to share the same traffic lane in

single file. Opened in June 2009, the five-foot-wide green strip is intended to encourage bicyclists to share traffic with automobiles in a middle lane, away from car doors that open into streetside lanes along parallel parking (Ulaszewski 2009).

- At intersections, the city has painted a green bicycle box in lanes to allow and encourage left-turning bicyclists to share the lane in front of motorists (Bike Long Beach n.d.).
- In June 2011 the city launched a program to create "bicycle friendly business districts" in four neighborhood-oriented retail areas. About 60 firms are participating in the two-year pilot program. With funds provided by a grant from the Los Angeles County Department of Health and Human Services, the districts will promote replacing short car trips with bicycle trips. Participating firms will be provided with free bicycles and gear to encourage cycling as a mode for small deliveries and business trips to banks, the post office, and similar destinations (Bikeable Communities 2011, Eaton 2011).

Elsewhere in metropolitan LA, regional and local agencies are experimenting with small zero-emission electric vehicles capable of speeds not more than 25 miles per hour. Known as Neighborhood Electric Vehicles (NEV) or Local Use Vehicles (LUV), they are typically used for trips of between one and five miles. The Riverside County cities of Corona, Norco, Riverside, and Moreno Valley, with funding from the Southern California Association of Governments (SCAG) and coordination from the Western Riverside Council of Governments (WRCOG), developed an NEV plan that identified lower-speed streets and prospects for coordinated NEV/bicycle lanes that would form a network connecting destinations (Urban Crossroads and Bennett Engineering Services 2010). The plan also surveyed residents about attitudes toward NEVs and offered suggestions for the safe implementation of NEV travel.

The South Bay Cities Council of Governments (SBCCOG) is similarly experimenting with NEVs. South Bay communities are home to more than a million persons living in auto-oriented, first-generation, post–World War II suburban development dotted by neighborhood-serving businesses (Solimar Research Group 2005). SBCCOG has focused on concentrating commercial and retail into neighborhood centers and nodes and encouraging LUV and NEV transportation (Boarnet et al. 2011, Siembab and Boarnet 2009). Since May 2010, SBCCOG has pursued a demonstration project in which households used a free NEV/LUV with geographic positioning system (GPS) devices to track all household travel. A year later, an analysis of eight households suggests that 28 percent of travel was by NEV/LUV. The sample size is exceptionally small, but the project was intended to place the vehicles on the street and create a demonstration effect in addition to the data collection effort. SBCCOG now has a waiting list of more than 200 households for the NEV/LUV demonstration (draft NEC/LUV Demonstration Project Preliminary Final Report, June 2011).

These and other similar projects exist within an evolving framework that has shifted transportation governance from centralized infrastructure construction to an increasing focus on local demonstrations. SCAG provides funding to support local innovation through its CMPASS Blueprint demonstration program. That and related efforts have supported a large number of projects, including the WRCOG NEV plan and the re-

Figure 5.7. A shared bicycle-vehicle (sharrow) lane in Long Beach

search that led to the South Bay NEV/LUV demonstration. SCAG has also supported plans for TOD around BRT in Orange County, a nonmotorized transportation plan in the exurban high desert municipality of Victorville (almost 70 miles from downtown LA), and three studies examining the feasibility of covering highways to recover land that divides neighborhoods in downtown Ventura, downtown LA, and Hollywood.[8] Senate Bill 375, which requires metropolitan planning organizations to develop sustainable communities strategies (SCS) that will document progress toward reductions in greenhouse gas emissions, will provide an additional and complementary framework for canvassing, publicizing, and encouraging local, context-sensitive transportation and land-use planning.

Even in the politically conservative and car-oriented communities of Orange County, transportation planning is not an auto-only endeavor anymore. The Orange County SCS recognizes seven jurisdictions that have implemented TOD policies and discusses preferential parking for alternative fuel vehicles in Huntington Beach; a bike-sharing program in Garden Grove; complete streets policies being implemented in Irvine, Huntington Beach, and Santa Ana; and the identification of 69 miles of potential BRT routes in three high-traffic transit corridors (LSA Associates 2011).

The Future
The car has not vanished from LA, nor will it in any foreseeable future. Yet transportation planning in the region has moved far from a single-minded focus on automobility. In doing so, the process has returned to the more normal exigencies of the era before

the interstate highways. LA led the nation into an auto-oriented vision of transportation planning; perhaps not ironically, LA is now leading the way out. Transportation in the LA metropolitan area is increasingly locally financed, through whatever practical instruments are available, and tied to local land use and community development. Concomitantly, transportation is tied to visions of place and community, implying experimentation and variation. Transportation practices that seem sensible in one locale will appear inappropriate in other places, and justifiably so. Transportation is increasingly a tool not only for mobility but for local visions of amenities, economic development (often tied to those amenities), and quality of life.

While this community-based vision is important, there is a need to somehow knit together local action into a metropolitan system that accommodates regional mobility while addressing problems of air quality and the global commons. In that respect, the evolving regional framework of demonstration programs nested within metropolitan planning—encouraged by the SCAG COMPASS Blueprint program and required under SB 375—is a positive departure from even the preinterstate era. Local planning is nested within loosely knitted governance at the scale of a metropolitan region that has 189 cities and almost 19 million persons. That metropolitan governance is not formal, in that metropolitan entities have no land-use or taxing authority, and navigating the necessary processes of collaboration and cooperation will be the challenge of the coming years. In its increasing emphasis on localism and alternatives to the automobile, and in the nascent methods for combining local efforts with metropolitan plans and systems, LA continues to point the way forward.

Regional Planning in Southern California

Robert A. Leiter, FAICP, and Elisa Barbour

The Southern California Association of Governments (SCAG), formed in 1965, is now the largest of nearly 700 metropolitan-area councils of government (COGs) in the United States. This essay traces the evolution of SCAG's roles and responsibilities in response to federal and state laws as well as significant planning issues.

SCAG's responsibilities have grown over the decades to reflect new requirements for integrated planning for growth and development. As the metropolitan planning organization (MPO) for Southern California, SCAG is responsible for developing federally and state-mandated regional plans for transportation. SCAG also conducts planning for growth management, greenhouse gas (GHG) emissions reduction, housing development, air quality, and other issues. Furthermore, SCAG has developed a strong role in formulating and implementing economic development policies for the region, tied to transportation. Among California MPOs, SCAG excels in serving as a forum for connecting economic development with social equity.

The history of SCAG reflects the challenge of achieving regional coordination through an organizational structure emphasizing local home rule. In SCAG's case, this task is made difficult by the sheer size and complexity of the region, which contains 191 cities across six large counties in a territory the size of Ohio. SCAG's structure reflects this diversity, with substantial responsibility devolved to subregional agencies. Five county transportation commissions (CTCs), the Tribal Government Regional Planning Board, and the Imperial Valley Association of Governments hold primary authority for programming and administering transportation projects and programs in their respective jurisdictions. In addition, 14 subregional COGs plan land-use aspects of SCAG programs.

SCAG's multilayered, federated structure can inhibit planning coordination. The agency faces formidable challenges in meeting new demands for integrating land-use, transportation, and environmental planning at a regional scale. At the same time,

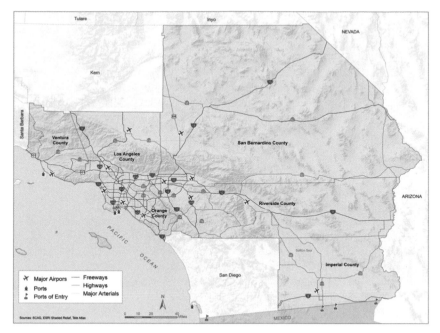

Figure 5.8. The SCAG Region covers a wide swath of the southern portion of the state.

SCAG's substantial accomplishments, in the face of such structural challenges, point to lessons for other agencies in complex, large urban areas.

Reluctant Regionalism: SCAG's Formative Years

Regional planning during SCAG's formative years emerged largely due to federal and state mandates. Starting in the 1960s, the federal government required regional planning as a condition for funding highways, transit, housing, and other purposes. California state legislation favored emphasizing voluntary cooperation among local governments. In 1963, the California legislature passed the Regional Planning Act, enabling a limited form of regional government in each area unless a voluntary association of governments existed. In response, SCAG was formed as such a voluntary association, as were 25 other COGs throughout the state (Douglas 1968, Johnson 1976). Federal legislation also called for regional review of transportation investment plans by MPOs in urban areas with populations of 50,000 or more. MPOs, which typically coincide with COGs, were made responsible for "continuing, comprehensive, and cooperative" planning for transportation.

California directed greater authority to county-level agencies than did the federal approach. The California Transportation Development Act of 1971 provided each county the proceeds of a quarter-cent state sales tax increase, earmarked mainly for transit. Regional transportation planning agencies (RTPAs) were designated, mainly at the county level, to allocate the funds and submit plans to the state. Although SCAG was designated the LA region's RTPA, CTCs were subsequently established for four (later five) counties in the region, to aid in plan preparation (Wilshusen 1992, Bollens 1993). SCAG also designated five subregional "mini-COGs" to assist in plan preparation (Johnson 1976).

Thus, federal and state actions prompted the creation of the current system of cross-jurisdictional planning collaboration. Regionalism was not vigorously promoted from the bottom up in the SCAG region, reflecting its decentralized pattern of development. Given their size, county governments long had acted somewhat as regional planning entities, but they resisted planning integration across borders. Reflecting these realities, SCAG emerged as a voluntary regional planning agency governed by local officials, with substantial power devolved to county-level transportation agencies.

Mounting Pressures and Expectations: SCAG's Evolution, 1980–2000

During the 1980s and 1990s, local planning-related stresses increased, including rapid population growth, decentralization of jobs and housing, and environmental and fiscal constraints. Meanwhile, the rise of a global economy focused attention on economic competitiveness. These factors drew attention to the regional consequences of local land-use decision making, such as urban sprawl and lengthening commutes.

Although the federal government had encouraged a regional multimodal approach since the 1970s, in reality MPOs had little discretion over the types of

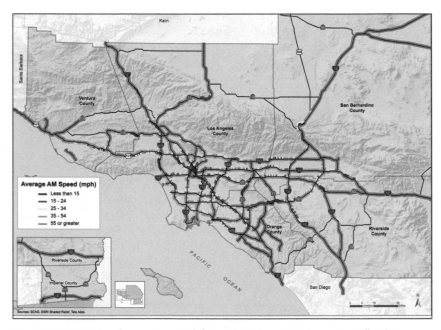

Figure 5.9. Motorists have become increasingly frustrated with the region's slow-moving traffic. This map shows morning freeway speeds.

projects in their plans. With most federal and state funds allocated as categorical grants for specific purposes and geographic areas, MPOs primarily served as brokers, helping to align local preferences with funding availability (Wachs and Dill 1999). New federal legislation strengthening the MPOs changed this situation in the 1990s, but California policy counterbalanced this outcome by strengthening the county-level role.

The federal government adopted a new approach to transportation with the Intermodal Surface Transportation Efficiency Act (ISTEA) of 1991 and successor legislation, which redirected federal policy from highway building toward a more multimodal approach. The law allocated about half of federal funds for flexible use across modal categories, with more going directly to MPOs—about one-fifth of funds in California (CLAO 1998, Innes and Gruber 2001).[1] MPOs were required to take the lead in preparing long- and short-range transportation plans for their region and were mandated to demonstrate the conformance of their plans to air quality goals, essentially establishing an "air pollution budget" (Lewis and Sprague 1997).

While the new federal approach aimed to strengthen MPOs, a series of California policies and programs redirected some authority back to the county level. Shortly after ISTEA's passage, state legislation required SCAG to suballocate to the CTCs its ISTEA funds, weakening SCAG's autonomy, compared to other multicounty MPOS (Lewis and Sprague 1997, Innes and Gruber 2001). A state ballot measure passed in 1990 doubled the gas tax to fund a new Congestion Management Program, allocating funds to existing county-level transportation agencies using a county-based formula based on population and road-miles. (Nash 1992, Wilshusen 1992, Rothblatt and Coleman 1995, Innes and Gruber 2001). This program rendered county plans more important in multicounty MPO areas. Soon after ISTEA, the state legislature defined its own new framework for transportation policy, with passage of SB 45 in 1997. Like ISTEA, the law established more flexible block grants and devolved authority down from the state level, specifically to RTPAs.[2] However, the state system repeated the pattern of strengthening county agencies, because funds were allocated using the county-based formula (Innes and Gruber 2001).

County-level authority was also enhanced substantially by optional "self-help" sales taxes. Starting in the 1980s, the state government authorized counties to adopt half-cent sales taxes for transportation programs. These measures, enacted by five counties in SCAG's jurisdiction, require approval by a two-thirds majority of voters. The measures must specify expenditure packages and plans and are administered by county transportation authorities. By the 1990s, as transportation needs in the state increasingly outstripped available revenue, the self-help taxes formed the largest source of local transportation funds. With most large-scale transportation projects dependent on funding from multiple sources, county sales tax programs influenced the allocation of state and federal dollars, prompting one analyst to call the sales tax plans "de facto transportation plans for this region" (Giuliano 2004, 153). The county measures permit substantial intraregional variation in investment priorities; for example, Los Angeles County has invested far more in transit than its more suburban neighbors. While this approach orients investments to differing voter preferences at the subregional scale, it also inhibits SCAG's role in defining and

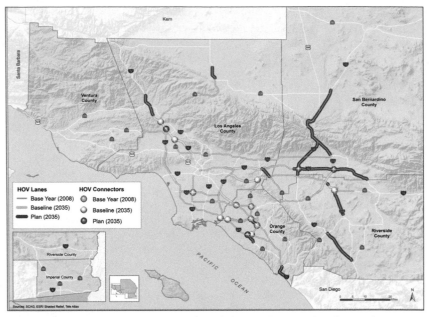

Figure 5.10. One response to congestion is incentives for drivers to become riders. This map shows SCAG Region HOV lanes projected for 2030.

implementing overarching, integrated regional priorities and policies. Transportation patterns and problems, as well as solutions, do not stop at county borders.

The state legislation that strengthened county transportation agencies during the period was particularly influential for the SCAG region, where CTCs already wielded considerable authority. In spite of federal efforts to strengthen MPOs, SCAG's primary authority continued to rest with its rarely exercised ability to veto local projects (U.S. DOT 1993, Lewis and Sprague 1997). County transportation agencies grew powerful, bolstered by ISTEA funding and sales tax revenue. As focus on air quality increased, SCAG did not attain a lead regional role in managing the issue. The South Coast Air Quality Management District dominated air quality planning and its relations with SCAG were sometimes strained (Grant 1995). Proposals to integrate regional agencies (SCAG and the air district, among others) were met with resistance from many SCAG member organizations (Innes et al. 1994, Saltzstein 1996, Fulton 2001). The primary organizational outcome for SCAG during the period was greater devolution of governance, through a tripling of its board of directors to 70 members, and creation of 14 subregional COGs.[3]

21st-Century Regionalism: SCAG's Role Since 2000
Since the dawn of the new century, significant environmental and economic challenges have arisen in the SCAG region, calling for integrated planning across traditional geographic and institutional boundaries. SCAG has responded effectively to certain issues but in some cases has been hampered by its federated structure.

Transportation and Land-Use Integration

Regional planning in California has evolved toward greater integration of transportation and land use. This process was led by the large MPOs, which launched "blueprint" planning by the early 2000s to invest scarce resources strategically and achieve multiple goals, including air quality conformity. During the second half of the decade, the state government stepped in to provide grants for blueprint planning statewide and adopted SB 375, a landmark law orienting the blueprint process toward helping achieve the state's ambitious climate policy goals.

Regional Blueprint Planning

By the early 2000s, the MPOs in the four largest California metro regions (LA, San Francisco Bay, San Diego, and Sacramento) had all initiated blueprint processes (Barbour and Teitz 2006). The approach relies on public outreach and scenario analysis of modeled alternative land-use and transportation futures to arrive at a "preferred regional alternative" development scenario. Blueprint plans improve transportation system performance by identifying helpful land-use strategies, such as locating compact development near transit. Blueprint implementation requires close coordination of MPO investments with local land-use policy making, because land use is governed locally.

SCAG launched a blueprint process in 2000, with a yearlong discussion on growth visioning principles, development of a regional map with consistent land-use designations, and public outreach meetings throughout the region. The process culminated in 2004 with adoption of SCAG's Compass Blueprint Program, aimed at focusing growth in existing and emerging centers and along transportation corridors, promoting mixed use development and walkable communities, and preserving open

Figure 5.11. Regional solutions seem difficult to develop, save for the freeways.

space. Implementation strategies have included an annual awards program and technical assistance to local governments.

SCAG has been considerably limited in implementing its blueprint, compared to the other large MPOs, by its inability to provide financial incentives to local jurisdictions for supportive land uses. The three other MPOs have adopted competitive incentive grant programs, for example, funded at $10 million annually or more, for local projects that support their blueprints (Barbour and Teitz 2006). SCAG has not adopted a similar program because the devolution of discretionary funds to the CTCs leaves the agency with few resources for such purposes.

The blueprint process illuminates the challenge SCAG's decentralized structure presents for coordinating transportation, land-use, and environmental policies. The five Southern California CTCs have traditionally done little to connect their plans to local land-use policy (see Barbour and Teitz 2006). Meanwhile, the 14 subregional COGs are institutionally separate from the CTCs. Blueprint planning requires integrating plans across policy domains that are fragmented in SCAG's organizational structure.

Senate Bill 375

SCAG's organizational challenge was brought into even sharper relief with passage of SB 375 in 2008. This landmark planning law was adopted to help achieve the state's climate policy goals—namely, to reduce statewide GHG emissions to 1990 levels by 2020, and to 80 percent below 1990 levels by 2050.[4] Under SB 375, MPOs must develop sustainable communities strategies (SCSs) as components of regional transportation plans, explicitly building upon the blueprint planning process. In their SCSs, MPOs must demonstrate how they will achieve state-mandated GHG reduction targets through strategies to reduce vehicle-miles traveled (VMT) and other system efficiencies. In this regard, recent MPO scenario modeling aligns with emerging academic evidence indicating that the most effective approach for reducing VMT involves a combination of policies that promote higher-density development near transit, invest in alternatives to solo driving, and adjust pricing so as to raise the cost of driving and parking (Cambridge Systematics 2009, Rodier 2009).

SCAG's challenge was illustrated by a 2010 controversy within its governing council over the emissions reduction target the region proposed to the state Air Resources Board (ARB) for adoption under SB 375. The SCAG board called for a target by 2035 that was significantly less ambitious than the one ARB ultimately adopted for the region.[5] The controversy highlights ongoing tensions within the region over the feasibility and desirability of smart growth plans and policies.

SB 375 tests the limits of SCAG's federated organizational structure, particularly SCAG's ability to integrate land-use policies with CTCs. Some CTCs are rising to the challenge of SB 375; for example, LA Metro spearheaded passage in November 2008 of a county sales tax measure committing $40 billion over 30 years mainly (65 percent) to transit. The question still remains how Metro, and other CTCs, can promote policies with supportive land uses—something that CTCs do not control.

Goods Movement Planning for the Southern California Megaregion

SCAG can also point to achievements over the past decade in designing plans and programs for the Southern California megaregion, particularly goods-movement strategies developed to address mounting congestion problems and promote economic development.[6] The goods-movement issue emerged after the region's severe recession of the early 1990s, which featured a deep loss in aerospace jobs and led to economic restructuring. With more than one-third of all U.S. containerized trade passing through the region's two ports, the region's role as gateway for the movement of international goods is central to its global competitiveness. However, associated traffic congestion and air pollution threaten economic competitiveness and quality of life.

With a possible tripling in the volume of goods predicted by 2035, SCAG has forcefully engaged the challenge of defining a goods-movement strategy. SCAG, the CTCs, and the San Diego area MPO developed a multicounty goods-movement plan in 2008 (SCAG 2010). Strategies include improving intermodal linkages and promoting land uses such as inland warehousing and transloading facilities. In addition, SCAG has assertively called for state and federal aid and private-sector financing through user fees and other techniques.

SCAG's approach to goods movement underscores the central role that transportation can play in broader efforts to promote the "three Es" (environment, social equity, and economy) of sustainable development. SCAG's strategy aims to simultaneously strengthen the regional economy; address widening income divides; mitigate environmental, health, and social equity effects of port practices; and relieve growing traffic congestion. Port-related negotiations have involved multiple parties, including labor, neighborhood, and environmental activists; port owners, shippers, and truckers; and state, federal, and regional air quality agencies (Boarnet et al. 2009, Pastor and Benner 2011). Initially focused on the ports themselves, negotiations have widened

Figure 5.12. Freeways define downtown's borders, hemming it in as well as providing access for suburbanites.

in recent years to encompass a more systemic look at widespread regional impacts, including rail and freeway congestion and associated costs for human health, the environment, and the economy. In 2007, a multiagency cooperative agreement established the Southern California National Freight Gateway Collaboration to refine and coordinate strategies. This flexible structure, operating outside of traditional boundaries of jurisdictions and disciplines, points to the continuing usefulness of voluntary, collaborative approaches in the region (Boarnet et al. 2009). At the same time, the goods-movement issue places SCAG in a pivotal role as convener of deliberations across agencies and interests from the local to the state and even federal scales.

A comparison of SCAG's success in developing megaregional goods-movement strategies with its challenges in implementing local land-use integration strategies highlights the strengths and weaknesses of its organizational structure. SCAG's decentralized structure need not necessarily inhibit an effective role for the agency. Instead, in this case, the widespread perception among stakeholders of the need for concerted action to address a shared concern galvanized momentum, and SCAG has seeded the process with new ideas and a forum for developing solutions. SCAG's more limited progress in implementing smart growth strategies indicates that, in relation to more contested policy topics, a decentralized decision structure can be an impediment to convincing multiple partners to promote innovative strategies.

Conclusion

SCAG's evolution over the past 45 years has led to a distribution of responsibilities that has at times limited the agency's agility and effectiveness. Not surprisingly, SCAG's collaborative structure works best for issues such as goods movement on which multiple stakeholders agree a solution is needed. In that context, SCAG has filled a much-needed role in defining strategies and providing a deliberative forum, a role that its subregional partners cannot fulfill on their own. For policy areas where that consensus does not exist, such as around the adoption of smart growth principles and programs, SCAG has not been as successful in developing assertive strategies.

Which policy and institutional reforms could help SCAG adapt to current demands? Our analysis points to some key concerns that must be addressed, many of them long-standing for regional planning in general. These challenges include how to craft a federated planning system that preserves local land-use authority while still integrating land use with transportation at a regional scale. A potentially promising avenue for reform would be to coordinate CTC and subregional COG efforts more closely. At the same time, SCAG's regional role should be strengthened through access to more resources and autonomy at the regional scale. In addition, effective SB 375 implementation by SCAG and other MPOs is likely to require more concrete support from the state and federal levels, for example through programs that reward MPOs and jurisdictions that reduce GHGs through coordinated transportation and land use. Given the regional challenges confronting LA and its satellite counties, SCAG has an important role to play. The agency can meet the challenges most effectively if it works to overcome the limitations created by its traditional governing structure.

Ballot Box Planning for Transit

Lisa Schweitzer

Los Angeles County voters passed Measure R in 2008 to raise between $30 and $40 billion over the next 30 years primarily for transit projects. Measure R exemplifies a strategy of funding public transit using local option sales taxes as a means to make regional transit agencies less dependent on state and federal revenues. These "self-help" jurisdictions have taken up the cause of public transit with their local voters.[1]

I use Measure R to discuss the promise and challenges associated with sales tax methods of financing transit. As a caveat, Los Angeles County is exceptional because of its population size, tax base, and policy constraints, which should be considered when applying the lessons from this case to other regions. Measure R, however heavily celebrated by its promoters, illuminates a set of problems around transit financing through political deals that can disperse funding and present problems of equity and the increased fiscalization of land use.

The Burgeoning Urban Tax Base

Measure R built on four decades of success and failure at the ballot box for sales tax financing. By the time LA sales tax proponents began promoting Measure R, LA voters had considered six sales tax initiatives dedicated to transit funding since the early 1960s. The voters repeatedly (in 1968, 1974, and in 1976, on two measures) rejected ballot measures that would have built new rail lines and expanded transit (Stipak 1973, Dorothy Peyton Gray Transportation Library n.d.).

In 1980, Los Angeles County voters approved Proposition A, a half-cent sales tax in perpetuity to support regional transit and road projects. Ten years later, voters again passed another half-cent measure, Proposition C, in perpetuity for the same general purposes. In 1993, the Los Angeles County Transportation Commission and the Southern California Rapid Transit District merged into the Los Angeles Metropolitan Transportation Authority (Metro), which is currently the state-chartered transit provider

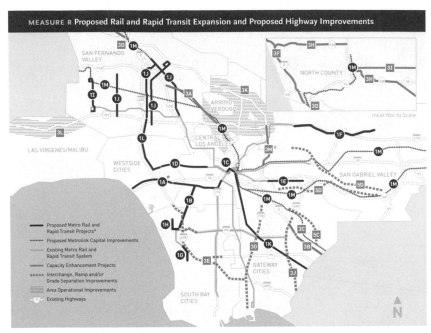

Figure 5.13. Routes covered by Measure R

for the county (Dorothy Peyton Gray Transportation Library n.d.). By 2008, when proponents were gearing up for Measure R, a little less than half of Metro's $3 billion budget came from the two sales tax initiatives passed in 1980 and 1990 (LA Metro Office of Management and Budget 2007). For Metro, Measure R promised billions of additional dollars after an 18-year dry spell of local initiatives.

Building the Project List and the Ballot Box Coalition

The campaign for Measure R illustrates some of the thornier aspects of tax politics. In 2005, Antonio Villaraigosa ran for mayor in part on the promise that he would complete the "Subway to the Sea," a subway line down Wilshire Boulevard previously thwarted by Westside Los Angeles home owners. The failure had resulted in the truncated Purple Line, which originates in downtown LA and terminates on Western Avenue in Koreatown, with the remainder of the line rerouted as the Red Line through Hollywood and into the San Fernando Valley (Taylor, Kim, and Gahbauer 2009). Completing the line became a focal point for Westside transit advocates.

By the time Villaraigosa came along, finding new funds required more than getting voters on board. Los Angeles County was already charging local option sales taxes up to the state's legal limit. In response, Assemblyman Mike Feuer (D–Los Angeles) put forth a bill to authorize the county to exceed the state cap through voter approval; the bill passed the state legislature in 2008 (City News Service 2008a). Feuer also worked with Villaraigosa and Metro board member Richard Katz to build a coalition of LA county supervisors to support Measure R.

Expanding the Measure R coalition meant spreading the funds across a sufficiently large geographic area and across transportation modes so that it would attract a coalition of voter support (Sellers, Grosvirt-Dramen, and Ohanesian 2009), but not so much that the funds would become too dispersed to pay for the county's share of the Subway to the Sea.[2] The final project listing contained a geographic cross section of transportation improvements ranging from freeway sound walls and large-scale rail projects to pedestrian and bicycle improvements. The centerpiece of Measure R would be the Subway to the Sea itself, which stood to get $4.1 billion from the measure. The second-biggest project was $2.8 billion for an 11-mile extension of truck lanes on the I-5 freeway. Boosters also constructed the measure to appeal to those left off the project list: each year, 15 percent of the Measure R revenue (so far roughly $100 million a year) would be set aside for city funds for discretionary improvements (LA Metro 2008b). The resulting project list heavily benefitted the affluent Westside of LA.

Under the leadership of County Supervisor Mark Ridley Thomas, predominately African American and Latino South LA already had projects either finished, under way, or programmed from other funding: the Blue Line light rail connecting downtown to Long Beach had been serving downtown Compton and Watts for more than two decades. Metro was in the process of building the Expo Line light rail through West Adams into Culver City on the northern edge of South Central. Finally, the Crenshaw light rail would also serve traditional African American communities. The projects moved ahead even though some community criticisms of the individual projects' designs lingered. Thus, the coalition backing Measure R could assemble a project list that avoided redistributing tax funds from white or Latino suburbs to African American districts. And because South LA already had transit projects under way by the time Measure R came around, it became possible to leave this jurisdiction off the project list without a priori shortchanging democratic and geographic minority groups like African Americans.

Serving Voters Rather Than Passengers?

The potential political minefield associated with local financing for transit was evident in the Measure R campaign. As Metro geared up for the initiative, a spokesperson for Los Angeles County Supervisor Michael Antonovich (R–San Fernando Valley) argued that the agency was misusing public funds by producing a 16-page color brochure of the measure's proposed project lists and descriptions. The agency labeled the brochure as "informational," but an outraged Antonovich, joined by Gloria Molina (representing San Gabriel Valley and eastside LA) referred to it as "propaganda" and demanded that Metro stop issuing information about Measure R (City News Service 2008b).

The legislators' challenge raised questions about the proper agency role in transit planning and marketing. Metro and the coalition supporting Measure R were simply following the conventions of tax politics and ballot box planning: if you are going to ask for a supermajority vote on a tax, you have to tell voters where the money is going. For Metro, spending $4 million to convince voters to pass a measure that would over time yield over $30 to $40 billion would pass any benefit-cost rationale. Just as transit agencies like Metro have for years paid lobbyists, development staff, and industry associations to further the agency's budgetary goals within statehouses across

Figure 5.14. One of many brochures produced on behalf of Measure R

the country, setting money aside to get voters' approval make sense fiscally for the agency. Yet Antonovich and Molina contended that the investment plan associated with Measure R constituted campaign materials—not mere planning information.

At the same time, Metro was setting aside millions for the campaign, just as it was facing a deficit in its operating budget that would, over the subsequent years, prompt it to cut bus routes and hours for existing passengers. The campaign also raises the question of the distributional equity of using agency money to market future projects to voters, likely more affluent than average Metro riders, while cutting service for existing riders.

These questions were sidestepped rather than resolved when, in September 2008, propelled by Antonovich's challenge, Mayor Villaraigosa began managing the "Yes on Measure R" campaign out of his own organization with support from a large coalition of LA businesses and nonprofits (Cavanaugh and Sanchez 2008, Doyle and Cavanaugh 2008, Perkins 2008). The solution was a rare political win-win: Villaraigosa could more closely associate himself with the ultimate victory of Measure R, and the agency avoided further criticisms that it overstepped its role.

Still, if the uproar over Measure R is any indicator, transit agencies seeking funding at the ballot box will experience more scrutiny of their communications. That scrutiny means that agencies will need a robust set of political and nongovernmental partners campaigning for them. Equipped with just such a coalition, the Yes for Measure R campaign moved forward without, ostensibly, Metro at its center.

The battle was not over even after the Villaraigosa campaign staff took over. In the weeks coming up to the election, opponents from the city's suburban valleys argued that Measure R was designed to take money from the suburbs while neglecting their transit projects. "With Measure R, downtown's 'big dogs' carefully crafted a scheme to keep the meat to themselves," groused Paul Little for the *Los Angeles Business Journal* late in October (Little 2008). Supervisor Molina's constituent San Gabriel Valley cities of Monrovia and Duarte lined up in opposition to Measure R (California Newsletter 2008) since the proposed Gold Line extension into the valley was to receive only $750 million. That funding was enough to get the line to the suburban cities of Azusa/Glendora but not enough to extend it to Claremont. *The Daily News* carried an indictment from Supervisor Michael Antonovich: "Of the $7.5 billion project funding proposed for the City of Los Angeles, only 13 percent of that is allocated for the San Fernando Valley. However, 37 percent of all Los Angeles city residents and 40 percent of all Los Angeles city jobs are located in the Valley" (Antonovich 2008). Ironically, the controversy over who would receive their due dominated the equity discussion prior to the election, while major news outlets neglected to raise the question of the effects of new sales taxes on families in a region hit hard by the emerging national foreclosure crisis and double-digit unemployment.

Despite the dissent, when the November 4 election day came, 64 percent of Los Angeles County voters supported Measure R. Metro moved ahead with plans for the funding.

The Win, the Future(s), and the Analysis for Planning

After the election, however, a new issue illustrated concerns about sales tax financing. As the California state budget crisis worsened, the state raised the sales tax by another 1 percent for three years. That move, along with Measure R, raised the total sales rate in LA from 8.25 percent to 9.75 percent (Doyle and Anderson 2009). The discussion finally turned to the tax's effect on low-income families. LA County consumers now faced out-of-pocket retail prices nearly 2 percent higher at a time with no real wage or employment growth.

In general, public finance research suggests that since low-income families tend to consume most of their income, sales tax payments are regressive—that is, poor families pay a higher portion of their income than do higher-income families (Poterba 1996, Derrick and Scott 1998). Nonetheless, public policy analysts are divided about the equity effects of sales taxes, particularly those targeted for transit investment. Sales taxes penalize spending up front rather than saving, earning, or investing, which are all activities that can promote long-term wealth acquisition. Unlike income taxes, consumers pay sales taxes at point of purchase, a little at a time, which stretches out the expense to cash-strapped families more than lump-sum taxes do.

Some sales tax research suggests that over a lifetime, sales taxes may be less hard on low-wage earners than cross-sectional analysis suggests. As individuals grow older, they buy fewer taxable goods (Feenberg, Mitrusi, and Poterba 1997, Schweitzer and Taylor 2008). Thus sales taxes may be less of a concern for low-income, house-rich seniors than property taxes (Mullins and Wallace 1996). But this equity benefit has its own consequences for localities, as an aging population can also mean a shrinking consumer base for sales taxes.

Despite the possible advantages of sales taxes for transit, the pursuit of sales tax dollars for transit measures remains a controversial subject for those interested in social justice. As important as it is to provide public transit for impoverished urban residents, ballot box measures and sales tax financing can prioritize politicians' and districts' needs for projects over riders' needs for service. The Los Angeles Bus Riders Union formed in the 1990s partly because of the perception that Metro's rail programs were throwing money at pursuing riders among better-off Angelenos who already had cars at the expense of impoverished bus riders (Brown 1998, Grengs 2002). Rail advocates tend to respond by arguing that all riders will benefit from a complete system, even if the investment is going to more affluent places. After all, West LA has many jobs and amenities, such as the ocean, that transit riders could benefit from.

Even if one can make a social justice argument in favor of rail investment, should general consumers pay to provide that service through taxable sales? In the case of rail investment, study after study has shown that landowners near stations can be major beneficiaries because of higher land values. For the Subway to the Sea project, that meant landowners in affluent West LA would benefit, probably a lot, and those gains in wealth are sheltered from taxation by Proposition 13 rules. Substituting sales taxes for land value capture redistributes money toward more affluent groups, even if the sales tax itself is not overly burdensome.

Even though 35 percent of Measure R's revenue goes to transit, 65 percent of the projects are road, freight, and local street/bike/pedestrian changes that could easily be funded out of ad valorem taxes on gasoline, tolls, or other user fees rather than through general sales taxes. Again, the beneficiaries of highway projects are likely to have higher incomes than transit riders or general consumers, and using sales taxes here rather than tolls again promises redistribution from lower to higher incomes. It also relieves system users of the costs associated with their infrastructure (Schweitzer and Taylor 2008). That may be a defensible policy for biking and walking, which are mode choices that society wants to encourage. But for freeway and freight infrastructure, both of which are polluting and potentially profit-making facilities, shifting the costs of driving and shipping onto consumers as a whole and away from those driving the demand for such facilities makes little sense from a social justice perspective.

Among the potential equity problems associated with sales taxes for local finance, perhaps none has been more apparent in California than the fiscalization of land use. With property taxes limited, revenue-hungry jurisdictions throughout the state have turned to sales tax measures just as Los Angeles County did (Lewis 2001, Byun and Esparza 2005). The result has been a direct fiscal incentive for jurisdictions to court retail development and discourage housing development, in particular low-end housing. Critics have argued that the sales tax finance and fiscal land-use policy have contributed to urban sprawl in California, with big-box retail stores, hotel complexes, and entertainment districts promising much higher returns to both developers and city coffers than housing for families. Tying transit funding to the sales tax adds a perverse element to the mix: those in most need would benefit from both transit and affordable housing, but the more you discourage the latter in favor of retail and commercial uses, the better the revenue opportunities from sales taxes.

In addition to all the potential equity problems, sales taxes have both opportunities and problems for the transit agencies themselves. As desperate as agencies are for new revenues, sales tax revenues are volatile, and they move in parallel with the larger regional economy. As a result, agencies that rely on sales taxes have little financial cushion when retail sales begin to plummet in a recession. Transit agencies thus lose revenues right when residents need comprehensive services the most—when they have lost work and need to cut back on using a car. Prior to Measure R, Metro already received half of its revenues from sales taxes. The recession beginning in 2008 contributed to large agency budget deficits, prompting the agency to raise fares temporarily and cut some bus services permanently—the opposite of enabling transit agencies and local governments to function as safety net services when individuals fall on hard times. Sales taxes do not allow agencies much discretion in how they provide service during economic downturns.

For the most part, the equity, incentive, and managerial arguments against sales tax financing have not gained much traction. Agencies and legislators throughout California have had few other options for raising revenues. It remains to be seen whether sales taxes continue to grow in importance to transit agencies, or whether things like Measure R stay a California strategy. If, as systems mature, agencies move both politicians and voters away from projects and toward operations, own-source local revenues like the sales tax could contribute to stabilizing transit agencies' budgets for both capital investment and operating revenues. If, however, ballot box planning requires agencies to shill new projects to far-flung, voter-rich suburbs while cutting existing services, sales taxes will simply reinforce transit's current, unsustainable finance structure.

Reducing Pollution at the Port

Meredith Drake Reitan

The American Lung Association recently reported that the communities surrounding the Port of Los Angeles and Long Beach rank among the worst in the nation for ozone and particulate matter exposure, two air pollutants closely associated with diesel trucks (American Lung Association 2011). In response to the dangers, the Port of Los Angeles established the Clean Trucks Program in 2008 (www.portoflosangeles .org/idx_environment.asp). Despite some early challenges, the program is one of the country's most successful antipollution measures.

Hailed by environmental groups and labor unions, the Clean Truck Program was the first program to be initiated under the port's Clean Air Action Plan (CAAP). It uses a combination of regulations and incentives to gradually replace older, polluting trucks with newer models that meet more stringent emission standards. The trucking fleet was included in the CAAP because the independent owner-operator trucking system that had evolved after trucking was deregulated in the 1990s resulted in a fleet of nearly 17,000 dirty trucks regularly entering and exiting the port.

Since the program's implementation, more than 6,600 clean trucks are operational at the port, including at least 600 natural gas, electric and hybrid trucks. Upgrading the truck fleet is estimated to reduce diesel particulate matter by at least 30 tons per year, the equivalent of removing nearly 250,000 automobiles from Southern California highways (Apollo Alliance 2010). The National Resources Defense Council (NRDC) has suggested that in the last three years, the Clean Truck Program has reduced air pollution at the port and in communities along freight transportation corridors by nearly 80 percent, a goal the Port of Los Angeles had originally planned to achieve by 2012 (NRDC 2010).

A key component of the Clean Truck Program is the "concession agreements" that make trucking companies responsible for truck maintenance. The agreements are supported by an estimated $1.6 billion in incentives to help companies make the transition to clean trucks. Another element of the program is the requirement that trucking companies make their drivers employees rather than independent contractors. According to LAANE, a local labor advocacy organization, the program has profound implications for drivers, more than 10,000 of whom will see major improvements in their working conditions (LAANE n.d.).

While the program has strong supporters, full implementation had been slowed by legal challenges. The American Trucking Association argued against the program, citing the Federal Aviation Administration Authorization Act, which restricts local governments from regulating the prices, routes, or services of trucking companies. However, in 2010, the U.S. District Court upheld the legality of the program's key features. Melissa Lin Perrella, senior attorney with NRDC's Southern California Air Program, says that "millions of people in port communities across the country are forced to subsidize the operations of outdated port operations with their lungs." The court's decision to allow the port to require cleaner trucks "sets the stage for healthier communities nationwide" (NRDC 2010).

Systemic Change Through CicLAvia

Aaron Paley and Amanda Berman

Ephemeral Intervention as a Tool for Urban Reform

Many visitors and Angelenos alike view the city as a massive, disconnected agglomeration, an unsustainable city. Their iconic images of LA are the Hollywood sign, the Pacific Ocean and its vast shoreline, twinkling lights emanating from the hills, and a sweeping overhead image of the intricate and infinite network of congested freeways and streets that cover the city's 490-some square miles. Rarely do they include the intimacy of a walkable, tree-lined neighborhood with an active street life; such an image is often saved for more European-style cities like New York, Chicago, Boston, and Philadelphia.

They do not imagine an LA with a compact, easily navigable urban environment. Still, countless efforts are under way to change these perceptions and alter the reality. In the last five years, such notable urban planning projects as Metro's Expo Line and Gold Line extensions, the Los Angeles Streetcar, the Los Angeles Bicycle Plan, the Downtown Urban Design Guidelines, and the Los Angeles River Revitalization Master Plan have pushed forward an agenda to make LA a more sustainable city—with an emphasis on walkability, public transit, the making of complete streets and vibrant neighborhoods, and the incorporation of public spaces.

A planning tool helping to redefine LA in the minds of its inhabitants is an "ephemeral intervention"—a temporary demonstration of how the city might function and feel with a radically redesigned transportation infrastructure. Impermanent events are part and parcel of the life of cities, but their ability to impact long-term planning as well as brick-and-mortar infrastructure is less documented. CicLAvia, a five-hour Sunday event during which downtown streets are closed to auto traffic, has created a lasting impact on the direction of LA planning and a sea change in public attitudes.

CicLAvia took place on October 10, 2010, occurred again in April and October 2011, and promises to reemerge in April 2012. Its organizers intend to move

Figure 5.15. An 1895 bicycle club

CicLAvia from a biannual event to a quarterly or monthly one within two years. They also hope to grow the route from an initial 7.5 miles to 10 and then 30 miles over the same period. In one of the most car-centric cities in America, CicLAvia temporarily transforms a section of LA from a sprawling, disconnected megalopolis to a cohesive and manageable city. For five brief hours, it acts as an ephemeral monument to the responsibility that the city holds to its own future, as well as the progress it has made

Figure 5.16. Some of the thousands of participants in CicLAvia

thus far—a new piece of LA iconography to which both Angelenos and "outsiders" can connect. As a result, it helps propel the larger conversation about creating a sustainable LA—often saved only for urbanists and policy makers—beyond the typical boundaries. A dialogue has begun around navigating this almost limitless city—a conversation that has grabbed the attention of the public and the media as well as academia.

Redrawing the Mental Map of Los Angeles

For many participants, CicLAvia radically alters their mental map of LA. Normally, Angelenos perceive their city in terms of time and aggravation, not space and mobility. The distance between two points is not about absolute mileage but instead is measured by the time necessary to get to the destination, as well as the emotional energy expended. CicLAvia makes part of the city suddenly feel intimate and pedestrian-scaled.

CicLAvia also stitches together a widely diverse set of dense, historic city center neighborhoods rarely thought of as an urban unit.[1] During rush hour, the drive along the CicLAvia route can take 45 minutes, giving drivers and passengers a sense they will never reach their destination. However, during CicLAvia, participants were pleasantly surprised to be able to ride a bicycle the 7.5-mile distance in about the same amount of time it would normally take them to drive. Neighborhoods that seemed too far away suddenly felt easy to reach. Most downtown workers would never imagine walking across the Fourth Street Bridge to stroll over to Boyle Heights' Hollenbeck Park for a break. Likewise, a resident of MacArthur Park would not likely bike to East Hollywood for an espresso at Cafecito Orgánico. But they do during CicLAvia.

Most surprisingly, CicLAvia makes the ride or stroll possible for all types of people. One story from the April 2011 CicLAvia illustrates the way the event repositions the city for participants: at the northern end of the route in East Hollywood, a father lost sight of his youngest daughter. Two hours later, he contacted the police because he still had

not found her. The police were sure they would find the girl close to where she was last seen. To everyone's surprise, she was located within 10 minutes—but at the opposite end of the CicLAvia route. She had ridden the 7.5 miles from East Hollywood through MacArthur Park, Downtown, Little Tokyo, and across the river into Boyle Heights by herself. Following the flow, she had no problems navigating the city and told officers that she had never felt afraid. CicLAvia is not just for hardy urban explorers; senior citizens, folks in wheelchairs, dog walkers, and even kids are able to easily use the route.

From Ciclovía to CicLAvia: Reframing the Project Beyond Bicycles

The idea to open city streets to bicycles and pedestrians on a regular basis was originally developed in Bogotá in 1974. Jaime Ortiz Mariño, a graduate student of urban planning at Case Western Reserve University in Ohio, had returned to his native Colombia inspired by the antiwar demonstrations and counterculture of the United States. Hoping to bring some of that American rebelliousness to his hometown, Jaime and several other activists launched *ciclovía* (a term the organizers coined that roughly translates as "bicycle path"). Ciclovía entered the lexicon of urban planners and urban activists throughout Latin America and then worldwide.

Gil Peñalosa greatly expanded ciclovía in the 1990s during his brother Enrique's mayoral term. Bogotá's ciclovía has grown to encompass 80 miles of contiguous roadway open to the public each Sunday and holiday of the year. Today, as many as 1.5 million Bogotanos take advantage of this public space every week of the year. Many other municipalities throughout Latin America adopted the model. Mexico City; Guadalajara; Puebla; Santiago, Chile; Quito, Ecuador; and Rosario, Argentina, are just some of the cities that run a regular ciclovía. Other cities have banned traffic on certain boulevards on a regular basis, including the internal streets of New York's Central Park, the riverfront of Cambridge, Massachusetts, and Paris's Right Bank. Winnipeg, Baltimore, Atlanta, New York, Portland, Oakland, San Francisco, and Melbourne, to name just a few, have since adopted "car-free" days along select streets.

When organizers in LA decided to adopt this form of "urban ephemera" they did not present CicLAvia as merely a temporary solution to the city's transportation issues through a day of cycling.[2] Instead, the all-volunteer group behind the program framed CicLAvia as a program to address multiple LA dilemmas: improving public health, increasing available public space, enhancing community and economic development, and promoting pedestrian and bicycle advocacy.

By looking at the project as a comprehensive urban intervention, CicLAvia's organizers managed to reframe the funding parameters, as well as open up the policy implications of the program. In its first attempt to raise funds for the initial event, CicLAvia successfully offered the following set of rationales to the California Endowment, a health-oriented philanthropy:

IMPROVING PUBLIC HEALTH: In the past decade, public health has become an overwhelming concern for health professionals, civic leaders, and urban planners, as well as the public at large. . . . CicLAvia has the potential to shift the public's perception of the Los Angeles landscape . . . [allowing those] usually intimidated by the vehicular traffic, including children, families, and seniors, to experience the joys of outdoor activity.

INCREASING AVAILABLE PUBLIC SPACE: Los Angeles is considered the most park-poor major city in the United States. For many neighborhoods—particularly in LA's communities of color—public park space is scant or non-existent. CicLAvia will temporarily ease this problem by providing an ad hoc public space for such neighborhoods—a newfound common ground on which to congregate and enjoy this democratic, outdoor activity. . . .

ENHANCING COMMUNITY AND ECONOMIC DEVELOPMENT: . . . CicLAvia will likely bring different populations and neighborhoods together, working to celebrate [LA's] diversity and multiculturalism. . . . By connecting several diverse city neighborhoods, CicLAvia will encourage residents to explore resources within and beyond their own communities. . . . The increased pedestrian traffic associated with CicLAvia events will translate into higher revenue for restaurants, cafés, and shops. . . . Miami business owners along that city's ciclovía route have noticed increased sales. . . . In fact, when the city proposed to implement a migrating route, business owners protested the move.

PROMOTING PEDESTRIAN AND BICYCLE ADVOCACY: . . . [CicLAvia] sends an iconic message to all that the city belongs to its people, not its vehicles. CicLAvia will offer all Angelenos a safe environment in which to recreate and enjoy their urban landscape. . . . CicLAvia will present the streets as a space for recreational and physical activity, while offering a more sustainable alternative to driving.[3]

The California Endowment presented CicLAvia with its first grant—$25,000 for its pilot program and $25,000 more for its second incarnation. The contextualization of CicLAvia through these four core issues helped the program receive funding from a variety of other foundations. The Rosenthal Family Foundation and the Metabolic Studio at the Annenberg Foundation came on board as general supporters to help jump-start change on multiple levels. Bikes Belong supported the project for its bicycle advocacy, while Metro, the region's public transit purveyor, clearly hoped to nurture new users for its trains and buses.[4]

CicLAvia was presented to Mayor Villaraigosa's office in October 2009 and was immediately adopted as a program goal by the mayor and his staff. Working with the mayor's team (led by Deputy Mayor for the Environment Romel Pascual), the CicLAvia team spent the next year working through the implementation details.

The city agreed to cover services including police, fire, and transit (approximately $200,000 per event), while the CicLAvia organization agreed to find approximately $110,000 to cover marketing, branding, event production, insurance, route expansion, and community relations. This division of funding and responsibilities continues.

Even with the support of the mayor, organizers had a complicated journey as they took CicLAvia from theory to reality. Serious obstacles continuously threatened the project. The four difficult hurdles were:

Proof of concept: an event with no beginning or end, no start or finish, taxed the imaginations of most everyone in positions of power. Because few had ever witnessed a similar event, it was difficult to explain to them just what CicLAvia would look like, let alone how it would run. The idea was so foreign that it appeared quixotic.

Risk and liability: Fearful of an accident between an automobile and cyclists or pedestrians—with ghosts of the Santa Monica Farmers Market tragedy on people's minds—the Department of Transportation insisted on total separation of cars and people.[5] Only after the volunteers' continued insistence that this was nonnegotiable and the mayor's intervention was a compromise fashioned allowing car traffic to cross the CicLAvia route. The decision came at a steep expense: four LAPD officers and four LADOT officers at each such intersection.

Funding: the city paid for its share of services through state funds earmarked for improving mobility and not usually used for temporary events. The nonprofit managed to scrape together its first set of funders mostly on the strength of individual board relationships with donors.

Audience: The emphasis on CicLAvia as a bicycle event threatened to overpower the more diverse and less easily grasped concept of CicLAvia as a program with manifold benefits. This singularity of purpose could, in the long run, undermine future funding as well as diverse participation.

CicLAvia's Initial Reception

CicLAvia's launch on October 10, 2010, was widely hailed as a success that affirmed LA's desire for such an ephemeral intervention. The coverage welcomed the event not only for the immediate happiness it gave its participants but also, as hoped, for how it exemplified the possibilities for urban design and social life change in the city.

An October 13, *Los Angeles Times* editorial estimated the crowd at 100,000 and stated, "Angelenos are used to street closures for events like the L.A. Marathon, but they've never seen anything like CicLAvia." Joel Rubin reported, "Unstructured by design, CicLAvia had no planned events. Organizers set up first-aid and information stations, along with portable toilets, at a few points along the route, but for the most part, they left it up to those who showed up to use the streets as they saw fit." Critically, he found, "It all made for a strangely quiet, serene scene. The city's police and fire departments reported no major incidents. Several people said the experience of gliding or strolling along streets empty of motor vehicles amounted to more than just a chance to get some exercise. "'We're alone in our cars. We pass above whole neighborhoods on freeways and never actually see them. Today, I've seen buildings I never took the time to lay eyes on before. Today gave people a chance to just slow down and it connected the neighborhoods of the city in a new way. That's important,'" said Rafael Navar (Rubin 2010). The *Times's* annual year-end editorial, "They Made Our Days," exceeded the hopes of the organizers when it stated simply: "More, please."

With a marketing budget of only $44,000 per event (which includes on-site signage, design, and public relations fees), CicLAvia organizers have been able to launch a new brand with widespread recognition in a market of 10 million people. CicLAvia received widespread traditional press coverage on traditional television, radio, and print, yet this old-school media coverage was only the most visible part of the media iceberg. With thousands of Facebook friends and Twitter followers, and an equal number of e-mail addresses, the CicLAvia organizers built up an impressive cadre of virtual fans—a YouTube search shows more than 425 videos posted by participants. This grassroots, viral following has characterized the program since its launch. Not only did it work to spread the CicLAvia message, it helped to attract a crowd that truly embodied the diversity of LA. The three rides brought together thousands of participants of all ages and ethnicities drawn from the entire LA basin.

CicLAvia offers Angelenos a glimpse into a possible alternative future, a demonstration of what life could be like without the constant traffic that characterizes LA. Those who took part were able to see their city in a new way. The *Los Angeles Times* reported the day after the pilot event that "people . . . talked with a sense of surprise that the city felt smaller and more manageable [during CicLAvia] . . . they had expected the journey from East Hollywood to Boyle Heights would take far longer and be far more arduous than it was" (Rubin 2010).

CicLAvia has helped fuel a campaign for change. Organizers are currently working with funding from the Los Angeles County Department of Public Health to provide technical assistance to six additional cities within Los Angeles County to expand the concept. Additionally, Santa Monica, Long Beach, Culver City, Pasadena, the San Fernando Valley, and many other cities and regions are all lining up for their own CicLAvias. With three ephemeral interventions, CicLAvia has inserted itself into the warp and woof of LA's consciousness and provoked a new perspective in the corridors of city hall and throughout its neighborhoods.

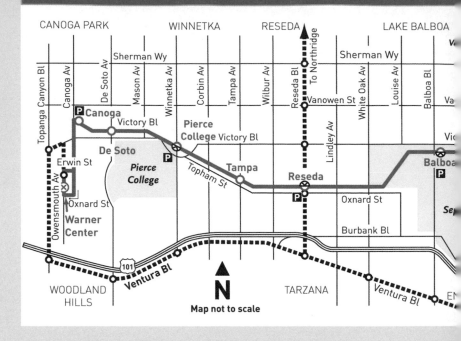

Map not to scale

A Train on Rubber Tires

Meredith Drake Reitan

Following a visit in 1998 to the pioneering public transit community of Curitiba, Brazil, Los Angeles Metro officials proposed constructing a similar system in Southern California. The Orange Line, which opened in October 2005, is one of the first full-featured bus rapid transit lines in the United States. A two-lane, 14-mile dedicated busway, the line includes an exclusive bus lane, high-capacity vehicles, extended distances between stops, frequent service, rail-like stations, and off-vehicle fare collection. The Orange Line connects the Red Line subway running from Union Station in downtown LA to the San Fernando Valley and allows workers living in the western edge of the city to take public transit to the city center. As a result the Orange Line has exceeded ridership projections; it performs so well that many commentators believe people are shifting from cars to public transit in an area of LA long considered auto-dependent (Vincent and Callaghan 2007, Stanger 2007).

The service operates 22 hours per day, seven days a week. Vehicles depart every five to six minutes during the morning and evening rush hours, every 10 minutes at midday, and every 15 to 20 minutes on weekends and other nonpeak times. The Orange Line runs along an existing but abandoned train line. It parallels the 101 Freeway through the San Fernando Valley, and land use along the line is mostly residential, including both single-family and low-rise multifamily housing. The corridor's commercial activity is focused around the Warner Center, Los Angeles County's third-largest employment center. A second commercial center is located in North Hollywood where the line meets the western terminus of the Red Line.

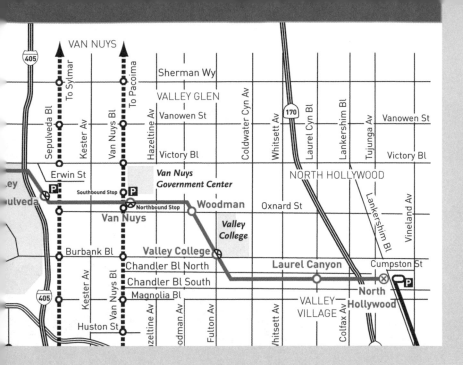

Initially, Metro faced opposition from a number of community groups that argued for the addition of more traditional busses rather than the Orange Line. A lawsuit was filed alleging that Metro overestimated the Orange Line's benefits and that an expansion of the existing rapid bus service would provide comparable time savings at a significantly lower cost. MTA had projected an average of 5,000 to 7,500 weekday boardings for the first year of Orange Line service and 22,000 by 2020. Remarkably, by May 2006, only seven months after opening, the Orange Line had almost achieved its 2020 goal, attracting more than 21,000 weekday boardings on average. Metro estimates that the Orange Line logged about six million boardings in its first 12 months.

While usage is high, the Orange Line's travel time goals have not been met. The Orange Line crosses 34 streets and at least five midblock pedestrian crosswalks. Detectors were installed to give traffic signal priority to the Orange Line. Soon after the busway opened, however, several collisions occurred, most frequently caused by cars running red lights. In response, Metro has reduced speed through intersections from 25 mph to 10 mph, affecting overall efficiencies.

Despite the longer trip time, the Orange Line appears to be performing better than other rail lines which cost more but carry fewer passengers. As a result of its success, Metro's board of directors has recently approved an extension. Scheduled to be completed in summer 2012, the line will be extended north to the Chatsworth Metrolink Station and will include the construction of four new stations. Additional bike and pedestrian paths will also be built along the dedicated busway.

PARKS AND PUBLIC SPACE

6

Green Spaces in the Auto Metropolis

Anastasia Loukaitou-Sideris

Many decades before landscape urbanists started urging us to look holistically at metropolitan landscapes, emphasizing and privileging their existing natural systems (Waldheim 2006), the Olmsted Brothers and Harland Bartholomew Associates presented a sweeping green vision for the LA basin. As documented by Hise and Deverell (2000 and later in this chapter), their report *Parks, Playgrounds, and Beaches for the Los Angeles Region,* published in 1930, envisioned an interlaced network of about 70,000 acres of existing and proposed parks, playgrounds, forests, parkways, and waterways. These multiple lungs, the planners believed, would ensure the livability of the growing metropolis.

As we all know, the plan's vision was never realized in LA. Another network, not of parks and open spaces but of freeways, was superimposed on the region. An alternative vision was promoted for the City of Angels, and the thousands of acres of parkland that the Olmsted Brothers had suggested be reserved were quickly paved over, the embankments of the city's river concretized, and its extensive public transit network dismantled.

In the last decade, a number of activist voices have been raised from different circles (environmentalists, smart growth advocates, transit advocates, bikers, and park advocates) arguing for an overhaul of this unfettered, car-centric development. They call for a more compact and mixed use urban form, a reinvented transit system, a "complete streets" network that can accommodate different modes of transportation and support walking and biking, and more parks. The greening of the city through the acquisition of new parkland and the reclaiming of the Los Angeles River loom high in this activist agenda.

Few people would disagree with a greener vision for LA. However, creating an open space network in the region faces a variety of challenges. My purpose here, therefore, is to lay out the specific challenges but also the opportunities that

Angelenos are facing in regards to parks. I will discuss four interrelated aspects of park provision and use: (1) the inadequate supply of parks and open spaces; (2) their inequitable distribution throughout LA; (3) the phenomenon of nonuse and relative underutilization of some parks; and (4) the challenges of addressing different and competing open space needs for an increasingly heterogeneous public. I will close with a discussion of opportunities and suggestions.

Why Parks?

Incontestably, urban parks are desirable assets for cities. Parks, playgrounds, and urban greens are valued as physical settings because they can satisfy certain leisure, recreational, and social needs. Parks offer visual and psychological relief in high-pace urban communities and contribute to the quality of life and overall sense of well-being of urban dwellers. Parks can also serve as a substitute for nature in cities, offering important environmental benefits. Their trees and vegetation reduce ambient heat levels and offer sequestration of air pollution, while their "softscape" allows natural water filtration and absorbs runoff.

Additionally, parks are considered important settings for the social and cognitive development of young children (Hart 1979, Saegert and Hart 1978) and for the physical activity of children and adults. They can offer younger children opportunities for free play, discovery, and exploration of nature, allowing them to interact in environments that are less restrictive than those of the school and the home (Proshanski and Fabian 1987). Recently and increasingly, evidence has linked park visits to health benefits for active users. In light of the recent and alarming epidemic of obesity in the United States, parks have the potential to increase physical activity for both children and adults because they offer active-recreation facilities close to where people live (Floyd et al. 2008, Cohen et al. 2007 and 2006).

Further, in a rather insular society characterized by privateness and individualism, the public space of parks provides settings for socializing with peers and chances for encounters with a larger public. The more interactive and public experiences offered by parks are in sharp contrast to the more passive and insular behaviors encouraged by television, computers, and electronic games (Burgess, Harrison, and Limb 1988).

In general, parks and open spaces offer a variety of aesthetic, psychological, social, educational, and physiological benefits to their users, and different social groups are found to enjoy or privilege different park qualities (Loukaitou-Sideris 1995). Nevertheless, LA officials encounter increasing difficulty in providing the appropriate amount of park acreage with the right mix of park services.

Inadequate Supply

In densely built urban areas, large repositories of open land have almost disappeared, and the cost of the few remaining pieces is quite prohibitive. The dramatic fiscalization of land and decreasing property tax revenues have made the creation of new parks and the expansion and upgrading of existing ones difficult and expensive propositions. California's Proposition 13, which passed in 1978, and similar tax-cut measures in 37 other states have seriously challenged municipal budgets. At the same time, parks and open spaces do not represent a profitable use of land in a monetary sense, as they do not produce property or sales tax revenue for cities, even though they have been often shown to increase the values of adjacent properties. As a result, the supply of public parks has severely lagged behind the growth of urban population in many cities.

In the fast-growing cities of the West Coast, particularly LA, the growth in urban park acreage is nowhere near proportional to the growth of urban areas. A recent report on parks in the largest U.S. metropolitan areas found that LA, which has only 7.9 percent of the total land devoted to parks, ranks last of all the big cities of the West Coast (Trust for Public Land 2010) (see Table 6.1) and is close to the bottom when compared to other large U.S. cities (Harnik 2000). The LA Parks and Recreation Department's $60 per resident spending for parks in 2010 is well below the per capita spending of San Diego ($120), San Francisco ($192), Portland ($157), and Seattle ($252). Park acreage in Los Angeles is just 6.2 acres per 1,000 residents, lower than the national standards that recommend up to 10 acres (National Recreation and Parks Association 2000).[1]

Table 6.1: Comparison of parkland among major West Coast cities						
City	City population (2010)	Pop. density (persons/ acre)	Park acreage per 1,000 residents	Park space as % of city area	Park play- ground per 10,000 residents	Park expenditures per resident (FY 2008)
Los Angeles	3,833,995	12.8	6.2	7.9	1.0	$ 60
San Diego	1,305,754	6.3	36.1	22.7	1.8	$120
San Francisco	808,976	27.1	6.7	18.0	1.8	$192
Seattle	598,541	11.1	9.1	10.2	2.2	$252
Portland	557,706	6.5	24.2	15.7	1.9	$157
Source: Trust for Public Land 2010						

Public financing for park creation and maintenance has been uneven, though always limited. Even though a variety of options may be used to finance parks, ranging from property taxes, general obligation and revenue bonds, special assessment districts, impact fees, user fees, and real estate transfer taxes, parks compete with other public goods and services, such as education, policing, and public libraries, for limited public funds. In the first years after the passing of Proposition 13, the City of LA had to close 24 recreation centers and reduce the funds or cut the operating hours of the remaining centers (Schwadron and Richter 1984). Between 1972 and 1998 the city acquired fewer than 1,000 acres for parks (Wolch, Wilson, and Fehrenbach

2002). The good economic climate of the early 1990s brought some funding to LA parks. In 1992, Los Angeles County voters passed Proposition A, which assured $550 million for parks, with $126 million dedicated to parks in the city of LA.

In 1996, voters approved Proposition K, a park bond assuring $750 million in park improvements for Los Angeles County and $25 million per year for 25 years for the city. But many Proposition K projects faced delays and cost overruns. Proposition K funding, which was allocated through a competitive process, did not reach all neighborhoods equally. Examining the impact of Proposition K, Wolch et al. (2002, 27) found that "communities of color [and] areas with the largest shares of young people received half as much Proposition K funding on a per youth basis than areas with the least concentration of children, and more privileged sub-areas with the highest rates of accessibility received as much if not more bond funds."

California voter support for parks and open spaces continued into the new century, with electoral approval of a number of general obligation bonds to fund parks. In 2000, Proposition 12 allocated $519 million for additions and improvements to California state parks and $845 million to local park grants. In 2002, Proposition 40 provided $2.2 billion for a variety of environmental needs, which included funds for the acquisition of new parklands and the improvement of existing ones. In 2006, Proposition 84 included $400 million in park funds.

Despite this infusion of bond funds for parks, a 2006 audit by the LA city controller's office found: "Overall, the Department has sufficient authorized staff to effectively maintain the recreation and park assets. However, the City has not allocated sufficient ongoing funding to preserve, rehabilitate, and renew these assets" (City of LA 2006). Continuing criticism also questioned the equity in the distribution of bond funds for parks to underserved communities (Planning and Conservation League Foundation 2005, Garcia et al. 2009).

Some rare opportunities for substantial and centrally located new development of park space in LA appeared when the state acquired the 32-acre site of the Cornfields, north of Chinatown, and by the Santa Monica Mountains Conservancy's purchase of parcels of industrial land at the confluence of the Los Angeles River and the Arroyo Seco (also the confluence of freeways I-10, I-110, and I-5). But the deep economic crisis of recent years has postponed any significant work on these sites.[2] The most recent communitywide needs assessment conducted by the Recreation and Parks Department (2009) found unmet citizen needs for neighborhood and community parks and open space.

Uneven Allocation

The inadequate supply of parks and open spaces in LA is more pronounced in some neighborhoods than others (Table 6.2). While at first glance the parks seem to be quite uniformly distributed throughout the metropolitan region, examining the allocation of open space in relation to need shows a different picture (Figure 6.1).[3] Los Angeles inner-city neighborhoods have the highest need for parks yet enjoy a much lower acreage of neighborhood parks per capita than the more affluent suburban neighborhoods of the San Fernando Valley. Site visits to the parks in the two districts revealed differences in their quality. While the inner-city parks had more sport fields and indoor facilities, their levels of maintenance and cleanliness were lagging far behind their counterparts (Loukaitou-Sideris and Stieglitz 2002).

Table 6.2: Neighborhood park acreage and child obesity by council district				
Council district	Total population	Total acres of parks[1]	Park acreage/ 1,000 residents	% of obese children
1	232,156	1,115	4.80	28.2
2	255,446	4,695	18.38	24.1
3	258,751	1,565	6.05	19.3
4	249,774	4,026	16.12	24.3
5	262,165	3,197	12.19	18.1
6	239,516	1,691	7.06	29.0
7	230,406	1,426	6.19	28.8
8	243,269	387	1.59	29.3
9	238,924	142	0.59	29.1
10	245,150	106	0.43	25.9
11	255,674	14,748	57.68	20.3
12	239,188	3,794	15.86	21.2
13	244,777	236	0.97	27.8
14	236,224	501	2.12	26.6
15	252,219	946	3.75	27.3
Sources: City Project 2006, Los Angeles County Department of Public Health 2007				

Inner City District

[1]Includes the Los Angeles National Forest and the Santa Monica Mountains National Recreation area

Following the passage of Proposition 13, the ensuing loss of revenue for park acquisition and operations did not affect neighborhoods equally. Parks in affluent suburban coastal and valley areas were able to absorb the impact by imposing user fees for park programs and classes (e.g., swimming and water polo classes) or by allowing different groups to use the athletic fields. Parks in low-income inner-city communities, however, saw a dramatic reduction of their staff, space, and services (Schwadron and Richter 1984). Similarly, the Quimby Act, a state law passed in 1975 that requires developers to pay a fee for park development or set aside land for parks in the immediate vicinity of their project, has favored newer suburban subdivisions and has done little to increase the park supply in built-up inner-city areas (Wolch, Wilson, and Fehrenbach 2002).

As critics worried would happen, the recent infusion of bond funds has not helped to close the open-space gap between wealthy and poor areas of the city. Thus, Latino

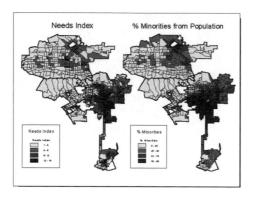

Figure 6.1. Needs index and percentage of minority population in the inner city and valley regions of Los Angeles

neighborhoods on average have only 1.6 acres per 1,000 residents, African American neighborhoods enjoy on average 0.8 acres per 1,000 residents, and Asian–Pacific Islander–dominated neighborhoods have 1.2 acres per 1,000 residents, while white-dominated neighborhoods have on average 17.4 acres per 1,000 residents, partly because they encompass the Santa Monica Mountains (Wolch, Wilson, and Fehrenbach 2002). In its 2006 audit, the controller's office concluded that "lower income neighborhoods, including those predominantly populated by Latinos, African American and Asian/Pacific Islander communities, have dramatically less access to park resources than more affluent areas" (City of LA 2006).

Inequity in parklands and resources is particularly distressing because many inner-city children lack alternative play spaces. For many inner-city kids the neighborhood park serves as an extension of their house, a viable alternative to the often absent backyard and private play space. They frequent the park after school and on weekdays and weekends to meet with their peers and find space for play and sport activities. In contrast, suburban children enjoy the neighborhood park as a place for family picnics and Little League games, primarily on weekends. Their attachment to the neighborhood park is weaker because the park is only one of many possible venues for recreation and play (Loukaitou-Sideris and Stieglitz 2002).

Inequity in park distribution may also translate into health disparities. A 2007 survey conducted in 128 cities and communities by the county Department of Health and Human Services found that obesity was strongly associated with economic hardship. Cities with fewer parklands, playgrounds, and other recreational areas, trails, or wilderness areas were more likely to have a higher prevalence of obese children.

Nonuse and Underutilization

Ironically, despite the scarcity of green open spaces in the region, many parks remain underutilized and devoid of social uses and activities. We hypothesized that this paradox exists because some parks suffer from poor accessibility, a perception of lack of safety, and lack of programs or facilities appealing to the needs and values of a diverse population. We conducted a systematic observation of 50 inner-city and 50 valley parks during May and June 2007 (Loukaitou-Sideris and Sideris 2009). In general, inner-city parks were more heavily utilized than valley parks because of higher population densities, residential overcrowding, and the relative lack of backyards and private open spaces in the inner city. Eight of the observed parks in the San Fernando Valley contained no children at all during our observation times, while another 10 parks contained fewer than 10 children each (Figure 6.2). Half of all the parks observed each contained fewer than 50 children. Only five parks in the inner city and four parks in the valley had more than 200 children (Figure 6.3).

Since we were not going to find nonusers at the parks, we surveyed 897 children and 348 parents in 12 Los Angeles Unified School District (LAUSD) middle schools located in close proximity to some of the observed parks. We found that 20 percent of these children never go to the park for a variety of reasons, which include lack of time, lack of interest, negative perceptions about the park, availability of other alternatives for recreation, and challenges of accessibility.

The vast majority of parents interviewed did not allow their middle-school children to go to the park alone or stay there without adult supervision. Not surprisingly, the lack of parental time for visits to the park emerged as a most important reason for nonuse. Some children, primarily girls, said that they had outgrown the park, elaborating that they found the park "boring" and preferred other activities such as spending time at friends' houses or at the mall or playing video games at home. A number of children, primarily from more affluent backgrounds, reported being physically active in alternative settings such as athletic clubs, private pools, or private ballet classes.

Other children viewed the park as "unsafe," "dirty," or "too far from home." A survey of park users by the city controller's office reported that half of the respondents were reluctant to visit neighborhood parks out of concern for their personal safety (City

Figure 6.2. Empty playground at Bee Canyon Park, in the San Fernando Valley

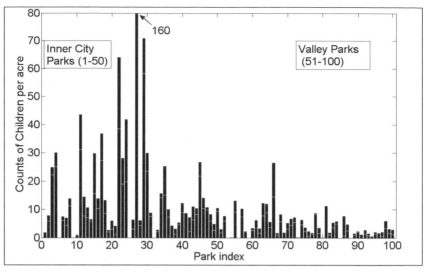

Figure 6.3. Distribution of children, normalized by park acreage

of LA 2006), while a study by the RAND Corporation found that the most common user response for suggested improvements to neighborhood parks was safety (Cohen et al. 2006). In our survey, more than three-quarters of all parents in both the inner city and suburban regions stated that they do not allow their children to go to the park without an adult, mostly because of concerns about crime and traffic. Girls had decidedly less independent mobility than boys.

Lack of easy access to parks may be an additional reason for nonuse. Since the origins of urban planning in the early decades of the 20th century, planners have envisioned parks and playgrounds as important neighborhood assets that had to be in close proximity to residences. But good accessibility to parks remains challenging in California, where more than a quarter of teenagers report having no access to a safe park, playground, or open space for physical activity (Babey, Brown, and Hastert 2005). Most of them live in disadvantaged neighborhoods and have no access to private open space, either.

A study by the UCLA Center for Health Policy Research found that the complete lack of physical activity is higher for teenagers living in apartment buildings, presumably because they have no access to private open space. For adolescents who live in apartment housing, access to a safe park increases the prevalence of physical activity by almost 10 percent and cuts the percentage getting no physical activity by 50 percent (Babey, Brown, and Hastert 2005). In LA, poor accessibility to parks is more severe than in many other major cities. Only about a quarter of the city's population lives within a quarter-mile of a neighborhood playground or park facility (Yanez and Muzzy 2005). Only 33 percent of school children in LA live within a quarter-mile of a park, compared with 97 percent in Boston and 91 percent in New York City (Schoch 2007).

In our survey, however, proximity to a park was not found to be a very significant factor in park use by suburban children, presumably because of the availability of other open space alternatives. More Valley children (44 percent) than inner-city children (27 percent) reported living within five minutes of a park, yet a higher proportion of Valley children never visited parks. While people are commonly expected to walk to their neighborhood parks, most of the children interviewed in both regions of LA were driven to the park (Loukaitou-Sideris and Sideris 2009).

Misfit between User Needs and Park Offerings

The final challenge concerns a frequent lack of good fit between desirable park uses and their design and programming. The neighborhood park of the early 21st century is typically expected to serve myriad purposes and satisfy diverse users. Park suppliers try to respond to this challenge by following the norm of the "average user," but this often fails to satisfy the different use patterns and needs of men, women, children, young adults, the elderly, or different ethnic groups. The typical neighborhood park design mixes elements from past park models, providing greenery, athletic fields, and picnic areas. It tries to create an easily reproducible and standardized milieu, one that seeks to be multiuse but is also without context and possibly insensitive to cultural and social specificities (Loukaitou-Sideris 1995).

Nowhere is standardization more evident than in the playground facilities, which for the most part fail to provide any elements of discovery or surprise in children's play (Figure 6.4). Some attribute the uninspired playground design to overwhelming concerns about safety and the fear of lawsuits. As Arieff (2007) argues: "American playgrounds often seem anything but playful. Their equipment is designed not so much to let children have fun as to make sure they don't hurt themselves....Well-meaning efforts to reduce risk of injury have overwhelmed opportunities for self-expression and creativity." As a result, many children "vote with their feet," choosing not to utilize park facilities. This result is particularly true for girls, who are significantly underrepresented in neighborhood parks.

Studies have found that urban residents of different genders, races and ethnicities, and socioeconomic backgrounds have different park preferences (Loukaitou-Sideris and Sideris 2009). Yet typical park design and programming, which tends to favor the classical American sports and active recreation, does not account for these diverse needs. For example, many Chinese immigrants in Monterey Park, a suburb with high concentration of Chinese Americans, use their neighborhood parks very sparsely, and they view them as poorly landscaped. Their ideal of a park as an outdoor urban garden, richly landscaped with flowers and water elements, was not met by the utilitarian park design that featured baseball diamonds, basketball courts, and playgrounds (Loukaitou-Sideris 1995). The underrepresentation of certain age, gender, or ethnic groups at parks is likely partly the result of a misfit between their needs and preferences and the park offerings.

Emerging Opportunities

Despite the challenges surrounding the provision and allocation of parks in LA, there is also ground for some optimism. First, and despite American voters' widespread distaste for new taxes, California voters have shown their support for urban parks by approving ballot measures and taxing themselves for additional park resources.

Second, an important coalition of grassroots groups fighting for more parks and open spaces has emerged, which not only includes long-standing park advocates

Figure 6.4. Standardized playground design, Branford Park, in the San Fernando Valley

such as the Sierra Club, the Trust for Public Land, the Santa Monica Mountains Conservancy, and the Audubon Society but also smaller community and nonprofit organizations such as the Friends of the Los Angeles River, Alianza del Rio, North East Trees, People for Parks, the City Project, and Mujeres de la Tierra.

Third, for the first time in the last 50 years, the region has been able to identify and designate large pieces of land for park space. In South Central LA, the Santa Monica Mountains Conservancy has converted a former cement pipe storage yard into the 8.5-acre Augustus F. Hawkins Natural Park. At the western edge of downtown, the conservancy, in collaboration with the Mountains Recreation and Conservation Authority, the LAUSD, and the city, has developed the 10.5-acre Vista Hermosa Park. As a result of activist efforts, the abandoned 32-acre railyard near Chinatown has been claimed as the Cornfields Park, while the El Toro Marine Corps Air Station, between Irvine and Lake Forest, will be transformed into Orange County's Grand Park. While the weak economy has slowed down these two efforts considerably, they both represent significant land resources that have been dedicated as parklands.

Fourth, with vision, political will, and adequate funding, LA has the opportunity to convert an environmental liability to an environmental and green space asset. The Los Angeles River, which runs for about 52 miles, passes through many underserved and park-poor neighborhoods. Great opportunities for riverfront park development in these neighborhoods exist if parts of the river are restored.

Fifth, there is an emerging realization among the relevant city agencies that they need to "do better" in addressing the challenges and open space needs of a growing and diverse city. In 2006, the city controller's audit of the recreation and parks department emphasized the need to improve park services in all neighborhoods, mitigate the inequities in the allocation of parkland and resources through a fair system of park financing, and seek to understand and address the diverse needs of the residents. In 2008, the city established the Los Angeles Parks Foundation, a nonprofit that serves as the fundraising arm of the recreation and parks department. In 2009, the department initiated a communitywide needs assessment that involved focus groups, community forums, and resident surveys.

Rethinking Neighborhood Parks

These opportunities are encouraging, but how can parks appeal to a larger and more diverse segment of the public? The multiplicity of roles that the urban park is expected to play is challenging and at times creates conflict among competing user groups. More often, however, many potential park users simply do not go to the park because it does not satisfy their needs. What is the proper role or roles that urban parks should serve? Should they be designed as green oases for peaceful retreat, relaxation, and mediation? Should they be facilities for active recreation and fervent group play? Or should some be more simply social spaces for community involvement and cultural exchange?

Certainly, one size does not fit all. Instead of replicating the same standardized model, park providers should give some thought to the type of park activities and programming that suit the needs of different user groups. LA, as a diverse and multicultural city, needs a diversity of parks—large and small, centrally and peripherally located, for active and passive recreation, with "hardscape" and "softscape" settings. Parks should be within easy reach of neighborhoods, in particular the poorer parts of the city that are deficient in both public and private open spaces.

Large and centrally located parks are blessings for cities because they can host a variety of facilities and programs. But large expanses of open land are exceedingly difficult to find and acquire in dense and highly urbanized areas. And in large and sprawling cities like LA, even centrally located parks are far from many residents. Parks and recreation departments should not forget that small green spaces in neighborhoods can also offer recreational opportunities and environmental benefits. Los Angeles has a plethora of underutilized or empty lots and vacant spaces under freeways and along obsolete railway lines and the concrete banks of the Los Angeles River. They can be converted into miniparks and adventure playgrounds, jogging trails, and biking paths. Following Aldo van Eyck's example in Amsterdam, leftover spaces in between buildings of dense downtown districts and formerly unsightly urban artifacts can be transformed into urban playgrounds.[4] Partnerships among parks and recreation departments, nature conservancies, and school districts, along with shared uses, should be also considered in the most dense and undersupplied neighborhoods of the region. One could even think of mobile playgrounds, spaces whose equipment and furniture can be transported to other parts of the city as the need arises.

Parks should not be seen in isolation but rather in connection to one another and to other land uses, such as housing and schools. Planners should make parks as accessible as possible to children and adults by considering their links to the adjacent neighborhoods, the safety of the routes, and the pedestrian and bicycling environment leading to the park.

In addition to reshaping the traditional patterns of active and passive recreation, we should rethink park programming and activities and introduce less conventional uses in parks, if these are deemed appropriate by the surrounding communities. Cultural events, after-school programs, urban gardening, and even entrepreneurial activities and volunteerism can take place in some parks. At the same time, the educational and environmental potential of parks, presently quite unexplored and underdeveloped, can be cultivated to offer opportunities for learning more about ecology and nature. In particular, park designers should address the claims of some children who find the standardized playground and park setting "boring" (Loukaitou-Sideris and Sideris 2009). Other programs such as films, crafts, music, water games, skateboarding, rock climbing, and even electronic games may provide incentives for more children to use the park.

Studies have shown that some groups are more represented in parks than others (Loukaitou-Sideris 1995). To address the challenge of nonuse, we should consider who is not present at the park and why. The underrepresentation of girls in parks is particularly problematic. Not coincidentally, public health officials warn that teenage girls are more prone to sedentary lifestyles. Parents are more reluctant to leave their girls alone at the park, and in general girls are less satisfied than boys by the parks' equipment and programming (Loukaitou-Sideris and Sideris 2009). The increase of supervised activities in parks may appease parents' concerns about safety. Additionally, offering more programs geared toward girls and girls' sports may bring more girls to the park.

Eighty years ago, the Olmsted Brothers and Harland Bartholomew Associates plan prompted LA city fathers to preserve land and convert it into a network of green open spaces and playgrounds. Although LA has more than tripled its population since 1930, it has only about one-fifth of the parkland the plan was calling for. Today, LA parks are no longer sufficient to address the needs of a vastly expanded and heterogeneous public. Moreover, the needs of children and adults have significantly changed and cannot be captured by the early models of park design. Unfortunately, park suppliers have not always responded to the challenges of inadequate park supply, inequitable allocation, underutilization, and frequent misfit between park form and programming and the needs of some Angelenos. Nevertheless, the belief that parks and green open spaces are critical urban amenities that can fulfill a host of different recreational, social, educational, environmental, and health benefits has re-emerged and is now shared by a wide platform of nonprofits, environmentalists, and community groups. The time is right to rethink neighborhood parks and recapture the spirit of the Olmsted and Bartholomew plan.

The Afterlife of a Master Plan

Greg Hise and William Deverell

I DO NOT BELIEVE THERE IS A MORE CRYING NEED ANY PLACE IN THE
WORLD FOR PARKS THAN RIGHT HERE IN LOS ANGELES.
—CHAMBER OF COMMERCE DIRECTOR CAREY HILL, 1929

WE HAVE ALL THE PARKS WE WANT DOWN HERE AS I SEE IT.
—CHAMBER OF COMMERCE DIRECTOR WILLIAM LACY, 1929

Politics and a Big Plan

On March 7, 2000, 63 percent of California voters approved Proposition 12, a $2.1 billion bond initiative designed to fund park improvements and maintain the state's coastline and beaches.[1] Given the sums involved, readers should not be surprised to learn that Southern Californians who attended candidate forums that spring heard LA mayoral hopefuls refer to a comprehensive master plan as they touted the need for additional parks, playgrounds, and open space. On more than one occasion, opposing candidates James Hahn and Antonio Villaraigosa held such a master plan aloft while delivering forceful commitments to restore the Los Angeles River, create a new center city park at the Cornfield site near downtown, and cap toxic waste that endangered the health of children playing on Los Angeles Unified School District (LAUSD) playgrounds and sports fields.

What may surprise many is that the report they brandished was decades older than the politicos themselves. Dusted off after 70 years of neglect, a 1930 vision of a different landscape future seemingly had new life breathed into it. With an ambition belying its banal title, that report, *Parks, Playgrounds, and Beaches for the Los Angeles Region,* had at last gained some of the attention its authors, Olmsted Brothers and Harland Bartholomew and Associates, and their client, the Los Angeles Area Chamber of Commerce, first imagined in 1927. Three years of survey, analysis, and design by two of the leading planning firms in the nation and their local consultants had resulted in a proposal for neighborhood playgrounds and local parks linked to regional "reservations" along the Pacific coastline and interspersed across the surrounding foothills, mountains, and desert. Their bold vision encompassed an area of more than 1,500 square miles stretching from the Antelope Valley to the harbor in Long Beach, from the beaches in Malibu to Riverside County. Why their client came to see the study as dan-

Figure 6.5. The beach at the mouth of Santa Monica Canyon, which the report noted shows a private club and parking area competing with public uses.

gerous, as a threat to its authority and power, and how its members worked to suppress the product they had funded and that its Parks and Recreation Committee endorsed is the subject of the introduction in our book, *Eden by Design* (2000, 1–63).

That essay describes how, as greater LA grew through the first decades of the 20th century, civic awareness of a distinct lack of environmental planning (from both public and private sectors) grew as well. Urban and suburban expansion in the LA basin had occurred more quickly than did any broad awareness of planning deficits. Voices were and had been raised about the need to think through how LA expanded. By the mid-1920s, these disparate voices had coalesced into what we might call a minimovement to do something. Backed by private subscriptions primarily garnered from wealthy film and manufacturing elites, a committee spun from the LA Chamber of Commerce made a pitch to Olmsted Brothers of Massachusetts: Would you come to Southern California and design a new landscape future for the City of Angels?

Three years of on-the-ground planning ensued, with Frederick Law Olmsted Jr. and Harland Bartholomew presiding over a talented collection of landscape, engineering, and planning professionals. Regular updates went to the client committee as well as the umbrella body of the chamber. Experienced in the ways of planning, politics, and fiscal matters, the lead designers and their local representatives matched visionary landscape design with hardheaded financial and political exigencies.

Parks, Playgrounds, and Beaches contained fewer than 200 pages, yet it presented three essential paths toward a vastly different LA future. First, the plan linked open space and greenbelts in a bold, even brash, design that could be described

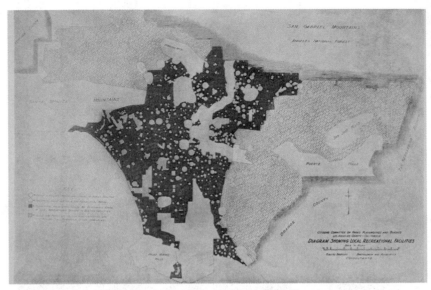

Figure 6.6. The map highlighted in dark the residential areas considered "outside the range" of local recreational facilities.

as laying an "emerald necklace" across Southern California. Second, it laid out the pathways that could bring together the bonded, borrowed, and other necessary financing. Third, the planners reminded their client that big plans necessitated big, or at least big-enough, governance. The report sketched out a superjurisdictional political organization needed to effectively manage their comprehensive vision.

Eighty years later, it all looks so straightforward, even dry, in its clarity. It makes sense. Yet visionary planning is good only if it can be implemented and, once executed, cared for. The downfall was dramatic. The plan was initially to be printed in hundreds, if not thousands, of copies so that distribution could be far and wide in public and governance constituencies in LA. But the presses were stopped just as they had started. Fewer than 200 copies of the plan were printed, its status thus instantly changed from primer to rare book.

Why? The planners had misread the reaction of the chamber, which controlled the client committee. They did not object to the plan or even to the way it was to be financed. The chamber, and especially its executive committee ruling body, did resent being barred any oversight role of a greenscape future they had caused to be imagined in the first place. Though Olmsted et al. were right to propose a superjurisdictional body to oversee what was expressly a superjurisdictional plan, the chamber proved entirely—adamantly—unwilling to cede any authority to an upstart body; that prospect was, to quote one chamber member, simply "terrifying" (Hise and Deverell 2000, 39). Lacking any animating reception whatsoever, the report languished and inexorably disappeared from sight and thought.

To be fair to the historical record, the plan did not *totally* disappear from view. It made occasional, even casual, appearances in this or that planning document of the World War II and Cold War eras; the references were rarely more than nods, even quaint nods, in the plan's direction. Occasionally, a facet or section of the plan would actually be instituted—a crafted boulevard here or a park project there—but in a sense even these projects belittled the plan because they were anything but comprehensive.

Only in 2000, with our republication of the plan, did a document limited to a paltry print run, that had been treated in 1930 more as a keepsake than as a working document, come to serve as a touchstone and to engender a public conversation about the uneven, and inequitable, distribution of playgrounds, parks, and outdoor recreation in the city and county (e.g., Garcia and White 2006, Wolch, Wilson, and Fehrenbach 2002).

Partiality and Appropriation

In our introduction, we asked readers to consider whether making the Olmsted-Bartholomew report available to a broad audience might encourage design professionals, elected officials, and citizen planners to use the document as a basis for a renewed public discourse about current and future development in LA, Southern California, and beyond. In other words, might discovery lead to a recovery; might learning *about* the report lead readers to learn *from* it? Whether the excitement of 10 years ago—the plan as mayoral election prop—has led to much of anything in the way of landscape reconstitution will be determined with time. Yet in the short term a variety of institutional, activist, public, and individual actors have begun to rethink and "re-scape" the Los Angeles River. That vision, or those visions, are indebted to the Olmsted-Bartholomew plan in many ways, and in their allegiance to that plan, as well as their willingness to think well beyond it, these actors are thinking big in their own right.[2]

Today, newer voices are dusting off the report. As we write this, the Urban Design Studio, a subunit within LA's Department of City Planning, is considering creation of a "Ten-Mile Loop" that would link parks with public transportation. Simon Pastucha, the head of Urban Design Studio (see Pastucha's essay in this chapter), informed us that reference to particular aspects of the Olmsted-Bartholomew report has facilitated his study of fundamental issues in the city and region: the need for additional neighborhood scale parks, how to encourage exercise, and how to stimulate ridership for mass transit. Whereas the Olmsted and Bartholomew proposal used roads and trails, Urban Design Studio's plan would rely on a rail network to connect parks included in the 1930 report (Echo and Elysian parks, for example) with parks, developed during the intervening 80 years (Vista Hermosa) or currently in development (Cornfields).

Pastucha has been appropriating selectively and partially from the Olmsted-Bartholomew plan, perhaps an indication that those who produced the report overshot the mark. One can acknowledge and appreciate a grand vision, broad scope, and extensive geographic reach and yet still ask: What value ought we to assign a plan that appears to have been too big to implement? Partiality is the fate that awaits all plans. The degree of partiality increases exponentially as the scope, scale, breadth, and reach are enlarged. Vagaries of financing and limited access to capital, change in political regimes, technological innovation, revised objectives, and resistance by those opposed to the intended outcomes are among the factors that stymie implementation. Stated succinctly, conditions are dynamic, and one ought to expect change. An ability to alter a plan in response to changed conditions or the appropriation of parts from the whole might be considered a type of success.

Partial appropriation has long been a sign of utility and worth. For design professionals cribbing is an honorific art. Think of Pierre Charles L'Enfant who, while he was preparing plans for a capital city that would convey the ideals of republican America, reportedly studied maps of European capitals—Rome, Vienna, and Versailles—for inspiration, he said, not imitation. Yet the lines he drew, and the city that generations of federal officials, institutions, and taxpayers struggled to construct, has drawn upon formal principles L'Enfant lifted directly from the plans of aristocratic Europe. The same has been true in the case of *Parks, Playgrounds, and Beaches*. Then, as now, discrete segments of the 1930 report have been implemented. The Olmsted-Bartholomew study provided a framework for future interventions and a benchmark for comprehensive investigation into planning and development in greater LA. Both firms continued to produce studies and propose alternatives for clients in the region.

Takeaways for Practice

For these reasons the 1930 Olmsted-Bartholomew report remains a useful case study, a textbook example of the distance that separates a plan, a vision of the future, from its realization. The report is also significant for having been completed in LA. Many observers, professional and lay alike, consider LA a case study of what a city ought not to be, an example Jane Jacobs, Lewis Mumford, and like-minded urbanists referred to when they spoke of an "anti-city" (Whyte et al. 1958). However, LA has been the subject of a surfeit of planning reports, studies, and proposals. To cite just one measure, Metro has been developing a bibliography of "Los Angeles Transit and Transportation Studies, 1911–1957." At present the list includes 68 documents and counting. Ten plans from 1949 alone record how the Pacific Electric Railway Company studied passenger-loading standards; the California State Assembly examined rapid transit for metropolitan areas; and the City of Los Angeles assessed street traffic management. A similar accounting for land use, zoning, infrastructure, and urban design would generate comparable lists.[3]

Despite an unevenness of power and authority in 1930 that has continued to the present (a lamentable yet predictable condition); despite the uncertainty of unanticipated phenomena and events ("natural" disasters, economic downturns, changes in political regimes); and despite changed norms in the planning profession (from an expectation of big plans to incrementalism, from Daniel Burnham or the Regional Planning Association (RPA) to process, procedure, and small-scale interventions), studying the Olmsted-Bartholomew report does reveal positive lessons for the present.

Close study of the 1930 plan has encouraged practitioners, scholars, and the general public to dispense with hoary myths that have informed thinking and guided planning in Southern California. A foundational myth holds that in 1781 Felipe de Neve and the *pobladores* (initial settlers) circumambulated the plaza site and fixed a grid pattern of lots and thoroughfares oriented in the cardinal directions according to principles codified in 1581 as the Laws of the Indies. In doing so, they determined future growth in the pueblo and city. Actually settlers in Alta California honored the

Figure 6.7. The central planning map, showing the existing recreational areas in green and the proposed parks, playgrounds, and beaches in red.

laws more in the breach than in application. Partiality was the norm. Within a generation residents of El Pueblo de la Reina de Los Angeles had removed their settlement to higher ground, reoriented the plaza, reconstructed the church, and recast the pattern of parcels for civic buildings and town lots, fields, and grazing. Their actions were the zoning map for an oral society.

If myths of exceptionalism are set aside, including the enduring myth of a city and its metropolitan region growing without control in an endless expanse of territory, we can proceed to interpret LA as a city with a long history of planning. In common with all cities, planning in LA can be understood best through attention to interdependency and contingency, rational and accidental causation. One might choose to ask: Which courses of action ought elected officials, design professionals, citizen planners, and others to consider and possibly to pursue? This shift leads us toward an unacknowledged but necessary observation: all cities occupy compromised sites. Los Angeles's dependence on water from sources in the Sierra and the Colorado River is anything but an anomaly. All cities tap exogenous supplies to service urban needs. For two decades, New York City has been constructing a third intake tunnel to augment the flow of water it has siphoned from the Croton system for a century and a half, and Chicagoans reversed the flow of the Chicago River in the 1890s to ensure that city a supply of potable water; comparable engineering feats are the norm elsewhere.

Rather than simply condemn LA for dependence on resources in excess of local supply, might it be productive to assess land use in terms of capacity? In 1930, Olmsted, Bartholomew, and their consultants urged the Chamber of Commerce and its Citizens Committee to avoid killing a "goose that lays golden eggs." The general

[118] PARKS, PLAYGROUNDS AND BEACHES FOR THE LOS ANGELES REGION

Figure 6.8. A sketch from the report depicts a 225-foot-wide parkway planned to extend from LA to Palos Verde.

reference was to nature, the landscape, and local ecologies that drew visitors and potential residents to Southern California. But booster success in attracting people to the region threatened its amenities, making it "less and less attractive, less and less wholesome" (Olmsted Brothers 1930, 1).

Asking questions about capacity would encourage planners and other design professionals to emulate their predecessors. The professionals who contributed to the 1930 report sought out and found opportunities for recreation, parkways, and reservations in unlikely sites. A proposal to convert the Arroyo Seco into a pleasure parkway that would revert to a watercourse when necessary during the rainy season is suggestive of recent multipurpose proposals for stretches of the Los Angeles River. More pointedly, the careful, technical analysis of administration, land rights, and financing developed in the appendixes of the 1930 report could serve as a model for those engaged in efforts to calculate the costs and benefits of investment in parks and open space today.

How else might we build upon and enlarge what Olmsted and Bartholomew achieved? Planners engaged in the survey effort foundational for the 1930 report recorded a city at the close of a decade that had been powered by the discovery of theretofore unmatched oil deposits, the emergence of aviation and film as key sectors in the region's economy, and the continued expansion of branch plants sent to greater LA from the nation's manufacturing heartland. Today's planners engaged in economic development seek similar vitality in a context that has changed significantly. Where will the 21st-century correlates of aviation and aerospace find physical space in a five-county region that in some sections has been developed with densities comparable to Manhattan's? Just as critical, how might we assure that the benefits of a third industrial revolution accrue to the many rather than favoring the few?

Although large-scale comprehensive plans are out of favor at the moment, the 1930 report reminds us these were once the norm. Yet big projects move forward— including, at present, regional plans for light rail and a state program for high-speed rail. Politics, bureaucracy, and greed are present whenever one plans at these scales, as is the potential for failure. A belief in the necessity and utility of big plans such as Burnham's proposal for Chicago or the RPA's designs for the New York region are one measure of a divide that separates us from the generations that came of age during the first decades of the previous century.

Knowing how our predecessors defined and responded to like challenges can provide insight for the present. Dust off those big plans. Peer into the past as a way to plan the future.

An Orchard Spirals Out

Meredith Drake Reitan

A new art park is emerging among the skyscraper-adjacent vacant lots of the Temple-Beaudry neighborhood. Spiraling Orchard, the second project of ARTScorpsLA (ACLA), is entering a new phase of development. From a single parcel leased in 1996, Spiraling Orchard has grown to include approximately 21,000 square feet of native plantings, vegetable gardens, murals, and mosaics. In the very near future, a sustainably designed, multipurpose community building will provide space for local residents, art classes, after-school tutoring, and a kitchen for healthy eating demonstrations. A stage and a small sports area are also in the works and, if the leaders of ACLA (www.aclaparks.org) get their way, the site may one day include 8 to 12 low to moderately priced town houses that will have the park at their front doors.

Spiraling Orchard is located just west of downtown LA in an area that had once been one of the most productive oil fields in Southern California. (The oil stopped pumping only in 2003.) Due to the high levels of contamination on the park site, progress has been both slow and expensive. ACLA founder Tricia Ward recalls, "When we first began work at Spiraling Orchard, the smell of methane was persistent." Ironically, the presence of methane, which delayed construction of the controversial Belmont High School (now the Edward Roybal Learning Center) for more than 20 years, had never been reported as a problem for the approximately 32,000 people living in Temple-Beaudry.

The largely Latino and Filipino residents of Temple-Beaudry are often overlooked by city leaders and real estate speculators. Envisioning an expansion of the Bunker Hill project, the Community Redevelopment Agency cleared most of the area's Victorian-era homes in the 1960s. During the 1980s, the area was considered a prime location for a growing Pacific Rim financial services sector, and the neighborhood's proximity to downtown LA has continued to shape plans for the area. Today, while some homes remain, the area is dominated by large institutional buildings and parking lots. Because of this historic disregard for the neighborhood, ACLA felt establishing a firm partnership with community members was especially important. As a result, the input of the Vecinos (neighbors) de Spiraling Orchard is an active and integral part of the park's design.

This focus on community engagement is a key element in ACLA's success. Founded by Ward and her partner John Maroney, ACLA has been a response to the quick fix solutions proposed by LA city leaders after the 1992 riots. The group's founders felt that true healing could only be the result of an active and vibrant democracy—of communities gaining a voice and taking control of their neighborhoods. At the heart of ACLA is the goal of redefining public art. As traditionally conceived, Ward explains, public art would be better described as "plop" art: public money buys something, which is then "plopped" in a public space. Instead, ACLA envisions public art as an ongoing act of creation both grounded in, and reinforcing, community identity, development, and empowerment. As Spiraling Orchard suggests, the arts can be a particularly powerful vehicle for communities to reclaim their urban spaces.

Reestablishing the Connection with Physical Planning and Design

Simon Pastucha

A transformative moment occurred in LA in 2007 when the city planning department decided to return to physical planning. The department created the Urban Design Studio to make the connection between policy, planning, and codes within the built environment. Reestablishing the link to urban design is central to good planning. Every new project should have as its primary objective creating a neighborhood based upon good urban design principles, not just constructing a building. Design needs to play a critical role in our contemporary conception of urban planning.

The understanding of urban planning's role in shaping the built environment is vital to the success of a city. The failure to embrace urban design as central to good planning over the last few generations has formed the basis for a substantive critique of city planning today. Evidence of bad results abounds: the zoning code confines the building envelope, eliminates flexible site design, and does not require an active connection to the public realm; the street standards narrow the sidewalk and widen the roadway, resulting in the loss of a pedestrian neighborhood character; and the fire code flattens the roof of soaring signature buildings while widening neighborhood streets. The resulting detrimental effects on neighborhood and city planning emerge from having urban design defined as a by-product of other—single-purpose—planning tools.

Instead, planners need to work as part of a team in alliance with many other disciplines, such as transportation and civil engineering, to create a better city. Urban design plays a critical—a central—role by serving as the glue that integrates land use, transportation, and regulations for unexpected, unpredictable, and glorious results. The mission of the Urban Design Studio is to bring about greater functionality, better design to all neighborhoods, and thus an improved image for LA.

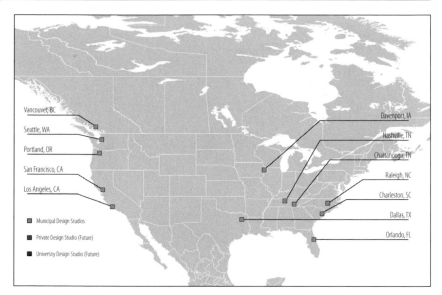

Figure 6.9. Municipal design studios nationwide

A Better City

People moving around a city often ask questions about why the city functions, looks the way it does, and how could it be improved. Many ask why the built environment is not more consistent with international and national trends led by citizens, elected officials, designers, and planners. Why doesn't it celebrate and reinforce inspired design and create better neighborhoods and more sustainable cities? People started to see such changes as adding value by enhancing the marketability of the city and improving its economy.

As a result, urban design is hot. Books, articles and blogs about design are proliferating. The Internet is filled with it; search "urban design" and you get over 165 million results. The air is filled with discussions and debates about street, project, neighborhood, and city designs. This discussion is supporting the creation of a stronger connection between planning and the physical environment.

Los Angeles is like other cities around the United States and Canada that have created a municipal design studio or center. Each design studio or center has shared goals to provide a better quality of life and improve the environment in their city. The Dallas CityDesign Studio, for example, recently finished a brief study of 12 cities (https:// texasarchitects.org/media/uploads/resourceDocs/111047_handout.pdf). Cities big and small are looking at improving their built environment by requiring their planning departments to develop and sustain efforts to improve design practices.

Background

The Urban Design Studio started with two staff members—me and Emily Gabel Luddy—with design education who were reassigned from within the planning depart-

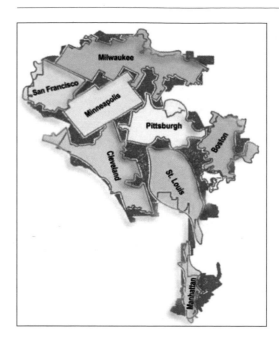

Figure 6.10. How big is LA? Big enough to fit the area of all the cities shown here

ment. We had more than 50 years of experience in the city and a thorough working knowledge of existing planning processes, city departments, and political structure. We started out by researching existing municipal models. The more we examined the city and its structure and compared it to other cities, the less we could find in common with them. Los Angeles is so big, at 470 square miles; so large, with over 3.8 million people; so physically diverse, with elevations ranging from ocean level to 4,000 feet including natural, rural, suburban, and urban spaces in seven climate zones. It has an automotive infrastructure that includes 6,500 miles of streets, 900 miles of alleyways, and 71 transit stations already built with another 43 funded (for a total of 114).

Within this world city, no one person or agency controls or monitors new additions to the built environment. Usually the public realm is regulated and controlled by different agencies or departments than private property is. Figure 6.11 illustrates the complexity of LA, with its many elected and appointed officials, neighborhood groups, and various regional and local government agencies that influence the development of the built environment. They all deal somehow with the future of the city. We held many discussions with residents, business representatives, elected officials, government staff, and community organizations. They expressed the need for improved mobility, enhancements of neighborhoods, historic preservation, equal attention, simpler permit processing, clear design standards, and learning opportunities.

Everyday decisions are being made that shape the built environment. A city of the size and complexity of LA is constantly dealing with the inevitability of change. Change is an ongoing and gradual process that comes in many forms. Some examples include new laws, policies, regulations, and developments, as well as a shifting

MANY POLICY MAKERS FOR THE BUILT ENVIRONMENT

• 1 Mayor
• 15 Council Members
• 9 Citywide Planning Commissioners
• 35 Area Planning Commissioners
• 110 Neighborhood Councils
• 5 Public Works Commissioners
• 7 Redevelopment Commissioners
• 7 Airport Commissioners
• 5 Harbor Commissioners
• 5 Building & Safety Commissioners
• 5 Rec & Parks Commissioners
• 7 Transportation Commissioners
• 5 Water & Power Commissioners
• 7 Cultural Affairs Commissioners
• 5 Cultural Heritage Commissioners
• 13 Metro Board Directors
• 7 School District Board Members

Figure 6.11

economy, new technology, and expanding knowledge. Each change, big and small, demands that a series of decisions be made that affect the eventual built environment. The need for a shared vision and a team approach is apparent. If the decisions on these changes could be informed by a shared vision, creating a direction for the city, the decisions would be better integrated and gain better results.

Urban Design Principles

Given the need for a shared vision, how could we use urban design principles as a part of one? The design of anything is based on a list of broad requirements that are the basis for the design solution. Some requirements are more flexible than others. One example is the design of a building, which calls for a list of requirements that is the foundation for the creation of the structure. The program shapes the entire project.

Thinking that it would be helpful to have an illustrated list of the permanent requirements, I developed the urban design principles. As I discussed them with stakeholders, they started to fall into broad categories, such as movement, health, and resilience. Ultimately I came up with 10 urban principles (see Figure 6.12, page 218). Not all of them are appropriate all the time; it depends on the project and the context. Examples of different types of projects might be a new ordinance requiring stormwater capture, a new development on a large property, or the reuse of an old commercial store. Each will have an effect on the built environments, but not all the principles will be applicable due to the scale, context, and the defined project.

This citywide vision became the basis of a design program for the city. The Urban Design Principles provide guidance in responding to questions such as: What city of los angeles urban design principles

10 urban design principles

prin•ci•ple: *(noun)* **1** a basic rule that guides or influences thought or action. **2** an essential element, constitute, or quality, especially one that produces a specific effect. **3** a general truth from which other truths follow.

Movement : a city of mobility

1. **develop inviting + accessible transit areas**
2. **ensure connections**
3. **produce great, green streets**

Health : a city of activity

4. **generate public open space**
5. **reinforce walkability, bikeability + wellbeing**
6. **bridge the past + the future**
7. **nurture neighborhood character**

Resilience : a city of responsibility

8. **stimulate sustainability + innovation**
9. **improve equity + opportunity**
10. **emphasize early integration, simple processes + maintainable long term solutions**

Summer 2011 3

Figure 6.12

are the values people want to be expressed in the built environment? What do they want to see, and what does the city want to be known for? They draw upon theoretical and practical efforts of the last few generations to rethink urban and suburban spaces. The outcome is the aspiration to make bike plans real and connect streets and developments to transit and make the city more generally walkable and bikeable. This vision creates an environment that promotes more physical activity, enhances and preserves neighborhood character, generates more and better quality public open space, and results in a more sustainable and socially responsible city.

The intention is to assist leaders, decision makers, community members, designers, developers, planners, and other stakeholders in their discussions about change. These principles provide guidance for new development and encourage projects to complement existing urban form in order to enhance the built environment in LA. While called "urban," the Urban Design Principles establish a design program for the entire city. They are intended to adapt to the variety of urban forms that exist within LA, from the most urban, concentrated centers to our suburban, even rural neighborhoods. Although the Urban Design Principles are broad, they will provide the framework when the city creates more specific design guidelines, polices, regulations, and requirements.

People Walk in Los Angeles

The first more specific guidelines created by the Urban Design Studio emerged from a community advisory group on pedestrian safety. The guidelines were developed to raise the level of design related to walkability prior to the submittal of projects to the planning department for review. The Walkability Checklist for Entitlement Review guides planning staff, developers, architects, engineers, and community members in creating enhanced pedestrian movement, access, comfort, and safety—contributing to the walkability of the city.

This checklist encourages pursuit of high-quality form. Stakeholders learn about the tools and techniques that improve curb appeal, beauty, and usability through a location-specific (or contextual) approach. Parts of LA retain their historic neighborhood character with low density, while other parts are modern local and regional centers with an array of small and large office buildings. Placemaking—designing buildings, streets, and open space to make them more attractive to and compatible with the people who inhabit them—is the primary foundation in creating walkable neighborhoods.

The Walkability Checklist provides a list of recommended strategies that projects may employ to improve the pedestrian environment. Each of the implementation strategies on the checklist should be considered in a proposed project, although each project will require an individualized approach. While the checklist is neither a requirement nor part of the zoning code, it provides a consistent response to the policies contained in the General Plan. Incorporating these guidelines will encourage pedestrian activity, which is good for business and the environment as well as the health of walkers.

Design Guidelines for the Whole City

The next specific guidelines were the Citywide Design Guidelines for Commercial, Mixed Use, Residential, and Industrial Uses, which serve as an implementation guide for the 10 Urban Design Principles. By offering more direction for proceeding with the design of a project, the Design Guidelines illustrate options, solutions, and techniques in an effort to achieve the goal of excellence in new design. An example is the difference between a badly designed building that is oriented to a rear parking lot where people walking or driving by are greeted by only blank walls versus a building with a distinguishable and attractive design, where pedestrian connections to the street and within the property are obvious, the driveways and utilities are minimized, and the site has enhanced open areas and landscaping. They are performance goals, not zoning regulations or development standards, and therefore do not supersede regulations in the municipal code.

A Livable Downtown

The third application example is area-specific guidelines, the Downtown Design Guidelines and Street Standards, which aim to create a more responsive built environment. This set of guidelines contains guidance for the development of a richer public realm with tailored street design standards and a set of private-property design guidelines unique to the specific area. The guidelines reflect a new emphasis on reinvigorating residential life in the city center. They advise developers and planners how to create context-sensitive streets, develop good buildings for good streets, enhance team building across multiple agencies, promote a sustainable community, and reduce bureaucratic obstacles. They were written using a team approach with the Urban Design Studio working with the Community Redevelopment Agency, planning department, and transportation and public works agencies as well as design consultants.

The team attempted to improve existing zoning codes, development requirements, streets standards, and the unique neighborhoods characteristics so stakeholders could better know how to plan and develop a downtown that reflected the increased residential population and richer transit infrastructure. The team worked together over a two-year period reviewing streets block by block, applying draft design guidelines and street standards on new projects to create a iterative process. When the draft guidelines and standards were finally applied, their great value became quickly apparent in streamlining the permitting process, eliminating excess roadway widening, and creating a great public realm. The end result was the adoption of revised planning policy documents, design standards, and context-sensitive street standards celebrated by resident, business, and development organizations.

Raising the Level of Design

Los Angeles has matured as a city, and most of its land is already developed. So the focus today is on infill projects. The return to physical planning for LA is a logical step at this moment in its evolution. People are looking with increasing doubt at the city built under the conventional and traditional zoning and standards. They are not satisfied with the results. They ask, How can we adapt existing regulations and codes in the city for drought, stormwater capture, and decreased car use to help make LA the greenest city in the United States? How do we change codes and standards created to regulate the city's more suburban developments—codes that conflict with the new goals of a revitalized downtown, an expanded transit system, more bikeable and walkable neighborhoods, and preservation concerns?

The Urban Design Studio has been instrumental in creating a more responsive built environment for LA. It is working to make everyone understand that all stakeholders in the city are part of creating the built environment. The Urban Design Studio has been creating and supporting new design guidelines, an improved review process for zoning codes, enhanced design and peer review, increased community planning, design assistance for other departments and agencies, innovative idea creation, new initiatives, and community outreach and education seminars. Studio personnel collaborate with elected officials; city, county, and state agencies; professional organizations; neighborhood associations; and education institutions on ways to improve the built environment. The Urban Design Studio aims at creating a better city by doing real planning.

Managing Development Through Urban Growth Boundaries

William Fulton, AICP

In 1994, residents of a new single-family subdivision in Ventura got mad. When they bought their houses, they had been promised that 87 acres of adjacent or-chard land would become a major city park. Now, they thought, the city was welshing on the deal.

As part of the deal to approve their subdivision, the developer had transferred the property to the city, and everyone in the neighborhood assumed the park would be built. The park was important to residents for recreational opportunities and what they viewed as the ambience of their neighborhood. For 40 years, the eastern part of Ventura had been developed in patchy fashion, with subdivisions adjacent to and sometimes surrounded by orchards. With orchards remaining on two sides, the resi-dents believed the park would help maintain the rural-like character of their otherwise standard-issue subdivision.

In 1994, however, the city began negotiating to give the 87 acres back to the developer in exchange for about 100 acres of more centrally located property. That property was already sewered and ready for development, but it was also a better location for a large, active sports-oriented park. To make the whole deal work, the city would rezone the 87-acre property from agriculture to residential, allowing another subdivision similar to the one already built. Frustrated with what they viewed as a breach of faith, the residents began gathering signatures to place an initiative on the ballot that would block the deal.

Elsewhere in the country, a citizen-led land-use initiative is almost unheard of. But in California, with its century-old tradition of direct democracy, the mid- to late 1990s was the peak of a boom in "ballot-box" zoning. Between 1986 and 2000, more than 600 ballot measures related to land-use issues appeared on local ballots around California. They came in all shapes and sizes—urban growth boundaries, numerical limits on housing units, limits on density, requirements that development be tied to

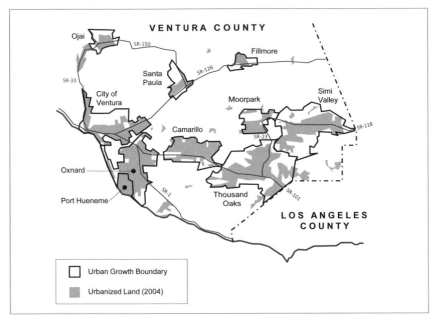

Figure 6.13. Map of Urban Growth Boundaries, Ventura

infrastructure. The most fashionable: a ballot measure requiring that future land-use changes be approved by voters. Though such ballot measures could be advertised as democracy in action, they had the clear effect of discouraging development.

It was not long before the angry Ventura residents contacted Richard Francis, a local lawyer and former mayor knowledgeable about writing ballot initiatives. By coincidence, the California Supreme Court had just upheld a Napa County initiative that required voter approval to rezone agricultural land for urban use. Instead of writing a new initiative to block development of the 87 aces, Francis thought, why not mimic Napa County and require voter approval in Ventura any time farmland was converted to urban use? "We just took Measure J," he liked to joke, "and wherever it said 'grapes' we just crossed it out and wrote 'fruits and nuts.'" In November 1995, led by Francis and Steve Bennett—an environmentalist on the Ventura City Council— the "Save Our Agricultural Resources" initiative got 53 percent of the vote.

The passage of the SOAR initiative was the leading edge of a land-use revolution—and an experiment in planning democracy that has had ramifications statewide and even across the nation. Over the next five years, voters in virtually every city in Ventura County and the county itself adopted versions of the SOAR initiative, making Ventura the only county in the nation with a comprehensive set of voter-imposed urban growth boundaries (Figure 6.13). Ventura County today still has 100,000 acres of cultivated farmland. The SOAR boundaries have virtually eliminated sprawl in a suburban county and, to some extent, have fostered smart growth–style infill development, especially in Ventura. And the idea of urban growth boundaries controlled by the voters themselves has spread around California.

History of Land-Use Regulation in Ventura County

Located northwest of LA on the way to Santa Barbara, Ventura County is the only one in Southern California that still retains a distinctly agricultural feel. Dating back to the 19th century, the county's economy was founded on oil and agriculture, especially in the older cities along the ocean such as Oxnard and Ventura. Around Ventura and in some of the county's interior valleys, orchards made the county a top national grower of both lemons and avocados. The Oxnard Plain contained some of the most productive farmland on the planet. Topsoil was 40 feet deep in some places, and the mild climate allowed a four-crop annual rotation for row crops, especially strawberries.

In the 1960s, California Highway 101 opened up Ventura County to LA commuters, and the county got caught up in a frenzy of home building. The planned executive suburb of Thousand Oaks, located close to the San Fernando Valley, took off, as did other suburban cities such as Simi Valley and Camarillo. Between 1950 and 1990, Ventura County's population quintupled, from 114,000 to 670,000.

Unlike Orange County, Ventura County retained its agricultural flavor, even along the Highway 101 corridor. Though new subdivisions did spread across the landscape, cities did not blend together as they did in Orange County. This was not an accident. Beginning in the early 1970s, local officials throughout the county worked together to accommodate urban expansion while protecting agriculture and open space. The county, the cities, and the Local Agency Formation Commission (LAFCO), a boundary-setting commission (required under California law since the 1960s) formulated a set of policies and agreements unique even in California—which, at the time, was creating some of the most trailblazing growth management approaches in the United States.

The principles were simple. Virtually all new development would be channeled into cities. But the cities would be small in number. In contrast to neighboring Los Angeles County—which had more than 80 cities—there would never be more than 14 cities in all of Ventura County. (At the time there were nine.) Although a hard urban growth boundary was not created, the cities reached a series of agreements to create greenbelts between them.

These principles were called the Guidelines for Orderly Development, or GOD. Except in a few preexisting hamlets, the county limited maximum density to one-acre lots that did not require water or sewer service. Annexations were governed by LAFCO for the County of Los Angeles, made up of elected city and county officials. To a large extent, they were simply carried out by custom, because the greenbelt agreements—while they had the force of a political agreement—were not binding. And they worked. Some 90 percent of all residents in Ventura County live inside city boundaries.

The result was a suburban/rural county with a large population but only 10 cities, many of which are large by suburban standards. The county now has about 800,000 people. The biggest city, Oxnard, has about 200,000 people. Three others—Thousand Oaks, Simi Valley, and Ventura—are between 100,000 and 130,000. None dominates the county.

By the mid-1990s, however, pressure for urban development in unincorporated areas was growing. Some "rural residential" development was permitted, such as the super expensive Lake Sherwood golf course housing development, where Tiger Woods hosts a tournament each December. The one-acre limitation—along with a hard-line attitude among Ventura County planners—was not enough to ward off the kind of sprawl that GOD was designed to prevent.

In the summer of 1995, while the Ventura city SOAR measure was pending, a split Ventura County Board of Supervisors gave the go-ahead to an environmental impact report on a proposed subdivision in the rural community of Somis, near Camarillo. The location was ground zero for agricultural protection in the county—fertile farmland on the Oxnard Plain, located in an unincorporated area near one existing subdivision yet miles away from the 101 freeway.

The Somis project was sprawl in the wrong place, but there wasn't much the county could do to stop it. With 189 houses on 195 acres, it met the one-acre-lot requirement. Water and sewer hookups were unlikely. The one thing the project did need was a zone change from agricultural to residential—the one thing, coincidentally, that a measure like the SOAR initiative would have required voters to approve. The county moved forward with a task force to reexamine GOD and its long-standing policies, but with the passage of SOAR in November 1995, a new era in growth management had begun in Ventura County.

Land-Use Initiatives in California

California has a long history of "direct democracy," dating back to a constitutional amendment in 1911 that enshrined the power of initiative, referendum, and recall in the state constitution. In the intervening decades, the initiative power had frequently been used for populist purposes – the most famous being Proposition 13, the property tax limit adopted in 1978 – though it had often become a tool of moneyed interests, simply because anyone who pay signature gatherers can place a measure on the state ballot.

The use of initiatives on the local level was widely considered a kind of sideshow to the main event, but beginning in the 1970s, as citizen concern about growth increased, local activists used the ballot to try to restrict development. In localities throughout the state, initiatives restricted height, density, and the amount of housing—and often required any further changes to be approved by voters. A series of court rulings in the late 1970s and early '80s clearly established that legislative land-use decisions (such as General Plan amendments and zone changes) were subject to initiative and referendum, though quasi-judicial decisions (conditional use permits, variances, and the like) were not. City measures won more often than county measures, for two reasons: voters related to local land-use issues better, and foot power could compete with developer money in a campaign.

SOAR Goes Countywide

After the Ventura victory, Francis, Bennett, and other environmentalists started working on writing a countywide SOAR-style initiative. It took a while to hit upon the right approach because the eastern part of the county—closest to LA—had little irrigated agriculture and many Republicans who had sympathy for property rights. And a developer could end-run a county SOAR requirement by simply annexing to a city using the GOD system.

SOAR advocates camp up with two ingenious wrinkles. The small wrinkle was to change the name of the movement, from Save Our Agricultural Resources to Save Open-space and Agricultural Resources. That change helped broaden SOAR's appeal in the eastern part of the county. The big wrinkle—a genius move, politically—was to place initiatives on the ballot simultaneously for the county and for each city. So, if a developer wanted to build in unincorporated territory, he had to go to a countywide SOAR vote for a zone change. But if that same developer wanted to annex property to a city, he had to go to a ballot within that city to expand the urban growth boundary.

The combined city-county approach also overcame the problem of a lack of local interest in countywide issues. By placing the city measures on the ballot, the SOAR advocates cleverly made the countywide measure into a local measure: Sure, you can create an urban growth boundary, but unless you vote for the countywide measure as well, developers can end-run it.

In November 1998, the county measure and four of the city measures—including measures in the conservative communities of Simi Valley, Thousand Oaks, and Camarillo—passed with at least 65 percent of the vote. It barely passed in Moorpark and failed in the poor and most Latino community of Santa Paula. Santa Paula passed a SOAR measure in 2000, and the city council in neighboring Fillmore, another small farming community, adopted SOAR in 2002. Only two cities do not have a SOAR measure in place: Port Hueneme, which is completely surrounded by Oxnard, and tiny Ojai, which has a slow-growth tradition dating back decades. All of the measures will require renewal in either 2020 or 2030.

How Has SOAR Changed Ventura County—and California?
Political Fallout

In the years that followed the passage of the SOAR initiatives, several subsequent elections—held to change growth boundaries and accommodate new development—provide insight into some of the difficulties of the SOAR system. The most significant message has been that voters are receptive to institutional development but mixed on residential growth.

In 1999, for example, Ventura voters approved the rezoning of 25 acres of agricultural land to accommodate construction of a new Assembly of God Church. But the blunt force of a ballot measure conflicted with the subtleties of a zoning ordinance, which had no district for a church. Since churches were permitted uses in all residential zones, Assembly of God sought a change to the lowest possible residential density—one unit per acre. The church vote also raised the question of when in the planning process the vote should take place, since the project was still subject to all the usual planning commission reviews and permits. Perhaps most important from a planning perspective, the 25 acres were part of a larger farm area that was not up for rezoning. In contemplating how to accommodate the church, the city could not predict whether the rest of the farmland would ever be developed.

Residential developers have had a more difficult time of it. In the suburbanizing community of Moorpark, for example, a long-standing controversy over a major greenfield residential development proposal became even more volatile after SOAR passed. The proposed project had been defeated on the ballot in 1998, and a SOAR override vote to approve a new version of the project failed by a 3:1 ratio in 2006. Meanwhile, in Santa Paula, one major SOAR expansion proposal failed and another one passed, while a smaller proposal by the highly respected Limoniera Company also passed. But Santa Paula, a struggling small city that is more prodevelopment than its neighbors because of its history as a poor farming town, has always been the exception that proves the rule in Ventura County.

Perhaps the most remarkable political shift has been the elections that have not taken place. Not a single SOAR election has ever been held in Simi Valley, Thousand Oaks, Camarillo, Oxnard, or Fillmore. Countywide discussions about future growth patterns rarely involve the possibility that the SOAR boundaries will ever be changed, or at least not changed very much.

SOAR's Impact on Land Use

Thanks to GOD, Ventura County has always had a fairly compact development pattern compared to the rest of Southern California. But the SOAR boundaries clearly have accelerated the trend toward more efficient use of urban land inside the boundaries and greater protection of farmland outside the boundaries.

About 20 percent of the county's nonfederal land—approximately 150,000 acres—is located inside the SOAR boundaries. According to a study in 2007 by Solimar Research Group, at the time the SOAR measures went into place, almost half of that was developed, while only 14,000 acres of the 400,000 acres outside the SOAR boundaries were developed. Of the county's 110,000 acres of farmland, 100,000 acres was protected outside the growth boundaries and 10,000 acres located inside the boundaries. Most of the rest of the undeveloped land outside the growth boundary was constrained by steep slopes anyway.

The Solimar report found that the presence of the SOAR boundaries appeared to have a significant impact on development patterns during the real estate boom of the early century. From 1996 to 2000, as the SOAR measures were being put into place, one acre of land was developed outside the SOAR boundaries for every three acres developed inside them. In the period 2000–2006—with the SOAR boundaries in place and a roaring development market—that ratio changed from 1:3 to 1:8. The amount of land developed outside the SOAR boundaries dropped by half (Figure 6.14).

SOAR clearly has had a significant impact on the density of urban development in Ventura County—though in most cases this has meant denser auto-oriented suburban development rather than more walkable urban development. Between 2000 and 2006, the urban density (the number of people divided by the amount of urbanized land) of Ventura County increased from 8.2 to 8.5 persons per urbanized acre. (California generally is at about seven persons per urbanized acre, double the national average.) The marginal density—the population added divided by the urbanized land added—was 10.9 persons per urbanized acre. At a time when much of the United States was urbanizing one acre of land for each person added to the population, traditionally suburban/rural Ventura County added 63,000 residents and consumed only 5,400 acres of land in the process.

Only in Ventura—the city with the county's tightest growth boundary, the strongest downtown, and a staunch political commitment to infill development—did this trend begin to lead to truly urban development. Although Ventura's overall urban density is similar to the county's (8.7), the marginal urbanized density was almost 21 persons per acre; during this period, Ventura added as many multifamily residential units as single-family units. In the rest of the county, the increase in density was due largely to the development of small-lot single-family subdivisions inside the SOAR boundaries.

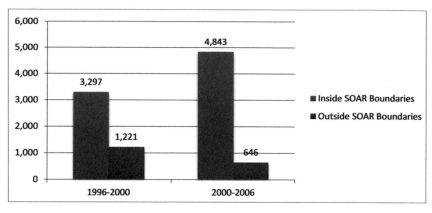

Figure 6.14. *Land developed, 1996–2006 (acres). Source: Solimar Research Group, based on California Farmland Mapping and Monitoring Program data*

SOAR's Impact on Agriculture

One change that SOAR's drafters may not have imagined was a significant change in cropping patterns that began to alter the county's scenic agricultural landscape. Deprived of the opportunity to develop their property, Ventura County farmers moved aggressively toward generating more revenue from agricultural operations. In general, they replaced orchards with more profitable row crops and greater use of greenhouses, especially on the Oxnard Plain. Row crops require less capital investment because harvests are available immediately, whereas orchards take several years to begin producing revenue. Row crops are also far more profitable on a per-acre basis.

Among the four historically largest crops—lemons and avocados among the tree crops and strawberries and celery among the row crops—the post-SOAR patterns shifted significantly. In particular, the lemon acreage dropped by 30 percent while the strawberry acreage increased by 35 percent (Figure 6.15). Between 2003 and 2010, the annual value of the county's agricultural production increased from $1.1 billion to $1.9 billion. Strawberries now outpace all other crops by a huge margin, and in 2010 the value of the celery crop exceeded the value of the lemon harvest for the first time ever. Avocados continue to do well because they can more easily be grown on hillsides than lemons can.

Conclusion: Push Will Soon Come to Shove

Almost two decades after the original SOAR debate, SOAR has changed the way people think about the future of Ventura County. With a few changes, the original SOAR boundaries remain in place. Virtually every debate about future growth in the county assumes that the SOAR boundaries will stay put indefinitely.

Yet Ventura County has not yet faced the really hard choices created by SOAR. The original boundaries were expansive enough to accommodate suburban-style development without too much difficulty, especially in Oxnard, Camarillo, Thousand

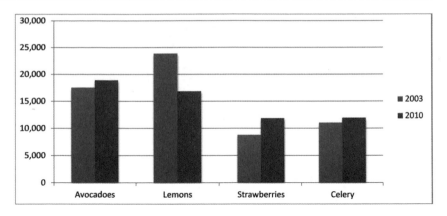

Figure 6.15. Cropping pattern, 2003 and 2010 (acres). Source: Ventura County Agricultural Commissioner's Office, Ventura County Crop Reports, 2004, 2010

Oaks, and Simi Valley, which together accounted for more than 80 percent of the county's population growth between 2000 and 2010.

But virtually every future analysis conducted by the Southern California Association of Governments has concluded that to accommodate future growth, Ventura County, whose housing stock is 70 percent single-family homes, will have to build mostly multifamily homes in the future. The 2007 Solimar report concluded that by 2030 Camarillo would be completely out of residentially zoned land, while all the other major cities except for Simi Valley would be running very low on residential land supply. The report also concluded that most of these cities were overzoned for commercial land—not surprising in a region where competition among cities for sales taxes is ferocious.

Some of the SOAR boundaries will expire in eight years unless they are renewed, and the hard choices ahead of pretty clear. The county and its cities will have to do one (or more) of three things:

- Expand the SOAR boundaries, which will have to occur on a city-by-city basis and will inevitably face stiff political opposition
- Rezone commercial land for residential use, losing potential sales tax revenue
- Significantly increase the amount of infill development and increase the density of greenfield development across the board, which would change the suburban character of the county

None of these choices is politically easy, especially in a county that still views itself primarily as rural and suburban. Confronting them directly over the next few years will be the next step in Ventura County's ongoing efforts to manage growth. The county's political leaders—and its citizen activists—need to craft a path forward that accommodates more growth and yet still maintains Ventura County's essence.

Unpaving Paradise:
The Green Visions Plan

Jennifer Wolch, Travis Longcore, and John Wilson

Southern California is a compelling region. Since the late 1800s millions of people hungry for the American Dream have arrived seeking its economic opportunities, social diversity, temperate climate, and abundant natural resources. Yet Southern California is perhaps the nation's most challenging urban region in terms of socioecological planning and environmental restoration. The metro area retains the distinction of having the most polluted air in the United States and suffers serious freshwater, groundwater, and coastal water pollution. Water supply shortages are growing worse, and the region is an endangered species hotspot. Deep-seated environmental injustices have yet to be remedied, and as a result of a long history of flood control the Los Angeles River is one of the most channelized rivers in the nation.

Awareness of the need for fundamental changes in urban development has grown rapidly in recent decades. Why?

- Long-overdue enforcement of the federal Clean Water Act, leading to tough new Total Maximum Daily Load restrictions, which in turn have engendered a push for integrated watershed management
- Conflicts over endangered species, with resulting defeats of major development projects
- Passage by voters of bonds to fund water quality projects and parks/recreational open space for metropolitan areas (not solely wilderness land acquisitions), as a means to address urban watershed health and park access goals
- The campaign to restore the Los Angeles River
- Concerns about the lack of open space for active living in the face of a looming obesity epidemic

- Passage of the Sustainable Communities and Climate Protection Act in 2009, which increases pressures on localities to increase densities and better integrate land use and transportation

A historical legacy of weak regional governance stands as a major barrier to re-weaving the green fabric of the region and enhancing its socioecology. The metropolitan planning organization, the Southern California Association of Governments, has a say in transportation planning and fund allocation, but little else; regional agencies such as the state's Regional Water Quality Control Board regulate but have limited resources for analysis; the counties and cities have strong powers of land-use control but few resources to engage in scientific analysis or detailed planning and limited project funding; the U.S. Army Corps of Engineers has initiated some major studies but focused solely on major river channels; and nonprofit organizations have made significant headway in terms of raising awareness but can mount only limited scientific projects. The result is a paucity of scientific study of the region's ecological and watershed health or geographically disaggregated data that would allow scientific, needs-based decisions on where to make strategic investments. The Green Visions Plan (GVP) for 21st Century Southern California launched in 2003 sought to fill some, if not all, of these gaps.

For state land conservancies, including the Coastal Conservancy, Rivers and Mountains Conservancy, Santa Monica Mountains Conservancy, and the small but centrally located Baldwin Hills Conservancy, the status quo constitutes a major chal-

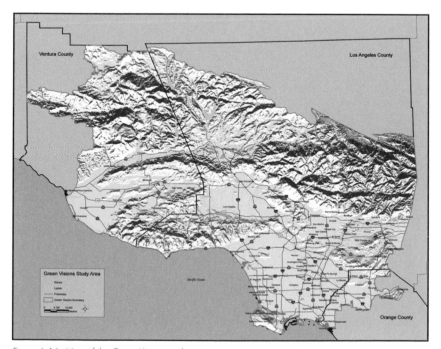

Figure 6.16. Map of the Green Visions study area

lenge. With large amounts of state bond funds to allocate, habitat protection duties, shared responsibilities for integrated watershed management planning, and a mandate to increase recreational open space access, the conservancies have long needed better science and planning tools to do their jobs well. Moreover, most state and local project funding has been based on competitive proposals, thereby disadvantaging poorer communities with fewer staff or consulting resources. Since such communities often have the worst park access, the least amount of natural habitat and open space, and the most polluted water, the seemingly merit-based, competitive resource allocation model actually serves to reinforce or even deepen environmental inequalities. Thus a motive for conservancy support of the GVP was to create data and planning tools as common-good resources, thereby leveling the playing field across communities with disparate abilities to produce the technical analyses needed to gain access to funding.

Curiously, LA has a unique history of powerful socioecological planning efforts. In the early 1930s, the Los Angeles Chamber of Commerce commissioned well-known landscape architects Olmsted and Bartholomew to create a regional plan for "parks, playgrounds, and beaches." Though the plan was never implemented, in the mid-1990s it resurfaced and became a beacon, stimulating a renewed vision for an ecological city connected by green corridors and major parklands. (See Hise and Deverell, this chapter.)

One outgrowth of this was the GVP with its study area covering 11,240 square kilometers and almost 11 million residents. Funded by a collaborative partnership among the region's land conservancies led by Belinda Faustinos of the Rivers and Mountains Conservancy, the purpose of the GVP was to use the best science and data available to characterize the major watershed, habitat, and recreational open space assets of the region and design a web-based planning tool for a variety of stakeholders. The tool was to offer a data-rich context for planning and a set of static and dynamic analytic capabilities for the exploration of alternative multibenefit projects that could further major social and ecological goals at regional and local planning scales.

Along the way, the GVP encountered many challenges including inadequate data, lack of appropriate scientific models, and political obstacles. Both the successes and limitations of the GVP offer a unique window into the challenges, complexities, and opportunities of using place-based science and planning to "unpave paradise." Here we provide an overview of the GVP analytic framework, the scope of empirical and modeling work, and web-based tool development. We conclude with lessons for future planning practice.

The Green Visions Plan Framework

The prospect of drafting an urban conservation plan for the three-county, multiwatershed GVP area was daunting and inspiring. The study area's many natural communities range from disturbed urban sites to wilderness, and stakeholders abound. Our objective was to create a template for "needs-based" conservation funding rather than "proposal-based" allocation of resources, which results in a mosaic of projects that may not achieve synergistic conservation goals. The GVP analytic framework and its Geographic Information System (GIS)–based methods had four parts: (1) habitat conservation; (2) watershed health; (3) recreational open space; and (4) a GIS toolkit.

Habitat Conservation

The LA region presents a dilemma for conservation planners. The least disturbed natural lands are found in the mountain ranges that ring and bisect the metropolitan areas while the most disturbed lands are found in the valley bottoms and large alluvial plain. Based on the current distribution of parklands, the mountains and foothills have historically received significant conservation attention, while the river valleys and plains have not. Greater emphasis is now being placed on the valleys and plains. This emphasis has evolved out of a desire to reclaim rivers as a part of public space, an increasing need to undertake watershed planning to meet regional water-quality goals, and proposals to increase access to open space.

The GVP habitat conservation component sought to build on this renewed attention to valleys and plains, as well as mountains and foothills. For the entire study area, we focused on species recovery, restoration based on historic and current conditions, maintenance of natural or seminatural disturbance regimes, and an incorporation of the scale-dependent nature of urban connectivity and its implications for harnessing the urban matrix for biodiversity. Methods included identifying and modeling target species ranges, historical analysis to promote representation of natural communities, and the development of tools to support the design of metropolitan corridor-reserve systems (Rubin, Rustigian, and White 2006, Stein et al. 2007, Longcore et al. 2011).

The use of target species is helpful since they act as surrogates for biodiversity, either directly or indirectly; provide guidelines for the spatial configuration (e.g., size, connectivity, and habitat types) of a reserve system to maintain biodiversity in wild to urban situations; and serve as benchmarks for evaluating the effectiveness of the plan over time. As a result, target species for urban conservation planning include some native species that have become increasingly rare as native habitats diminish in size and connectivity. We developed a modeling tool that predicts the distribution of the chosen target species based on the size and isolation of vegetation types predicted to support the species. These models produce predictive maps of habitat quality for each of the target species, which are then overlaid to produce a map of target spe-

Figure 6.17. Target species map

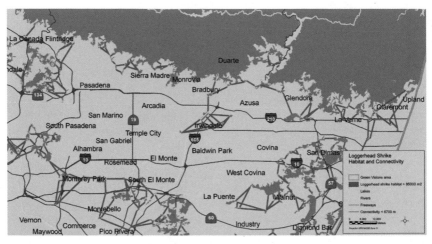

Figure 6.18. Map of the habitat and connectivity of the loggerhead shrike

cies density for the planning region that can be used to prioritize open space acquisition and reserve monitoring (Rubin, Rustigian, and White 2006).

Connectivity is an important goal to ensure long-term viability of sensitive species in fragmented reserve systems. Planners often focus on connectivity for large predators in intact landscapes, but such an approach provides little guidance for species that depend on natural fragments within urban landscapes. Planning for species that have less restrictive needs is appropriate to identify and plan for connectivity within cities.

We used the GVP area as a case study to identify and implement a connectivity analysis for five native species that persist in protected lands across the region and that are relatively tolerant of human proximity and urbanization (Longcore et al. 2011). The results allow open space planners to prioritize acquisition of a reserve system that provides connectivity for species appropriate to an urban region. Using these results, open space planners can prioritize acquisition of a reserve system that could provide connectivity for species. Further calculations, using habitat suitability assessment, could be used for the five species to identify those areas that are within existing corridors or are relatively easy to traverse, and those most isolated from habitats.

Connectivity in this application does not necessarily require contiguous habitat but rather can includes habitat stepping-stones that increase the probability that more mobile species (e.g., birds, coyotes) can traverse between larger habitat blocks. Findings can inform land acquisition decisions, develop corridor development strategies for key linkage areas, and create habitat stepping-stones within recreational open space or watershed projects.

Watershed Health

The natural hydrology in Southern California has been extensively modified and largely replaced by a paved drainage system that quickly carries away water following storm events while increasing discharges of reclaimed wastewater and other surface discharge—including lawn watering overflow and streetside car washing—into the regions' waterways, dramatically altering stream flow regimes and hence the nature and quality of downstream habitat. The GVP watershed health component focused on multiple-use project designs that would help to restore the scenic, recreational, and habitat values of streams and rivers, maximize groundwater detention and infiltration to reduce polluted runoff and enhance groundwater supplies, and reduce discharge of pollutants through source controls (e.g., Bina and Devinny 2006, Sayre, Devinny, and Wilson 2006). The methodological approach relied on a series of spatially explicit models implemented at a variety of regional and subregional scales to characterize the current flow and water quality conditions and evaluate the restoration potential of alternative projects based on a set of watershed and related metrics (Sheng and Wilson 2008).

For assessments of watersheds, GVP utilized the high-resolution National Hydrography Dataset (NHD), a geographically referenced spatial data system developed for this purpose that constitutes a major advance in detail and accuracy over previous such datasets. However, the "fitness for use" of these types of datasets varies with the choice of analytical tools and landscape settings, and we encountered problems with data describing stream features and flow patterns that occurred frequently but unevenly across this heavily urbanized landscape. GVP implemented several strategies for correcting errors and ultimately generated a superior, single-line natural flow network for the metropolitan LA area (Sheng et al. 2007).

Using the corrected NHD data, plus supplementary information, we assessed conditions in five Southern California watersheds (Sheng and Wilson 2009a–e). For each watershed, descriptions of general characteristics and hydrologic conditions are followed by an analysis of stream networks, watershed attributes, hydrologic features (dams, reservoirs, flood control facilities, debris basins, spreading grounds, etc.), flow and flood dynamics, and groundwater characteristics. Stream segments were linked

Figure 6.19. Assessing water quality is a critical part of the Green Visions Plan.

with their catchment and flow data from selected stream gauge stations to characterize annual mean daily discharge and flood magnitudes with different recurrence inter-
vals (Sheng and Wilson 2009f). Not surprisingly this assessment showed a radically
altered stream network with few remaining natural riparian landscapes, suggesting
the need for headwater preservation, conservation and restoration of open space
areas, a cadre of projects to improve water quality and mitigate urban flood magnitudes, and a modified approach to regional groundwater extraction and recharge to
improve hydrological health throughout this rapidly changing region.

Finally, we developed a series of catchment-level water quality models to allow
planners to simulate the hydrological cycle over metropolitan regions. The complications arising from extensive human modification of land cover and land use along with
a lack of long-term hydrological monitoring records made this task more challenging
and led to results that incorporate substantial uncertainty. We employed customized
water-quality models for planning, using data and case studies from the GVP study
area. The resulting model highlights current water quality problems and identifies
those areas that produce the most contaminants. Such models can describe the region's spatial heterogeneity to some extent, offering reasonably good representations
of its hydrologic system, but the many data gaps reduce accuracy and limit the success of hydrologic modeling as well as water quality model results.

Parks and Recreational Open Space

The GVP parks and recreational open space component highlighted environmental justice for communities with inadequate access to green space. Our framework
sought to help planners achieve several goals: enhance access to recreational open
space in communities of color; maximize connectivity of trail/bikeways to promote
physical activity and access to nature; and connect beaches to inland communities.
We also sought to make it easier to develop multibenefit park projects by incorporating data on habitat and watershed conservation features associated with existing and
potential park sites.

First, we developed a detailed audit instrument and methodology to characterize parks and open space along key dimensions (Byrne et al. 2005). Some aspects
were derived from remote data sources, while other features were obtained through
use of a field audit instrument, created to characterize a random stratified sample of
parks and open space in the GVP. The instrument covered facilities and amenities,
landscape features, and condition and safety and was designed for a variety of
recreational settings (e.g., campgrounds, beaches, piers, marinas). Questions were
included on specific landscape features that could be used to evaluate conservation
and restoration potential. A version of the audit tool was used to perform web audits
for all existing facilities not field audited.

We used two approaches to quantify access to parks: (1) the traditional radius
technique that identifies a distance threshold inside which populations are deemed to
have access, and (2) the park service area approach, which assigns residents to their
closest park and quantifies potential park congestion for every park (Sister, Wilson,
and Wolch 2007, 2008). The radius analysis revealed that minority and low-income
groups were as likely to have access as high-income groups or whites, while the park
service area approach showed that Latinos and blacks had up to six times less park

Figure 6.20. No one's definition of a high-quality park

acreage per capita compared to whites. Similarly, low-income and poor residents were park-poor (Sister, Wolch, and Wilson 2010).

The park service area approach facilitated the identification of areas with greater park need and provided a pragmatic way to redress existing disparities in park access. Built into the GVP web-based planning toolkit (described below) this approach uses "on-the-fly" features that can be utilized by a wide spectrum of users, including community-based nonprofits and other stakeholders involved in park provision.

The GVP park planning strategy, with its emphasis on multibenefit projects, raised questions about nature and culture in the megalopolis. What are the consequences of successful urban conservation efforts for people and wildlife when they try to share urban hydrological systems and native assemblages of plants and wildlife? What are the consequences of the repopulation of urban space by wildlife and its simultaneous use by humans? Restoration and associated recreation initiatives can generate positive and negative interactions with urban planning and management tools (see Seymour 2005 and Seymour et al. 2006 for additional details).

The GVP Web-Based GIS Toolkit

The result of the analysis was the development of the GVP Toolkit 1.0, a web-based GIS mapping system. The toolkit integrates these three focus areas and the accompanying data into scenario planning features, allowing users to interactively visualize and explore synergies and trade-offs (Ghaemi et al. 2009) as they consider the planning and development of multibenefit projects that could provide habitat conservation, watershed health, and recreational open space benefits (Newell et al. 2008). Its dynamic analysis tools allow planners to conduct "what if" assessments of alternative parks or open space sites, to ensure their projects have maximum impact.

Figure 6.21. A more useful and appealing park

The GVP Planning Toolkit website consists of a map viewer, customized toolbars, and approximately 80 GIS data layers in addition to dynamic analysis tools that provide on-the-fly reports for specific parcels, stream segments and catchments, parks, and modeled native wildlife diversity. For example, the park analysis tool allows users to identify a specific parcel that could become a park and conduct an analysis of the extent to which its conversion to park space would relieve user congestion in existing parks in neighboring areas. By comparing alternative sites, project developers are better able to select the site that will have the largest benefits for park accessibility. Similarly, the habitat conservation tool can rank locations by their contribution to wildlife linkages across the region and calculate what target species would be supported by the area's restoration.

Prospects for Unpaving Paradise: Lessons from the Green Vision Plan Experience

Urban ecological and watershed scientists are only just developing the theoretical models and empirical research base that will allow planners tasked with making important investment and management decisions to conduct metropolitan socioecological analysis and scenario assessments. For example, most ecological corridor studies ignore cities, yet creating "local linkages" for mobile species can revivify the city and enhance biodiversity. Similarly, watershed analysis has focused on wildland stream networks, avoiding the complexities of modeling urban hydrological dynamics and water quality that are ever more critical to making cities more resilient. And park equity studies are narrowly focused, using metrics focused on park acres rather than facilities, condition, or potential for multibenefit projects.

As local and regional planners, community organizations, and scientists use the findings and tools derived from the GVP, four challenges are emerging, three of which are operational, the other scientific. Operational challenges include the fragmentation of responsibility for planning and analysis, severe gaps in data on habitat and hydrology in urbanized areas, and the need for collaborative structures for data and web-tools maintenance. The key scientific challenge is how to integrate place-based science across time-space scales; for example, how do we link models of nutrient cycling or estimates of ecosystem services to larger landscape dynamics scenarios such as river restoration or habitat corridor-reserve configuration alternatives?

First, no one agency has authority over planning in Southern California. This fragmentation has led to a proliferation of one-off mapping systems and GIS tools. Some systems are extraordinarily basic in terms of their science and rely on inadequate information yet are marketed aggressively by engineering or planning consultants. Most systems are designed for idiosyncratic purposes and are not part of any larger framework since there is insufficient collaboration around data sharing and updating. Decision makers are confused by the multiplicity of systems. The situation calls out for strong local-regional coordination around data quality, maintenance, and modeling.

Second, the data gaps are profound. Scholars, activists, and policy makers trying to think regionally have to work across many jurisdictions, each with its own data collection systems and quality standards. The technical problems of data integration are significant, while some types of data simply are not available. For example, Los Angeles County's Department of Public Works only recently created digital files of the county's underground water infrastructure system. Moreover, crafting models that account both for natural runoff and runoff patterns over the surface of the city's built environment is complex. Similarly, detailed mapping and habitat suitability assessment of the area's wide variety of habitats, much of it dominated by exotic vegetation but still supportive of biodiversity, are seldom conducted. Our knowledge of urban wildlife dynamics remains patchy and inadequate for restoration planning.

Third, GVP immediately raised unanswered questions regarding collaborative structures to maintain and update datasets, models, and tools. As the project moved toward completion in the late 2000s, the economic recession and attendant fall in public funding deeply affected land conservancies and local governments. This situation left open how the GVP toolkit would be maintained and kept up-to-date and how users across the public, nonprofit, and private sectors would be trained.

Finally, socioecological processes span time and space. We currently lack both robust microlevel ecological models that can generate estimates of regional ecosystem services and analyses of urban water quality at the watershed level that can provide sufficient detail on which water quality projects to prioritize on the ground. Similarly, we need agent-based models of park utilization behavior that can inform public park investment and, in turn, how investments—or lack thereof—drive use or avoidance of open space in the city. The development of multiscale models that allow easily visualized scenario planning will be an increasingly important part of the planners' toolkit as we seek to build more resilient, fair, and ecologically sustainable metropolitan regions.

Planning a Great Civic Park

Meredith Drake Reitan

For many planners, as Todd Gish discusses in Chapter 2, LA remains the epitome of the unplanned, centerless, and fragmented city. The myth of the city without a heart remains particularly strong—even among Angelenos. They are surprised to discover that the public spaces surrounding the Los Angeles Civic Center have been the object of more than 100 years of planning. Beginning in 1909 with a plan from one of the profession's early pioneers, Charles Mulford Robinson, numerous plans and schemes have been advanced for the Civic Center. Some of the United States' most famous architects, including Lloyd Wright and Paul Williams, have designed buildings for the area. However, after initial fanfare, most of the proposals simply collect dust.

The current complex, with its monolithic public buildings and concrete plazas, was considered the pinnacle of mid-20th-century planning design. Despite those accolades, the Civic Center has been much maligned. The area became know in the popular press

as "Bumper Butte," "Auto Atoll," and "that gigantic parking lot with the tower" in the middle.[1]

Public dissatisfaction with the Civic Center led a 1970s architectural critic for the *Los Angeles Times* to call the area "pretentiously inept" and consider it to be a "strong contender for the title of America's worst complex of public buildings and public spaces." While obvious hyperbole, the critic's point that the arrangement suggested "an image of mutually hostile guests seated for a formal banquet from which the table has been removed" is quite appropriate (Pastier 1970). The Civic Center's various open areas have never come together as a complete entity. The interior orientation of the surrounding buildings conceals rather than reveals interior spaces, and much of the park is hidden from view.

The most recent vision for providing coherence to the area is the Los Angeles Grand Park. An element of the much larger Grand Avenue project, new plans aim for a complete transformation of the existing space. At an estimated cost of $56 million, the plan is an ambitious marriage of landscape architecture and cultural programming. The design firm of Rios Clementi Hale Studios has been tasked with unifying the 12-acre site. To accomplish this goal, the firm has proposed a tree-lined perimeter of pathways and a number of new performance venues. The hope is that the park will become an extended front lawn for the Los Angeles Philharmonic, the Los Angeles Opera, the Center Theatre Group, and other arts organizations located at or near the Los Angeles Music Center.

Perhaps the most dramatic change is the construction of a grand stairway leading from the Music Center to the park at Grand Avenue. With a commanding view downward toward City Hall, the stairway will replace auto ramps that previously led to an underground parking lot. For some, these new stairs symbolically mark the passing of LA's auto-oriented planning ethos. The plan also updates the Arthur J. Will Memorial Fountain, dedicated in 1966, by adding a new wading pool and proposed additional green space to the area currently known as the Court of Flags. With spaces for strolling, relaxing, and participating, planners and city leaders hope the Grand Park will finally enliven the Civic Center.

ECONOMIC DEVELOPMENT

7

Policy and Community in Los Angeles Development

Goetz Wolff

Arguably the "industrial policy" of LA over the decades has been driven by land developers and real estate interests—whether for housing or commercial sites, major entertainment-related "destinations," or, in rare cases, industrial sites. In 2011, for instance, the Los Angeles City Council tentatively approved moving forward the development plan for a $1.5 billion National Football League stadium in the downtown core, adjacent to the city's convention center and the privately owned Staples Center and entertainment center LA Live (Zahniser and Farmer 2011). This decision is yet another example of project-based, public-private partnership economic development achieved by affluent developers (in this case, AEG—Anschutz Entertainment Group), agreed to by optimistic public officials, and accepted by the public, thanks to enthusiastic, largely uncritical, media portrayals.

Of course, LA economic development involves a number of other tools besides projects. This brief overview contextualizes LA's spatial environment and distinguishes among the various tools that purport to advance economic development. Along the way, I suggest that "economic development" as a primary public focus coincides with broader, negative economic conditions that bring development to the forefront of the agenda. In addition, this chapter highlights changes that have taken place in the development process due to popular activism—community, environmental, and labor.

The LA Setting

Although Los Angeles County mirrors the industrial shifts affecting the nation as a whole, including the economic restructuring to service industries, LA remains the largest center of manufacturing employment in the nation (LAEDC 2011). Its GDP ranks between those of Belgium and Switzerland and is greater than those of Sweden and Taiwan. The composition of the region's industries largely resembles that of the nation, with the exception of agriculture, mining, and tobacco. Key industries include entertainment, aerospace/high tech, tourism, and the cluster of industries surrounding international trade. This diverse industrial profile means LA is not as vulnerable as some regions, or even states, whose economic well-being rests upon the success of only a few prominent industries.

The economy's combination of entrepreneurship and a broadly diverse labor force continues to provide the momentum for surprisingly strong economy, despite the loss of many larger firms from the region. The labor force reflects LA's "majority-minority" demographics and high percentage of immigrant population. Highly skilled (legal) immigrants combine with young, primarily male, undocumented immigrant workers to create a flexible workforce able to respond to needs in advanced biotechnology as well as the service economy.

LA unfortunately also reflects the nation's wealth and income inequality, a result of the impact of neoliberal policies. An analysis of the most recent list of the "Top 50 Wealthiest Los Angeles Residents" (Lee 2011) shows that their cumulative wealth was $108 billion, far more than the annual incomes of more than two million LA workers.[1] These figures help explain why economic development efforts in LA have not been left to the usual agencies and actors. As a counterbalance, numerous community, environmental, labor, and immigrant organizations are inserting themselves into the economic development process.

What Is "Economic Development"?

For planners, economic development represents the active effort to advance the economic prosperity of localities and regions through policies to change the status quo by altering the current economic direction. While the government is always involved in the functioning of the economy—from the basic defense of private property and the "rules of the market" to the determination of who benefits from direct and indirect public subsidies and benefits—some portray the status quo of political-economic power in the nation or a city as the "natural" state, resulting in the labeling of economic development efforts as economic "interventions." Previous and existing "interventions" that have shaped the economy are unrecognized or hidden from discourse. All too often, this lapse in memory sets the stage for those who oppose an economic outcome, especially when it applies to a shift that reduces the benefits to the affluent.

As a result, an informal consensus pervades the mainstream economic development community. The actors concerned with practical outcomes that arise from political necessity are informed by a seeming consensus to grow jobs and enlarge the tax base. In recent years, labor and community organizations have inserted additional elements, including the quality of jobs, environmental and sustainability standards, and the admittedly fuzzy concern with quality of life.

U.S. Economics, LA Economic Development

LA economic development efforts have closely mirrored national recessions and economic crises. In the 1973–1975 post-Vietnam recession, LA established an economic development agency in the mayor's office, foreshadowing repeated efforts to address job loss and to retain firms. The new office was charged with creating a "positive industrial and commercial development program that will first identify . . . new employers who could best serve the needs and utilize the resources of Los Angeles."

Additionally, the program aspired to "aggressively seek to interest [employers] in Los Angeles," establish "industrial parks to meet the needs of new as well as expanding industry," and identify the "negative or positive" factors that influence the establishment or relocation of firms within the city. The office offered a proposal to market the region, as well as develop a "manpower training and job placement program involving the cooperative efforts of the City and private industry" (Crowe 1974). The 1974 proposals foreshadowed future, almost reflexive responses by city leaders to such economic downturns and their challenges as the severe double-dip recession of 1980–1982.

Drawing upon the remarkable success of the 1984 Olympics, Mayor Tom Bradley reacted to the difficult recession of the early '90s by handing off economic development responsibilities to the privately run Rebuild L.A., which achieved more press attention than job creation. With the regional economy lagging far behind the nationwide recovery because of the major downturn in the defense industries and the period's social and seismic catastrophes, businessman Richard Riordan followed Bradley into the mayor's office in 1993, advocating for a "business-friendly" city. He established a Mayor's Office for Economic Development. (*Plus ça change, plus c'est la même chose!*) In addition, numerous economic development efforts were set loose, including the use of "Red Teams" organized by the state to assist and keep firms.

As the national and local economies gradually recovered, the sharp focus on economic development efforts diffused. Economic development efforts were not abandoned, but the attention by leadership to such planning receded. Soon, a renewed focus on economic development programs occurred thanks to the inherent cyclical nature of the economy—this time the dot-com collapse at the turn of this century led to a major recession. In 2001, newly elected mayor James Hahn gave additional responsibility to the city's Community Redevelopment Agency, which leveraged private development with public resources. Once again, the approach aspired to make LA more business friendly, leading to the creation of the Office of Housing, Homelessness, and Economic Development, which promoted small business. Hahn promoted business tax reforms, while also establishing—strongly supported by labor and community advocates—a $100 million housing trust fund that led to the construction of thousands of additional affordable housing units.

The worldwide economic crisis is the most recent reminder that the U.S. economic system trumps LA economic development. State and local governments have been caught up in the swirl of financial shortfalls, and the national economy experienced dramatic job losses. California and LA were among the most severely hit by the subprime mortgage scandal. Caught in this environment, the region's economic development efforts once again became the primary focus and activity.

This history shows that, rather than plan, actors again—and again—*reacted* and rediscovered the problems facing the economy of the city, rather than institutionalizing a coherent, ongoing economic development planning infrastructure and strategy.

Size and political fragmentation are major structural challenges to the region's economic development efforts. Given its geographic and population size, Los Angeles County should have some uniform or coordinated economic development programs. Yet county government does not provide the institutions for economic development planning. Of course, LA and Long Beach programs are not coordinated with the county, with each other, or the activities of other significant cites such as Pasadena,

Burbank, Santa Monica, and Torrance. To compound the absence of meaningful economic development coordination, the larger metro five-county region is also free of any significant integrated economic development planning.

Efforts to resolve these challenges have largely failed. At a regional level, the Los Angeles County Metropolitan Transit Authority (Metro), brings together LA city and county along with other governmental interests to shape the pursuit and disbursement of massive numbers of transportation dollars, through local taxing as well as federal funding. Metro arguably is the only regional planning agency that brings together the interests of multiple jurisdictions combined with resources to implement aspects of economic development—e.g., transit-oriented districts and rail routes that shape land-use development. The Southern California Association of Governments (SCAG), a voluntary quasi-governmental agency, can at best collect data, especially related to transportation planning issues (due to its federal government transportation funding). It has little authority around economic development and little direct impact except as an arena for discussion among municipalities. A local nonprofit, Los Angeles Economic Development Corporation (LAEDC), has sought to provide economic data, analyses, and occasional economic development exhortation focusing on key industries, such as entertainment, fashion, and manufacturing, primarily for LA but also including the region and even San Diego County.

The fragmentation also affects local efforts. In LA, the mayor's office and the city council often have differing visions and goals, as do the several administrative departments and the many proprietary agencies, such as the Port of Los Angeles, the Department of Water and Power, and the Los Angeles World Airports (which includes LAX, Van Nuys, and Ontario airports—the latter located in Riverside County!). These numerous, independent actors set a stage for fractionated economic development policies and programs.

Repeated efforts to establish new institutional arrangements have never succeeded. In Mayor Riordan's second term, he established an advisory committee with appointees selected by the mayor's office and the city council to study the problems of the fragmented economic development system. Out of respect for the many constituencies, one of the board's elected cochairs came from the business-oriented Central City Association, the other from the LA County Federation of Labor (LACFL) AFL-CIO. The board's hearing revealed the dysfunctional nature of the institutional structures and agencies' fundamental differences around values. In the end, they issued a report but took no action.

Mainstream Economic Development Tools and Strategies

Although rarely ever a part of planners' and advocates' formal discourse, a tension between a focus on "people" versus "place" is embedded in economic development (Crane and Manville 2008, Lemann 1994). In practice, the tools available for local economic development programs lead to a greater reliance on various forms of "place-based" development, especially since the resources and existing programs that address the "people" dimension rely largely upon federal policies and resources.

Business Climate: Attraction

A strategy of business attraction has been, and continues to be, central to LA local economic development. Practitioners hope for the "big catch," ranging from replacement manufacturing plants for the many that have closed down or departed the region—auto, aerospace, steel, rubber, glass, and the like—but are just as likely to accept enticing an auto dealership and big box retailer to move jurisdictions, all in the pursuit of fattening the local tax base.

Over the past several decades, the mayor's office has established a variety of programs and special offices to bring in commercial and industrial development. Depressingly, many efforts seem more likely to lead to employment for consultants and city staff than bring in new businesses. For instance, one mayor promoted a public-private partnership called "New LAMP" (the Los Angeles Marketing Partnership) to provide initially regional and eventually national promotion as "the place to do business." The program placed positive-thinking billboards around LA and multipage ads in *Fortune* following the last substantial recession (as well as the 1992 riots and the 1994 earthquake). The difficulty in assessing the effectiveness of such attraction efforts leads to the repetition of such undertakings—from administration to administration—unguided by an assessment of past efforts.

Business Climate: Retention

Retention efforts portray LA as a "high-cost" business environment, which presumably accounts for job losses—disregarding parallel job declines statewide and nationally, especially during recessions. The most common economic development response is to attack the "regulatory climate" (especially in the city) and to reduce business-related taxes. More recently, addressing the need of companies for a suitable labor force has been added to the mix of enticements with the added benefit of addressing unemployment and underemployment. Mayor Villaraigosa appointed former mayor Riordan and a team of volunteer advisors to represent the business community perspective to advance job growth by tempering "environmentalists and unions going in for their piece of the pie without looking at the fact that people are starving in the meantime" (Willon 2009).

Employment Training

Training has become an added quiver in the arsenal of economic development. The Workforce Investment Board (WIB)—the largest of seven WIBs in LA County—committed itself to focusing on jobs and industries that are aligned with expected growth and job demand in the region. However, federal funding for workforce investment programs is less than half of what it was a decade ago, precisely at a time when the number of clients seeking job training is escalating and companies are not finding applicants with appropriate skills.

Such a commitment is a dramatic change from as recently as the period of the Riordan administration (1993–2001). At that time, the mayor proposed restructuring the economic development functions and departments, including shifting the employment training role to a human resources function (Fulton 1994). The attempted maneuver treated employment training (then residing in the Community Development Department) as a social service/job placement function—distinct from a coherent program that integrates job training and provides trained workers for growing companies. Fortunately neither the proposal nor the perspective prevailed.

Place-Based Projects

Practitioners promoting such projects assume that economic development interventions can change the fortunes of communities and places, although there may be other factors that intervene (Reese and Ye 2011). The Los Angeles City Community Redevelopment Agency (CRA/LA), the largest such agency established by the state, leads the project-related economic development efforts in LA. CRA/LA identifies some 166 active projects, affordable housing construction, retail centers, and commercial and industrial projects involving $1 billion of CRA investment and claims that $9.4 billion in leveraged sources resulted (CRA/LA 2011).

However, due to a dramatic state revenue shortfall, Governor Jerry Brown successfully promoted legislation that resulted in all redevelopment agencies being eliminated. Consequently, a number of CRA/LA projects have been put in limbo, awaiting the final determination of the legal battle challenging the elimination of these agencies. The LA city council agreed to move some $97 million to county services and thus maintain the city's CRA. Meanwhile a lawsuit by the California Redevelopment Association hopes to block the state effort to redistribute CRA funds (Zahniser 2011).

Taking advantage of the momentum associated with the American Recovery and Reinvestment Act of 2009, Mayor Villaraigosa also proposed a major transit infrastructure program for LA. It compresses the timetable for the completion of transit projects from 30 years to 10 years, based on the assurance to the federal government that the federal loan advance would be secured by the already passed city bond issue Measure R. In addition to reducing traffic and consequent particulate emission, the project would result in the creation of an estimated 166,000 construction jobs (Rutten 2010).

Industry Targeting

This strategy usually involves an attempt to capture (or at least identify) critical industries that bring investment and growth with jobs. The focus goes beyond the typical big box or auto dealerships as tax generators by taking into account such industry clusters as entertainment, design, logistics, health care, manufacturing, and tourism.

CRA/LA and WIB have committed to this strategy, underpinned by proactive research reports from LAEDC. Influenced by the onset of the great recession, Mayor Villaraigosa announced that his second term would focus on attracting and retaining key industries such biotechnology, clean technology, and entertainment, although he acknowledged that the city alone does not have the tools to drive a recovery in the context of the economic crisis (Willon 2009). The effort to develop a "Clean Tech Corridor," providing space for a variety of green-related firms adjacent to downtown, was a major step toward growing "green" manufacturing (Estolano 2007). However, the effort stumbled when a major Italian railcar manufacturer withdrew from locating an assembly plant there. In addition, brownfield problems made the property vulnerable to costly environmental remediation.

The CRA chief executive officer, who had redirected the agency toward industry targeting, was attacked by probusiness interests seeking to reduce public sector industrial policy and regulations that were viewed as curtailing "free market" growth. The resulting outcome was the resignation—under pressure—of the CEO (Rothman 2010). Nevertheless, the Clean Tech Corridor incubator moved forward and has been able to attract several business tenants (Fine 2011). Currently the CRA is seeking to target "critical business/industrial sectors . . . [and] to create strategies and opportunities for economic development" (personal communication 2011).

Sustainable Development

In contrast to the temporary fumbling of the sectoral targeting of "clean technology," sustainable development is becoming a reference point for LA economic development efforts. LA added a new focus for green-related economic development in three areas: low-impact development addressing issues of water conservation; changing the waste disposal system as an economic development issue; and linking the local food system to alternative food sources beyond the corporate food industry. Each of these initiatives is in the emerging stage, but the mayor's office has added a point person (i.e., senior advisor on food policy and special projects in water) to develop legislation and bring together stakeholders who may provide support and momentum for these areas of sustainable economic development (LA Dept. of Public Works 2011).

Expansion of the Participants in the Economic Development Process

Edward Soja's *Seeking Spatial Justice* provides an empathetic survey of the emergence of community, environmental, labor, and immigrant-based social formations that are reshaping LA economic development (2010). While mainstream economic development textbooks remain bogged in pluralist models of decision making by formal government institutions, LA provides an alternative model of economic development shaped by "unconventional" actors: community organizations, environmental activist groups, labor groups (including unions and worker centers), and immigrant-based organizations.

Grouping these organizations into distinct categories is somewhat misleading because nearly all of these organizations pursue policies and rely on support that tends to blur these neat groupings. Consequently the following review of these alternative "planning" actors attempts to note their overlapping membership and policy interests.

Strategic Actions for a Just Society (SAJE); Strategic Concepts in Organizing and Policy Education (SCOPE); and the Labor Community Strategy Center, which includes the Bus Riders Union (BRU), are prominent community-based membership organizations that have sought to directly shape economic development policies. Community groups, such as Union de Vecinos, East Yard Communities for Environmental Justice, and the Community Coalition, focusing on quality of life issues (e.g., housing, education, crime, water, and pollution) have joined them in the effort.

Over the past two decades, LA communities increasingly rejected policies and practices that treated them as objects of development. They became more organized to voice their own interests and demands. In brief, since 1996 SAJE has become the voice of primarily poor and minority residents opposing the "steamroller" of private development—such as the Staples Center and related entertainment complex—typically supported by key political figures. SAJE pioneered the use of community benefits agreements while standing for the "right to the city" and advocating the development of community land trusts that seek to provide alternatives to land and development speculation.

SCOPE, established in 1993, has focused on targeted industries (entertainment, health care, and city public employment) that provide job opportunities for disadvantaged communities. SCOPE evolved from an advocacy organization that forced the city of LA to agree to job opportunities in the entertainment industry for its community when the city arranged a land deal for the DreamWorks development in Playa del Rey—to a partner in developing job programs with the WIB.

The Labor Community Strategy Center originated in the fight over the closing of the Van Nuys General Motors assembly plant. While the plant in the San Fernando Valley ultimately shut down, the closing was delayed for several years. Their major role in shaping economic development has come through the environmental and social justice challenges to Metro's plans by BRU. This project forced the retirement of old diesel buses and the purchase of 2,500 CNG buses, and it challenged the focus on the highly subsidized rail system.

The Strategy Center and BRU have joined other alternative planning voices in speaking out for stronger environmental policies, the second area of activity. Communities for a Better Environment was founded in 1978. It attempts to free low-income minority communities adversely affected by industrial and traffic pollution from the source of the danger. Currently the group is partnering with several other community groups to develop a city ordinance that would curtail polluting heavy metals in LA communities.

Community-Based Economic Development Resources

Readers who want to know more about the innovative community organizations expanding LA's economic development agenda should use the following resources:

- Asian Pacific American Legal Center (APALC), www.apalc.org
- Central American Resource Center (CARECEN), www.carecen-la.org
- Coalition for Humane Immigrant Rights of Los Angeles (CHIRLA), www.chirla.org
- Coalition for Clean and Safe Ports, http://cleanandsafeports.org/los-angeleslong-beach
- Community Coalition, www.cocosouthla.org/about/ourmission
- Communities for a Better Environment, www.cbecal.org
- East Yard Communities for Environmental Justice, http://eycej.org
- Korean Immigrant Workers Alliance (KIWA): http,//kiwa.org
- Los Angeles Alliance for a New Economy (LAANE), www.laane.org/about-us/what-we-do/major-accomplishments
- Labor Community Strategy Center and the Bus Riders Union (BRU), www.thestrategycenter.org/about
- Los Angeles County Federation of Labor, AFL-CIO, http://launionaflcio.org/section/about-us.who-we-are
- Strategic Actions for a Just Society (SAJE), www.saje.net/site /c.hkLQJcMUKrH/b.2315795/k.C925/About_Us.htm
- Strategic Concepts in Organizing and Policy Education (SCOPE), www.scopela.org/article.php?list=type&type=5.
- Thai Community Development Center, http://thaicdchome.org/cms
- Union de Vecino, www.uniondevecinos.org

Originating in response to the intense diesel pollution accompanying goods movement from the Ports of Los Angeles and Long Beach, the Coalition for Clean and Safe Ports has become a voice addressing similar issues across the nation. In its words, it is a "partnership of environmental, public health, community, labor, faith, business, civil rights, and environmental justice organizations that promote sustainable economic development at ports coast to coast to make the port trucking system a less polluting, more competitive generator of good quality jobs for residents, workers and business alike." The coalition brought pressure to bear on the local ports, forcing them to adopt a plan to require only low-polluting trucks to haul the shipping containers in and out of the ports.

Organized labor is a third planning and economic development force to the community and environmental organizations. In contrast to conventional economic development agencies, labor- and union-based social institutions mobilize their worker bases to advocate for policies and programs that are advancing the interests of the poor and the working class.

For example, the Los Angeles Alliance for a New Economy (LAANE) was the leader in the development of the "clean trucks" strategy for the Coalition for Clean and Safe Ports. LAANE evolved from its predecessor organization, the Tourism Industry Development Council (TIDC), founded in 1993. The start-up TIDC received significant initial union support from Hotel Employees and Restaurant Employees union. Although LAANE no longer describes itself as a "labor" organization, its mission parallels that of most LA unions: improving the standard of living of workers and their communities.

LAANE was at the forefront in establishing a living wage and related ordinances; brokering the major development agreement for the Hollywood and Highland project; developing community benefit agreements with the LAX expansion; creating a superstore ordinance in LA that requires economic impact analyses by such development projects; leading the successful community fight challenging Wal-Mart's proposal to do away with community planning procedures in the city of Inglewood; and moving to transform the city's private trash collection and recycling system.

The growth in power of organized labor has propelled the planning and economic development success of LA community, environmental, and labor advocacy organizations. The keystone organization in this success has been LACFL, the umbrella organization with some 350 affiliated union locals representing over 800,000 workers. LACFL has emphasized the connections between the conditions of workers and their communities and city ordinances, subsidies, and projects. Beginning in the 1990s, LACFL made a conscious commitment to enlist its members in the political process. The electoral success of this movement in local, state, and congressional elections transformed the character of elected officials from representatives of, to advocates for labor interests (Frank and Wong 2004). Developers are not the only ones who can influence economic development policies. Likewise, appointments to key boards and commissions include members from labor and labor-related organizations. Perhaps most strikingly, Mayor Villaraigosa appointed the head of LAANE to be one of the seven CRA board commissioners.

The Los Angeles/Orange Counties Building Trades Council, representing a subset of unions within LACFL, is another labor organization that is critical to shaping LA economic development projects. They advocate for, and are involved in, every construction plan, whether it is with Metro's light rail, a new rail facility for goods, a sports facility, school building expansion, or port expansion. However, their focus on construction jobs leads them to part ways with many community and environmental groups, who feel they sometimes disregard adverse environmental or community impacts.

Allied with the labor groups is another set of community-based organizations that focus on immigration issues. Many of the workers that unions are trying to attract are immigrants, and immigration issues are critical economic development issues in a city with an immigrant population the size of LA's. Organizations such as the Thai Community Development Center, the Korean Immigrant Workers Alliance, the Coalition for Humane Immigrant Rights of Los Angeles, the Central American Resource Center, and the Asian Pacific American Legal Center are not simply "interest groups," but rather actors that directly insert themselves in the planning process and help create economic development policies that would not occur otherwise.

The "New Landscape" of Economic Development

As with all metropolitan areas in the United States, LA remains in the grip of an economic catastrophe. The challenge for economic development centers on competing visions of how to advance the well-being of the residents (and businesses) of LA. The history of "rediscovering" economic development schemes is usually centered on a myopic view that the current job losses and revenue collapse can be attributed to local policy failures. Just as in past recessions, these adverse conditions serve as the opportunity for business interests to undermine advances in addressing the needs of (particularly) poorer communities and excluded populations. In contrast to the past, a countervailing force made up of community, environmental, labor, and immigrant groups has succeeded in challenging the clarion call for simple "probusiness" economic development policies that often leave the unrepresented to experience the consequences of such policies. These advocates of progressive economic development do not have all the answers, nor are they in command of the outcome. Rather than being subjects to economic development, however, the previously excluded are now more likely to be among the decision makers who question past methods. These new participants also are likely to temper economic development policies that disregard the immediate well-being of the residents. In some cases, the power of these groups will result in advances in wages, housing, education, and the environment. However, we need to acknowledge the vulnerability of the metropolitan region to national and global economic trends. Thus the plans and projects of the community "interlopers" in the economic development process may not be fulfilled.

A Planning Ordinance Injects New Life into Historic Downtown

Ken Bernstein, AICP

On an early Thursday evening in the summer of 1995, the corner of Spring Street and Sixth Street in the heart of downtown LA is deserted, except for clusters of drug dealers offering passersby the opportunity to buy crack cocaine. Fifteen years later, thousands of Angelenos have congregated at the same corner for a monthly Art Walk, stopping to eat at nearby food trucks serving gourmet fare. Passersby are strolling with dogs on leashes, ambling about their residential neighborhood, sometimes stopping to start a conversation at one of two coffeehouses near the corner.

What triggered this remarkable transformation? While many factors have contributed, most agree that a provision inserted in the city's zoning code—the Adaptive Reuse Ordinance (ARO)—played the most important role.

The ARO cleared away the most significant obstacles to the repurposing of dozens of historic structures downtown that had sat vacant for years, even decades. The ordinance allowed the reuse of these older, and often historically significant, buildings without triggering restrictive zoning code requirements.

The Abandonment of Downtown Los Angeles

For a city reputed to have no history, LA has retained one of the nation's most intact historic downtowns. In many downtowns around the country, new office towers sprouted between the 1960s and 1980s on the sites of older and historic commercial structures torn down in the name of urban renewal. In LA, renewal occurred to a limited extent in the southern portion of downtown, now called the Financial District. But from the late 1960s through the 1980s, LA did not demolish and replace the heart of its downtown. Instead, it essentially abandoned and forgot about it, creating instead an entirely new downtown on Bunker Hill, replete with glassy skyscrapers.

Bunker Hill's large late-Victorian-era mansions, connected to the bustling commercial center by the 1901 Angels Flight funicular, "the shortest railway in the world,"

Figure 7.1. The massive redevelopment of Bunker Hill eliminated a grand old neighborhood in favor of modernist planning for a new downtown.

had been downtown's residential core. By the late 1950s and early 1960s, Bunker Hill's mansions had largely been subdivided into rooming houses, and the neighborhood was termed "blighted." Using the tool of eminent domain available under state law, the Los Angeles Community Redevelopment Agency (CRA) created the Bunker Hill Redevelopment Area, cleared out the entire neighborhood for the new Los Angeles Music Center and developed a plan to fill the space with high-rise office buildings.

By the 1980s, people had difficulty remembering that downtown's Spring Street had been famed as the "Wall Street of the West," with stately Beaux Arts bank buildings, financial buildings, and the former Pacific Stock Exchange. Or that one street to the west, Broadway, the commercial and entertainment hub of downtown, had been home of a dozen ornate movie palaces constructed between 1911 and 1931, the 1917 Grand Central Market selling food and produce, and the city's flagship department stores, including the May Company (originally Hamburger's, at Eighth Street), Bullock's (at Seventh Street), and the Broadway (at Fourth Street).

Slowly, the entire line of 13-story commercial structures along Spring and Broadway emptied out above the ground floor. Broadway still retained a lively street life, with the city's burgeoning Latino community embracing the street as a lower-cost

Figure 7.2. The Atlantic Richfield Building   Figure 7.3. The Los Angeles Central Library

shopping district. While ground-floor rents were high, driven by the high weekend foot traffic, millions of square feet above were entirely vacant. Even the once-grand movie palaces were shuttered by the late 1990s, after more than a decade showing second-run films dubbed in Spanish.

Historic Preservation? In Los Angeles?!

While the ARO in 1999 became a successful tool to preserve this remarkable architectural legacy, LA's initial steps to protect that heritage started in 1962 with the passage of the Cultural Heritage Ordinance, three years before New York City's more renowned Landmarks Preservation law. The LA law provided for the designation of significant buildings and sites, including a handful of the Bunker Hill mansions, some of which were relocated to a site off the 110 freeway, dubbed "Heritage Square," in an initiative spearheaded by the city's Cultural Heritage Board.

Nevertheless, several significant LA structures were lost in the late 1960s and early 1970s, including the art deco Atlantic Richfield Building and Irving Gill's Dodge House, and the preservation movement citywide remained a fledgling. A proposal in 1978 to demolish the LA Central Library served as the catalyst to encourage preservationists to create a broad-based, citywide preservation advocacy and education nonprofit, the Los Angeles Conservancy. The conservancy had some important early successes, helping to engineer a transfer of development rights deal that allowed for the preservation and expansion of the Central Library and rescuing the art deco Wiltern Theater on Wilshire Boulevard.

In 1981, the conservancy's advocacy moved the city beyond saving individual buildings with the passage of the Historic Preservation Overlay Zone (HPOZ) Ordinance, enabling the creation of historic districts. The first HPOZ, in Angelino Heights

Figure 7.4. A residence on Carroll Avenue in Angelino Heights

in 1983, protected the city's finest extant collection of Victorian-era architecture, in one of LA's "original suburbs." HPOZs spread slowly around the city, with eight districts created between 1983 and 1998. In the late 1990s and early 2000s, an explosion of interest in HPOZs occurred, as a preservation ethic deepened and development pressures increased. Today, 29 HPOZs are located in every corner of the city, including three in the San Fernando Valley and two in the Harbor communities.

False Starts on Downtown Housing

By the late 1990s, with successes multiplying across the city, historic preservation was increasingly accepted as an economic revitalization tool, yet the many successes did not easily translate into a widespread revitalization of the historic downtown.

The success of the Adaptive Reuse Ordinance followed several abortive efforts to promote housing in downtown LA. For instance, the CRA helped finance housing on Spring Street during the 1980s. The Premiere Towers project combined two historic buildings (the 1923 California Canadian Bank Building and the 1931 E. F. Hutton Building) into a single condominium project. The effort ended in heartbreak and financial distress for the urban pioneer owners who came to downtown a few years too soon.

Next, the pioneering developer Ira Yellin pursued an ambitious project called Grand Central Square in the early 1990s. He attempted to redevelop the corner of Broadway and Third Street, converting the Laughlin Building into 121 units of mixed income housing, while also rehabilitating the 1917 Grand Central Market and the 1893 Bradbury Building, which boasts one of the nation's most stunning historic com-

Figure 7.5. The restored Bradbury Building

mercial interiors. Grand Central Square required heavy public subsidies, including a $44 million loan floated by the CRA and backed by the Metropolitan Transportation Authority (Metro) to reinforce its public investment in the Red Line. But while the project's rental units quickly filled up, eventually the CRA and Metro needed to provide additional financing for Yellin to avoid foreclosure (MacAdams 1998, 60).

Such were the false starts, widespread skepticism, and depressed downtown land values when Tom Gilmore entered the downtown scene in 1997, originally working with downtown real estate investor Judah Hertz. Gilmore quickly struck out on his own and began purchasing low-cost downtown commercial buildings, particularly around Fourth Street at Main and Spring streets. The gregarious Gilmore, with an urbanist's sensibility, promoted the vision of a lively, 24-hour downtown: a place where younger, creative residents, nontraditional households, and empty-nesters could find the authenticity, excitement, and convenience available only in traditional downtowns and historic buildings.

Gilmore's enthusiasm quickly ran up against code requirements that treated the conversion of older buildings to new uses—"adaptive reuse"—as equivalent to new construction. In 1996, the CRA and the Central City Association (CCA), the major advocacy organization for downtown businesses, convened an Adaptive Reuse, Live/Work Workshop, which grew into the Adaptive Reuse Task Force. The task force's work culminated in the 1999 passage of the ARO. City planning department staff planner Alan Bell took the lead in its drafting the original ordinance and subsequent amendments and interpretations. Gilmore's project, which he named the "Old Bank District," was the first to test the viability of the ordinance and the state of the downtown residential market.

The Provisions of the Adaptive Reuse Ordinance

The ordinance largely waived or grandfathered in zoning requirements for conversions of downtown buildings in a commercial or R5 (high-density) residential zone constructed before July 1, 1974. (A building constructed after this date was eligible for the incentives upon determination of a zoning administrator that the building was no longer economically viable.) These provisions addressed the following issues:

- **Parking:** No new parking spaces are required, but all existing spaces must be maintained.
- **Floor area, lot line setbacks, and heights:** Existing conditions that do not conform to current zoning regulations are grandfathered in.
- **Unit size:** The minimum size for each unit is 450 square feet, with a required average size of 750 square feet.
- **Density:** There is no limit on the number of units permitted if the project complies with the other standards.
- **Mezzanines:** Mezzanine spaces may be added so long as they do not exceed one-third the size of the floor below and comply with the building code.
- **California Environmental Quality Act:** Adaptive reuse projects permitted "by right" do not require environmental clearance; projects in historically significant buildings do require environmental review, solely to ensure that the project would not adversely affect the building's historic character.

In short, most adaptive reuse projects were now able to bypass the lengthy planning and zoning approval process altogether and proceed directly to the Department of Building and Safety for permits.

The Department of Building and Safety developed special guidelines for adaptive reuse projects, which it tested on Gilmore's Old Bank District project and other early applications. The guidelines were published for all projects in 2002 and ultimately codified (as amendments to Division 85 of the city's building code) in 2005. These provisions addressed occupancy requirements, fire/life safety, disabled access, and structural/seismic safety. In late 2002, the city council also extended the adaptive reuse incentive to five other areas of the city and then extended it citywide in 2003.

Marketing Adaptive Reuse

Even with the new ordinance, downtown and city leaders needed to overcome continued skepticism that the residential market would ever take hold. The Los Angeles Conservancy played a leadership role in implementing and marketing the ordinance.

The Conservancy partnered with Killefer Flammang Architects and Degenkolb Engineers to survey all buildings in the historic downtown, identifying 50 that had the appropriate conditions and configurations for residential conversions. The conservancy actively marketed these buildings, and adaptive reuse generally, to potential developers and lenders. The conservancy and the city joined forces in organizing lenders roundtables on adaptive reuse in 2002 and 2003. At the first roundtable in July 2002, one downtown LA bank representative echoed the prevailing sentiment of the time by asking, "How can we be sure that this revitalization is sustainable?"[1]

The CCA and its Downtown Center Business Improvement District also played

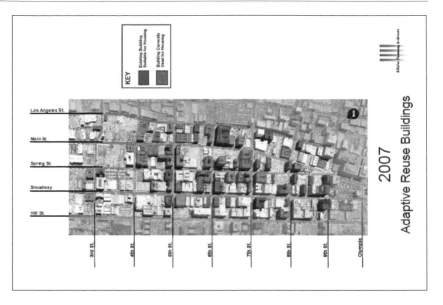

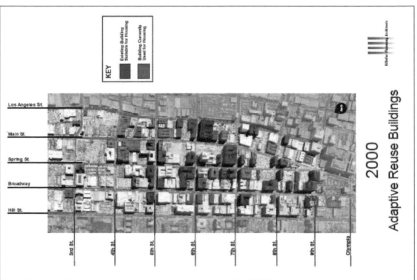

Figure 7.6a and 7.6b

a critical role, promoting adaptive reuse in the development community, organizing trips to New York to woo lenders and hosting bus tours of new loft housing with the conservancy. Downtown city council member Jan Perry also played a strong role in marketing the ordinance and facilitating key projects.

Perhaps the most important step in the implementation of the ordinance was the appointment of Hamid Behdad, formerly an engineer in the Department of Building and Safety, to serve as the point person for adaptive reuse in the Mayor's Office of Economic Development. Behdad actively promoted adaptive reuse, cut through bureaucratic impasses in addressing ongoing code challenges, and helped shepherd applicants through the permitting process.

Financial Incentives: The Historic Preservation Link

Even with the very best marketing and coordination, adaptive reuse projects would be successful only if they "penciled out" economically. Many early rehabilitations relied on two historic preservation financial incentives. The Federal Historic Rehabilitation Tax Credit offers a 20 percent credit applied to qualified expenditures on historic rehabilitation for buildings listed in the National Register of Historic Places. Because Spring Street and Broadway were National Register historic districts, all of the historic buildings on both streets qualified for this incentive.

Other downtown building owners sought local Historic-Cultural Monument designation of their buildings to qualify for the Mills Act incentive. The Mills Act, a state law passed in 1977 and applied in LA starting in 1996, can provide property tax relief to owners of historic properties. Owners contract with city government, agreeing to preserve the building in accordance with historic preservation standards and to pursue an agreed-upon maintenance schedule in return for an alternative property-tax assessment formula that typically results in a 20 to 80 percent reduction in property taxes.

Case Studies

Tom Gilmore's Old Bank District project, involving the renovation of the San Fernando, Continental, and Hellman buildings, opened in 2000–2001, utilized both of these incentives, and successfully demonstrated that the market existed, for urban living. Numerous other adaptive reuse projects followed on its heels, including these two:

Pacific Electric Lofts

In 1905, Henry Huntington constructed the Pacific Electric Building at the corner of Sixth and Main streets. At nine stories, the building was the largest in LA, and is considered the city's first skyscraper.[2] It was built as the transit hub and central offices for Huntington's Pacific Electric Railway, then the largest interurban railway system in the world. The building's top floors, with a grand, two-story rotunda, housed the exclusive Jonathan Club, a men's social club. The building, with its Richardsonian Romanesque and Beaux Arts design, yellow brick masonry, and arched Romanesque windows, is a Los Angeles Historic-Cultural Monument and is listed in the National Register of Historic Places yet had sat mostly vacant since 1989.

The award-winning transformation of the Pacific Electric into 314 residential lofts by ICO Investment Group and Killefer Flammang Architects created large penthouse units with exposed original steel trusses, a gym, rooftop pool, and garden. The Jonathan Club rotunda became a library, offering residents a place to gather and socialize. The project utilized Federal Rehabilitation Tax Credits to generate more than $5 million in equity, helping to make the rehabilitation feasible.

Figure 7.7. The restored Pacific Electric Building

Douglas Building Lofts

While the Pacific Electric was one of downtown's largest and most notable historic buildings, many smaller, yet still very significant, structures were transformed by adaptive reuse projects. The Douglas Building, located on the corner of Third and Spring streets, was built in 1898 as a memorial to Thomas Douglas Stimpson, a lumber baron and real estate mogul. James and Merritt Reid, San Francisco architects who were responsible for numerous commissions, including the original Fairmont Hotel in San Francisco and the Hotel Del Coronado, designed the classical revival building.[3]

Like the Pacific Electric Building, the Douglas Building had sat vacant for many years. In 2005, Metro Partners 5 and Rockefeller Partners Architects converted the building into 50 residential condominiums, among the first condominium projects to sign a Mills Act contract with the city.

Results

The stories of the Pacific Electric and the Douglas Building have been repeated in dozens of other projects downtown and around the city. The cumulative results of the ordinance and the accompanying activities have been nothing short of remarkable. As of 2011, the ordinance has resulted in 76 projects in downtown alone, producing 9,137 units of new downtown housing. Of these, 2,479 were for sale (condominium) units.[4]

Figure 7.8. The Douglas Building as seen from Third Street

Policy Issues

For all of its success, the ARO was not entirely free of controversy. Critics have been concerned that the ordinance has resulted in the gentrification of downtown, displacing nearby lower-income residents and not offering new affordable housing. The realities are mixed.

Adaptive reuse in the historic downtown was shadowed by the proximity of many potential building candidates to Skid Row or Central City East, with its high concentration of shelters and social services for the homeless just a few blocks to the east. However, the program has not resulted in the direct physical displacement of poorer residents: the vast majority of buildings converted had previously been in commercial use and had long been entirely vacant above the ground floor. Further, fears that Broadway would lose its pedestrian-friendly, Latino-oriented character have not materialized. Broadway's ground-floor uses remain very similar to the uses in 1999.

The revitalization spurred by the ARO did create some development pressure on single-room-occupancy (SRO) hotels and other residential hotels that typically rent to lower-income tenants on a weekly or monthly basis. The ARO incentives did not apply to residential-to-residential conversions. Nevertheless, five SRO hotels with 982 units were converted to market rate housing between 2000 and 2003.[5] The LA city council responded by passing a temporary moratorium on such conversions in 2006, followed by a permanent ordinance in 2008 requiring one-for-one replacement of converted units or payment of an in-lieu fee.

The most disappointing outcome has been the failure to provide new affordable housing. Early in the adaptive reuse boom, many downtown developers, including

Tom Gilmore, expressed enthusiasm for pursuing a mixed-income approach downtown, typically with a 20 percent mix of affordable housing. The state, partially inspired by the early success of LA's Adaptive Reuse Program, also passed a statewide Downtown Rebound Initiative to encourage these projects. But few actual mixed-income projects resulted: of the more than 9,000 units created downtown, fewer than 10 percent (797) were affordable units.[6]

Conclusion

Despite these reservations, LA's ARO and accompanying implementation program must be recognized as one of the most successful urban strategies pursued in recent decades. The program has preserved a remarkable collection of historic structures that would have otherwise been threatened with demolition or long-term obsolescence; created thousands of units of new housing in the city's neighborhoods best served by transit and existing infrastructure; and established entirely new residential communities downtown and in other neighborhoods, such as Hollywood, spurring new retail investment and nightlife.

While not every city has the high concentration of vacant historic downtown buildings that 1999 LA did, the ARO's formula—historic preservation as economic development tool—clearly offers a replicable model for urban regeneration across the nation.

The Evolution of Entertainment Retail

Sam Gennawey

In 1965, architect Charles Moore wrote that in LA "you have to pay for the public life" in a region where "hardly anybody gives anything to the public realm." The planners and architects, dreamers and schemers who have created the region's retail centers have repeatedly reinvented the formula by making their centers less about location and more about destination. The region has been the site of change from some of the first suburban shopping centers to the latest trend in entertainment retail. In LA—this "improbable" place, as journalist Carey McWilliams once called it—Hollywood set designers build houses, architects design movie sets, and many of our most cherished "public spaces" are actually privately owned and operated.

The region has long been a pioneer in the development of retail centers. As Richard Longstreth (1998, 227–38) has chronicled, the Broadway-Crenshaw Center (1947) is considered one of the earliest suburban retail centers anchored by a supermarket in the United States. When the Lakewood Center opened in 1952, it was the largest shopping center in the United States, according to the *Guinness Book of World Records*. Over the next three decades, shopping malls opened throughout the region, servicing the growing suburban crowds.

Many malls were uninspired, boring, formula-driven boxes of mass consumption drawing (often quite unfairly) on the designs of Victor Gruen, a Los Angeles architect. When Gruen designed the Northland Mall near Detroit (1954) and the enclosed Southdale Center near Minneapolis (1956), he was creating a new kind of communal space for postwar America (Hardwick 2004). Many of his imitators, here and around the nation, saw these structures only as machines for making money.

In more recent years, many older malls have declined as shopping preferences changed and the Internet and other alternatives rose. In a polycentric region such as LA, the many commercial business districts compete for local and regional markets, hoping to draw customers. As a result, the region's entrepreneurs have continued to adapt the retail center to emerging locations and activities. From CityWalk in Universal City to Hollywood and Highland along Hollywood Boulevard, new centers have emerged that integrate entertainment and shopping to satisfy new generations of LA residents and visitors.

The Pioneer: CityWalk

CityWalk at Universal City (1993) was the first center that tried to break the mold of the conventional shopping mall. German-Jewish immigrant Carl Laemmle had founded Universal City in 1915 for the purpose of making motion pictures. The property grew from 230 acres to more then 425 acres and became the site of a popular studio tour and theme park (1964) with a live concert venue (1972). Universal Studios went from being just a movie studio to becoming a major entertainment destination.

By 1989, legendary entertainment mogul and head of Universal Studios Lew Wasserman hired architect Jon Jerde to draft a master plan for the property. Jerde was well-known for his simple, effective architectural elements at the 1984 Los Angeles Olympics as well as the urban infill Horton Plaza shopping center in the Gaslamp District in downtown San Diego.

A major component of the new master plan was the entertainment retail center CityWalk. In a *Los Angeles Times* interview Jerde said, "I saw CityWalk as a venue for human intercourse." He agreed with Charles Moore that "all America is now private" and that only "New York and San Francisco held on to more foot-driven aspects of human interaction, but most of the country has been given over to separateness and loneliness." He wanted to create something different.

"Our enemies are artifice and the ersatz [with] fake this and that, like those theme restaurants," Jerde said. "But people reject it. It's exceedingly difficult to make sure that what you do isn't exceedingly synthetic and contrived." The result was a two-block-long pedestrian "street" that connects the theme park's front gate to the parking structures required by this isolated, compact hilly site. Jerde said he wanted to capture the emotional impact of Tuscany or North Beach in San Francisco.

"CityWalk had to be appropriately built on the architectural language of LA, as opposed to New York or Paris," he said. "And the language of LA is that there is no language except stucco buildings and layers put upon them. So the thematic element is layering." Juxtaposed facades, historic neon signs, and billboards frame the narrow street, which Jerde says creates "a sequential plan of orchestrated events." The massing of the buildings came from computer-compiled traces of local architecture. No one building is replicated. Instead you have a collage of images and traits of the city. Jerde wanted a space that is "self-consciously designed" yet tries to appear to have grown organically.

CityWalk does feel energetic, bordering on chaotic, as it tries to echo the visual disorder of a complete city within the space of a few yards. The street leads to a large central plaza capped by a steel-web canopy. Within this multistory space is a second level of nightclubs and restaurants dubbed CityLoft, centered around an interactive fountain by WET Design. More then a third of CityWalk's 540,000-square-foot building area is dedicated to offices and a satellite college campus.

Many critics disliked the design. Cultural critic Norman Klein wrote, CityWalk is "a Victorian-style separation of classes in our public life," while writer Lewis Lapham argued that it served consumers who "had no intention of going to see the original city four miles to the south." Mike Davis simply concluded, "It fulfills our worst prophecies."

CityWalk's second phase opened seven years after the original in 2000. Lighting is used as the signature architectural component. *Los Angeles Times* critic Nicolai Ouroussoff suggested that "the new structures offer fewer architectural quotations, leaning toward a more abstract aesthetic" with "images distilled from Los Angeles' own peculiar landscape of fantasy." He says "the effect is a 'Blade Runner'-like collage of commercial images, a tensely energetic mix of fantasy and reality." The new addition is best experienced at night, when the lighting provides an eerie effect.

Designing a Downtown for Disneyland

In 2001, Universal's longtime competitor, the Walt Disney Company, went in a very different direction from Jerde's sense of randomness, surprise, and disorder when it opened the entertainment retail center Downtown Disney in Anaheim as part of a major expansion of the Disneyland Resort that included a new theme park and hotel.

If the success of the early shopping centers established the components of the shopping mall model, Disneyland pointed the way to retail's future. John Hench, a 65-year Disney veteran, said, "the whole 'malling of America,' I think is the expression—comes from Main Street here in Disneyland. They suddenly discovered that they could . . . make it work a lot better by observing what happened here." However, he added, "Their observation . . . didn't penetrate too deeply, but they knew they wanted to make sense of the place."

Disneyland works, Hench explained, "simply because every member of the thing, every facility, agrees on what the place is. One building recognizes the existence of the other. There's plenty of diversity, but there isn't contradiction. Most urban environments are basically chaotic places, as architectural and graphic information scream at the citizen for attention." He warns: "A journey down almost any urban street will quickly place the visitor into visual overload as all of the competing messages merge into a kind of information gridlock."

Hench taught his designers that architectural chaos "does have some stimulation to it because it's a threat—you're stimulated by a threat, but how long can you continue that?" Instead, he said, "We stimulate them with another kind of emotion, with the kind of stimulus that says, 'You're going to be okay.'" The result is "not a threat, it's the reverse." This advice would influence many developers.

Downtown Disney has none of the harsh edges to be found at CityWalk. Timur Galen of Walt Disney Imagineering said the district "possesses its own unique 'sense of place,' evoking the feeling of stepping into a garden paradise." The shopping center is a long corridor that connects the Disneyland Hotel to the plaza in front of the two theme parks. The pathway meanders and is dotted with planters, fountains, and deflected views. The architecture along the frontage is mildly art deco but primarily serves as background. The pavement is embedded with leaves, and the street furniture continues to reinforce the garden theme. A resort hotel in the Arts and Crafts tradition is integrated into the mall along with numerous performance spaces. The center is not as highly detailed and theatrical as Main Street inside of Disneyland. However, the park's spirit of reassurance is captured in the new spaces.

Urban Infill on a Grand Scale: The Grove

As John Hench suggested, Disneyland's architectural vocabulary has influenced many other "invented" places, including The Grove in the Fairfax district of LA (2002). Developer Rick Caruso considers Walt Disney a hero, saying he is "one of the true geniuses in the world." Built adjacent to the historic Farmers Market (1934), The Grove is one of the most successful shopping centers in the region. It was Caruso's first urban infill project after constructing suburban "lifestyle" centers in Calabasas and Thousand Oaks. "What we are building are downtowns. It's not just the big ideas, it's also the little ideas that matter," Caruso said, adding that his goal was to build "a great street."

"It's a thousand different things you notice but you couldn't tell what it is," he said. "It's the scale of buildings and the width of the street. It's the rhythm of the trees and the lampposts. It's eye candy that your brain pick(s) up but you can't really say what makes a difference." He was inspired by the redevelopment of Rome's Via Veneto and wanted to capture the elegance and spirit of an Italian villa. The Grove features a musical fountain designed by WET Design and a double-decker trolley designed by former Disney Imagineer George McGinnis. All set along a curvy main street, as prescribed by the feng shui expert Caruso consulted.

Like Disneyland, The Grove features building facades framing a narrow corridor using forced perspective, a filmmaking technique that adds depth. Applied to the built environment, forced perspective can create an illusion of greater building height while maintaining an intimate atmosphere. At Disneyland, the first floor is generally nine-tenths scale while the upper floors get progressively smaller. At The Grove, the first floor is full-scale while the upper floors get progressively larger. The result is what the *Los Angeles Times* described as a "wildly popular amusement park-like shopping center," with a highly energized space, midway between Disneyland's Main Street and CityWalk.

The Grove is a single-use shopping center with little connection to the streets that surround it. When Caruso planned The Americana at Brand in Glendale (2008), he added housing, basing the design on 1940s Charleston, South Carolina. The decision to mix uses was, of course, a response to planning reform movements that advocated alternatives to the autocentric shopping center. The integration of housing within an entertainment retail center was pioneered at the Paseo Colorado in Pasadena (2001), designed by Ehrenkrantz Eckstut + Kuhn Architects.

Hollywood Actually in Hollywood: Hollywood and Highland

For decades, many tourists and local residents have asked themselves the same question, where do you go when you visit Hollywood? You can go to Anaheim, where Walt Disney captured a bit of Hollywood spirit with Disneyland. Or to Universal Studios, which successfully invited (paying) guests to peek behind the movieland curtain. David Malmuth asked himself, What if somebody celebrated Hollywood actually in Hollywood and did not charge admission?

Malmuth, working for the development arm of the Walt Disney Company, had been involved with the rehabilitation of the New Amsterdam Theater in New York City. He recognized how this investment became one catalyst in the revitalization of Times Square. Could Disney do the same thing for the heart of Hollywood, at the corner of Hollywood Boulevard and Highland Avenue?

Down the street from that corner is what many consider the center of Hollywood, the iconic Grauman's Chinese Theatre, famous for world premieres and the signatures, footprints, and handprints of popular motion picture personalities since the 1920s. Disney had already moved onto the block in 1989, acquiring and renovating the El Capitan Theater, only steps from the Chinese Theatre, as a showcase for its new entertainment offerings.

Hollywood had struggled economically for decades, especially after the movie industry spread throughout the region. The failing Hollywood Galaxy entertainment complex was a couple of blocks to the east of the El Capitan. Across the street was the rundown Hollywood Hotel. A new transit line offered hope for the future but pain in the meantime, as businesses struggled with construction delays and obstructions. Visitors looking for the myth of Hollywood constantly walked away disappointed when they visited the actual place. Malmuth said, "Visitors had money, they had interest, they were looking for something special, and their expectations were not being met."

Malmuth originally envisioned each of the major movie studios "adopting a block" of storefronts where guests could interact with the film industry as they do at Disneyland and Universal Studios. Each studio would have spaces in the new development where they could place studio-themed retail stores, restaurants, and opportunities to preview upcoming films. Many studios, such as MGM, Paramount, Warner Bros., and Sony had already experimented with place-based entertainment venues, so he thought this idea would be a natural extension. Hollywood and Highland would not be a suburban shopping mall planted in city, but it would be a safe, clean, gathering place for those seeking the "Hollywood" experience.

The property across the street from the El Capitan was perfect. Warner Bros. owned 50 percent of the Chinese Theatre. The city Community Redevelopment Agency (CRA) and Metro (the transit agency) owned the rest. The CRA was trying to consolidate surrounding properties for a large development. A subway station was planned for this location. In 1995, Malmuth began working with recently elected LA city council member Jackie Goldberg to bring the pieces together.

Confident that he was on to something big, in March 1996 Malmuth made a presentation to Disney CEO Michael Eisner and company president Michael Ovitz. Eisner responded that Disney did real estate deals only if they served the company's entertainment arm, and the theater already did that, so Disney was not interested. Soon the other studios lost interest. In June 1996, Malmuth brought the concept to Lou Wagman at TrizacHahn, a large real estate development firm. The city released an RFP for the redevelopment of the block adjacent to the Chinese Theatre in April 1997. TrizacHahn partnered with Ehrenkrantz Eckstut + Kuhn Architects and won the contract. An agreement was reached in April 1998 for a project with an estimated cost of $615 million. The CRA would contribute $90 million with $30 million set aside for the Kodak Theater, a critical piece of the project.

The Academy of Motion Picture Arts and Sciences was looking for a new home for the Oscars. The academy considered existing sites, such as Pantages Theater, as well as the Dorothy Chandler Pavilion, before deciding to build a state-of-the-art facility. The city agreed to retain ownership of the theater. Malmuth said, "What we talk about in describing our ambition here for Hollywood Boulevard is to create a place that's authentic." The Kodak Theater would add instant credibility to the commercial enterprise.

The architectural centerpiece of the five-story entertainment retail complex is a massive interior courtyard inspired by the Babylon set from D. W. Griffith's film *Intolerance*, one of the largest movie sets ever built in Hollywood. The archway of the courtyard frames the Hollywood sign. Vaughan Davies, an architect on the project, commented that this view is the project's most compelling aspect. Tying everything together internally is a series of mosaics called *The Road to Hollywood* by Erika Rothenberg.

The exterior has none of the flash expected in Hollywood. Instead, it is laminated with billboards, which have been granted exempt status from city standards until 2022 (a critical part of the development's financial plan). The billboards hide the lack of quality architecture in this money-making machine. As on a movie set, one side is to be filmed (the interior) and the other side just holds up the facade (the exterior).

Critics have dismissed the center as filled with commercial and architectural compromises. The innovative original plan to create a showcase for the studios remains only in the confusing circulation pattern. In addition to the subway station, the complex has a bowling alley, nightclubs, a broadcast studio, and a 65,000-square-foot ballroom. However, Hollywood and Highland has helped attract considerable new development in the surrounding area, fulfilling one of the original project goals.

What is the next step in the evolution of the entertainment retail center? With constant pressure to reinvent the genre, it may not be long before we find out.

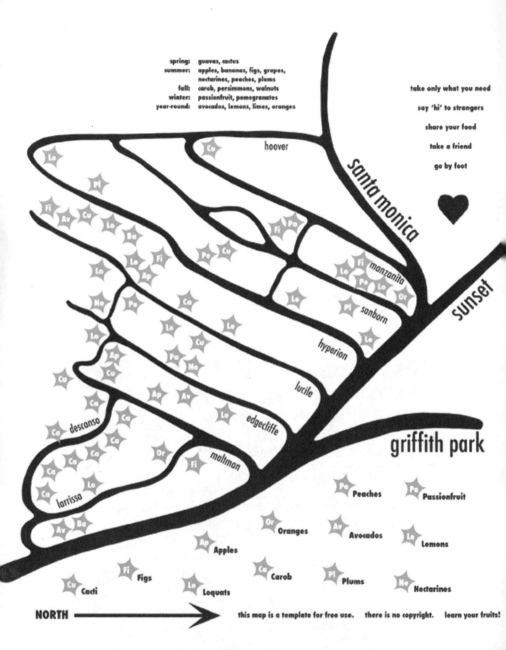

spring: guavas, cactus
summer: apples, bananas, figs, grapes, nectarines, peaches, plums
fall: carob, persimmons, walnuts
winter: passionfruit, pomegranates
year-round: avocados, lemons, limes, oranges

take only what you need

say 'hi' to strangers

share your food

take a friend

go by foot

hoover

santa monica

sunset

manzanita

sanborn

hyperion

lucile

griffith park

edgecliffe

descanso

maltman

larrissa

Peaches

Passionfruit

Oranges

Avocados

Lemons

Apples

Carob

Plums

Nectarines

Figs

Cacti

Loquats

NORTH

this map is a template for free use.   there is no copyright.   learn your fruits!

FALLEN FRUIT OF SILVER LAKE

more information at http://www.fallenfruit.org

Politics of Food and Culture

Meredith Drake Reitan

Southern California has long been known for its agricultural abundance, with the prototypical suburban home set in a garden full of fruit trees and a home to a chicken coop. The Irvine Ranch in Orange County (now home to the master planned community of Irvine) once housed over 300,000 Valencia orange trees, along with miles of lima beans and other fruit and vegetable crops. Similarly, much of LA and Hollywood was once blanketed by orchards, traces of which can be found in streets named for lemons, oranges, and other citrus.

Yet the role of fruit has been obscured in our urbanized society, which is one reason why the art group Fallen Fruit (www.fallenfruit.org) has used fruit as a means to investigate urban space, conceptions of neighborhood, and the tensions surrounding citizenship, property, and community. They have whimsically interrogated traditional planning concepts, like the use of public space and community engagement, by trying to involve and educate residents about the natural environment that surrounds them through inventive, even subversive events and projects. At the core is their questioning of the boundary between public and private property, which has led them to investigate alternative forms of shared property and resources, such as the commons.

A collaboration of artists David Burns, Matias Viegener, and Austin Young, Fallen Fruit has produced an ongoing series of narrative photographs, videos, public events, and collaborative performances. The team has created public service posters for bus shelters as well as interactive installations and murals. They have planted "love apples" (tomatoes) on traffic islands and opened "bars" where their docents serve "neighborhood infusions" of vodka and fruit fallen from local trees. Their ongoing project of mapping the fruit trees in local neighborhoods so people can learn about plants, and eat a little fruit, has gone worldwide, with maps from Sweden, Spain, Colombia, Mexico, and Denmark. In each instance, the idea is to increase the residents' awareness of the plants around them, while ensuring they remember, as Fallen Fruit asks, to "share your food" and "say hi to strangers." By pointing out where the trees are and are not, they remind us of those who have resources, and those who don't.

Only recently, planners have begun to see food as a local, regional, national, and international planning issue. Communities are implementing new regulations through the planning process, as well as establishing urban farmers, farmers markets, community gardens, and other positive alternatives to commercialized food systems. Fallen Fruit is one of a legion of art and planning groups interrogating our assumptions about the industrialized food system, its impact on local communities, and how it represents power and politics in our society, even as they remind us that art does not have to be confined to galleries and museums.

Community Benefits, Negotiations, and (In)Justice

Gilda Haas

Not until a few days after we had signed the Community Benefits Agreement (CBA) on May 31, 2001, with the Anschutz Entertainment Group (AEG), owner-developers of the proposed Staples Center and the LA Live project, did I feel the weight of our accomplishment. Actually, the day after the signing I felt uneasy and introspective. At first I attributed the sensation to the kind of postpartum depression that often follows the end of the all-engaging atmosphere of a campaign. But nagging in the back of my mind was something else—ambivalence. Ambivalence never plays well in politics. It muddles messaging and undermines the righteousness that propels us through David and Goliath battles.

I was ambivalent about negotiation in general, about the terms that are accepted by simply sitting down with the "other side." I was ambivalent about the goal, which was to extract benefits from a megaproject for a community that was never regarded as such by the people in positions of power in corporate boardrooms, in City Hall, or even by the media. I was ambivalent because what I really wanted—community control over development whose primary purpose is to serve human needs—was never actually on the table.

Later in the week, exuberant articles in the *Los Angeles Times*, the *Wall Street Journal*, and the *Nation*; congratulatory messages from colleagues and comrades; and my own recollection that this agreement was connected to a much larger strategy lifted the cloud. I could own that we had won something big, and we celebrated.

A decade has passed since AEG signed the community benefits agreement with the Figueroa Corridor Coalition for Economic Justice (FCCEJ—pronounced "fick-age"—a name that only a mother could love) that stipulates how the developer will provide living wage jobs, local hiring, affordable housing, and other community needs in exchange for FCCEJ's nonopposition during project's entitlement phase.[1]

At the time, the media and its proponents hailed the "Staples Agreement" as the "the most comprehensive community benefits agreement in the country." It still stands as a touchstone for comparison and discussion about CBAs, evoked as a key example at many conferences and trainings about CBAs.

But in July 2011, I facilitated a gathering of 50 diverse, mostly young LA organizers and activists trying to figure out how to integrate equity into the current urban planning fad called "transit-oriented development." During the closing circle of the meeting, participants presented their dreams and desires for working together, and the question of community benefits agreements came up several times as a topic that evoked ambivalence and, with that, curiosity, confusion, and some anger. I dedicate this to their questions and my desire to end ambivalence on the matter.[2]

Working Backward from a Goal

There is an old expression, "If you don't know where you're going, any road can take you there," and with that in mind, while many things about CBAs are interesting, their meaning is elusive without a goal. In other words, if CBAs are the answer, then what is the question?

In the case of the Staples Agreement, the individual members of FCCEJ had different overlapping goals that converged during the campaign. For example, one can imagine that the unions and labor-based organizations wanted more leverage for the labor movement in LA and to elevate the prospects of workers; the environmental members hoped to insert environmental concerns and consciousness into the economic justice movement; and, grassroots organizations in the coalition—for the immigrants and tenants who lived in the area and were referred to as "invisible" by the Los Angeles Times—demanded respect, recognition, and the placement of their issues and concerns in the public dialogue.[3]

At the time of the agreement, I was the executive director of Strategic Actions for a Just Economy (SAJE), a member and the convener of FCCEJ. For SAJE, the goal of the CBA was community control over development, a goal that resides in a larger human rights development framework we call urban land reform—a people-centered development framework that establishes a right to the city for all.[4]

With this in mind I will (re)locate CBAs as a tactic within a larger strategy about land and rights and justice by describing where it fits into an array of basic tactics and strategies for reducing inequality and increasing democracy in the city.

Over the last 30 years I have used three methods, often simultaneously, sometimes sequentially, in the service of reducing economic inequality and increasing people's control over economic resources. All of them involve organizing, forming alliances, and building coalitions to create the necessary leverage that can change power relationships as well as relationships in the market.

For example, the 1977 Community Reinvestment Act outlawed redlining—the Jim Crow of the banking system where banks drew lines around undesirable working-class neighborhoods often of color and refused them credit or charged them exorbitant rates—but did not provide regulators with serious enforcement powers. The act did, however, offer activists the leverage of a public forum if we organized smart campaigns.

Banking is a private-sector activity that provides multiple public benefits (low-cost loans, insurance, and periodic bailouts). We used the public laws to challenge big private banks' mergers and acquisitions and to demand that the Federal Reserve and Congress regulate them, and we turned out large groups and well-informed speakers.

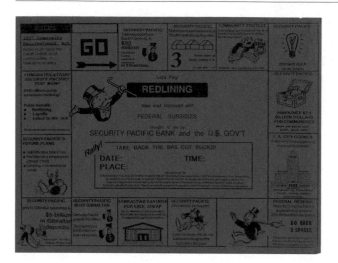

Figure 7.9. If only redlining was a game...

We demonstrated and engaged the media. Our attacks on the banks' highly valued (and expensive) public relations led to a meeting with bank presidents and a negotiated agreement. The agreement set the tone for new relationships with the community, created new banking products, and established internal policies whereby some very large financial institutions began to consider and meet some of our needs.

We went further, starting our own bank—the South Central People's Federal Credit Union. Part of a larger vision, it was a financial institution serving only its members—the community (not Wall Street). Our success was relatively short-lived. Over the last two decades, the tiny credit union, visionary though it was, passed into oblivion along with some of the giants from the other side of the negotiating table like Security Pacific and Washington Mutual. We never imagined that a lethal combination of Wall Street and subprime loans would replace redlining with approvals of the very worst loans, resulting in the largest reduction of black wealth since there was such a thing.

It was a harsh lesson—not the last one. Still, it represented the reality that we could find many spaces and places in the economy to reduce inequality with different combinations of policy campaigns, negotiated agreements, and community-controlled economic institutions.

To understand the need for a larger vision, take the area of jobs. One could focus on the policy arena and the issues of minimum wage, employment discrimination, local hiring, or even simply the right to negotiate with an employer. One could negotiate collective bargaining agreements between workers and owners. Or one could start a cooperative, reversing the roles of capital and labor—where workers hire capital. Cooperatives are popular today as they often are in the times of economic collapse. They can help us practice what a democratic economy might look like at the same time that we provide people with needed jobs.

The Staples CBA must be evaluated in those longer terms. I will wager than no reader wants a stadium or a 50-story hotel in his or her neighborhood. Those are things that belong somewhere else, like the "invisible" neighborhoods around

Staples Center. Within that larger frame, the Staples CBA was not a big success for its community creators. What people want is not the leftovers of high-end real estate development. They want control over their communities. They want affordable housing and good jobs and supermarkets and great schools and libraries and better futures for their children. We did win some of those things in our CBA. Still, many residents and much of the community were displaced and replaced, rather than cared for and repaired.

CBAs like the Staples Agreement should be embedded in a larger strategy. They can exist as the negotiated agreement part of a bigger idea, deriving its sense and meaning from that historical context, such as SAJE's idea of urban land reform. That vision holds a future where redevelopment raises up people rather than real estate values; where slumlords, rather than poor tenants and their children, are criminalized; where public money is used to produce public goods and to provide people with good jobs and needed services. If we view the Staples CBA in this context, as a tactic of a much larger campaign, it becomes a single step in very long-term struggle for urban land reform in LA.

That struggle is a brilliant example of what it takes to align values and relationships in order to produce complementary new institutions, infrastructure, and campaigns from the grassroots. From this view, the CBA complements the work of the Trust South LA land trust, which is dedicated to removing land from the speculative market for affordable housing and other community needs; the United Neighbors In Defense Against Displacement (UNIDAD) coalition that recently signed a new CBA with developer Geoff Palmer, who must now include rent-free space for a community clinic, job training, affordable housing, and health promotion in his luxury housing development that will be built on a former hospital site; and the criminalization of the notorious slumlord Frank McHugh, who is now forbidden by law to manage any buildings in the city and is court-ordered to fund the repair of his 100 apartment buildings.

These efforts achieved necessary scale by reconfiguring trusted networks to approximate the capacity of a large and powerful organization bound together by a proactive vision of change. Given the neoliberal forces that shape city politics favoring private property over public goods, much of our work is defensive. In many ways, good CBAs are defensive maneuvers that offer limited proof of what is possible. No large developer ever went under because they fulfilled a CBA.

That reminds me of the nature of negotiation. CBAs are as much the product of the developer as the community coalition. The 2001 AEG and FCCEJ press releases about the Staples Agreement were identical, except for the name of the protagonist credited with the accomplishment.

In his short, seminal book, from *Dictatorship to Democracy* (2002), Gene Sharp lays out the argument for why nonviolent struggle is the best means for unseating a dictator or oppressive regime. He speaks to negotiating with an oppressive regime in relationship to a larger goal: "Negotiations are a very useful tool in resolving certain types of issues in conflicts and should not be neglected or rejected when they are appropriate. In some situations where . . . a compromise is acceptable, negotiations can be an important means to settle a conflict." He argues that solving a labor strike through negotiations might "provide an increase somewhere between the sums originally proposed by each of the contending sides."

However, negotiations sometimes are not appropriate: "When the issues at stake are fundamental, affecting religious principles, issues of human freedom, or the whole future development of the society, negotiations do not provide a way of reaching a mutually satisfactory solution." Sharp argues that on some issues one should never compromise. "Only a shift in power relations in favor of the democrats can adequately safeguard the basic issues at stake. Such a shift will occur through struggle, not negotiations." The rub, of course, is what *are* non-negotiable issues?

How many times can a community member be forcibly evicted or moved before "relocation" becomes a nonnegotiable issue? How many foreclosures can be allowed to transform the character of our communities and destroy the hard-earned wealth of people for whom wealth inequality has always been the empirical result of structural racism? How many more building permits can the city issue to high-end developments that will predictably remain vacant for many years because the market for high-end housing is saturated while the supply of housing that working families, young, and elderly people can afford is virtually nonexistent?

A few times, negotiations between AEG and FCCEJ broke down, but at the end of the day we were all so invested in the process they resumed. What impressed me so much about the organizers who attended July's meeting about transit-oriented development and equity is that they were asking these questions *before* they formed a coalition or alliance.

In my mind, the extent to which a nascent coalition is born out of these deeper agreements will define its value to the movement landscape of LA. LA has many coalitions and alliances, since they are a practical requirement of most power analyses; they are often a requirement for external funding; and—in the best of them—there are spaces where we learn from one another, stretching our thinking and growing our movement. Very few large alliances, however, begin with a deep shared confidence about the question of what is absolutely nonnegotiable.

Learning how to create this depth is precisely what is needed to rescue the city and ourselves from the current neoliberal stranglehold: as a means of widening, rather than narrowing, our membership; of affirming the values and principles of the many; and of replacing fear with a hopeful, visionary plan.

CBAs are still useful and important. Gene Sharp clarifies that his message is "not to say that negotiations ought never to be used," and I concur. With that in mind, I offer a few lessons that I believe might be useful from the experience of the Staples Agreement CBA.

Take a Long-Term View

The FCCEJ; its first formation, the Coalition for a Responsible USC; and its successor, UNIDAD, were not created with the idea of producing a CBA. They were created to serve as a long-term vehicle to insert community voice and values into plans and development that affected the place and lives of its members.

Indeed, FCCEJ brought together leaders and institutions who had been struggling with issues of displacement and disrespect from redevelopment and the ever-expanding adjacent university for decades with relative newcomers to the fray (including SAJE).

The deep understanding of the past combined with the threat of the present led to commitment to a long-term view being an early first principle of the organization.

This principle produced practical results. The Staples Agreement was signed in May 2001. A few months later, the terrible events of September 11 greatly affected LA tourism—a key market for the proposed LA Live. While a few "ground-breaking" events occurred over the ensuing years, not a teaspoon of earth was turned on the site for about eight years. Meanwhile, the promised benefits were tracked and delivered per the contract. When the project eventually did break ground, the coalition was still there, maintaining oversight and protection over its agreement.

Consider the Timeline

Time and sequence matter in a complex megadevelopment like LA Live. As a result, an important structural component of the CBA was it had its own timeline and triggers separate from the actual construction timeline of the project.

For example, specific parts of the agreement were to be fulfilled by AEG whether the project was built or not, including a poor people's preferential parking district, a park planning and investment program, an affordable housing revolving loan pool, and a small job training fund. Further, the agreement required that certificates of occupancy for the required affordable housing had to be available before a certificate of occupancy for the associated luxury housing could be issued.[5] The developer was thus motivated to invest in affordable housing right a way so that the requirement sold parcels of entitled property to other developers.

As it turned out, those developers' lenders did not like the requirement: "Do you mean that if an affordable housing project is delayed, our big condo has to stand empty? No can do!" At the end of the day, AEG and FCCEJ ended up negotiating new language that benefited the new community land trust while creating an alternative for the developers.

The separate timeline meant the lengthy delay did not slow the community benefits, just as the coalition's commitment to a long-term life that was grounded in the community made everything possible.

Make Inclusion Work

Finally, from AEG's point of view, two factors made the FCCEJ an interesting negotiating partner. First, it was broad enough to gain City Hall's respect and, city officials hoped, to marginalize any later opposition from outside the coalition's ranks. Second, the developer was anxious to obtain entitlement approvals before the election of a new mayor and half of the city council later in the year. The coalition agreed to a very rapid time frame, compressed from 24 to 36 months to three to six months, in exchange for a serious and robust negotiating effort by AEG.

This decision required FCCEJ to quickly create a negotiating body with the knowledge, relationships, and capacity to get the job done. The Steering Committee came up with five criteria for selecting team members, including "past success negotiating with a major corporation" and "strong technical knowledge and experience in one of the key areas of discussion (i.e. housing and jobs)." These pragmatic requirements eliminated any of the approximately 300 local neighborhood activists, most of whom were working-class Latino immigrant tenants. We all felt that the accelerated timeline would not accommodate the preparation typically needed for our grassroots participants to authentically lead the negotiations.

Instead, the negotiations became a teachable moment. Every negotiating session included the five-member negotiating team, four or five grassroots leaders from the community, one or two organizers, and a professional simultaneous interpreter. We frequently caucused. The community leaders were responsible for reporting back to the 300 residents. This chain of participation and reporting from neighbor to neighbor served to elevate the credibility of negotiations.

Many other examples of "best practices" and not-so-great practices occurred in the ongoing lifetime of the Staples Agreement. And for better and for worse, other CBAs have been negotiated around the country.

If I had to identify one lesson to impart about this experience, I would ague that the meaning and influence of a CBA is entirely determined by how deeply it is connected to a larger campaign strategy and how deeply it is rooted in deeply shared larger long-term goals. So, any present consideration of a CBA must consider the harsh structural conditions that are increasing inequality in our city and our country. As more and more people become effectively excluded from full participation in the economy, the question of what and who we are negotiating for stands in stark relief.

For the growing economically disenfranchised, the slumlord, the sweatshop, the developer who denies that your community even exists, the university that refers to the community as an "environmental threat," the police that attack rather than protect your children all merge into a cloud of omnipresent oppression by a dictator that is distinguished only by its form of capital. Moments occur when this reality is concrete and seeable. And when that happens, and when we see yet again that the beauty of what is possible has again been denied, negotiation may not be possible.

From Barbie to Banksy

Elizabeth Currid-Halkett

I AM AMUSED BY FANCY ART-WORLD TYPES WHO BREEZE INTO LOS AN-
GELES PLANNING TO "GET" THE SCENE IN A FEW DAYS. THEY WOULD
HAVE BETTER LUCK READING "IN SEARCH OF LOST TIME" OVER A LONG
WEEKEND. AMERICA'S SECOND-LARGEST CITY SPRAWLS—PHYSICALLY,
AESTHETICALLY, SOCIALLY—OVER NEARLY 500 SQUARE MILES. SO ANY
ATTEMPT TO NUTSHELL THE BURG AND ITS CULTURAL BAZAAR TAKES
ON COMIC ASPECTS. —HAINLEY 2006

In the early autumn of 2006, under the sweltering LA sun, a quarter-mile-long line of people stretched around an abandoned downtown warehouse. Unlike downtowns in other global cities, LA is a latecomer to the urban renaissance. Only in the past few years have city residents witnessed an influx of young professionals, artists, and amenities. Even today, the downtown walks a line, quite literally, between its blighted Skid Row heritage and the now bustling and buzzy Art Walk and LA Live development. Thus, the stretch of hipsters and art aficionados patiently waiting for hours seemed a highly curious event. The spectacle worth waiting for turned out to be Banksy, the notorious, anonymous British graffiti artist, who had chosen downtown LA for his new exhibition *Barely Legal*. The show was attended by the glittering stars of Hollywood (who purchased his artwork by the armful) and featured a live elephant "in the room" as it were, painted in red with gold fleurs-de-lis and wandering slowly around. (This particular facet of the exhibition unsurprisingly catalyzed the ire of PETA.)

Banksy is arguably one of the most famous graffiti artists of all time; only Jean-Michel Basquiat and Keith Haring have attained such global attention as street artists. Open for only three days, the exhibition sold out before it closed. More recently Banksy's work has fetched over a half-million dollars at auction. For city planners, however, the most interesting bit of this story must be that Banksy, as one of the most obsessed-about artists of his generation, could have chosen any city in the world and yet he chose LA—not New York, not San Francisco, Chicago, or London—for one of his rare exhibitions.

The Banksy exhibition is somewhat an emblem for LA's cultural economy.[1] Once associated primarily with film, LA's creativity now extends to fashion, industrial design, architecture, music, art, and video games. And while this larger symbiotic economy seems like something new, LA has been pursuing diverse cultural production for many years now, just seemingly under the radar. Barbie, the modern VW Beetle, and the Eames lounge chair were all created in LA (LAEDC 2010). More recently, LA's cultural economy has been both recognized and quantified in terms of its economic and social impact. Today the city is thought of as a leading global hub of cultural production, generating billions of dollars and thousands of jobs. The city itself has benefited tremendously from its unique position as a highly profitable cultural juggernaut. Like Banksy's artwork, the city's creativity is more than just "art for art's sake"; it is also big business.

In the past decade, the cultural economy has emerged as a defined aspect of economic development (Pratt 1997, Markusen 2004, Grodach and Loukaitou-Sideris 2007, Currid 2007b). Yet how do we capture the more tangible contributions of the arts to our regional and urban economies? The impact of art is not simply a long line of art aficionados waiting outside of an abandoned warehouse. The extant research on the arts demonstrates that it provides meaningful economic contributions to society. This essay considers how we might understand the economic dynamics of the cultural economy. As a case study, I use the *Otis Report on the Creative Economy of the Los Angeles Region*. The report describes the entire landscape of art and cultural industries in LA and provides tools for capturing the contribution and economic impact of the cultural economy. In discussing the cultural economy, I consider the extant methodological approaches for measuring their economic impact and the accompanying challenges. Drawing from my own qualitative research I discuss the mechanisms by which art "works" in a regional economy. Understanding these dynamics is essential in the cultivation of the cultural economy and its positive developmental effects.

The Cultural Economy and Economic Development

Recent planning literature has demonstrated the overall economic importance of the arts (Florida 2002, Lloyd 2006, Markusen and Schrock 2006, Rantisi 2004, Caves 2000, Currid 2007a). My own research on LA demonstrates that the city's greatest strength is in fashion, film, and media—all over four times more concentrated in LA than in other cities and spatially concentrated in specific neighborhoods (Currid 2006, Currid and Williams 2010). By the middle of the first decade of the 21st centur, cultural industries accounted for 20 percent of the region's high-skilled workforce, who work for the third-biggest employer behind only finance and professional services (Figure 7.11). Quite simply, LA demonstrates a unique advantage in the arts compared to other metropolitan areas.

Unequivocally, art and culture matter to LA. Yet the difficulty in understanding their true impact to the regional economy revolves around definition and means to appropriately count cultural workers. Debate surrounds how art and culture are defined and what occupational and industrial groups ought to be included (NESTA 2008, Markusen and Schrock 2006, Markusen et al. 2008, Currid 2007a), whether analyzing the cultural economy specifically or including the arts within the more broadly constructed "creative class" (Florida 2002). Additionally, artists are often undercounted in economic surveys, and quantified as either an occupational group or industrial sector (see Markusen and King 2003, Markusen et al. 2004, and Currid 2006). Yet the study of occupations often misses the important synergies between artistic and "nonartistic" workers that make up larger cultural industry agglomerations (Scott 2005, Keegan et al. 2006, Scanlon et al. 2007, Currid and Williams 2010). More recently, scholars have been arguing for a multitier analysis that includes various types of occupational and industrial data reported by both individuals (the cen-

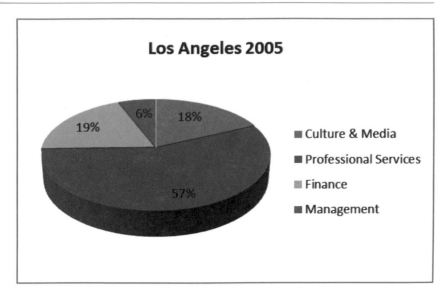

Figure 7.10. Aggregate chart on the distribution of occupations by sector in LA's high-skill economy (2005). Source: Currid 2009

sus) and firms (Bureau of Labor Statistics) (Barbour and Markusen 2007, Renski, Koo, and Feser 2007, Currid-Halkett and Stolarick 2011). For example, Stolarick and I (2011) find that more than 50 percent of artists do not work in art-related industries and that cultural industries rely on a density of artistic and "nonartistic" workers.

The Cultural Economy of Los Angeles: Documenting the Evidence

The *Otis Report on the Creative Economy of the Los Angeles Region* provides the most systematic and comprehensive analysis of this research on LA's cultural economy. Produced annually for the past four years, it is the most succinct account of the city's creative economy and its future projections. This report is demonstrative of the growing appreciation of the cultural economy as a significant variable in the economic development of LA and the wider understanding of the arts' positive developmental effects on urban and regional prosperity.

To that end, *Otis* finds that one in six jobs within Los Angeles County is within the cultural economy.[2] The cultural economy is one of the largest business sectors in the county, generating $113 billion in sales revenue and $4.6 billion in state and local tax revenues. Within these broad, sweeping statistics we find a very synergistic and diverse economic dynamism that demonstrates the full swath of industries responsible for upholding the cultural economy of LA. While entertainment is certainly significant (generating 118,000 direct jobs, $48.3 billion in sales, and $2.4 billion in taxes), other sectors including fashion, the visual and performing arts, art, and digital media are all major players in the city's cultural production. For example, the visual and performing arts produce 32,300 jobs, $9.8 billion in direct sales revenue, and $653.3 million in taxes. Fashion, often thought of as a small player compared to its New York counterpart, generates almost 7,000 jobs, $32 billion in direct sales, and $577.6 million in tax revenue (Table 7.1). *Otis* also projects that the creative economy will be a key component to LA economic recovery in the aftermath of the recession. Between 2009 and 2014, *Otis* expects the creative industries will grow by 6.9 percent with digital media (video games, phone applications) growing the fastest, generating a 10 percent growth in employment over the five-year period.[3] The entertainment sector, driven primarily by film production, is projected to grow by 9 percent.

The *Otis* analysis demonstrates the extent to which the cultural economy meaningfully affects the urban and regional economy of LA. For some time both scholars and practitioners have been making a case for the developmental effects of the arts. While some of this research has measured aspects of the economic benefits of the arts (e.g. jobs, industrial diversity, competitive advantage), the full extent of the direct and indirect impact is not fully captured. The *Otis* report, however, reports the economic contribution through quantifiable means that show the surprisingly dominant role that the arts play in shaping the local economy. For example, the entertainment industry's overall economic impact (direct and indirect) generates 345,900 jobs and $129 billion in economic output.[4] Fashion generates 199,100 direct and indirect jobs and $62.4 billion in economic output (Table 7.1). Thus art and culture are not simply contributing directly to the economy. But while art and culture clearly matter to LA, the question remains: How does the cultural economy work?

How the Cultural Economy Works: Los Angeles and Beyond

In 1993, the indie musician Beck released the cult single "Loser." In subsequent years, he went on to produce seven major-label albums along with multiple contributions to movie soundtracks. Beck remains one of the iconic musicians of Generation X. His rapid rise to cultural demagoguery is a window into how the cultural economy works more broadly. As Beck told *LA Weekly* in a 2006 interview, his success depended on complete chance. When hanging out in one of LA's music venues, Beck would jump on stage and practice while the main band was getting ready. "I would get up and play my *quote* folk songs. I did this one night and this guy came up to me [the record producer Tom Rothrock] and kept saying 'I like that rap you were doing.' I said 'Thanks—I was just making it up.' He said 'I know a guy who makes some beats.'" About six months later, Beck met the beat expert, Carl Stephenson, whom he collaborated with to write "Loser." As Beck put it, "He [Stephenson] had a beat, and I wrote some lines, you know what I mean? And I put some of my slide guitar on there and that was 'Loser.' The whole thing was so ridiculously simple, how it came together . . . but [*sic*] the best known thing."

What Beck may call chance one could also say was the musician maximizing the probability of being discovered by simply spending time in an LA music venue. Creativity becomes economically meaningful when the right people and institutions are in place. Consider the counterfactual: if Beck had been rapping on a lone stage in a small town in North Dakota, he would not have likely met Rothrock, nor would he have been able to pop by Stephenson's house to trade ideas and ultimately produce a worldwide hit. The success of Beck lies within the larger success of LA's cultural economy. The city's dense clustering allows cultural workers, industries, and institutions to efficiently exchange information and ideas. The diversity of LA's

Table 7.1. Economic impact of the creative economy						
Los Angeles County				Total (Direct + Indirect) Impact		
Industry	Establishments	Jobs (1,000s)	Payroll (million $)	Output (billion $)	Jobs	Taxes (millions $)
Architecture/ Interior design	1,697	9,800	730	4.5	19,400	97.0
Art galleries	246	900	37	0.9	1,300	5.5
Communication arts	1,653	16,100	1,522	5.9	35,200	215.2
Digital media	170	5,800	787	7.2	17,300	105.6
Entertainment	5,626	118,700	11,370	129.4	354,900	2,407.9
Fashion	6,689	87,000	3,227	62.4	199,100	577.6
Furniture/ Home furnishings	1,803	28,400	1,097	18.9	62,400	186.8
Toys	245	4,700	390	7.6	12,700	64.0
Product/ Industrial design	128	600	39	0.2	1,000	5.3
Visual and performing arts	8,522	32,300	4,928	24.0	55,200	653.3
Total	26,779	304,400	24,127	260.9	758,500	4,318.1
Source: LAEDC 2010						

creative economy means that diverse skills and jobs are always available. Those who determine "good art" (e.g., editors, gallery owners, critics, and journalists) are present when an artist has an exhibition, a fashion runway show is held, or, in the case of Beck, a musician releases an eccentric but brilliant single. In other words, all of these processes and interactions occur within the same place—LA.

The cultural economy operates like other agglomerations, except for the great premium on informal transactions like the one described by Beck. In my many interviews with those who produce art and evaluate it, the social scene becomes the nexus point for many economic transactions (Currid 2007a). By extension, a high concentration of creative sectors, workers, and gatekeepers is essential to making these dynamics work. Scott (1996, 2000, 2005) and Molotch (1996) have found that this dense agglomeration within LA has enabled the region to become one of the world's leading cultural hubs, both producing and shaping art and culture for the global marketplace: "While they are choosy and fickle, L.A.'s indigenous immigrants from everywhere act as a proxy for world taste as well as sources of creativity" (Molotch 1996, 262). The dynamic is recursive: as more cultural producers and industries locate in the city, the influence of LA and efficiency of its cultural economy increases, thus catalyzing more of the same social and economic activity.

There are three key aspects to how the cultural economy works: (1) the ease of networking to mobilize one's career; (2) the interlocking of industrial sectors that allows for skills and capital to transfer easily across sectors, enabling what I call "flexible career paths" for artists; and (3) the lowered transaction costs and accidental serendipity of simply being in the same place with likeminded firms and workers (Currid 2007a, 2007b). When these processes work simultaneously they facilitate cultural producers and industries to participate in numerous combinations of skills and production of innovative goods and services. The *Otis* report relays the sheer extent of this creative concentration, and within this cluster these mechanisms can occur. In other words, Beck's casual encounter with a record producer and ensuing collaboration is emblematic of a process that goes on continuously in the cultural economy but is possible only because of LA's densely concentrated array of industries and workers.

LA's story demonstrates that the cultural economy is of great significance to the cities and regions in which it resides. The story also illuminates the unique processes at play within the cultural economy: the genesis of creativity is only part of the story. Creativity is everywhere, but the ability to translate it into a commodified product or a source of income requires a dense and diverse agglomeration of many cultural industries and workers. We know that culture matters to economic development, and places like LA, New York, and London disproportionately benefit from the cultural economy. However, other locales interested in cultivating a cultural economy ought to look to LA—not to be another LA but to see how the cultural economy works on a micro level, right down to the informal milieu where it all happens, whether a grungy music venue or an abandoned warehouse. In both these cases, the cultural economy seemed to emerge unconventionally, but as long as the right people and a good concentration of them are in place, anything can happen.

What the (Economic) Tide Left Behind

Christian L. Redfearn

The United States experienced an extraordinary bubble in real estate markets between 2000 and 2010. The lingering effects are still roiling world capital markets. Lenders will eventually work through the pools of bad loans, but the new housing units that are the physical manifestation of the bubble in our metropolitan areas will be with us for decades. How these new units were allocated geographically within those metropolitan areas reveals something interesting about the underlying land-use processes. In the LA metropolitan area, the bubble produced approximately 600,000 new housing units. Over half of them were built in Riverside and San Bernardino counties, even though these areas held just 20 percent of the existing housing units at the beginning of the period. By contrast, Los Angeles County grew by just 174,000 housing units, despite being home to almost 10 million people.

The units in the peripheral counties require long commutes, expensive infrastructure requirements, and in most cases greenfield development. More pertinently, these new units are now ground zero for loss in values and foreclosure activity. The loss is so severe at least one federal government program offers funding for the demolition of vacant units as way to prevent blight from persisting and further damaging surrounding home values. That the bubble produced excess would be less interesting if the LA region had not begun the period underhoused and remains so. The question then becomes, Where housing is scarce, why did so much housing end up where so many don't want to live? The tsunami of capital that washed through the region in the first half of the decade offers the opportunity to see how the fluid nature of mortgage capital is translated into geographically specific development and how local municipal land-use policies and institutions shape the aggregate urban form of the metropolitan area.

One significant contributing factor to the bubble was a dramatic increase in access to mortgage credit. In 2000, approximately 19 million mortgages were originated nationwide; this number rose to approximately 35 million in both 2005 and 2006. Changes in credit market underwriting standards—such as lower down payment requirements, lower income standards, weaker credit histories, and less required supporting documentation—unambiguously increased the pool of households who qualified for more debt. In the five counties that form the Los Angeles Metropolitan Statistical Area (MSA)—Los Angeles, Orange, Riverside, San Bernardino, and Ventura—these underwriting changes led to an astonishing rise in mortgage borrowing: the dollar volume of originated mortgages climbed from just over $76 billion in 2000 to more than $313 billion in 2006.

This huge wave of capital led to a significant increase in the effective demand for owner-occupied units. The wave did not create a symmetric increase in the stock of units around the LA metropolitan area—cities did not simply scale up to meet demand. Quite the opposite, the demand to build new units disproportionately manifested itself in places where development was relatively easily accommodated. As such, the dramatic increase in credit led to significant expansion of development in the periphery of metropolitan LA—a sudden change in urban form not generally considered consistent with good planning practices. The development at the periphery was not unplanned; rather, entitlements were more easily obtained at the edge of the metropolitan area than in infill areas.

I will show here that the variation in local land-use policies and approval processes among cities within the metropolitan area resulted in capital flows and development that is arguably far from optimal. Demand-driven development deemed inappropriate by one city does not evaporate when it is thwarted but rather ends up elsewhere in the region and brings with it externalities not generally considered by all of those affected. In this situation, while individual cities erected planning policies and regulations that suited their preferences, the collective result at the metropolitan level may be a spatial organization of people and jobs that leaves much to be desired for everyone. This dynamic is not new, but the scale of the change in demand for owner-occupied housing was huge and occurred over a relatively brief period, allowing the relative barriers to development to be brought into sharp relief. We can track the wave of capital that washed through the LA metropolitan area from 2000 to 2006 to see where it flowed and what the high tide left behind.

Development as Transformer of Fluid Capital into a Fixed Durable Investment

Housing is expensive to build and therefore expensive to buy. In addition to significant construction costs, the land required to build a unit can be very costly in urban areas. As such, dense development is generally required in urban areas to minimize the per-unit cost of land and to make new construction feasible. Whether the home is a unit in a condominium building in the urban core or a single-family detached home in the exurbs, the scale of required investment typically entails financing via mortgages. Where households do not have cash available to purchase a home outright, they often have an income that could support servicing the debt needed to buy a home. This circumstance means that the cost of debt and access to debt are important contributors to the aggregate demand for owner-occupied housing.

The status of both these contributors changed between 2000 to 2005. First, interest rates fell from 8 percent at the beginning of the decade to 6 percent by 2005, · so households could borrow more and still service the debt. The change in rates is deceptively large on its own but highly significant in light of the second trend: the loosening of underwriting standards. A traditional down payment of 15 to 20 percent shrank to 3 percent and in many cases to no down payment at all. Credit score thresholds slipped. Irregular incomes were not penalized as they had been. Mortgage "innovations" like loans with low teaser rates became available. The result was that many households previously well below the traditional threshold for home ownership became eligible for financing and joined the ranks of those looking for their version of the American Dream. Nationally, these changes pushed the home ownership rate from 64 percent to almost 70 percent during this period—representing millions of new owner-occupied units. In Southern California, development pressure grew significantly against a backdrop of an existing housing affordability problem. The LA metropolitan area was ranked 166th out of 184 metropolitan areas in the National Association of Homebuilders' index of affordability in 2001; by 2011 the ranking had fallen to 219th out of 223.

These tectonic changes in lending are fundamentally aspatial. The region's planning and development processes channel the flows to particular locations. Unlike capital markets, real estate and the markets in which properties are traded and developed are geographically specific, with investment flowing to where investors see the most opportunity. In the case of housing and other real estate, the developer reacts to the demand for housing and transforms the liquid mortgage capital into something durable and fixed in space. The easing of debt pricing and qualifying requirements meant that essentially everyone had access to more capital, increasing the demand. Developers responded by seeking to maximize return while minimizing risk.

Consider a parcel in one of the region's cities. On this site the market demands a use for which the developer could earn a good return. If the local land-use norms prevent this use, the developer could negotiate to build the use desired by the market. This process is an uncertain one—in terms of final outcomes, time to resolution, and additional burdens in the form of mitigations demanded by the municipalities. The developer assesses the prospect of a good return against the marked risk of pursuing a change in use. Depending on the outcome of the assessment, the developer may look elsewhere to build. The metropolitan area of Los Angeles has 191 cities as well as unincorporated county lands. Another location may have a more transparent development process. Location choice is therefore a function not only of construction costs and market demand but also of the approval process. Local processes may be narrowly "optimal" but leave a regional urban form that is not.

Consider an apartment dweller in Orange County. He lives near his place of work and other significant amenities of coastal California: the beach, good air quality, and many choices of restaurants and entertainment that come with denser and mature urban areas. By 2003, mortgage rates had fallen far enough that he qualified for a mortgage. However, he is not alone; others now qualify as well, driving up local house prices—so the loan he now has access to is not enough to purchase a nearby house. The loan is tied to the borrower, not to its use in Orange County. A developer eager to meet his housing demand could try to build in Orange County but faces several obstacles. Little vacant land remains undeveloped. Redevelopment is an option, but only by significantly increasing densities, which nearby residents oppose. The developer sees risk in trying to rezone single-family residential lots to higher density. However, when he looks over the mountains to greenfields in Riverside, he finds available land, with fewer neighbors to complain and a supportive local city council. The apartment dweller ends up in a new home in a low-density development far from his workplace. The negative externality, his extra commuting induced by the move, was not part of the approval process in either development-resistant Orange County or development-friendly Riverside.

This example is admittedly highly stylized, but it illustrates the way local decision makers overlook important development impacts embedded in the process by which developers pursue new projects to meet new demand. When the bubble grew, households throughout the region were faced with a new set of circumstances. The development process is the link between national and international capital markets and individual borrowers and specific locations. The phrase "drive to qualify" became part of the residential real estate vernacular during the bubble because of the regularity with which households could become home owners by extending their commutes to the exurbs. Two empirical questions are then: (1) Where did capital flow? and (2) Where did new development occur? These two questions lead us to the larger one: is this outcome any sort of "best practice"?

Mapping Capital and Development

The following analysis relies on Home Mortgage Disclosure Act (HMDA) data files and the U.S. Census. In an attempt to track racial profiling among mortgage lenders, HMDA requires all but the smallest mortgage lenders to disclose at the census tract level a variety of data about each loan application they receive and loan origination they make. These data are reported annually, but only three cross sections are used here: 2000, 2006, and 2009—marking the beginning of the decade, the peak of the bubble, and the end of the period. The U.S. Census is used to measure changes in housing stock and populations in the LA metropolitan area from 2000 to 2010.

The HMDA files allow us to track the flow of mortgage funds within and across the region. Once a household qualifies for mortgage lending, the dollars need not flow to the location where the application was started. Rather, they go where the household ends up. Thus, increases in demand for housing among households in Santa Monica may not be met by development in Santa Monica. Further, all mortgage originations do not result in new purchases or directly in new construction. Indeed, the drop in mortgage rates induced a series of refinancing waves with households staying put. Other mortgages financed renovations on existing homes. Table 7.2 reports purchase mortgage origination flows by county.

Table 7.2 makes clear the full extent of the bubble. The growth in purchase lending is huge—more than doubling through the first six years of the decade. The bust is equally apparent; purchases fall 40 percent from 2006 to 2009. Table 7.2 also shows that the broad change in demand for housing ended up disproportionately in the periphery: roughly 40 percent of the purchase mortgage volume of almost $70 billion ended up in Riverside and San Bernardino counties.

Table 7.2. Purchase Mortgage Flows					
Purchase Mortgage Value (million $)				Purchase Mortgage Value (million $)	
County	2000	2006	2009	2000-2006	2006-2009
Los Angeles	24,788	55,905	20,964	125.5	(62.5)
Orange	12,779	20,914	8,845	63.7	(57.7)
Riverside	5,524	22,463	6,686	306.6	(70.2)
San Bernardino	4,009	13,989	4,349	248.9	(68.9)
Ventura	3,492	5,774	2,471	65.3	(57.2)
Total	50,592	119,045	43,315	135.3	(63.6)
Source: HMDA					

The flows spurred uneven development throughout the region. In 2000, the population of the five-member counties was 16.37 million people who were housed in 5.68 million housing units. Table 7.3 reports the distribution of population and housing units across the five counties before and after the surge in purchase lending. Los Angeles is by far the largest in both categories, followed by Orange County and the others. While the population data are available only for 2000 and 2010, the vast majority of development clearly occurred in the first six years of the decade. Table 7.3 makes evident that Riverside and San Bernardino counties were the recipients of a disproportionate amount of development. Over half of the region's 597,000 unit increase occurred in the same two counties that received extranormal capital flows. One conclusion from these data would be that people were hungering to move to Riverside and San Bernardino counties. What counterevidence would suggest that this spatial distribution of new development is less than optimal? The argument here does not consider the variety of criticisms of this low-density spread of population, relying instead on the simple economic performance of the units themselves. Did the

Table 7.3. Population and Housing Evolution		
County	Population Change 2000–2010	Housing Units Change 2000–2010
Los Angeles	3.14%	5.32%
Orange	5.76%	8.19%
Riverside	41.69%	37.95%
San Bernardino	19.06%	16.34%
Ventura	9.31%	11.91%
Total	9.18%	10.53%

Table 7.4 Average House Price Trends by County						
	Average House Price			House Price Change (%)		
	Peak	Trough	Current			
County	2007, Q2	2009, Q1	2011, Q3	Peak to Trough	Trough to Present	Peak to Present
Los Angeles	555,499	300,178	317,133	−46.0	5.6	−42.9
Orange	634,062	380,332	431,694	−40.0	13.5	−31.9
Riverside	392,750	188,813	188,872	−51.9	0.0	−51.9
San Bernardino	355,344	162,144	159,920	−54.4	−1.4	−55.0
Ventura	583,333	333,135	358,393	−42.9	7.6	−38.6
MSA Average	503,267	249,370	272,969	−50.4	9.5	−45.8

increases in mortgage lending reflect an underlying demand for more units in the far reaches of the metropolitan area? If not, and the development was the response of builders looking to find a place to capture capital market-driven demand, then prices should fall farthest where inherent demand was weakest. Table 7.4 reports average price trends for the metropolitan area and its member counties.

Table 7.4 shows the extraordinary loss of value the whole region felt when the bubble burst. In all five counties house prices remain above where they were when the bubble started; the same retention is not true when we look at changes from the peak of the bubble. After the second quarter of 2007, house prices in all five counties tumbled over the next two years. They fell the farthest in Riverside and San Bernardino counties—the recipients of the lion's share of the new development. Over the four-year period from 2007 to 2011—a period that is less dominated by the panic present in the immediate postbubble period—Riverside and San Bernardino counties have had house price declines in excess of 50 percent. Orange, Los Angeles, and Ventura counties have seen significant price rises even in the absence of genuine economic recovery. Respectively, these three counties had peak-to-current price declines of 32 percent, 43 percent, and 39 percent—far less than Riverside and San Bernardino.

These three sets of basic statistics—on mortgage flows, new construction, and price dynamics—are consistent with the hypothesis that a large increase in the demand for housing was shunted to the periphery even though these locations were not the preferred ones. Rather, households wanted to be in more primary and secondary markets, but developers could not meet demand in these locations. The foreclosure crisis is telling about the markets. Certainly foreclosure has occurred throughout the region, but when a foreclosure occurs in interior submarkets sufficient demand takes that unit back into the hands of new home owners. Fewer purchasers are willing to do so at the periphery. In addition, in aggregate the region remains underhoused, suggesting that peripheral construction was far from an optimal allocation of resources.

Conclusion

Coordination in planning across American regions has always been difficult, but planners and economists have presumed the costs associated with a lack of coordination were small relative to the benefits of local control of planning. These data suggest that local planning controls did little to allocate resources effectively. The thousands of single-family homes scattered in the periphery did meet the need of households who desperately wanted to be home owners and the investment criteria of developers who built in response to that demand, but they were not based on good principles of planning. If we had a better way to allocate resources, could we have built enough housing and met good planning principles (used loosely given our lack of a consensus on what that actually is)? The obvious failure of local land-use controls to provide a good regional solution suggests that city-by-city planning can have large costs. Whether these exceed the benefits of the current system is an open question. But in the debate over how best to plan, planners need to acknowledge that local decisions have aggregate impacts and that these may swamp local planning.

Clearly, the region experienced a huge influx of mortgage capital; new development was disproportionately peripheral; and this new development has performed the worst since the bust. These factors together suggest that new development might have been better built along transit, in existing communities with better amenities, in denser configurations, and so on. Given a development industry that is relatively footloose and able to build anywhere in the region, why didn't these things happen? The development processes in infill areas can be markedly more byzantine than those involved with greenfield development. Where many neighbors and many competing stakeholders live, land use becomes wholly more political but not necessarily more rational. The environmental impact report prepared by Universal Studios for its internal redevelopment is more than 39,000 pages long. This document has more to do with defensive legal strategy than it does with meaningful environmental protection. But this is how development proceeds in many cases in existing areas with land-use changes to higher densities.

California has this problem, and it affects housing affordability, job creation, and the environment. Housing demand is certain to rise in the future. Native births alone will add millions to the state's population. If cities thwart development in the name of good local planning, the result will be more development at the periphery with all the incumbent infrastructure costs and negative externalities. This outcome conflicts with California's Senate Bill 375 and Assembly Bill 32, which codify the goals of sustainable communities via higher density development. This outcome appears to be at odds with good planning practice—even if the local processes are functioning "optimally" in the narrow view of local residents. And, this outcome appears to be odds with an efficient market outcome, with markets failing due to the presence of unpriced externalities. The epilogue is still being written on the housing bubble and bust, but the same local processes that pushed development to the periphery remain in place.

From KAOS Comes Community

Meredith Drake Reitan

South Los Angeles is home to the majority of the region's African Americans. The area has been ignored by retailers, is portrayed as a wasteland by Hollywood, and is currently the site of a dramatic demographic shift toward becoming a Latino LA. The neighborhood of Leimert Park, along Crenshaw Boulevard, stands in the center of these swings. Today the area, which began as a racially covenanted community prohibiting African Americans and other minorities, has emerged as the essential heart of the African American community, replacing the lamented and lost vibrancy of Central Avenue.

In Leimert Park's commercial district, documentary filmmaker Ben Caldwell created KAOS Network in 1984. A community-based arts center dedicated to providing training in digital and multimedia arts, the KAOS Network offers workshops in video production, website development, CD production, Internet exploration, animation, and video teleconferencing. Other classes available on-site include acting, capoeira, and yoga. Besides these offerings, KAOS Network is probably most well-known for Thursday night's Project Blowed, a hip hop and rap open-mike night that gave birth to rappers and rap groups such as Aceyalone, Medusa, Busdriver, Freestyle Fellowship, and Jurassic Five.

For Caldwell, KAOS is the culmination of a long and sustained interest in film and new media. While assisting his grandfather, a projectionist at a small New Mexico movie theater, Caldwell saw hundreds of films that inspired him. According to a 2009 interview in the *San Francisco Bay News*, Caldwell earned a master of fine arts degree at the UCLA film school in the mid-1970s and, after a brief period teaching at Howard University in Washington, D.C., returned to LA to settle in Leimert Park.

According to Caldwell, an important principle in developing the network was to provide youth in the community with knowledge and understanding of the 21st century's cyber technology. KAOS offers the opportunity for families to participate in hands-on courses in video production and website development. Such a forum has provided access to technology previously thought out of reach for many youth and adults in the community. The center is a safe place to learn art and to work, create, and produce. It serves as a living resource for the entire Leimert Park community.

In his Recession Series (2002–), David Yamamoto photographs the evolving economic landscape. These locations are haunted by recent commercial failures and memories of more prosperous times.

ENDNOTES

Multiciplicities/Multiple-cities

1. McWilliams (1973, 2) borrowed the phrase from the legendary novelist Helen Hunt Jackson, author of *Ramona* (1884), an advocacy novel that ironically birthed generations of nostalgic mythmaking about the Spanish treatment of the Native Americans.

Challenging the Myth of an Unplanned Los Angeles

1. Adamic 1932, 219, emphasis in original.
2. Banham 1971, 137.
3. For example, Mumford 1961 describes LA as "an undifferentiated mass of houses walled off into sectors by many-laned expressways" (510).
4. Just the myths about LA and Southern California have spawned an entire body of literature. See, e.g., Robinson 1963, 83–94; Reid 1994; McClung 2000; Hise 2006, 8–26, 62–64; and Klein 1997. Klein's discussion of the social imaginary, or myth construction, is helpful in its explanation of the messiness and multiplicity of the process: many participants, differing viewpoints, internal contradictions, and, importantly, elements of truth all have a part in mythmaking.
5. For illustrated examples and analysis, see Elias 1983; Davis 1992, 357–86; and Gish 2007a, 391–415.
6. Accounts of LA's urbanization sometimes mention aspects of its planning, but mainly to criticize reported shortcomings. See, e.g., Fogelson 1967; Fishman 1987, 155–81; and Fulton 2001.
7. Architect Richard Neutra, responsible for the LA maps at the meeting, is quoted in Mumford 2002, 84.
8. See, e.g., Krueckeberg 1983. One eastern city unassociated with an instantly identifiable plan or planner is Boston, though it has been planned continuously for centuries, as has LA. See Kennedy 1994.
9. For a more detailed account of planning in the city over the last two centuries, see Hise and Gish 2007; Gish 2007b, chap. 6. See also Weiss 1987, Hise 1999, and Axelrod 2009.
10. These local surveys, though separate projects, reflected the work of national surveyors implementing the federal public land survey in the upper Midwest, authorized by the 1785 National Land Ordinance. That work oriented new survey lines to the cardinal points. See, e.g., Johnson 1976.
11. The emphasis on the connection between business elites and early city planning work is made in Blackford 1993.

12. Fogelson 1967, 42, credits "private enterprise ... and not public officials" with "the decisive role in urban expansion" in LA. Fogelson does recount Progressive political reform in the early 1900s, dwelling on electoral implications and the introduction of civil service to municipal government. But the expanding activities of citizen commissions and civil servants working to control rapid urban development are left undescribed. For a general critique of privatism, see Warner 1987.

13. See Hise and Gish 2007, 331–38, for analysis of a sampling of council meeting minutes from the 1890s.

14. "Industrial Plants to be Pulled up by Roots," *Los Angeles Times*, Jan. 5, 1913, II1.

15. Designation of districts as "residential" or "industrial" was nominal and, though groundbreaking at the time, left plenty of room for exceptions allowing a wide spectrum of nonresidential uses in so-called residential areas. This pragmatic but promiscuous reality meant that true segregation of ostensibly incompatible land uses would wait for further planning and legal innovations in zoning. During the 1910s, impatience over delays in a more rigorous land-use regime was a major impetus for a formal, empowered city planning commission. See Weiss 1987, chap. 4. See also Kolnick 2008.

16. See Riis 1971. On Riis's visit, see "Jacob A. Riis on Slum and Paradise," *Los Angeles Times*, Jan. 4, 1905, II1.

17. *Los Angeles Almanac*, U.S. Census data, available at www.laalmanac.com/population/index.htm.

18. City of LA, Ordinance 14113, 1907; Los Angeles County Housing Commission 1906–1908; see also DeForest and Veiller 1903. For an historical overview, see Lubove 1962, chap. 5.

19. Charles Mulford Robinson, "The City Beautiful," in LA Municipal Art Commission 1909. See also Blackford 1993, chap. 3.

20. "Marble Vision of Bunker Hill," *Los Angeles Times*, Feb. 1, 1917, II2; City of LA, City Planning Commission 1928.

21. William H. Pierce to the LA City Planning Commission, in the minutes of the commission's meeting of July 7, 1920. See also City of LA, Ordinance 39906, 1920.

22. LA City Planning Commission, *General Meeting Minutes*, July 7, 1920.

23. Ibid., Aug. 5, 1924.

24. This was a multivolume work published between 1927 and 1931. See, e.g., Committee on the Regional Plan of New York and Its Environs 1929.

25. Weiss 1987 termed such fly-by-night developers "curb-stoners." The other type was the much more rare and better-financed "community builder," who took the long view and developed not only home sites and (sometimes) homes but also a full range of communal functions, integrated street systems, and coordinated infrastructure. In Los Angeles, developers such as Walter Leimert, Fred Marlow, Fritz Burns, and others demonstrate this larger community-building approach—many of their tools became standard practices in emerging city planning agencies. See Hise 1999.

26. "A Community Plan," in County of LA 1931, 122. An additional 40 acres of hypothetical industrial land (not part of the units themselves)—off to one side and buffering an imaginary railroad line—completes the plan's thousand acres.

27. "Garden Cities for Laborers," *Los Angeles Times*, Sept. 7, 1913, II12.

28. City of LA, City Planning Commission, *Planning for the San Fernando Valley* (repr. from *Pencil Points*, June 1945), 93–94. Application of neighborhood unit planning mentioned above to urbanizing parts of the Valley would not have conflicted with this overall approach.

29. "Garden City for San Fernando Valley," *Los Angeles Times*, July 20, 1913, VI1.

30. Phelps 1995 argues that Torrance bore little resemblance to Howard's vision of the garden city, but this was true of virtually all garden city experiments of the time, including the most revered English exemplars of Letchworth and Welwyn.

31. *Los Angeles Times*, Jan. 15, 1913, II3, display advertisement.

32. City of LA, City Planning Commission, *General Meeting Minutes*, Nov. 17, 1942.

33. LA Community Redevelopment Agency, "Opening Rebuttal Statement" at City Council hearing, Nov. 12, 1958. Quoted in Cohen-Marks 2007, 427.

34. "City Planners Ready to Check on Bunker Hill," *Los Angeles Times*, May 15, 1958, 27.

35. For example, see City of LA, City Planning Commission, *General Meeting Minutes*, Oct. 27, 1955.

36. City of LA, City Planning Commission 1952. A compilation of then-recent guest registers at the Dept. of City Planning revealed visits from planners based in San Francisco; Phoenix, Arizona; San Antonio, Texas; Kansas City, Missouri; Boston; Honolulu; Washington, D.C.; Berlin; Copenhagen; Paris; Milan; Bangkok; Rome; Manila; Okinawa; and Melbourne.

The 1970 Centers Concept Plan for Los Angeles

1. Their planning approach contradicted the prevailing conventional wisdom of the concentric zone model of urban growth postulated by sociologist E. W. Burgess (1925). Burgess suggested that cities were monocentric, grew around their Central Business District (CBD), and had declining densities from the center. However, the subsequent multiple nuclei model proposed by geographers C. D. Harris and E. L. Ullman (1945) had a less dominant CBD and included multiple centers of density and activity. It more closely resembled Los Angeles's emerging pattern and what its planners were proposing.

2. In California, "master" or "comprehensive" plans are known as the general plan. In 1927, cities and counties were authorized to develop master plans, and in 1937, the state legislature began requiring local governments to adopt such plans (Fulton 1999, 102–3). Master plans in California were subsequently renamed as general plans in 1965 (Fulton 1999, 103). The City of LA, however, did not start developing a comprehensive citywide plan until the mid-1960s. The formal process for developing the general plan and its underlying concept was initiated by the planning department's new director, Calvin Hamilton, who had previously been the director of planning of the City of Pittsburgh (1960–1964) and of Metropolitan Indianapolis (1955–1960).

3. It exempted Downtown, Century City, the Hollywood redevelopment area, and the Wilshire Corridor. These areas together form LA's regional core and were the neighborhoods where towers already existed. LA was not the only city where residents were revolting against growth. Also in 1986, San Francisco residents voted in favor of Proposition M, which placed an annual floor-space cap on major developments of commercial space. These initiatives challenged the prevailing intellectual idea of local growth machines (Molotch 1976, Logan and Molotch 1987), which suggested that growth-based coalitions and real estate interests dominated the shaping of cities.

4. Research on employment distribution in the region indicates that although the regional core is dominant in jobs, and many centers offer concentrations of employment opportunities, the majority of the region's employment is outside its centers (Giuliano et al. 2007, Giuliano and Small 1991).

Everyday Los Angeles

1. The group included John Kaliski and John Chase, both writers, architects, and urban designers, along with other teachers and students at SCI-Arc, the city's independent school of architecture.

2. Contributors included: Barbara Kirshenblatt-Gimblett, a folklorist; Mona Houghton, a writer; Dennis Keeley, a photographer; Camilo Jose Vergara, a sociologist and photographer; Walter Hood, a landscape architect; and architects Phoebe Wall Wilson and Norman Millar.

3. Monacelli published a second, expanded edition in 2008.

Metropolis of Dispersed Diversity

1. Hereafter, whites and all other race groups are non-Hispanic. We will use "black" and "African-American" as interchangeable terms, similarly for "Hispanic" and "Latino"; "Asian" includes Pacific Islanders, even if not specified. American Indians or Native Americans and persons of multiple or other races are not generally specified because their shares amount in total to less than 3 percent.

2. UCLA sociologist Ivan Light (2006) emphasizes stricter labor and housing enforcement, while Massey and Capoferro (2008) emphasize border controls and better jobs elsewhere. Myers (2007, chap. 5) gives primacy to the shock of the deep California recession of the early 1990s.

3. This information is derived from comparisons of home owners by age and race or Hispanic origin in 2010 with data from 2000. For more explanation, see Pitkin and Myers 2011.

The Ambiguous Legacies of the 1992 Riots

1. For scholarship on the 1992 Los Angeles riots, see Gooding-Williams 1993, Cannon 1997, DiPasquale and Glaeser 1998, and Chang and Diaz-Veizades 1999.

2. For a description of Rebuild LA's accomplishments in the post-Ueberroth era, see "History of Rebuild LA," *Rebuild LA Collection* (Thomas and Dorothy Leavey Center for the Study of Los Angeles Research Collection, Loyola Marymount University), available at http://library.lmu.edu/Collections/specialcollections/CSLA_Research_Collection/Rebuild_LA_Home/Rebuild_LA_Collection__CSLA-6__History.htm.

3. The geographic boundaries of South LA, here and henceforth, refer to the census tracts bounded by Alameda Street on the east, Imperial Highway on the south, Crenshaw Boulevard on the west, and Martin Luther King Boulevard on the north. These boundaries conform to the Census Bureau's definition of the area and inform previous studies, most notably Myers 2002.

4. For a thoughtful discussion of arrest statistics in the LA riots, see Morrison and Lowry 1993, esp. 17.

5. Cannon 1997; on the increase in labor force participation rates in South LA since 2000, see Ong et al. 2008, 14; Porter 1997; and Cuomo 1999.

6. Black family median income in LA increased from approximately 80 percent of the countywide median in 1999 to approximately 83 percent in 2009. U.S. Census 2000; U.S. Census 2009, Tables B19113, B19113B.

Minority-Majority Suburbs Change the San Gabriel Valley

1. San Gabriel Valley Council of Governments, "About the San Gabriel Valley"; available at www.sgvcog .org/index.cfm/About.cfm.

One Hundred Years of Land-Use Regulation

1   See "City Planning," *Pacific Municipalities* 45(1) (1931): 63.

2. Some of the most significant literature focusing on the parochial management of zoning and planning in the United States and its outcomes has included Babcock 1966, Delafons 1969, K. Jackson 1981, and Toll 1969. Partial histories of zoning in LA have most notably been written in Fogelson 1967, Fulton 2001, and Weiss 1987.

3. My use of the term "regime" follows from Clarence Stone's work on regime theory (1989).

4. City of LA, Ordinance 18565, adopted Aug. 3, 1909.

5. City of LA, Ordinance 9774, adopted July 25, 1904.

6. City of LA, Ordinance 42666, adopted Oct. 19, 1921.

7. City of LA, Dept. of City Planning 1931–1932: 12; each commercial cluster could serve a few of these communities and would be limited in size to preserve the value of commercial land. Designer Charles Cheney pointed out that in a low-density urban area, commercial centers should be smaller and farther apart to maximize the concentration of purchasing power necessary to sustain businesses, see "Business Area Analysis Made," *Los Angeles Times*, Oct. 13, 1929.

8. "Plans Hearing for Zoning in Wilshire," *Los Angeles Times*, Oct. 31, 1920; Whitnall 1923.

9. "Too Much Business Zoning," *Los Angeles Times*, Oct. 10, 1928.

10. "Association Hits Zoning Alteration," *Los Angeles Times*, Feb. 26, 1925.

11. "Los Angeles City Plan Association Honors Gordon Whitnall," *Pacific Municipalities* 44(7) (1930): 252; "Notes and Events," *National Municipal Review* 13(5) (1924): 318–20.

12. "Zoning Graft in Wilshire District Told," *Los Angeles Times*, Dec. 17, 1938. The York Valley Taxpayers Association referred to spot-zoning as a "racket" in its resolution for amending Section 4 of the zoning code in Resolution of York Valley Taxpayers Association to City Council, Sept. 12, 1932, in Petition No. 4224, 1932 (Box A-0526 LACA).

13. "Realty Board Sifts Zoning," *Los Angeles Times*, Sept. 19, 1926.

14. "Too Much Business Zoning," *Los Angeles Times*, Oct. 10, 1928.

15. See "Survey" of John P. Nield, June 29, 1933 in Petition No. 6374, 1932 (Box A-0539 LACA).

16. "Factors Cited in Appraisals," *Los Angeles Times*, March 4, 1928; City of LA, City Planning Commission, "Letter to Edward W. Hopkins," LA County Assessor, Apr. 12, 1932, in Petition No. 1830, 1932 (Box A-0516 LACA).

17. "Councilmen's Zoning Action is Approved," *Los Angeles Times*, Apr. 29, 1923.

18. There was in fact an increase in the number of variances from 189 to 463 between 1927 and 1931; see City of LA, Dept. of City Planning 1930–1931, 12.

19. City of LA, Dept. of City Planning 1932–1933, 14, and 1928, 6.

20. The FHA also incorporated social characteristics into its evaluations such as the presence of minorities, this reflecting the social norms of the days. See the discussion of FHA lending standards in Jackson 1981, 197–203.

21. See, e.g., Communication No. 14773 (Box A-827 LACA) on rezoning 3.5 square miles in Playa del Rey; in industrial Wilmington near the port, the City Planning Commission's continued work began in 1933 to reduce the amount of commercial zoning, rezoning much of the area for residential property to accommodate incoming defense workers and arguing that "the proposed zoning map should afford sufficient protection to encourage the FHA to insure loans and reputable lending agencies to finance multiple residential improvements." in letter to City Council, Sept. 27, 1943 in Communication No. 15797 (Box A-834 LACA); City of LA, Ordinance 83070, adopted Dec. 23, 1943.

22. "San Fernando Valley" in LA Dept. of City Planning 1942–1943, n.p.

23. The city introduced the "RS" Residential Suburban zone in 1950 mandating a 7,500-square-foot lot minimum; see Communications No. 44357 (Box A-1053 LACA), City of LA, Ordinance 97201, adopted Oct. 27, 1950; City of LA, Dept. of City Planning 1949–1950, 2, 36; for early examples of rezoning to the "RS" designation, see Communications Nos. 50990 (Box A-1115 LACA), 56766 (Box A-1167 LACA), 57254 (Box A-1172 LACA), or 58042 (Box A-1181 LACA); regarding the "RE" Residential Estate Zone, see Communication No. 66318 (Box A-1266 LACA); City of LA, Ordinance No. 105652, adopted May 24, 1955; City of LA, Dept. of City Planning 1954–1955, 14.

24. Los Feliz Improvement Association, "Letter to City Council," Oct. 24, 1962, in Council File 110260 (Box A-1737 LACA).

25. Council File 110260 (Box A-1737 LACA).

26. Concerning Height District 1-VL, see City of LA, Ordinance 145486, adopted Jan. 2, 1974; concerning Height District 1-XL, see Council File 77-2251 (Box B-814 LACA), and City of LA, Ordinance 151564, adopted Sept. 21, 1978.

27. Council Files 115144 (Box A-1796 LACA), 117977 (Box A-1829 LACA), and 117977 S1 (Box A-1829 LACA); City of LA, Ordinance 127777, adopted June 16, 1964, and Ordinance 130132, adopted May 17, 1965.

28. "Zoning Plan Protested as '$40,000 Slum,'" Los Angeles Times, June 3, 1969.

29. Council File 141493 (Box A-2166 LACA); City of LA, Ordinance 140934, adopted Sept. 3, 1970; Council File 71-1902 (Box A-2401 LACA); City of LA, Ordinance 142690, adopted Nov. 3, 1971, allowed the Planning Commission to recommend changes of "M" classified land to "MR."

30. "For Mayor of Los Angeles," Los Angeles Examiner, January 15, 1961.

31. Council File 116846 (Box A-1816 LACA); City of LA, Ordinance 129334, adopted Jan. 19, 1965.

32. See motion 21 Aug. 1969 in Council File 146712 (Box A-2237 LACA); City of LA, Dept. of City Planning, Staff Report, and City Planning Commission Recommendation for Oct. 30, 1969 in Council File 146712 (Box A-2237 LACA); Building Industry Association of California to John S. Gibson, January 27, 1970, in Council File 146712 (Box A-2237 LACA).

33. See Garrigues 1966; Baker 1966; "Council Would Waive Zoning for Head Start," Los Angeles Times, February 24, 1966.

34. "Zoning Regulations Hamper Land Use," Los Angeles Times, Apr. 2, 1961; "Premise behind Zoning Laws Obsolete, City Planners Charge," Los Angeles Times, Sept. 24, 1961; "Zoning Waived in Favor of Optimum Land Use," Los Angeles Times, Feb. 18, 1962.

35. "First Report to the Mayor and City Council," in City of LA Citizens' Committee on Zoning Practices and Procedures 1968, vol. 3, 8–14.

36. Baker 1969a and 1969b; "YES on City Zoning Reform," Los Angeles Times, May 21, 1969; City of LA, Ordinance 138800, adopted May 29, 1969; City of LA 1969, Article VIII, Secs. 95, 95.5, 96.5, 96.6, 97.1, 97.2, 98, and 99; Council File 70-1137 (Box A-2286 LACA); City of LA, Ordinance 141821, adopted Mar. 30, 1971.

37. Regarding the "Crisis 1972" workshop, see "Zoning is Subject of Two-Day Forum," Los Angeles Times, Aug. 20, 1972.

38. "Role of Planning" in City of LA, Dept. of City Planning 1969–1970, n.p.

39. Most downzoning took the form of rezoning multifamily "R3" districts to one of the "Residential Density" districts, an action the Dept. of City Planning argued satisfied the community plans that made up the General Plan's Land Use Element but still promised to provide more affordable, multifamily options; see City of LA, Dept. of City Planning, "Staff Report" on Residential Density zones, 8 Aug. 1974 in Council File 117977-S2 (Box A-1829 LACA).

40. AB 283 (Alperin 1987); LA's tradition of home rule had enabled it to circumvent the state requirement that zoning conform to general plans in existence since AB 1301.

41. *Friends of Mammoth v. Board of Supervisors*, 8 Cal. 3d 247 (1972).
42. *Friends of Westwood v. Los Angeles*, 191 Cal. App. 3d 259 (1987); Shapiro 1988.
43. Motion June 10, 1987, and report of Mayor Tom Bradley July 27, 1987, in Council File 87-0986 (Box C-1707 LACA).
44. City of LA, Ordinance 165951, adopted May 29, 1990.
45. Fulton 2001, 260–63, reports that in 1978, before Proposition 13, the cities of Oxnard, Ventura, and Camarillo collected $8 million in property taxes and $10 million in sales taxes. One year later they were collecting $3.7 million in property tax and $12 million in sales tax. With Proposition 13, Fulton argues, retail became the "cash crop" of California cities.
46. Council File 71-2915 (Box A-2424 LACA); City of LA, Ordinance 145927, adopted Dec. 16, 1971.
47. Council File 83-1020 (Box C-692 LACA); City of LA, Ordinance 159532, adopted Nov. 20, 1984.
48. Council File 81-6052 (Box C-123 LACA); City of LA, Ordinance 161716, adopted Dec. 6, 1986.
49. City of LA, Ordinance 156279, adopted Jan. 12, 1982.
50. See report of Intergovernmental Relations Committee, Item 5 Dec. 12, 1988, and attachments 1–5, in Council File 88-2194 (Box C-2149 LACA).
51. AB 1863; regarding city conformance with the new density bonus legislation, see Council File 90-1034; the density bonus program has again been altered by SB 1818 to allow a by-right 20 percent density bonus given the reservation of 5 percent of units for very low-income households with a 2.5 percent additional bonus for every additional percentage point reserved up to a maximum density bonus of 35 percent. Alternatively it allows a by-right 20 percent density bonus given the reservation of 10 percent of units for low-income households with a 1.5 percent additional bonus for every additional percentage point reserved up to a maximum density bonus of 35 percent. A minimum density bonus of 5 percent can also be granted given the reservation of 10 percent of units for medium-income earners in condominium projects, with a 1 percent additional bonus for every additional percentage point reserved up to a maximum density bonus of 35 percent.
52. City of LA, Dept. of City Planning 1996, 3; motion July 25, 2006 in Council File 06-1725 regarding the need for a definition of "transit corridors" by Ordinance (LA City Clerk Connect).
53. "Breaking the Code: 'Local Control' Means the Valley Wants a Say in Zoning Issues. What a Concept!" *LA Daily News*, Nov. 17, 1998.
54. City of LA, Dept. of City Planning, report to the Planning and Land Use Committee of City Council. Nov. 15, 1990, in Council File 90-1878 (Box C-2438 LACA).
55. Council File 99-1753 (LA City Clerk Connect).
56. Residential Accessory Services zones "RAS3," permitting "R3" residential uses, and "RAS4," permitting "R4" residential uses, see City of LA, City Planning Commission to the Planning and Land Use Management Committee of City Council, 3 June 2002 in Council File 02-1240 (Box B-2914 LACA); LA (City) Ordinance 174999, adopted Nov. 26, 2002.
57. Ordinance 172571, adopted Apr. 14, 1999.
58. Council File 02-0177 (LA City Clerk Connect); Ordinance 175038, adopted Dec. 20, 2002.
59. City of LA, Ordinance 171427, adopted Nov. 20, 1996.

Almost New Urbanism

1. Stefanos Polyzoides in a private conversation with the author, July 2012.
2. "Hooray for Hollywood, but Playa Vista More than a Dream." 1996. National Real Estate Investor, February 1. Available at http://nreionline.com/mag/real_estate_hooray_hollywood_playa.
3. See Playa Vista Community, "The Village," available at www.playavista.com/our-community/the-village .php. On March 31, 2010, the LA City Council approved the second phase of the planned community's 111-acre mixed use component by a 12–2 vote.
4. See Playa Vista Community, "Riparian Corridor," available at www.playavista.com/parks-open-space /riparian-corridor.php.
5. See "Playa Vista: A Place for Everyone," *LA Architect*, Supplement N-D, 2005, 13.
6. The Downtown Strategic Plan was initiated by the Community Redevelopment Agency of Los Angeles. It was completed in 1989. The team comprised Moule & Polyzoides as lead consultant, with Duany Plater-Zyberk, Solomon, Inc., Peter de Bretteville, Susan Haviland, and Hanna/Olin.
7. For more on these projects, see Chase 2005, 125–28.

Planning a Tool for Battling the Fast-Food Invasion

1. California Health and Safety Code, Part 7; California Retail Food Code, Sec. 113705.
2. City of LA, Ordinance 180103, Sept. 14, 2008.

Back to the Future in Transportation Planning

1. Muller 2004 classifies the high-speed, limited-access freeways of the Interstate era as a different technology from the lower-capacity, slower-speed road that preceded the interstates.
2. The development of electric vehicles will likely not change this story, as electric vehicles appear not to require large infrastructure investments, unless issues of power distribution change that.
3. The early sales-tax increments did not have expiration dates, hence LA County Propositions A and C do not expire.
4. Information on the current length of the LA MTA rail system is from "Facts at a Glance," available at www.metro.net/news/pages/facts-glance/#P37_586. Information on planned rail lines is from the LA County Metropolitan Transportation Authority 2009, 66–68. Information on the Washington Metro, which currently covers 106 miles, is from "Metro Facts," available at www.wmata.com/about_metro /docs/metrofacts.pdf.
5. The account of the State Route 91 toll lanes in this paragraph is based on Boarnet, DiMento, and Macey 2002 and Boarnet and DiMento 2004.
6. For examples of theoretical and policy analyses of congestion pricing, see Vickrey 1963 and Small, Winston, and Evans 1991.
7. See www.metro.net/projects_studies/joint_development/images/JDP_completed_projects.pdf and http: //metro.net/projects/joint_dev_pgm.
8. Sources include e-mail communication from Marco Anderson of SCAG, May 2011, and the following webpages: www.compassblueprint.org/tools/hollywood, www.compassblueprint.org/tools/park101, www.compassblueprint.org/tools/ventura, www.compassblueprint.org/tools/brea, and www.compass blueprint.org/tools/victorville.

Regional Planning in Southern California

1. More specifically, the state government was required to "sub-allocate" Congestion Mitigation and Air Quality Improvement (CMAQ) and Surface Transportation Program (STP) funds in the largest metro regions to projects programmed by MPOs.
2. Under SB 45, 75 percent of the state's transportation improvement funds are designated for projects selected by RTPAs, and the remaining 25 percent for projects are selected by Caltrans, the state Department of Transportation.
3. Four of the subregional councils are coterminous with county boundaries, whereas Riverside County is divided into two parts and LA County into eight.
4. These goals are embodied in the Global Warming Solutions Act (Assembly Bill 32) adopted in 2006, and Executive Order S-3-05, signed in 2005.
5. For a more detailed discussion of the SB 375 target-setting process, see Barbour and Deakin forthcoming.
6. A megaregion refers to a clustered network of American cities whose population ranges or is projected to range from about 7 to 63 million by 2025, according to America 2050, an organization that conducts and sponsors research on this topic. America 2050 has identified 11 megaregions in North America, including "Southern California," which encompasses the SCAG region and San Diego County.

Ballot Box Planning for Transit

1. See the Self-Help Counties Coalition at www.selfhelpcounties.org.
2. The proposed subway does not extend through the west side all the way to the ocean. Instead, the proposed project stops in Westwood. But "the Subway to the Sea" makes for a much snazzier moniker than does "the Subway to the Veterans Administration Hospital in Westwood," and transit advocates sincerely hope to see the line expanded someday to the ocean so that it merits the name they have given it.

Systemic Change Through CicLAvia

1. These neighborhoods include Boyle Heights, the Arts District, Little Tokyo, the Old Bank District, the Historic Core, the Seventh Street Corridor, the Financial District, MacArthur Park/Westlake, Koreatown, and East Hollywood.
2. Renowned urban historian Sam Bass Warner Jr. succinctly summed up the elusive concept of "urban ephemera": "Urban ephemera are organized, momentary, repeated urban public presentations. They include parades, festivals, celebrations, outdoor performances, and rituals of all kinds. Because they impress themselves upon the public images of cities in small ways and large, Mark Schuster, a cultural policy analyst, urges city designers and planners to add ephemera planning to their list of tools" (2001).
3. This language was included in a proposal to the California Endowment, Feb. 23, 2010.
4. The full list of sponsors, supporters, and partners for the 10/10/10 CicLAvia event includes the City of LA, the LA County Bicycle Coalition (LACBC), the LA County Metropolitan Transportation Authority, the Metabolic Studio at the Annenberg Foundation, the California Endowment, the Rosenthal Family Foundation, Bikes Belong, Boeing, Kaiser Permanente, Northrop Grumman, Southern California Gas Company, and USC Government and Community Engagement.
5. In May 2003, an 86-year-old man plowed into pedestrians at the farmers market, killing 10; see Winton and Groves 2008.

Green Spaces in the Auto Metropolis

1. A recent communitywide needs assessment commissioned by the City of LA Dept. of Recreation and Parks in 2009 found that park acreage in the city is only four acres per 1,000 residents if only urban parkland is taken into account. This number increases to 9.7 acres per 1,000 residents if additional open space preserves are included, such as the Los Angeles National Forest, Santa Monica Mountains, and open spaces maintained by LA County and the State of California (LA Dept. of Recreation and Parks 2009).
2. A 0.5-acre circular plaza with an interactive water feature designed by Mia Lehrer + Associates and WET design has recently opened under the freeway at the Confluence Park site (at the corner of North San Fernando Road and North Figueroa Street). Thirteen of the 32 acres of the Cornfields site have been turned into a temporary park.
3. The study constructed a "needs index" for each neighborhood, taking into account its median household income, percentage of households under poverty, density of children, and average number of people per household (Loukaitou-Sideris and Stieglitz 2002).
4. From 1947 to 1978, Aldo van Eyck designed more than 700 playgrounds in Amsterdam transforming odd elements of urban space into usable and architecturally interesting playgrounds (Novak et al. 2002).

The Afterlife of a Master Plan

1. Proposition 12 is the "Safe Neighborhood Parks, Clean Water, Clean Air, and Coastal Protection Bond Act of 2000." The text is available at http://primary2000.sos.ca.gov/VoterGuide/Propositions/12text.htm.
2. Many an individual and organization have rethought the LA River in larger and smaller ways; the key organization in the private sector is Friends of the LA River; see folar.org as an introduction.
3. MTA bibliography at www.metro.net/about/library/archives/visions-studies/los-angeles-transit-and-transportation-studies; Hise and Gish 2007.

Planning a Great Civic Park

1. "Civic Center? A Big Parking Lot, New Custom House Would Worsen Jam," *Independent Press-Telegram*, April 9, 1961.

Policy and Community in Los Angeles Development

1. Based on my calculations, the $108 billion is equivalent to the annual income of 2,225,000 LA workers in the following industries: construction, manufacturing, trucking, retail trade, motion pictures, health services, restaurants, professional services, miscellaneous services, and real estate (California Employment Development Dept., Labor Market Information Division 2011).

A Planning Ordinance Injects New Life into Historic Downtown

1. Notes from Amy Anderson, Broadway Initiative Coordinator of LA Conservancy, on Adaptive Reuse Lenders Roundtable, July 24, 2002.
2. Pacific Electric Lofts website, http://pelofts.com.
3. Office of Historic Resources staff report on Historic-Cultural Monument application for Douglas Building, July 16, 2009.
4. Downtown Center Business Improvement District database on adaptive reuse, as of May 27, 2011.
5. City of LA, Ordinance 177577, an Interim Control Ordinance temporarily prohibiting the Conversion or Demolition of Residential Hotels, citywide.
6. Downtown Center Business Improvement District database on adaptive reuse, as of May 27, 2011.

Community Benefits, Negotiations, and (In)Justice

1. For the more details and a full copy of the "Staples" CBA, see www.saje.net/site/c.hkLQJcMUKrH /b.4489979/k.6E84/The_Staples_Agreement.htm. For more on the nuts and bolts of CBAs see: Gross et al. 2005. On CBAs and the Staples Agreement in particular as examples of community economic development, see Cummings 2006. For case studies of the Staples Agreement along with two other LA CBAs, see Kaye and Lopez Mendoza 2008. For more recent and visual material on CBAs, see the poster from the Center for Urban Pedagogy on the Atlantic Yards agreement in New York at www.hatmax.net /urbanspaces/centerforurbanpedagogy and the work-in-progress website the ABCs of CBAs at http: //test.nogginlabs.com/lincoln/ASKSystem/home.html, which organized video clips of community benefit "experts" (including me) as answers to specific questions.
2. My thanks to Sunyoung Yang and the Bus Riders Union, who provided me with a list of questions that helped me frame this article.
3. One of the headlines about the agreement was "Staples Plan Spotlights Invisible Communities," *Los Angeles Times*, June 2, 2001.
4. SAJE's map/brochure of the Figueroa Corridor Strategy for Urban Land Reform describes a platform that includes reform redevelopment, expand tenants' rights, eliminate slum conditions, and increase people's control over land. SAJE is a cofounder of the national Right to the City Alliance (www.righttothecity.org).
5. The affordable housing stipulated in the Staples Agreement was to be built off-site and in the neighborhood, as was the stated preference of local residents.

From Barbie to Banksy

1. Throughout this essay the terms "cultural economy," "creative economy," "art," and "culture" are used interchangeably.
2. The cultural or "creative economy," according to *Otis* includes the following: architecture/interior design, art galleries, communication arts, digital media, entertainment, fashion, furniture/home furnishings, product/industrial design, toys, visual and performing arts.
3. Excluding any accompanying manufacturing.
4. Direct jobs are those within the identified industrial sector, while indirect jobs are those in firms and sectors in supplier industries or consumer product suppliers.

References

Adamic, Louis. 1932. *Laughing in the Jungle: The Autobiography of an Immigrant in America*. New York: Harper and Brothers.

Adams, Tom, Amanda Eaken, and Ann Notthoff. 2009. *Communities Tackle Global Warming: A Guide to California's SB 375*. Los Angeles: National Resources Defense Council.

Adler, Sy. 1991. "The Transformation of the Pacific Electric Railway: Bradford Snell, Roger Rabbit, and the Politics of Transportation in Los Angeles." *Urban Affairs Quarterly* 27(1): 51–86.

Alba, Richard, and Victor Nee. 2003. *Remaking the American Mainstream: Assimilation and Contemporary Immigration*. Cambridge, Mass.: Harvard University Press.

Alonso, William. 1980. "The Population Factor in Urban Structure." In *The Prospective City*, edited by Arthur P. Solomon, 32–51. Cambridge, Mass.: MIT Press.

Alperin, Anthony Saul. 1987. "AB 283—A Zoning Consistency Odyssey." *Southwestern University Law Review* 17(1): 1–22.

American Lung Association. 2011. *State of the Air*. Available at www.stateoftheair.org.

Anderson, Dave. 2007. "Time Doesn't Relieve the Pain, or Change the Facts." *New York Times*, September 30. Available at www.nytimes.com/2007/09/30/sports/baseball/30anderson.html.

Antonovich, Michael D. 2008. "Let's Not Be Taken for a Ride with Measure R." *LA Daily News*, Valley edition, November 3.

Apollo Alliance: Clean Energy and Good Jobs. 2010. "Los Angeles Clean Ports Program Benefits Environment, Workers, and Local Community, as it Creates Demand for Clean Trucks." Available at http://apolloalliance.org/rebuild-america/los-angeles-clean-ports-program-benefits-environment-workers-and-local-community-as-it-creates-demand-for-clean-trucks.

Arieff, Allison. 2007. "Danger: Playground Ahead." *New York Times*, May 29. Available at www.nytimes.com/2007/05/29/opinion/29arieff.html.

Axelrod, Jeremiah. 2009. *Inventing Autopia: Dreams and Visions of the Modern Metropolis in Jazz Age Los Angeles*. Berkeley, Calif.: University of California Press.

Babcock, Richard. 1966. *Zoning Game: Municipal Practices and Policies*. Madison, Wisc.: University of Wisconsin Press.

Babey, Susan H., E. Richard Brown, and Theresa A. Hastert. 2005. *Access to Safe Parks Helps Increase Physical Activity among Teenagers*. Los Angeles: UCLA Center for Health Policy Research.

Baiocchi, Gianpaolo. 2001. "Participation, Activism, and Politics: The Porto Alegre Experiment and Deliberative Democratic Theory." *Politics and Society* 29(1): 43–72.

Baker, Elizabeth A., Mario Schootman, Ellen Barnidge, and Cheryl Kelly. 2006. "The Role of Race and Poverty in Access to Foods that Enable Individuals to Adhere to Dietary Guidelines." *Preventing Chronic Disease* 3(3): 1–11. Available at www.cdc.gov/pcd/issues/2006/jul/05_0217.htm.

Baker, Erwin. 1966. "Council Liberalizes Foster Home Zoning." *Los Angeles Times*, April 13.

———. 1969a. "City Council Approves Zoning-Planning Shifts." *Los Angeles Times*, February 20.

———. 1969b. "Planning-Zoning Shift Amendment Ordered." *Los Angeles Times*, February 25.

Banham, Reyner. 1971. *Los Angeles: The Architecture of Four Ecologies.* London: Allen Lane.

Barbour, Elisa, and Elizabeth Deakin. Forthcoming. "Smart Growth Planning for Climate Protection: Evaluating California's Senate Bill 375." *Journal of the American Planning Association.*

Barbour, Elisa, and Ann Markusen. 2007. "Regional Occupational and Industrial Structure: Does One Imply the Other?" *International Regional Science Review* 30(1): 72–90.

Barbour, Elisa, and Michael B. Teitz. 2006. *Blueprint Planning in California: Forging Consensus on Metropolitan Growth and Development.* San Francisco: Public Policy Institute of California.

Barboza, Tony. 2010. "Long Beach Makes Way for Bicycles." *Los Angeles Times*, January 26. Available at http://articles.latimes.com/2010/jan/26/local/la-me-outthere26-2010jan26.

Bartlett, Dana W. 1907. *The Better City: A Sociological Study of a Modern City.* Los Angeles: Neuner Company Press.

Beale, Lauren. 2011. "Housing Crisis Hasn't Touched San Marino." *Los Angeles Times*, January 31. Available at http://articles.latimes.com/2011/jan/31/business/la-fi-san-marino-housing-20110131.

Bean, Frank D., and Gillian Stevens. 2003. *America's Newcomers and the Dynamics of Diversity.* New York: Russell Sage.

Berg, Nate. 2011. "It's Never Too Soon to Start." *Planning.* February. Available at www.planning.org/resources zine/2011/spr/nevertoosoon.htm.

Bernstein, Sharon. 1997. "Plan Would Allow Some Garage Housing." *Los Angeles Times*, May 3.

Berry, Jeffrey M., Kent E. Portney, and Ken Thomson. 1993. *The Rebirth of Urban Democracy.* Washington, D.C.: Brookings Institution Press.

Bikeable Communities. 2011. "Long Beach Launches First 'Bicycle Friendly Business Districts' in the U.S." June 4. Available at http://bikeablecommunities.org/?p=929.

Bike Long Beach. 2011. "Broadway and Third Separated Bikeways Completed." April 23. Available at www.bikelongbeach.org/News/Read.aspx?ArticleId=85.

———. N.d. "Bicycle Boxes." Available at http://admin.longbeach.gov/civica/filebank/blobdload.asp?BlobID=24658.

Bina, Aarash, and Joseph S. Devinny. 2006. *Stormwater Quality Control through Retrofit of Industrial Surfaces"* Green Visions Plan for 21st Century Southern California, no. 10.

Birkinshaw, Jack. 1982. "Cities May Open Door to 'Granny Housing.'" *Los Angeles Times*, July 18.

Blackford, Mansel G. 1993. *The Lost Dream: Businessmen and City Planning on the Pacific Coast, 1890–1920.* Columbus, Ohio: Ohio State University Press.

Block, Jason P., Richard A. Scribner, and Karen B. DeSalvo. 2004. "Fast Food, Race/Ethnicity, and Income: A Geographic Analysis." *American Journal of Preventive Medicine* 27(3): 211–17.

Blumenfeld, Jane. 2010. "L.A. Zoning Turns 100: Now What?" Lecture. The Huntington, San Marino, Calif. March 27.

Boarnet, Marlon G., and Randall Crane. 2001. *Travel by Design: The Influence of Urban Form on Travel.* New York: Oxford University Press.

Boarnet, Marlon G., and Joseph F. DiMento. 2004. "The Private Sector's Role in Highway Finance: Lessons from California's SR 91." *Access*, no. 25: 26–31. Available at www.uctc.net/access/25/Access%20 25%20-%2005%20-%20Lessons%20From%20SR%2091.pdf.

Boarnet, Marlon G., Joseph F. DiMento, and Gregg P. Macey. 2002. *Toll Highway Finance in California: Lessons from Orange County.* Berkeley, Calif.: California Policy Research Center, University of California.

Boarnet, Marlon G., Kenneth Joh, Walter Siembab, William Fulton, and Mai Thi Nguyen. 2011. "Retrofitting the Suburbs to Increase Walking: Evidence from a Land-use-Travel Study." *Urban Studies* 48(1): 129–59.

Boarnet, Marlon G., Lindell Marsh, Chris Lunghino, and Lucy Olmos. 2009. "Sustainable Goods Movement in Southern California: The Promise of Collaborative Planning." In *Transportation Infrastructure: The Challenges of Rebuilding America*, ed. Marlon G. Boarnet. Planning Advisory Service report no. 557. Chicago: American Planning Association.

Boarnet, Marlon G., Emily Parkany, and Eugene Jae Kim. 1998. "Measuring Traffic Congestion." *Transportation Research Record* 1634: 93–99.

Bollens, Scott. 1993. *Metropolitan Transportation Governance in Orange County.* Irvine, Calif.: Department of Urban and Regional Planning, University of California.

Boone-Heinonen, J., Penny Gordon-Larsen, Catarina I. Kiefe, James M. Shikany, Cora E. Lewis, and Barry M. Popkin. 2011. "Fast Food Restaurants and Food Stores: Longitudinal Associations with Diet in Young to Middle-Aged Adults: The CARDIA Study." *Archives of Internal Medicine* 171(13): 1161–70.

Bottles, Scott. 1987. *Los Angeles and the Automobile: The Making of the Modern City.* Berkeley, Calif.: University of California Press.

Bowman, Shanthy A., and Bryan T. Vineyard. 2004. "Fast Food Consumption of U.S. Adults: Impact on Energy and Nutrient Intakes and Overweight Status." *Journal of the American College of Nutrition* 23(2): 163–68.

Box, Richard C., and Juliet A. Musso. 2004. "Experiments with Local Federalism: Secession and the Neighborhood Council Movement in Los Angeles." *American Review of Public Administration* 34(3): 259–76.

Boyer, Paul. 1978. *Urban Masses and Moral Order in America, 1820–1920.* Cambridge, Mass.: Harvard University Press.

Brown, Eleanor, and James M. Ferris. 2002. *Philanthropy and Social Capital in Los Angeles.* Los Angeles: Center on Philanthropy and Public Policy.

Brown, Jeffrey. 1998. "Race, Class, Gender, and Public Transportation: Lessons from the Bus Riders Union Lawsuit." *Critical Planning* 5: 3–20.

Brown, Jeffrey A., Eric A. Morris, and Brian D. Taylor. 2009. "Planning for Cars in Cities: Planners, Engineers, and Freeways in the 20th Century." *Journal of the American Planning Association* 75(2): 161–77.

Bryer, Thomas A., and Terry L. Cooper. 2007. "Challenges in Enhancing Responsiveness in Neighborhood Governance." *Public Performance & Management Review* 31(2): 191–214.

Buck, A. E. 1924. "Notes and Events." *National Municipal Review* 13(5): 318–20.

Burgess, Ernest W. 1925. "The Growth of the City." In *The City*, ed. Robert E. Park, Ernest W. Burgess, and Roderick D. McKenzie, 47–62. Chicago: University of Chicago Press.

Burgess, Jacquelin, Carolyn M. Harrison, and Melanie Limb. 1988. "People, Parks, and the Urban Green: A Study of Popular Meanings and Values for Open Spaces in the City." *Urban Studies* 25 (6): 455–73.

Burleigh, Irv. 1967. "Encinans Choose Up Sides in War over Development." *Los Angeles Times*, February 9.

Burnham, Daniel, and Edward Bennett. 1970 [1909]. *Plan of Chicago.* New York: Da Capo Press.

Bush, Carl. N.d. "Zoning, Its Possibilities, Purposes, and Difficulties," *Los Angeles Realtor* (June), 24, 28–32.

Byrne, Jason, Jennifer Wolch, Jennifer Swift, and Christine Ryan. 2005. *SAGE (Systematic Audit of Green-Space Environments) Audit Form and Instructions.* Green Visions Plan for 21st Century Southern California, no. 7.

Byun, Pillsung, and Adrian X. Esparza. 2005. "A Revisionist Model of Suburbanization and Sprawl: The Role of Political Fragmentation, Growth Control, and Spillovers." *Journal of Planning Education and Research* 24(3): 252–64.

California, State of, Legislative Analyst's Office (CLAO). 1998. *Transportation Equity Act for the 21st Century: What the New Federal Act Means for California.* August 26. Available at www.lao.ca.gov/1998/082698_tea_21/082698_tea_21.html.

California, State of, Newsletter. 2008. "Monrovia Council Opposes Sales Tax Hike for LA's 'Subway to the Sea'." *Targeted News Service.* October 8.

California Employment Development Department (EDD), Labor Market Information Division. 2011. "Quarterly Census of Employment and Wages." Available at www.labormarketinfo.edd.ca.gov/qcew/CEW-Major_NAICS.asp.

Cambridge Systematics. 2009. *Moving Cooler: An Analysis of Transportation Strategies for Reducing Greenhouse Gas Emissions.* Washington, D.C.: Urban Land Institute.

Cannon, Lou. 1997. *Official Negligence: How Rodney King and the Riots Changed the LAPD.* New York: Times Books.

Cavanaugh, Kerry, and George B. Sanchez. 2008. "Donations Slow for Local Issues: Taxes, Bonds Take Backseat to Bigger Campaigns." *LA Daily News*, Valley edition. October 7.

Caves, Richard E. 2000. *Creative Industries: Contracts Between Art and Commerce.* Cambridge, Mass.: Harvard University Press.

Central Intelligence Agency (CIA). 2011. "Life Expectancy at Birth." *The World Fact Book.* Available at www.cia.gov/library/publications/the-world-factbook/rankorder/2102rank.html.

Chang, Edward T., and Jeanette Diaz-Veizades. 1999. *Ethnic Peace in the American City: Building Community in Los Angeles and Beyond.* New York: New York University Press.

Chase, John. 2005. "Playa Vista: A New Urbanist Bog." In *Los Angeles: Building the Polycentric Region,* ed. Alan Loomis and Gloria Ohland. Chicago: Congress for the New Urbanism.

Chase, John, Margaret Crawford, and John Kaliski. 2008 [1999]. *Everyday Urbanism.* New York: Monacelli Press.

City News Service. 2008a. "Governor Signs AB2321." September 25.

———. 2008b. "Measure R Informational Campaign Funding." October 7.

City Project, The. 2006. "Healthy Parks, Schools and Communities."

Cohen, Deborah A., Thomas L. McKenzie, Amber Sehgal, Stephanie Williamson, Daniella Golinelli, and Nicole Lurie. 2007. "Contribution of Public Parks to Physical Activity." *American Journal of Public Health* 97(3): 509–14.

Cohen, Deborah, Amber Sehgal, Stephanie Williamson, Roland Sturm, Thomas L. McKenzie, Rosa Lara, and Nicole Lurie. 2006. *Park Use and Physical Activity in a Sample of Public Parks in the City of Los Angeles.* Santa Monica, Calif.: Rand Corporation.

Cohen-Marks, Mara A. "Community Development." In Rudd and Sitton 2007, 415–45.

Committee on the Regional Plan of New York and Its Environs. 1929. *Regional Plan of New York and Its Environs.* New York: Regional Plan of New York and Its Environs.

Connell, Rich. 1986a. "Prop U Backers See It as Start of Land-Use Revolt." *Los Angeles Times,* October 12.

———. 1986b. "Prop U Backers Hit Mail Hard to Blunt Critics." *Los Angeles Times,* October 31.

Construction Industry Research Board. 2010. *Residential Building Permits for Selected Place by Year.* Place: Los Angeles, County: Los Angeles.

Council on Development Choices in the 80s. 1983. "Factors Shaping Development in the 80s." In *Land Use Issues of the 1980s,* ed. James H. Carr and Edward E. Duensing, 3–17. New Brunswick, N.J.: Rutgers University Press.

Crabbe, Amber E., Rachel Hiatt, Susan D. Poliwka, and Martin Wachs. 2005. *Local Transportation Sales Taxes: California's Experiment in Transportation Finance.* Berkeley, Calif.: University of California Transportation Center. Available at www.uctc.net/papers/737.pdf.

Crouch, Dora P., Daniel J. Garr, and Axel I. Mundigo. 1982. *Spanish City Planning in North America.* Cambridge, Mass.: MIT Press.

Crowe, B. S. 1974. *Report of Mayor Bradley's Ad Hoc Committee on Economic Development.* Submitted by the Ad Hoc Committee, August 12, 1974.

Cuff, Dana. 2002. *The Provisional City: Los Angeles Stories of Architecture and Urbanism.* Cambridge, Mass.: MIT Press.

Cummings, Scott. 2006. "Mobilization Lawyering: Community Economic Development in the Figueroa Corridor." In *Cause Lawyers and Social Movements,* ed. Austin Sarat and Stuart Scheingold. Stanford: Stanford University Press.

Cuomo, Andrew. 1999. *New Markets: The Untapped Retail Buying Power in America's Inner Cities.* Washington D.C.: U.S. Department of Housing and Urban Development.

Currid, Elizabeth. 2006. "New York as a Global Creative Hub: A Competitive Analysis of Four Theories on World Cities." *Economic Development Quarterly* 20(4): 330–50.

———. 2007a. *The Warhol Economy: How Fashion, Art, and Music Drive New York City.* Princeton, N.J.: Princeton University Press.

———. 2007b. "How Art and Culture Happen in New York: Implications for Urban Economic Development." *Journal of the American Planning Association* 73(4): 454–67.

———. 2009. Los Angeles as a Global Creative Hub: Findings and Implications. Prepared for the John Randolph Haynes Foundation, Los Angeles. In *Measuring and Quantifying the Economic Impact of Culture: Limitations and New Directions.*

Currid, Elizabeth, and Sarah Williams. 2010. "Two Cities, Five Industries: Similarities and Differences within and between Cultural Industries in New York and Los Angeles." *Journal of Planning Education and Research* 29(3): 322–35.

Currid-Halkett, Elizabeth, and Kevin Stolarick. 2011. "The Arts: Not Just Artists (and Vice Versa): A Comparative Regional Analysis for Studying the Composition of the Creative Economy." In *The Handbook of Creative Cities,* ed. David Andersson, Åke E. Andersson, and Charlotta Mellander. Northampton, Mass.: Edward Elgar.

Danielson, Michael N., and Jameson W. Doig. 1982. *New York: The Politics of Urban Regional Development*. Berkeley, Calif.: University of California Press.

Davis, Clark. 1992. "From Oasis to Metropolis: Southern California and the Changing Context of American Leisure." *Pacific Historical Review* 61(3): 357–86.

— — —. 2000. *Company Men: White-Collar Life and Corporate Cultures in Los Angeles, 1892–1941*. Baltimore: Johns Hopkins University Press.

Davis, Mike. 1990. *City of Quartz: Excavating the Future in Los Angeles*. New York: Verso.

DeForest, Robert W., and Lawrence Veiller, eds. 1903. *The Tenement House Problem: Including the Report of the New York State Tenement House Commission of 1900*. New York: Macmillan.

Delafons, John. 1969. *Land Use Control in the United States*. Cambridge, Mass.: MIT Press.

Derrick, Frederick W., and Charles E. Scott. 1998. "Sales Tax Equity: Who Bears the Burden?" *Quarterly Review of Economics and Finance* 38(2): 227–37.

Deverell, William. 2004. *Whitewashed Adobe: The Rise of Los Angeles and the Remaking of Its Mexican Past*. Berkeley, Calif.: University of California Press.

DiPasquale, Denise, and Edward L. Glaeser. 1998. "The Los Angeles Riot and the Economics of Urban Unrest." *Journal of Urban Economics* 43(1): 52–78.

Dorothy Peyton Gray Transportation Library. N.d. "Los Angeles Transit History." Available at www.metro.net /about/library/about/home/los-angeles-transit-history.

Douglas, Peter. 1968. *The Southern California Association of Governments: A Response to Federal Concern for Metropolitan Areas*. Los Angeles: Institute of Government and Public Affairs, UCLA.

Dowall, David E. 1996. "An Evaluation of California's Enterprise Zone Programs." *Economic Development Quarterly* 10(4): 352–68.

Doyle, Sue, and Troy Anderson. 2009. "Are You Ready to Pay 9.75 Percent for Sales Tax in Los Angeles? A 1 Percent Hike Added to the 1/2 Cent Approved for Measure R." *LA Daily News*, February 13.

Doyle, Sue, and Kerry Cavanaugh. 2008. "Measure R Targets Road Congestion." *LA Daily News*, Valley edition, October 7.

Dreier, Peter. 1997. "Rent Deregulation in California and Massachusetts: Politics, Policy, and Impacts." Paper presented at the Housing '97 Conference, New York. May 14.

Duhl, Len J., and Andrea Kristin-Sanchez. 1999. *Healthy Cities and the City Planning Process: A Background Document on Links between Health and Urban Planning*. Copenhagen, Denmark: World Health Organization.

Eaton, Allison Jean. 2011. "New Long Beach Bicycle Business District Program Unveiled." *Long Beach Post*, June 8. Available at www.lbpost.com/news/allison/11777.

Egan, Timothy. 2010. "Rise of the Suburbs." *New York Times*, March 10.

Einstoss, Ron. 1966. "Tighter Zoning Control Needed, Yorty Tells Jury." *Los Angeles Times*, December 9.

Elias, Judith W. 1983. *Los Angeles: Dream to Reality, 1885–1915*. Northridge, Calif.: Santa Susana Press.

Erie, Steven P. 1992. "How the Urban West Was Won: The Local State and Economic Growth in Los Angeles, 1880–1932." *Urban Affairs Quarterly* 27(4): 519–54.

Estolano, Cecilia. 2007. "Sustainable Green Urbanism." Los Angeles Community Redevelopment Agency Presentation. Available at www.crala.org/internet-site/Media/index.cfm.

Fagotto, Elena, and Archon Fung. 2006. "Empowered Participation in Urban Governance: The Minneapolis Neighborhood Revitalization Program." *International Journal of Urban and Regional Research*, 30(3): 638–55.

Feenberg, Daniel R., Andrew W. Mitrusi, and James M. Poterba. 1997. "Distributional Effects of Adopting a National Retail Sales Tax." *Tax Policy and the Economy* 11: 49–89.

Fine, Howard. 2011. "L.A.'s Cleantech Incubator Adds Two Tenants." *Los Angeles Business Journal*, December 7. Available at http://labusinessjournal.com/news/2011/dec/07/ls-cleantech-incubator-add-two-tenants.

Fishman, Robert. 1987. *Bourgeois Utopias: The Rise and Fall of Suburbia*. New York: Basic Books.

Florida, Richard. 2002. *The Rise of the Creative Class*. New York: Basic Books.

Floyd, Myron F., John O. Spengler, Jason E. Maddock, Paul H. Gobster, and Luis J. Suau. 2008. "Park-Based Physical Activity in Diverse Communities of Two U.S. Cities: An Observational Study." *American Journal of Preventive Medicine* 34(4): 299–305.

Fogelson, Robert M. 1993 [1967]. *The Fragmented Metropolis: Los Angeles, 1850–1930*. Berkeley, Calif.: University of California Press.

Fong, Timothy P. 1994. *The First Suburban Chinatown: The Remaking of Monterey Park, California*. Philadelphia: Temple University Press.

Forsyth, Ann. 2005. *Reforming Suburbia: The Planned Communities of Irvine, Columbia, and the Woodlands*. Berkeley, Calif.: University of California Press.

Foster, Mark S. 1971. "The Decentralization of Los Angeles During the 1920s." PhD diss., USC.

Frank, Larry, and Kent Wong. 2004. "Dynamic Political Mobilization: The Los Angeles County Federation of Labor." *WorkingUSA* 8(2): 155–81.

Fulton, William. 1994. "The State: Riordan Quietly Kills the CRA, Thereby Starting a Jobs-vs.-Revitalization Debate." *Los Angeles Times*, April 24. Available at http://articles.latimes.com/1994-04-24/opinion/op-49970_1_economic-development.

———. 1999. *Guide to California Planning*. Point Arena, Calif.: Solano Press.

———. 2001 [1997]. *The Reluctant Metropolis: The Politics of Urban Growth in Los Angeles*. Baltimore: Johns Hopkins University Press.

Fulton, William, Rolf Pendall, Mai Nguyen, and Alicia Harrison. 2001. *Who Sprawls Most? How Growth Patterns Differ Across the U.S.* Washington, D.C.: Brookings Institution.

Fung, Archon. 2004. *Empowered Participation: Reinventing Urban Democracy*. Princeton, N.J.: Princeton University Press.

Gabriel, Stuart A., and Gary Painter. 2008. "Mobility, Residential Location, and the American Dream: The Intrametropolitan Geography of Minority Homeownership." *Real Estate Economics* 36(3): 499–531.

Galaskiewicz, Joseph. 1979. *Exchange Networks and Community Politics*. Thousand Oaks, Calif.: Sage.

Garcia, Robert, Zoe Rawson, Meagan Yellot, and Christina Zaldaña. 2009. *Healthy Parks, Schools, and Communities for All: Park Development and Community Revitalization*. Los Angeles: City Project.

Garcia, Robert, and Aubrey White. 2006. *Healthy Parks, Schools, and Communities: Mapping Green Access and Equity for the Los Angeles Region*. Los Angeles: The City Project. Available http://greenlacoalition.org/wp-content/uploads/2011/01/Mapping-Green-AccessEquity.pdf.

Garrigues, George. 1966. "Foster Home Zoning Rule May be Eased." *Los Angeles Times*, March 22.

Garvin, Alexander. 1996. *The American City: What Works, What Doesn't*. New York: McGraw-Hill Professional.

Ghaemi, Parisa, Jennifer Swift, Chona Sister, John P. Wilson, and Jennifer Wolch. 2009. "Design and Implementation of a Web-Based Platform to Support Interactive Environmental Planning." *Computers, Environment and Urban Systems* 33(6): 482–91.

Gish, Todd. 2007a. "Building Los Angeles: Urban Housing in the Suburban Metropolis, 1900–1936." PhD diss., USC.

———. 2007b. "Growing and Selling Los Angeles: The All-Year Club of Southern California, 1921–1941." *Southern California Quarterly* 89(4): 391–415.

Giuliano, Genevieve. 2004. "Where Is the Region in 'Regional Transportation Planning'?" In *Up Against the Sprawl: Public Policy and the Making of Southern California*, ed. Jennifer Wolch, Manuel Pastor, and Peter Dreier, 151–70. Minneapolis: University of Minnesota Press.

Giuliano, Genevieve, Christian L. Redfearn, Ajay Agarwal, Chen Li, and Duan Zhuang. 2007. "Employment Concentrations in Los Angeles, 1980–2000." *Environment and Planning A* 39(12): 2935–57.

Giuliano, Genevieve, and Kenneth A. Small. 1991. "Subcenters in the Los Angeles Region." *Regional Science and Urban Economics* 21(2): 163–82.

Glaeser, Edward L., and Janet E. Kohlhase. 2004. "Cities, Regions, and the Decline of Transport Costs." *Papers in Regional Science* 83(1): 197–228.

Gooding-Williams, Robert. 1993. *Reading Rodney King/Reading Urban Uprising*. New York: Routledge.

Gottlieb, Robert, Mark Vallianatos, Regina M. Freer, and Peter Dreier. 2005. *The Next Los Angeles: The Struggle for a Livable City*. Berkeley, Calif.: University of California Press.

Granovetter, Mark S. 1973. "The Strength of Weak Ties." *American Journal of Sociology* 78(6): 1360–80.

Grant, Wyn. 1995. *Autos, Smog, and Pollution Control: The Politics of Air Quality Management in California*. Brookfield, Vt.: Edward Elgar.

Greene, Robert. 2003. "Power to the Valley." *L.A. Weekly*, December 12.

Grengs, Joe. 2002. "Community-Based Planning As a Source of Political Change: The Transit Equity of Los Angeles' Bus Riders Union." *Journal of the American Planning Association* 68(2): 165–78.

Grodach, Carl, and Anastasia Loukaitou-Sideris. 2007. "Cultural Development Strategies and Urban Revitalization: A Survey of US Cities." *International Journal of Cultural Policy*, 13(4): 349–69.

Gross, Julian, with Greg LeRoy and Madeline Janis-Aparicio. 2005. *Community Benefits Agreements: Making Development Accountable*. Washington, D.C.: Good Jobs First/Center for Working Partnerships. Available at www.communitybenefits.org/downloads/CBA%20Handbook%202005%20final.pdf.

Guo, Chao, and Juliet Musso. 2007. "Representation in Nonprofit and Voluntary Organizations: A Conceptual Framework." *Nonprofit and Voluntary Sector Quarterly* 36(2): 308–26.

Haefele, Marc B. 1998. "Jersey West." *L.A. Weekly*, December 18.

Hainley, Bruce. 2006. "Artquake." *New York Times Magazine*. October 1.

Hall, Peter. 1988. *Cities of Tomorrow: An Intellectual History of Urban Planning and Design in the Twentieth Century*. Oxford: Wiley-Blackwell.

Hamilton, Calvin S. 1986. "What Can We Learn from Los Angeles?" *Journal of the American Planning Association* 52(4): 500–507.

Hammack, David. 1988. "Comprehensive Planning Before the Comprehensive Plan: A New Look at the Nineteenth-Century American City." In *Two Centuries of American Planning*, ed. Daniel Schaffer, 139–65. Baltimore: Johns Hopkins University Press.

Hardwick, M. Jeffrey. 2004. *Mall Maker: Victor Gruen, Architect of an American Dream*. Philadelphia: University of Pennsylvania Press.

Harnik, Peter. 2000. *Inside City Parks*. Washington D.C.: Urban Land Institute.

Harris, Chauncy D., and Edward L. Ullman. 1945. "The Nature of Cities." *Annals of the American Academy of Political and Social Science* 242: 7–17.

Harris, Richard. 1996. *Unplanned Suburbs: Toronto's American Tragedy, 1900–1950*. Baltimore: Johns Hopkins University Press.

Harris County Toll Road Authority. N.d.a. "Toll Road Information—Overview." Available at www.hctra.org /tollroads.

———. N.d.b. "Katy Freeway Managed Lanes." Available at www.hctra.org/katymanagedlanes.

Hart, Roger. 1979. *Children's Experience of Place*. New York: John Wiley and Sons.

Haughwout, Andrew F., Richard Peach, and Joseph Tracy. 2010. "The Homeownership Gap." *Current Issues in Economics and Finance* 16(5): 1–10.

Hawthorne, Christopher. 2011. "Reading L.A.: A Reyner Banham Classic Turns 40." *Los Angeles Times*, April 22. Available at http://latimesblogs.latimes.com/culturemonster/2011/04/reading-la-banhams-four-ecologies-turns-40.html.

Hines, Thomas S. 1974. *Burnham of Chicago: Architect and Planner*. Chicago: University of Chicago Press.

———. 1982. "Housing, Baseball, and Creeping Socialism: The Battle of Chavez Ravine, Los Angeles, 1949–1959." *Journal of Urban History* 8(2): 123–43.

Hise, Greg. 1999. *Magnetic Los Angeles: Planning the Twentieth-Century Metropolis*. Baltimore: Johns Hopkins University Press.

———. 2006. "Sixty Stories in Search of a City." *California History* 83(3): 8–26, 62–64.

Hise, Greg, and William Deverell. 2000. *Eden by Design: The 1930 Olmsted-Bartholomew Plan for the Los Angeles Region*. Berkeley, Calif.: University of California Press.

———. 2005. "Introduction: The Metropolitan Nature of Los Angeles." In *Land of Sunshine: An Environmental History of Metropolitan Los Angeles*, ed. William Deverell and Greg Hise, 1–12. Pittsburgh: University of Pittsburgh Press.

Hise, Greg, and Todd Gish. 2007. "City Planning." In Rudd and Sitton 2007, 329–69.

Hogen-Esch, Tom. 2001. "Urban Secession and the Politics of Growth: The Case of Los Angeles." *Urban Affairs Review* 36(6): 783–809.

Howard, Ebenezer. 1965 [1902]. *Garden Cities of To-Morrow*. Cambridge, Mass.: MIT Press.

Independent Commission on the Los Angeles Police Department. 1991. *Report of the Independent Commission on the Los Angeles Police Department*.

Innes, Judith E., and Judith Gruber. 2001. *Bay Area Transportation Decision Making in the Wake of ISTEA: Planning Styles in Conflict at the Metropolitan Transportation Commission*. Berkeley, Calif.: University of California Transportation Center.

Innes, Judith, Judith Gruber, Michael Neuman, and Robert Thompson. 1994. *Coordinating Growth and Environmental Management through Consensus Building*. Berkeley, Calif.: California Policy Seminar.

Jackson, Helen Hunt. 1884. *Ramona: A Story*. Boston: Roberts Brothers.

Jackson, Kenneth. 1981. *Crabgrass Frontier: The Suburbanization of the United States*. Oxford: Oxford University Press.

Jackson, Richard H. 1981. *Land Use in America*. New York: V. H. Winston and Sons.

Jacobs, Jane. 1961. *The Death and Life of Great American Cities*. New York: Random House.

Johnson, James H., Jr., and Walter C. Farrell Jr. 1993. "The Fire This Time: The Genesis of the Los Angeles Rebellion of 1992." *North Carolina Law Review* 71(1):1403–20.

Johnson, Joke H. W. 1976. *The Southern California Association of Governments: A Study of Its Record and Possible Future*. Claremont, Calif.: Claremont Graduate School.

Kaplan, Sam Hall. 1986. "Citizens Want a Hand in Zoning." *Los Angeles Times*, April 6.

Kaye, Laurie, and Jerilyn Lopez Mendoza. 2008. *Everybody Wins: Lessons from Negotiating Community Benefits Agreements in Los Angeles*. New York: Environmental Defense.

Keegan, Robin, Neil Kleiman, Beth Seigel and Michael Kane. 2006. *Creative New York*. New York: Center for an Urban Future.

Kennedy, Lawrence W. 1994. *Planning the City upon the Hill: Boston since 1630*. Amherst, Mass.: University of Massachusetts Press.

Klein, Norman M. 1997. *The History of Forgetting: Los Angeles and the Erasure of Memory*. New York: Verso.

Kochanek, Kenneth D., Jiaquan Xu, Sherry L. Murphy, Arialdi M. Miniño, and Hsiang-Ching Kung. 2011. "Deaths: Preliminary Data for 2009." *National Vital Statistics Reports* 59(4): 1–51.

Kolnick, Kathy. 2008. "Order before Zoning: Land Use Regulation in Los Angeles, 1880–1915." PhD diss., USC.

Koslow, Jennifer. 2001. "Eden's Underbelly: Female Reformers and Public Health in Los Angeles, 1889–1932." PhD diss., UCLA.

Krueckeberg, Donald A., ed. 1983. *The American Planner: Biographies and Recollections*. New York: Methuen.

Leavitt, Jacqueline. 1997. "Charlotta A. Bass, the *California Eagle*, and Black Settlement in Los Angeles." In *Urban Planning and the African American Community: In the Shadows*, eds., June Manning Thomas and Marsha Ritzdorf, 167–186. Thousand Oaks, Calif.: Sage Publications.

Lee, Alfred. 2011. "The 50 Wealthiest Angelenos." *Los Angeles Business Journal*, May 16.

Lemann, Nicholas. 1994. "The Myth of Community Development." *New York Times Magazine*, January 9. Available at www.nytimes.com/1994/01/09/magazine/the-myth-of-community-development.html.

Leovy, Jill. 2002. "A New Way of Policing the LAPD." *Los Angeles Times*, February 3.

Lewis, LaVonna Blair, David C. Sloane, Lori Miller Nasciemento, Allison L. Diamant, Joyce Jones Guinard, Antronette K. Yancey, and Gwendolyn Flynn. 2005. "African Americans' Access to Healthy Food Options in South Los Angeles Restaurants." *American Journal of Public Health* 95(4): 668–73.

Lewis, Paul G. 2001. "Retail Politics: Local Sales Taxes and the Fiscalization of Land Use." *Economic Development Quarterly* 15(1): 21–35.

Lewis, Paul G., and Mary Sprague. 1997. *Federal Transportation Policy and the Role of Metropolitan Planning Organizations in California*. San Francisco: Public Policy Institute of California.

Li, Wei. 1998. "Anatomy of a New Ethnic Settlement: The Chinese Ethnoburb in Los Angeles." *Urban Studies* 35(3): 479–501.

Light, Ivan. 2006. *Deflecting Immigration: Networks, Markets, and Regulation in Los Angeles*. New York: Russell Sage.

Little, Paul. 2008. "Cash Would Benefit Westside, L.A. to Detriment of County." *Los Angeles Business Journal*, October 20.

Lloyd, Richard D. 2006. *Neo-Bohemia: Art and Commerce in the Postindustrial City*. New York: Routledge.

Logan, John R., and Harvey L. Molotch. 1987. *Urban Fortunes: The Political Economy of Place*. Los Angeles: University of California Press.

Long Beach, City of, Department of Public Works. N.d. *Bicycle Master Plan*. Available at www.longbeach.gov/pw/traffic/projects/bicycle_master_plan.asp.

Longcore, Travis, Christine Lam, Mona Seymour, and Alina Bokde. 2011. *LA Gardens: Development of a Municipal Strategy for Community Gardens*. Los Angeles: USC GIS Laboratory. Available at spatial.usc.edu/Users/christineslam/USCLANTgardens.pdf.

Longstreth, Richard W. 1998. *City Center to Regional Mall: Architecture, the Automobile, and Retailing in Los Angeles, 1920–1950*. Cambridge, Mass: MIT Press.

Los Angeles Alliance for a New Economy (LAANE). N.d. "Port of Los Angeles Clean Trucks Program." Available at www.laane.org/b1294p521b10.

Los Angeles, City of. 1969. *Charter of the City of Los Angeles as Adopted January, 1925 … and Amended May 1969.*
———. 1999. *Charter of the City of Los Angeles as Adopted January, June 1999.*
Los Angeles, City of, Citizens' Committee on Zoning Practices and Procedures. 1968. *A Program to Improve Planning and Zoning in Los Angeles.*
Los Angeles, City of, City Controller's Office. 2006. *Analysis of the Maintenance Activities of the Department of Recreation and Parks.*
Los Angeles, City of, City Planning Commission. 1928. *Annual Report.*
———. 1931–1932. *Annual Report.*
———. 1944. *Annual Report.*
———. 1945. *Planning for the San Fernando Valley.*
———. 1952. *Annual Report.*
———. 1954. *Annual Report.*
———. 1955. *Annual Report.*
Los Angeles, City of, City Council. 1925. *Los Angeles Municipal Atlas: Official Zoning Maps.*
Los Angeles, City of, Department of City Planning. 1927–1928. *Annual Report.*
———. 1928. *Annual Report.*
———. 1929–1930. *Annual Report.*
———. 1930–1931. *Annual Report.*
———. 1931–1932. *Annual Report.*
———. 1932–1933. *Annual Report.*
———. 1934–1935. *Annual Report.*
———. 1937–1938. *Annual Report.*
———. 1942–1943. *Annual Report.*
———. 1949–1950. *Annual Report.*
———. 1954–1955. *Annual Report.*
———. 1956–1957. *Annual Report.*
———. 1957–1958. *Annual Report.*
———. 1965–1966. *Annual Report.*
———. 1966. *Staff Report.* February 3.
———. 1967. *Concepts for Los Angeles.* Los Angeles.
———. 1969–1970. *Annual Report.*
———. 1970. *The Concept for the Los Angeles General Plan.* Los Angeles.
———. 1971–1972. *Annual Report.*
———. 1972. *Density Adjustment Study: An Examination of Multiple Residential Zoning in the City of Los Angeles.*
———. 1974. *Concept Los Angeles: The Concept of the Los Angeles General Plan*
———. 1985a. *Annual Report.*
———. 1985b. *Framework Element Public Comments.*
———. 1986. *Housing Element: An Element of the General Plan of the City of Los Angeles.*
———. 1993. *Housing Element: An Element of the General Plan of the City of Los Angeles.*
———. 1995. *The Citywide General Plan Framework: An Element of the City of Los Angeles General Plan.*
———. 1996. *The Citywide General Plan Framework: An Element of the City of Los Angeles General Plan.* Prepared by Envicom Corporation in association with Anil Verma Associates.
———. 2009. *The New Comprehensive Sign Ordinance.* Available at http://cityplanning.lacity.org/Code_Studies/other/IllustratedBrochure.pdf.
Los Angeles, City of, Department of Public Works. 2011. "Los Angeles Puts the Lid on Stormwater Pollution: Los Angeles City Council Unanimously Passes Low Impact Development Ordinance." September 28. Available at www.lastormwater.org/siteorg/program/LID_Ordinance_Passes.pdf.
Los Angeles, City of, Department of Recreation and Parks. 2009. *2009 Citywide Community Needs Assessment.* Available at http://laparks.org/planning/pdf/exeSum.pdf.
Los Angeles, City of, Los Angeles Housing Crisis Task Force. 2000. In *Short Supply: Recommendations of the Los Angeles Housing Crisis Task Force:* 49–66.

Los Angeles Community Redevelopment Agency (CRA/LA). 1958. "Opening Rebuttal Statement." City Council hearing. November 12. Quoted in Cohen-Marks 2007.

———.2011. *Active CRA/LA Board Approved Projects.* Available at www.crala.org/internet-site/upload /ActivityReportJuly2011.pdf.

Los Angeles, County of. 1929. Regional Plan of Highways: Section 2-E, San Gabriel Valley.

———. 1931. Regional Plan of Highways: Section 4, Long Beach-Redondo Area.

Los Angeles County, Department of Public Health. 2007. *Preventing Childhood Obesity: The Need to Create Healthy Places.* Office of Health Assessment and Epidemiology.

———. 2009. *Key Indicators of Health by Service Planning Area.* Available at www.publichealth.lacounty .gov/docs/keyindicators.pdf.

Los Angeles County, Housing Commission. 1906–1908. *Annual Report.*

———. 1908–1909. *Annual Report.*

Los Angeles County Metropolitan Transportation Authority. 2008a. *Multi-County Goods Movement Action Plan.*

———. 2008b. "Proposed One-Half Cent Sales Tax for Transportation Outline of Expenditure Categories: Attachment A." August 13. Available at www.metro.net/measurer/images/expenditure_plan.pdf.

———. 2009. *2009 Long Range Transportation Plan, Technical Document.* Available at www.metro.net /projects_studies/images/2009_lrtp_techdoc.pdf.

Los Angeles County, Metropolitan Transportation Authority, Office of Management and Budget. 2007. *Adopted Budget, FY2008.* Available at www.metro.net/about_us/finance/images/budget_adopted_fy08.pdf.

Los Angeles County, Office of Health Assessment and Epedemiology. 2010. *Life Expectancy in Los Angeles County: How Long Do We Live and Why?*" Available at http://zev.lacounty.gov/pdfs/Life-Expectancy-Final_web.pdf.

Los Angeles County, Office of the Assessor. 2010. *2010 Annual Report.* Available at http://assessor.lacounty .gov/extranet/news/rollrls2010.pdf.

Los Angeles County, Regional Planning Commission. 1929. *Annual Report.*

———. 1941. *A Comprehensive Report on the Regional Plan of Highways.*

Los Angeles Economic Development Corporation (LAEDC). 2010. *2010 Otis Report on the Creative Economy of the Los Angeles Region: The Power of Art and Artists.* Available at www.otis.edu/creative_economy /download/2010_Creative_Economy_Report.pdf.

———. 2011. *Manufacturing: Still a Force in Southern California.* Los Angeles: Kyser Center for Economic Research. Available at www.laedc.org/reports/Manufacturing_2011.pdf.

Los Angeles Municipal Art Commission. 1904. *Annual Report.*

———. 1909. *Report of the Municipal Art Commission for the City of Los Angeles, California, Made to the Mayor, the City Council, the Board of Public Works.* Los Angeles: W. J. Porter.

Loukaitou-Sideris, Anastasia. 1995. "Urban Form and Social Context: Cultural Differentiation in the Uses of Urban Parks." *Journal of Planning Education and Research* 14(2): 89–102.

Loukaitou-Sideris, Anastasia, and Gail Sansbury. 1995–1996. "Lost Streets of Bunker Hill." *California History* 74(4): 394–407.

Loukaitou-Sideris, Anastasia, and Athanasios Sideris. 2009. "What Brings Children to the Park? Analysis and Measurement of the Variables Affecting Children's Use of Parks." *Journal of the American Planning Association* 76(1): 89–105.

Loukaitou-Sideris, Anastasia, and Orit Stieglitz. 2002. "Children in Los Angeles Parks: A Study of Equity, Quality, and Children's Satisfaction with Neighborhood Parks." *Town Planning Review* 74(4): 467–88.

LSA Associates. 2011. *Orange County Sustainable Communities Strategy.* Prepared for Orange County Transportation Authority and Orange County Council of Governments. Available at http://oc-scs.org /images/stories/draft_documents/Final_OC_SCS_2011-06-14.pdf.

Lubove, Roy. 1962. *The Progressives and the Slums: Tenement House Reform in New York City, 1890–1917.* Pittsburgh: University of Pittsburgh Press.

Lynch, Kevin. 1960. *The Image of the City.* Cambridge, Mass.: MIT Press.

MacAdams, Lewis. 1998. "Prophet of Boom." *Los Angeles Magazine* 43(3): 58–65.

Markusen, Ann. 2004. "Targeting Occupations in Regional and Community Economic Development." *Journal of the American Planning Association* 70(3): 253–68.

Markusen, Ann, and David King. 2003. *The Artistic Dividend: The Arts' Hidden Contributions to Regional Development.* Minneapolis: University of Minnesota, Hubert H. Humphrey School of Public Affairs.

Markusen, Ann, and Greg Schrock. 2006. "The Distinctive City: Divergent Patterns in Growth, Hierarchy, and Specialization." *Urban Studies* 43(8): 1301–23.

Markusen, Ann, Greg Schrock, and Martina Cameron. 2004. *The Artistic Dividend Revisited*. Minneapolis: University of Minnesota, Hubert H. Humphrey School of Public Affairs.

Markusen, Ann, Gregory H. Wassall, Douglas DeNatale, and Randy Cohen. 2008. "Defining the Creative Economy: Industry and Occupational Approaches." *Economic Development Quarterly* 22(1): 24–45.

Massey, Douglas S., and Chiara Capoferro. 2008. "The Geographic Diversification of American Immigration." In *New Faces in New Places: The Changing Geography of American Immigration*, ed. Douglas S. Massey, 25–50. New York: Russell Sage.

McClung, Alexander. 2000. *Landscapes of Desire: AngloMythologies of Los Angeles*. Berkeley, Calif.: University of California Press.

McWilliams, Carey. 1973 [1946]. *Southern California: An Island on the Land*. Layton, Utah: Gibbs Smith.

Meyerson, Harold. 1999. "Caretakers Take Charge: 75,000 Workers (in 75,000 Work Sites!) Form a Union." *L.A. Weekly*, March 4. Available at www.laweekly.com/content/printVersion/30583.

———. 2001. "A Place for Us?" *L.A. Weekly*, November 16.

Molina, Natalia. 2006. *Fit to Be Citizens? Public Health and Race in Los Angeles, 1879–1939*. Berkeley, Calif.: University of California Press.

Molotch, Harvey. 1976. "The City as a Growth Machine: Toward a Political Economy of Place." *American Journal of Sociology* 82(2): 309–32.

Molotch, Harvey. 1996. "L.A. as Design Product: How Art Works in a Regional Economy." In *The City: Los Angeles and Urban Theory at the End of the Twentieth Century*, ed. Allen J. Scott and Edward W. Soja. Berkeley, Calif.: University of California Press.

Moore, Charles, Peter Becker, and Regula Campbell. 1998 [1984]. *The City Observed: Los Angeles*. Santa Monica: Hennessey and Ingalls.

Morland, Kimberly, Steve Wing, Ana Diez Roux, and Charles Poole. 2002. "Neighborhood Characteristics Associated with the Location of Food Stores and Food Service Places." *American Journal of Preventive Medicine* 22(1): 23–9.

Morrison, Peter A., and Ira S. Lowry. 1993. *A Riot of Color: The Demographic Setting of Civil Disturbance in Los Angeles*. Santa Monica, Calif.: RAND.

Muller, Peter O. 2004. "Transportation and Urban Form: Stages in the Spatial Evolution of the American Metropolis." In *The Geography of Urban Transportation*, ed. Susan Hanson and Genevieve Giuliano, 59–85. New York: Guilford Press.

Mullins, Daniel R., and Sally Wallace. 1996. "Changing Demographics and State Fiscal Outlook: The Case of Sales Taxes." *Public Finance Review* 24(2): 237–62.

Mumford, Eric. 2002. *The CIAM Discourses on Urbanism, 1928–1960*. Cambridge, Mass.: MIT Press.

Mumford, Lewis. 1961. *The City in History: Its Origins, Its Transformations, and Its Prospects*. New York: Harcourt, Brace, and World.

Munro, William B. 1931. "A Danger Spot in the Zoning Movement." *Annals of the American Academy of Political and Social Science* 155(2): 202–6.

Musso, Juliet, Christopher Weare, Thomas Bryer, and Terry L. Cooper. 2011. "Toward 'Strong Democracy' in Global Cities? Social Capital Building, Theory-Driven Reform, and the Los Angeles Neighborhood Council Experience." *Public Administration Review* 71(1): 102–11.

Musso, Juliet, Christopher Weare, Mark Elliot, Alicia Kitsuse, and Ellen Shiau. 2007. *Toward Community Engagement in City Governance: Evaluating Neighborhood Council Reform in Los Angeles*. Los Angeles: Neighborhood Participation Project, School of Policy, Planning, and Development, USC. Available at www.usc-cei.org/pdfs/Full%20Brief%208%5B1%5D.0.pdf.

Myers, Dowell. 2002. *Demographic and Housing Transitions in South Central Los Angeles, 1990–2000*. Los Angeles: Population Dynamics Research Group, School of Policy, Planning, and Development, USC.

———. 2007. *Immigrants and Boomers: Forging a New Social Contract for the Future of America*. New York: Russell Sage.

Myers, Dowell, Janna Goldberg, Sarah Mawhorter, and Seong Hee Min. 2010. "Immigrants and the New Maturity of Los Angeles." In *State of the City: Los Angeles 2010*, ed. Ali Modarres, 12–27. Los Angeles: Pat Brown Institute of Public Affairs.

Myers, Dowell, and John Pitkin. 2009. "Demographic Forces and Turning Points in the American City, 1950–2040." *Annals of the American Academy of Political and Social Science* 626: 91–111.

———. 2010. *Assimilation Today: New Evidence Shows the Latest Immigrants to America Are Following in Our History's Footsteps.* Washington, D.C.: Center for American Progress.

Myers, Dowell, and SungHo Ryu. 2008. "Aging Baby Boomers and the Generational Housing Bubble: Foresight and Mitigation of an Epic Transition." *Journal of the American Planning Association* 74(1): 17–33.

Nash, Andrew. 1992. "California Congestion Management Program." *ITE Journal* 62(2): 29–32.

National Asian American Pacific Legal Consortium. 2003. *The Politics of Language: Your Guide to English Only Laws and Policies.* Available at www.ailadownloads.org/advo/NAPALC-PoliticsOfLanguage.pdf.

National Recreation and Parks Association. 2000. "National Park Land Standards." April 18. Available at www.ci.big-spring.tx.us/Recreation/park_standards.html.

Natural Resources Defense Council (NRDC). 2010. "Court Ruling: Los Angeles Clean Truck Program Legally Sound." Available at www.nrdc.org/media/2010/100827.asp.

Nelson, Arthur C. 2006. "Leadership in a New Era." *Journal of the American Planning Association* 72(4): 393–409.

Newell, Josh, Chona Sister, Jennifer Wolch, Jennifer Swift, Parisa Ghaemi, John Wilson, and Travis Longcore. 2008. *Creating Parks and Open Space Using Green Visions Planning Toolkit 1.0.* Green Visions Plan for 21st Century Southern California, no. 18.

Newman, Morris. 2004. "Playa Vista Doesn't Meet Expectations." *California Planning and Development Report* 19(8).

Ni, Ching-Ching. 2011. "In Arcadia Real Estate, 4 is a Negative Number." *Los Angeles Times,* May 21. Available at http://articles.latimes.com/2011/may/21/local/la-me-arcadia-numbers-20110521.

Nicolaides, Becky M. 2002. *My Blue Heaven: Life and Politics in the Working-Class Suburbs of Los Angeles, 1920–1965.* Chicago: University of Chicago Press.

Novak, Anja, Debbie Wilken, Liane Lefaivre, Ingeboorg de Roode, and Aldo van Eyck. 2002. *Aldo van Eyck: Designing for Children, Playgrounds.* Amsterdam: NAI Publishers / Stedelijk Museum.

Olmsted Brothers and Harland Bartholomew and Associates. 1930. *Parks, Playgrounds, and Beaches in the Los Angeles Region.* Los Angeles: Los Angeles Chamber of Commerce.

Olmsted, Frederick Law, Harland Bartholomew, and Charles Henry Cheney. 1924. *A Major Traffic Street Plan for Los Angeles.* Los Angeles: Committee on the Los Angeles Plan of Major Highways of the Traffic Commission of the City and County of Los Angeles.

Olshansky, Robert B., Laurie A. Johnson, Kenneth C. Topping, Yoshiteru Murosaki, Kazuyoshi Ohnishi, Hisako Koura, and Ikuo Kobayashi. 2005. *Opportunity in Chaos: Rebuilding after the 1994 Northridge and 1995 Kobe Earthquakes.* Urbana-Champaign, Ill.: University of Illinois, Department of Urban and Regional Planning. Available at www.urban.uiuc.edu/faculty/olshansky/chaos/Opportunity-in-Chaos-March2011.pdf.

Ong, Paul, Theresa Firestine, Deirdre Pfeiffer, Oiyan Poon, and Linda Tran. 2008. *The State of South LA.* Los Angeles: UCLA School of Public Affairs.

Orange County Transportation Authority. N.d. "Measure M2." Available at www.octa.net/M2Home .aspx?entryid=332.

Park, Annie, Nancy Watson, and Lark Galloway-Gilliam. 2008. *South Los Angeles Health Equity Scorecard.* Los Angeles: Community Health Councils.

Park, Kyung. 2004. "Confronting the Liquor Industry in Los Angeles." *International Journal of Sociology and Social Policy* 19(7/8): 103–36.

Parson, Don. 2005. *Making a Better World: Public Housing, the Red Scare, and the Direction of Modern Los Angeles.* Minneapolis: University of Minnesota Press.

Pastier, John. 1970. "L.A.'s Civic Center: Accent on Quantity Rather than Quality." *Los Angeles Times,* November 22.

Pastor, Manuel, and Chris Benner. 2011. "Planning for Equity, Fighting for Justice: Planners, Organizers, and the Struggle for Metropolitan Inclusion." In *Regional Planning in America: Practice and Prospect,* ed. Ethan Seltzer and Armando Carbonell, 81–113. Cambridge, Mass.: Lincoln Institute of Land Policy.

Perkins, R. 2008. "Board Notes." *City News Service,* October 23.

Perry, Clarence. 1929. "The Neighborhood Unit." In Committee on the Regional Plan of New York and Its Environs 1929, 22–140.

———. 1939. *Housing for the Machine Age.* New York: Russell Sage Foundation.

Phelps, Robert. 1995. "The Search for a Modern Industrial City: Urban Planning, the Open Shop, and the Founding of Torrance, California." *Pacific Historical Review* 64(4): 503–35.

Pickrell, Don H. 1992. "A Desire Named Streetcar: Fantasy and Fact in Rail Transit Planning." *Journal of the American Planning Association* 58(2): 158–76.

Pitkin, Hanna F. 1972. *The Concept of Representation.* Berkeley, Calif.: University of California Press.

Pitkin, John, and Dowell Myers. 2011. "A Summary Period Measure of Immigrant Advancement in the U.S." *Demographic Research* 24(12): 257–92.

Planning and Conservation League Foundation. *California Park Bond Analysis: An Examination of the Per Capita, Roberti-Z'berg-Harris, and Murray-Hayden Grant Programs under Proposition 12.* Sacramento, Calif.: PCLF.

Polyzoides, Stefanos. 1997. "The Streets of Playa Vista." *Places* 11(2): 22–27.

Porter, Michael E. 1997. "New Strategies for Inner-City Economic Development." *Economic Development Quarterly* 11(1): 11–27.

Portes, Alejandro, and Min Zhou. 1993. "The New Second Generation: Segmented Assimilation and Its Variants." *Annals of the American Academy of Political and Social Science* 530: 74–96.

Poterba, James. 1996. "Retail Price Reactions to Changes in State and Local Sales Taxes." *National Tax Journal* 49(2): 165–76.

Pratt, Andy C. 1997. "The Cultural Industries Production System: A Case Study of Employment Change in Britain, 1984–91." *Environment and Planning A* 29(11): 1953–74.

Pristin, Terry. 2007. "A Glimpse of a More Vertical Los Angeles." *New York Times*, March 21.

Proshanski, Harold M., and Abbe Fabian. 1987. "The Development of Place Identity in the Child." In *Spaces for Children: The Built Environment and Child Development*, ed. Carol S. Weinstein and Thomas G. David. New York: Plenum Press.

Pugsley, William. 1977. *Bunker Hill: Last of the Lofty Mansions.* Corona del Mar, Calif.: Trans-Anglo Books.

Putnam, Robert D. 2000. *Bowling Alone: The Collapse and Revival of American Community.* New York: Simon and Schuster.

Rantisi, Norma M. 2004. "The Ascendance of New York Fashion." *International Journal of Urban and Regional Research* 28(1): 86–106.

Rasmussen, Cecilia. 2006. "Family Stood up to Restrictive Covenants: Henry and Texanna Laws Built Their Dream Home in What Was Then a Whites-Only Area near Watts: Then the Court Battle Began." *Los Angeles Times*, December 3.

Reese, Laura A., and Minting Ye. 2011. "Policy versus Place Luck: Achieving Local Economic Prosperity." *Economic Development Quarterly* 25(3): 221–36.

Reid, David, ed. 1994. *Sex, Death, and God in LA.* Berkeley, Calif.: University of California Press.

Renski, Henry, Jun Koo, and Edward Feser. 2007. "Differences in Labor versus Value Chain Industry Clusters: An Empirical Investigation. *Growth and Change* 38(3): 364–95.

Revell, Keith. 2003. *Building Gotham: Civic Culture and Public Policy in New York City, 1898–1938.* Baltimore: Johns Hopkins University Press.

Riis, Jacob. 1971 [1891]. *How the Other Half Lives: Studies among the Tenements of New York.* New York: Scribner's Sons.

Riverside County Transportation Commission. 2002. *Ordinance No. 02-001: Riverside County Transportation Commission Transportation Expenditure Plan and Retail Transaction and Use Tax Ordinance.* Available at http://rctc.org/downloads/RenewedMeasureA_Plan.pdf.

———. N.d. "Measure A." Available at http://rctc.org/measurea.asp.

Robbins, George W., and L. Deming Tilton, eds. 1941. *Los Angeles: Preface to a Master Plan.* Los Angeles: Pacific Southwest Academy.

Robinson, W. W. 1948. *Land in California: The Story of Mission Lands, Ranchos, Squatters, Mining Claims, Railroad Grants, Land Scrip, Homesteads.* Berkeley, Calif.: University of California Press.

———. 1963. "Myth-Making in the Los Angeles Area." *Southern California Quarterly* 45(1): 83–94.

Rodier, Caroline. 2009. "Review of International Modeling Literature." *Transportation Research Record* 2132: 1–12.

Rohrlich, Ted. 1998. "Neighborhood Councils Plan May be Losing Ground." *Los Angeles Times*, May 24, 1998.

Roth, Matthew. 2007. "Los Angeles Transportation." In Rudd and Sitton 2007, 447–80.

Rothblatt, Donald N., and Steven B. Colman. 1995. "An Approach to Urban Transportation Planning: California's Congestion Management Policy." *IATSS Research* 19(2): 26–34.

Rothman, Tibby. 2010. "City Hall's Revenge on Cecilia Estolano: Villaraigosa and His Boys Pushed out the One Woman Who Topped Them All." *LA Weekly*, January 7.

Rubin, Esther S., Heather L. Rustigian, and Michael D. White. 2006. *Target Species Habitat Mapping.* Green Visions Plan for 21st Century Southern California, no. 13.

Rubin, Joel. 2010. "An Estimated 100,000 Turn Out for L.A.'s Inaugural CicLAvia Event." *Los Angeles Times,* October 11.

Rudd, Hynda, and Tom Sitton, eds. 2007. *The Development of Los Angeles City Government: An Institutional History, 1850–2000.* Los Angeles: Los Angeles City Historical Society.

Rutten, Tim. 2010. "Mayor Villaraigosa's 30/10 Plan: Moving Forward." *Los Angeles Times,* June 9.

Saegert, Susan, and Roger Hart. 1978. "The Development of Sex Differences in the Environmental Competence in Girls and Boys." In *Studies in the Anthropology of Play,* ed. Phillips Stevens. Cornwall, N.Y.: Leisure Press.

Saltzstein, Alan L. 1996. "Los Angeles: Politics without Governance." In *Regional Politics: America in a Post-City Age,* ed. H. V. Savitch and Ronald K. Vogel. Thousand Oaks, Calif.: Sage Publications.

Sandweiss, Eric. 2001. *St. Louis: The Evolution of an American Landscape.* Philadelphia: Temple University Press.

[San Gabriel Council of Governments]. N.d. "Language of Participation and Growth Projections in the San Gabriel Valley." Presentation. Available at http://yoursitecontrolpanel.com/sites/site1765/documents /Language_of_Participation_and_Growth_Projections_in_the_SGV.pdf.

Sansbury, Gail. 1993. "Lincoln Place: A Case Study of a Multi-Family Rental Complex." Master's thesis, UCLA.

Sassen, Saskia. 1994. *Cities in a World Economy.* Thousand Oaks, Calif.: Pine Forge Press.

———. 2000. "The Global City: Strategic Site/New Frontier." In *Democracy, Citizenship and the Global City,* ed. Engin F. Isin, 48–61. London: Routledge.

Sayre, Jaime M., Joseph S. Devinny, and John P. Wilson. 2006. *Best Management Practices (BMPs) for the Treatment of Stormwater Runoff.* Green Visions Plan for 21st Century Southern California, no. 11.

Scanlon, Rosemary, Catherine Lanier, Johanna Arendt, Amos Ilan, Eugene Spruck, and Anthony Morris. 2007. *Arts as an Industry: Their Economic Impact on New York City and New York State.* New York: Alliance for the Arts.

Scheid, Ann. 2009. "Pasadena's Civic Center: A Grand Vision Realized, Despoiled, and Revived." *Southern California Quarterly* 91(4): 389–412.

Schoch, Deborah. 2007. "How Can LA Create Better Places to Play?" *Los Angeles Times,* June 1.

Schrank, David, Tim Lomax, and Shawn Turner. 2010. *Urban Mobility Report 2010.* College Station, Tex.: Texas Transportation Institute. Available at http://mobility.tamu.edu.

Schultz, Stanley K. 1989. *Constructing Urban Culture: American Cities and City Planning, 1800–1920.* Philadelphia: Temple University Press.

Schwab, Jim, et al. 1998. *Planning for Post-Disaster Recovery and Reconstruction.* PAS Report nos. 483/484. Chicago: American Planning Association.

Schwadron, Terry, and Paul Richter. 1984. *California and the American Tax Revolt: Proposition 13 Five Years Later.* Berkeley, Calif.: University of California Press.

Schwarz, Benjamin, and Christina Schwarz. 1999. "Going All Out for Chinese." *Atlantic Monthly* 283(1). Available at www.theatlantic.com/past/issues/99jan/chinese.htm.

Schweitzer, Lisa, and Brian D. Taylor. 2008. "Just Pricing: The Distributional Effects of Congestion Pricing and Sales Taxes." *Transportation* 35(6): 797–812.

Scott, Allen J. 1996. "The Craft, Fashion, and Cultural-Products Industries of Los Angeles: Competitive Dynamics and Policy Dilemmas in a Multisectoral Image-Producing Complex." *Annals of the Association of American Geographers* 86(2): 306–23.

———. 2000. *The Cultural Economy of Cities.* Thousand Oaks, Calif.: Sage Publications.

———. 2005. *On Hollywood: The Place, the Industry.* Princeton, N.J.: Princeton University Press.

Scott, Anna. 2009. "Lawsuit Ruling Puts Housing Plan in Question." *Downtown News,* July 24. Available at www.ladowntownnews.com/news/lawsuit-ruling-puts-housing-plan-in-question/article_e70397e6-2f40-59a7-86b9-8c76ff4d2dbd.html.

Scott, Mel. 1971. *American City Planning Since 1890.* Berkeley, Calif.: University of California Press.

Seaver, Robert. 1963. "The Albatross of Localism." *House and Home* 24(6): 99–107, 195, 198–99, 202–3.

Secor, Walt. 1964. "Sherman Way Zoning Proposal Draws Fire." *Los Angeles Times,* August 13.

Sellers, Jefferey M., Doreen Grosvirt-Dramen, and Lillyanne Ohanesian. 2009. *Metropolitan Sources of Electoral Support for Transportation Funding.* Los Angeles: METRANS Transportation Center. Available at www.metrans.org/research/final/06-10%20Final%20Report.pdf.

Seymour, Mona. 2005. "Nuisance" Urban Wildlife. Green Visions Plan for 21st Century Southern California, no. 6.

Seymour, Mona, Jason Byrne, Diego Martino, and Jennifer Wolch. 2006. Recreationist-Wildlife Interactions in Urban Parks. Green Visions Plan for 21st Century Southern California, no. 9.

Shaffer, Amanda. 2002. The Persistence of L.A.'s Grocery Gap. Los Angeles: Urban and Environmental Policy Institute, Occidental College.

Shapiro, Dan. 1988. "Citizen Review Now Can Save Zoning Outrage Later." Los Angeles Times, August 4.

Sharp, Gene. 2002 [1993]. From Dictatorship to Democracy: A Conceptual Framework for Liberation. East Boston, Mass.: Albert Einstein Institution.

Sheng, Jingfen, and John P. Wilson. 2008. Watershed Assets Assessment Report. Green Visions Plan for 21st Century Southern California, no. 16.

———. 2009a. Hydrology and Water Quality Modeling of the Santa Monica Bay Watershed. Green Visions Plan for 21st Century Southern California, no. 19.

———. 2009b. Hydrology and Water Quality Modeling of the San Gabriel River Watershed. Green Visions Plan for 21st Century Southern California, no. 20.

———. 2009c. Hydrology and Water Quality Modeling of the Calleguas Creek Watershed. Green Visions Plan for 21st Century Southern California, no. 21.

———. 2009d. Hydrology and Water Quality Modeling of the Los Angeles River Watershed. Green Visions Plan for 21st Century Southern California, no. 22.

———. 2009e. Hydrology and Water Quality Modeling of the Santa Clara River Watershed. Green Visions Plan for 21st Century Southern California, no. 23.

———. 2009f. "Watershed Urbanization and Changing Flood Behavior across the Los Angeles Metropolitan Region." Natural Hazards 48(1): 41–57.

Sheng, Jingfen, John P. Wilson, Ning Chen, Joseph S. Devinny, and Jaime M. Sayre. 2007. "Evaluating the Quality of the National Hydrography Dataset for Watershed Assessments in Metropolitan Regions." GIScience and Remote Sensing 44(3): 283–304.

Shigley, Paul. 2010. "California Struggles with its Legal Yoke." Planning 76(4): 12–15.

Siembab, Walter, and Marlon Boarnet. 2009. Sustainable South Bay: An Integrated Land Use and Transportation Strategy. Prepared for South Bay Cities Council of Governments and Los Angeles County Metropolitan Transportation Authority. Available at www.southbaycities.org/files/Sustainable%20South%20Bay%20Strategy.09.08.09_0.pdf.

Sister, Chona, John Wilson, and Jennifer Wolch. 2007. Park Congestion and Strategies to Increase Park Equity. Green Visions Plan for 21st Century Southern California, no. 15.

———. 2008. Access to Parks and Park Facilities in the Green Visions Plan Region. Green Visions Plan for 21st Century Southern California, no. 17.

Sister, Chona, Jennifer Wolch, and John Wilson. 2010. "Got Green? Addressing Environmental Injustice in Park Provision." GeoJournal 75(3): 229–48.

Sloane, David C. 2006. "From Congestion to Sprawl: Planning and Health in Historical Context." Journal of the American Planning Association 72(1): 10–18.

———. Forthcoming. "Combating Social Hazards in the South Los Angeles Environment." In Post-Ghetto: Reimagining South Los Angeles, ed. Josh Sides. Berkeley, Calif.: University of California Press.

Small and Knust. 1980. California Local Government and CEQA, 1979: A Report Submitted to the Assembly Committee on Rules. San Diego: Small and Knust.

Small, Kenneth A., Clifford Winston, and Carol A. Evans. 1991. Road Work: A New Highway Pricing and Investment Policy. Washington, D.C.: Brookings Institution Press.

Soja, Edward W. 2010. Seeking Spatial Justice. Minneapolis: University of Minnesota Press.

Solimar Research Group. 2005. Mixed-Use Centers in the South Bay: How Do They Function and Do They Change Travel Demand? Ventura, Calif.: Solimar Research Group. Available at www.southbaycities.org/node/255.

Son, Joonmo, and Nan Lin. 2008. "Social Capital and Civic Action: A Network-Based Approach." Social Science Research 37(1): 330–49.

Sonenshein, Raphael J. 2006. The City at Stake: Secession, Reform, and the Battle for Los Angeles. Princeton, N.J.: Princeton University Press.

South Coast Air Quality Management District (SCAQMD). 1997. The Southland's War on Smog: Fifty Years of Progress toward Cleaner Air. Diamond Bar, Calif.: SCAQMD. Available at www.aqmd.gov/news1/Archives/History/marchcov.html.

Southern California Association of Governments (SCAG). 2010. *Comprehensive Regional Goods Movement Plan and Implementation Strategy.* Los Angeles, Calif.: SCAG.

Southern California Studies Center and the Brookings Center on Urban and Metropolitan Policy. 2001. "Sprawl Hits the Wall." In *The Atlas of Southern California.* Los Angeles: USC.

Spencer, James H., and Paul Ong. 2004. "An Analysis of the Los Angeles Revitalization Zone: Are Place-Based Investment Strategies Effective Under Moderate Economic Conditions?" *Economic Development Quarterly* 18(4): 368–83.

Stanger, Richard. 2007. "An Evaluation of Los Angeles's Orange Line Busway." *Journal of Public Transportation* 10(1): 103–19.

Stein, Clarence. 1957. *Toward New Towns for America.* Cambridge, Mass.: MIT Press.

Stein, Eric D., Shawna Dark, Travis Longcore, Nicholas Hall, Michael Beland, Robin Grossinger, Jason Casanova, and Martha Sutula. 2007. *Historical Ecology and Landscape Change of the San Gabriel River and Floodplain.* Whittier, Calif.: Southern California Coastal Water Resources Project.

Stipak, Brian. 1973. "An Analysis of the 1968 Rapid Transit Vote in Los Angeles." *Transportation* 2(1): 71–86.

Stone, Clarence N. 1989. *Regime Politics: Governing Atlanta, 1946–1988.* Lawrence, Kans.: University Press of Kansas.

Talen, Emily. 2008. "Beyond the Front Porch: Regionalist Ideals in the New Urbanist Movement." *Journal of Planning History* 7(1): 20–47.

Taylor, Barbara. 1981. "Inclusionary Zoning under Study." *Los Angeles Times,* August 16.

Taylor, Brian D. 1995. "Public Perceptions, Fiscal Realities, and Freeway Planning: The California Case." *Journal of the American Planning Association* 61(1): 43–56.

———. 2000. "When Finance Leads Planning: Urban Planning, Highway Planning, and Metropolitan Freeways in California." *Journal of Planning Education and Research* 20(2): 196–214.

———. 2006 "Putting a Price on Mobility: Cars and Contradictions in Planning." *Journal of the American Planning Association* 72(3): 279–84.

Taylor, Brian D., Eugene J. Kim, and John E. Gahbauer. 2009. "The Thin Red Line: A Case Study of Political Influence on Transportation Planning Practice." *Journal of Planning Education and Research* 29(2): 173–93.

Teaford, Jon C. 1984. *The Unheralded Triumph: City Government in America, 1870–1900.* Baltimore: Johns Hopkins University Press.

———. 1986. *The Twentieth-Century American City.* Baltimore, Johns Hopkins University Press.

Toll, Seymour I. 1969. *Zoned American.* New York: Grossman Publishers.

Transportation Corridor Agencies (TCA). 1999. *1999 Annual Report.* Irvine, Calif.: TCA. Available at www.thetollroads.com/home/images/publications/tca_ar99.pdf.

Trust for Public Land (TPL). 2010. *2010 City Park Facts.* San Francisco: TPL. Available at http://cloud.tpl.org/pubs/ccpe_CityParkFacts_2010.pdf.

Ulaszewski, Brian. 2009. "The Sharrow's National Discussion." *Long Beach Post,* November 3. Available at www.lbpost.com/brian/7156.

Urban Crossroads and Bennett Engineering Services. 2010. *Western Riverside Council of Governments 4-City Neighborhood Electric Vehicle Transportation Plan.* Riverside, Calif.: Western Riverside Council of Governments.

U.S. Census Bureau. 2000. Summary File 4 (SF4) – Sample Data, table PCT119.

———. 2009. 2005–2009 American Community Survey 5-Year Estimates.

———. 2010. "Los Angeles, Selected Housing Characteristics, 2009." American FactFinder, American Community Survey. Available at http://factfinder.census.gov.

U.S. Department of Transportation (DOT). N.d. "Electronic Tolling / Congestion Pricing." Washington, D.C.: U.S. DOT, Federal Highway Administration. Available at www.etc.dot.gov/index.htm.

———. 1993. *Review of the Transportation Planning Process in the Southern California Metro Area.* August. Available at http://libraryarchives.metro.net/DPGTL/longrangeplans/1993_review_transportation_planning_process_socal_metro_area.pdf.

U.S. Government Accountability Office (GAO). 2006. *Empowerment Zone and Enterprise Community Program: Improvement Occurred in Communities, but the Effect of the Program is Unclear.* Washington D.C.: U.S. GAO.

Vance, James E. 1991. "Human Mobility and the Shaping of Cities." In *Our Changing Cities,* ed. John Fraser Hart, 67–85. Baltimore: Johns Hopkins University Press.

Verba, Sidney, Kay Lehman Schlozman, and Henry E. Brady. 1995. *Voice and Equality: Civic Voluntarism in American Politics.* Cambridge, Mass.: Harvard University Press.

Vickrey, William S. 1963. "Pricing in Urban and Suburban Transport." *American Economic Review* 53(2): 452–65.

Vincent, William, and Lisa Callaghan. 2007. *A Preliminary Evaluation of the Metro Orange Line Bus Rapid Transit Project.* Washington D.C.: Breakthrough Technologies Institute. Available at www.gobrt.org /Orange_Line_Preliminary_Evaluation_by_BTI.pdf.

Wachs, Martin. 1984. "Autos, Transit, and the Sprawl of Los Angeles: The 1920s." *Journal of the American Planning Association* 50(3): 297–310.

Wachs, Martin, and Jennifer Dill. 1999. "Regionalism in Transportation and Air Quality: History, Interpretation, and Insights for Regional Governance." In *Governance and Opportunity in Metropolitan America,* ed. Alan Altshuler, William Morrill, Harold Wolman, and Faith Mitchell. Washington, D.C.: National Academy Press.

Waldheim, Charles, ed. 2006. *The Landscape Urbanism Reader.* New York: Princeton Architectural Press.

Warner Sam Bass. 1987. *The Private City: Philadelphia in Three Periods of Its Growth.* Philadelphia: University of Pennsylvania Press.

———. 2001. "Overview." In J. Mark Schuster, "Ephemera, Temporary Urbanism, and Imaging," in *Imaging the City: Continuous Struggles and New Directions,* ed. Lawrence J. Vale and Sam Bass Warner. New Brunswick, N.J.: Center for Urban Policy Research.

Weiss, Marc A. 1987. *The Rise of the Community Builders: The American Real Estate Industry and Land Planning.* New York: Columbia University Press.

Westside Cities Working Group. 2008. *Workforce Housing Study: Westside Sub-Region.* November. Available at www.westsidecities.org/WestsideWorkforceHousingStudy_111908.pdf.

Whitnall, G. Gordon. 1923. "History of Zoning Told." *Los Angeles Times,* November 18.

Whyte, William, Jr. 1958. "Urban Sprawl." *Fortune* 57 (January): 103–9.

Whyte, William, Jr., Jane Jacobs, Francis Bello, Seymour Freedgood, and Daniel Seligman. 1958. *The Exploding Metropolis: A Study of the Assault on Urbanism and How Our Cities Can Resist.* New York: Fortune.

Willon, Phil. 2009. "Villaraigosa Retools His Second-Term Message to Focus on Jobs." *Los Angeles Times,* December 25. Available at http://articles.latimes.com/2009/dec/25/local/la-me-lamayor-jobs25-2009dec25.

Wilshusen, Linda. 1992. *The Effect of Government Organization on Coordination of Transportation and Land Use Planning: The Role of California's Regional Transportation Planning Agencies.* Washington, D.C.: Transportation Research Board.

Wilson, William H. 1989. *The City Beautiful Movement.* Baltimore: Johns Hopkins University Press.

Winton, Richard, and Martha Groves. 2008. "Case Is Closed on Deadly Day at Market." *Los Angeles Times,* May 22. Available at http://articles.latimes.com/2008/may/22/local/me-market22.

Wolch, Jennifer, John P. Wilson, and Jed Fehrenbach. 2002. *Parks and Park Funding in Los Angeles: An Equity-Mapping Analysis.* Los Angeles: USC, Sustainable Cities Program. Available at biodiversity.ca.gov /Meetings/archive/ej/USC.pdf.

Wolfe, Tom. 1968. "The New Life Out There: Electro-graphic Architecture." *New York* 1(36): 47–50.

Wong, Dorothy Fue. 2001. *National Landmark Application for Baldwin Hills Village.*

Yanez, Elva, and Wendy Muzzy. 2005. *Healthy Parks, Healthy Communities: Addressing Health Disparities through Public Financing of Parks, Playgrounds, and Other Physical Activity Settings.* San Francisco: Trust for Public Land.

Zahniser, David. 2011. "Los Angeles' Redevelopment Agency Still Alive after Budget Deal." *Los Angeles Times,* August 11. Available at http://articles.latimes.com/2011/aug/11/local/la-me-redevelop-20110811.

Zahniser, David, and Sam Farmer. 2011. "Los Angeles OKs Outlines of Downtown Football Stadium Deal." *Los Angeles Times,* August 10. Available at http://articles.latimes.com/2011/aug/10/local/la-me-stadium-vote-20110810.

Zunz, Olivier. 1982. *The Changing Face of Inequality: Urbanization, Industrial Development, and Immigrants in Detroit, 1880–1920.* Chicago: University of Chicago Press.

Contributors

Elisa Barbour is a PhD student in the Department of City and Regional Planning at the University of California–Berkeley and a former policy analyst at the Public Policy Institute of California.

Amanda Berman is an LA–based cultural planner and an alumna of the Price School of Public Policy at the University of Southern California.

Ken Bernstein is the principal planner for policy planning and historic resources in the City of Los Angeles's Department of City Planning.

Vinayak Bharne is the director of design at Moule & Polyzoides Architects & Urbanists and an adjunct faculty in urban design at the University of Southern California

Marlon G. Boarnet is a professor of urban planning in the Price School of Public Policy at the University of Southern California.

Janis Breidenbach, a former executive director of the Southern California Association of Non-Profit Housing (SCANPH), currently has her own consulting company while serving as an adjunct faculty member at the Price School of Public Policy at the University of Southern California.

Margaret Crawford is a professor of architecture in the School of Environmental Design at the University of California–Berkeley.

Elizabeth Currid-Halkett is an assistant professor of urban planning in the Price School of Public Policy at the University of Southern California.

William Deverell is director of the Huntington-USC Institute on California and the West and a professor of history at the University of Southern California.

Meredith Drake Reitan received her doctorate in urban planning at the University of Southern California, where she is currently a lecturer on public space and the assistant dean for graduate fellowships.

William Fulton, AICP, recently concluded his term as mayor of the City of Ventura and has joined Smart Growth America as vice president for policy and programs, while remaining a senior fellow in the Price School of Public Policy at the University of Southern California.

Lark Galloway-Gilliam is the executive director of Community Health Councils, a policy advocacy organization in Los Angeles.

Sam Gennawey is a senior associate at Katherine Padilla & Associates, an author, and a public speaker.

Todd Gish, who received his doctorate in urban planning from the University of Southern California, is a fifth-generation Angeleno, a licensed architect, and practicing urban designer.

Gilda Haas is an organizer, educator, and urban planner who has been helping grassroots organizations build economies from the ground up for 30 years.

Greg Hise is professor of history at the University of Nevada–Las Vegas.

Anna Jacobsen is pursuing master's degrees in urban planning and public administration in the Price School of Public Policy at the University of Southern California.

Martin Krieger is a professor of urban planning in the Price School of Public Policy at the University of Southern California.

Robert A. Leiter, FAICP, is an urban and environmental planning consultant and former director of land-use and transportation planning for the San Diego Association of Governments.

Travis Longcore is an associate professor of research at the University of Southern California Spatial Sciences Institute.

Anastasia Loukaitou-Sideris is a professor of urban planning and design in the Luskin School of Public Affairs at the University of California–Los Angeles.

Doug McCulloh is a Southern California photographer whose work has shown in exhibitions in the United States as well as in Europe, China, and Mexico.

Sarah Mawhorter is a doctoral student in urban planning and development in the Price School of Public Policy at the University of Southern California.

Vinit Mukhija is an associate professor of urban planning in the Luskin School of Public Affairs at the University of California–Los Angeles.

Juliet Musso is an associate professor of public policy in the Price School of Public Policy at the University of Southern California.

Dowell Myers is a professor of urban planning and demography in the Price School of Public Policy at the University of Southern California.

Aaron Paley is the cofounder and president of Community Arts Resources (CARS).

Simon Pastucha directs the City of Los Angeles's Urban Design Studio within the Department of City Planning.

Steven A. Preston, FAICP, the city manager of San Gabriel, has served as president of the American Planning Association's California chapter and on APA's national board.

Christian L. Redfearn is an associate professor of urban economics and real estate development in the Price School of Public Policy at the University of Southern California.

Lisa Schweitzer is an urban planner who studies social justice in the Price School of Public Policy at the University of Southern California.

Josh Sides is the Whitsett Chair of California History and the director of the Center for Southern California Studies at California State University–Northridge.

David C. Sloane is a professor and director of undergraduate programs in the Price School of Public Policy at the University of Southern California. He serves as an associate editor of the *Journal of the American Planning Association* and recently completed his second term as a regional representative on the governing board of the Association of Collegiate Schools of Planning.

Kenneth C. Topping, FAICP, former Los Angeles city planning director, is president of Topping Associates International, lecturer at California Polytechnic State University–San Luis Obispo, and a San Luis Obispo County planning commissioner.

Joshua Wheeler is pursuing master's degrees in urban planning and real estate development in the Price School of Public Policy at the University of Southern California.

Andrew H. Whittemore is an assistant professor of city and regional planning at the University of Texas–Arlington.

John Wilson is a professor of geography and sociology and director of the Spatial Sciences Institute at the University of Southern California.

Jennifer Wolch is a professor of city and regional planning and William W. Wurster Dean in the College of Environmental Design at the University of California–Berkeley.

Goetz Wolff is lecturer in urban planning at Luskin School of Public Affairs at the University of California–Los Angeles and has an economic-development consulting practice working for labor, community organizations, and public agencies.

David Yamamoto is an assistant professor and head of photography department at Glendale Community College in Glendale, California.

Credits

The editor and publisher extend their profound thanks to the following photographers, illustrators, and institutions for providing their work for use here:

Archives–Los Angeles County Metropolitan Transportation Authority: Fig. 5.1

Vinayak Bharne: Figs. 4.7–4.9

Bike Long Beach; Fig. 5.6

Anne Bray: Fig. 5.4 and pp. 91, 221

City of Los Angeles: Figs. 2.5–2.7, 6.11, 6.12

City of Los Angeles Office of Historic Resources: Figs. 7.2, 7.4, 7.5

City of Los Angeles Planning Department: Fig. 6.10

Dallas CityDesign Studio: Fig. 6.9

Dorothy Peyton Gray Transportation Library: Fig. 5.13

Fallen Fruit of Silver Lake: p. 270

Field Operations: p. 190

Todd Gish: p. ix and Figs. 2.11, 6.13

Green Visions Plan: Figs. 6.16–6.21

The Huntington Library, San Marino, California: Figs. 2.3, 2.4, 3.17, 5.15, 6.5–6.8 and p. 161

J. Paul Getty Trust, © and used with permission, Julius Shulman Photography Archive, Research Library at the Getty Research Institute (2004.R.10): Fig. 7.1

Doug Jamieson, courtesy of Rios Clementi Hale Studios, pp. 240–41

Leo Jarzomb / Los Angeles Herald-Examiner Collection, Courtesy of the Los Angeles Public Library: Fig. 4.5

Killefer Flammang Architects: Figs. 7.6a–b, 7.7

Martin Krieger: p. 146

L.A. Eco-Village Blog: Fig. 5.7

Gary Leonard: Fig. 5.16 and pp. 182, 184, 185, 187

Alan Loomis / Glendale Urban Design Studio: Figs. 4.10, 4.12, 4.14

Los Angeles City Archive: Figs. 2.1, 2.2

Los Angeles County Metropolitan Transportation Authority: pp. 188–89

Los Angeles Fire Department Museum: Fig. 7.3

Los Angeles Public Library Photo Collection: Fig. 5.3

Anastasia Loukaitou-Sideris: Figs. 6.1–6.4

Doug McCulloh: Figs. 2.9, 2.10, 2.16 and pp. viii, 34, 68, 106

Juliet Musso: Figs. 2.14, 2.15

Damien Newton / LA Streetsblog: Fig. 5.14

Mike Nilsson / Glendale Urban Design Studio; Fig. 4.11

Aaron Paley: Figs. 2.17, 2.18 and pp. 18, 33, 85, 144, 203, 269

PBy Collaborative Design Group, pp. 137, 138

Tom Queally: p. 105

Rockefeller Partners Architecture: Fig. 7.8

James Rojas: p. 67

Public Matters: p. 145

Shimoda Design Group: Fig. 4.15

David C. Sloane: Figs. 1.1–1.13, 5.5, 5.11, 5.12 and pp. 177, 178, 292

Southern California Association of Governments: Figs. 5.8, 5.9, 5.10

University of Southern California Libraries, California Historical Society Collection: Fig. 5.2

University of Southern California Libraries, Title Insurance and Trust / C.C. Pierce Photography Collection, 1860–1960: Fig. 2.8

Strategic Actions for a Just Economy (SAJE): Fig. 7.9 and p. 278

Tricia Ward/ACLA: pp. 212–13

Withee Malcolm Architects: Fig. 4.13

Andrew H. Whittemore: Fig. 4.6

David Yamamoto: pp. 121, 242, 293